Performing

Performing Menken uses the life experiences of controversial actress and poet Adah Isaacs Menken to examine the culture of the Civil War period. Menken succeeded by playing with her identity off-stage and on, portraying herself as both respectable and daring and claiming various racial and ethnic identities. Playing male roles on stage, she became the reigning femme fatale. Yet she was also known as an intellectual, publishing poetry and essays. She shared friendships with the greatest writers of her time, including Walt Whitman, Mark Twain, and Alexandre Dumas, père.

Performing Menken also looks at what Menken's choices reveal about her period. It explores the roots of the cult of celebrity that emerged from the crucible of war. While discussing Menken's racial and ethnic claims and her performance of gender and sexuality, *Performing Menken* focuses on contemporary use of social categories to explain patterns in America's past and considers why such categories remain important.

Renée M. Sentilles is Assistant Professor of History and Director of American Studies at Case Western Reserve University. She is a former Mellon Post-Dissertation Fellow at the American Antiquarian Society.

This book is published in association with the American Antiquarian Society (AAS), in Worcester, Massachusetts, which supported the author's research and writing through a Mellon Post-Dissertation Fellowship, funded by a grant to AAS by the Andrew W. Mellon Foundation.

PERFORMING MENKEN

Adah Isaacs Menken and the Birth of American Celebrity

RENÉE M. SENTILLES
Case Western Reserve University

CAMBRIDGE
UNIVERSITY PRESS

CAMBRIDGE UNIVERSITY PRESS
Cambridge, New York, Melbourne, Madrid, Cape Town,
Singapore, São Paulo, Delhi, Mexico City

Cambridge University Press
The Edinburgh Building, Cambridge CB2 8RU, UK

Published in the United States of America by Cambridge University Press, New York

www.cambridge.org
Information on this title: www.cambridge.org/9780521527606

First published 2003
First paperback edition 2011

A catalogue record for this publication is available from the British Library

Library of Congress Cataloging in Publication Data
Sentilles, Renée M.
Performing Menken : Adah Isaacs Menken and the birth of American celebrity /
Renée M. Sentilles.
p.   cm.
Includes bibliographical references and index.
ISBN 0-521-82070-7
1. Menken, Adah Isaacs, 1835–1868.   2. Actors – United States –
Biography.   1. Title.
PN2287.M6 S46   2003
792´.028´092–dc21
[B]   2002031074

ISBN 978-0-521-82070-7 Hardback
ISBN 978-0-521-52760-6 Paperback

Dedicated to my parents
Dennis Sentilles and Claire Zeringue Tassin

Infelix

Adah Isaacs Menken

Where is the promise of my years;
Once written on my brow?
Ere errors, agonies and fears
Brought with them all that speaks in tears,
Ere I had sunk beneath my peers;
Where sleeps that promise now?

Naught lingers to redeem those hours,
Still, still to memory sweet!
The flowers that bloomed in sunny bowers
Are withered all; and Evil towers
Supreme above her sister powers
Of Sorrow and Deceit.

I look along the columned years,
And see Life's riven fane,
Just where it fell, amid the jeers
Of scornful lips, whose mocking sneers,
For ever hiss within mine ears
To break the sleep of pain.

I can but own my life is vain
A desert void of peace;
I missed the goal I sought to gain,
I missed the measure of the strain
That lulls Fame's fever in the brain,
And bids Earth's tumult cease.

Myself! Alas for theme so poor
A theme but rich in Fear;
I stand a wreck on Error's shore,
A spectre not within the door,
A houseless shadow evermore,
An exile lingering here.

Contents

Acknowledgments

If one can run up a deficit in karma, I believe I have done so with this book. This project has spanned the ten years when I went to graduate school, took several visiting positions and a postdoctoral fellowship, and finally found a place to put down roots. Consequently, this book bears the mark of many individuals and institutions.

In terms of institutions, I thank the American Antiquarian Society, the Mellon Foundation, the American Jewish Archives, the College of William and Mary, Franklin and Marshall College, Case Western Reserve University, the Historical New Orleans Collection, and the Harvard Theatre Collection. Their funding and collections made this book possible. I also thank Frank Smith and Cambridge University Press for seeing the value of this book while it was still in the rough.

In terms of individuals, let me begin by thanking my advisors and mentors. When I was an undergraduate at Mount Holyoke College, Johnny Mack Faragher introduced me to the wonderful creativity of American Studies, for which I am ever grateful. As my master's advisor at Utah State, Anne M. Butler taught me how to pull together a long research project and to remember that work is only one aspect of a life well lived. Bob Gross at the College of William and Mary was the one who advised me through my dissertation project on Menken. I cannot thank him enough for his high expectations and generosity of time and spirit. I can say the same about Kathleen Brown, who put me through my paces on American women's history and gave generously of her time when she was toiling with the final stages of her own book. I feel blessed that these four people have touched upon my life and scholarship in so many ways.

I was blessed in other ways by the advice and support of other professors, such as Clyde Milner, Carol A. O'Connor, and David Rich Lewis at Utah State and Arthur Knight, Bruce McConachie, Leisa Meyers, and Joanne Braxton at William and Mary. Fredrika Teute of the Omahundro Institute also gave unselfishly of her time and helped me through early drafts. Karla Goldman of Hebrew Union College helped me get a handle on American Jewish women's history.

I finished my dissertation during my first year of full-time teaching at Franklin and Marshall College, where my colleagues encouraged me every step of the way. I owe particular thanks to Abby Schrader, David Schuyler, and John Andrew for reading my work and giving advice. I am especially indebted to Adrian Davis for his support and friendship during those exhausting final months when I was so bleary-eyed he worried that I might walk out into traffic.

I cannot imagine how this book would have ever come into fruition had I not been awarded the Mellon Post-Dissertation Fellowship at the American Antiquarian Society in 1998, where I experienced the most exciting intellectual year of my life. AAS is simply a treasure and I value any time I get to spend there. The institution could not possibly be so wonderful without the presence of John Hench, Caroline Sloat, Joanne Chaison, Marie Lamoureux, Ellen Dunlap, Georgia Barnhill, and Laura Wasowicz. They not only helped me with my research but gave generously of both criticism and support. While at AAS I also met exceptional scholars, many of whom have become good friends and contributed to this book by sharing their own interests: Brett Mizelle, Jean O'Brien, Scott Casper, Paula Bennett, Lucia Knoles, Barbara Cutter, Brian Roberts, Laura Schiavo, Kate Haulman, Sarah Messer, Tim Marr, Tom Doughton, and Nicole Cooley. I owe particular thanks to Paul Erickson, Ann Fabian, Drew McCoy, Helen Lefkowitz Horowitz, Bob Lockhart, and Jay Fliegelman for reading through drafts and sharing ideas. Karen Halttunen went a step further, reading through the manuscript at two different stages and offering detailed advice on every chapter. Grey Osterud was the last of these to read the manuscript and helped me to solve problems that had plagued the project throughout.

Annette Fern, librarian at the Harvard Theatre Collection, was wonderfully helpful over the years as she saw this project move from idea to dissertation to manuscript to book. I had no official connection to the Houghton Library but I felt like an honorary fellow by the time Annette helped me sharpen citations in the final draft.

The support of family and friends was critical for me. They listened patiently to long accounts of this woman called Menken and encouraged my work, despite the fact that I was constantly saying, "I don't have time – I have to write" or "I'm sorry I can't visit longer – I have to finish this draft." I thank Benny Bach for his support and belief in me throughout graduate school and beyond. I am also grateful to Emily Mieras, who saw the magic of the project despite those dreadful early drafts. I am also grateful to Bert Ashe, Susan Foster Garton, Robin Craggs, Tim Barnard, and Susie Bonta.

Here, finally, at Case Western Reserve University, I have landed in a wonderful department. I thank my stars daily for having such supportive colleagues and friends. I especially thank Jonathan Sadowsky, who acts as my official mentor, and Alan Rocke, Rhonda Williams, Angela Woollacott, Ken Ledford, Carroll Pursell, and Ted Steinberg, who often play that role less officially. I thank Dean Samuel Savin for providing support, material and otherwise.

I also thank Ormus Davenport, descendant of magician William Davenport, and Frank Dailey, who introduced us and shared his own research. Gregory Eiselien, Daphne Brooks, and Maria-Elena Buszek shared in the excitement over scholarship on Menken.

My family, of course, deserves the most gratitude of all. After all, my parents and brother are the ones with whom I spent the first two decades of my life. My father led me to believe I was capable of doing anything and introduced me to a wider world. My mother provided the wisdom that sustained me through the worst times and helped me appreciate the best. Because of my older brother all of my early memories seem to be of laughter and mischief, and I admire few people as much as I admire and emulate him. I am daily thankful that he married Katie Cowan, who has become one of my closest friends and brought her parents, George and Anne Cowan, into my life. Since the first day I met him, George Cowan has been one of my staunchest supporters. I also give special thanks to my cousin, Kristen Scarborough, for driving me to Texas to look through old newspapers. I am one of those fortunate people who comes from a large family filled with kind, interesting people, and I am always appreciative of my grandmother, Emily Sentilles, and my many uncles, aunts, and cousins who enrich my life and make the holidays true celebrations.

But my nieces, Claire and Frances, well, they simply make the whole adventure worthwhile; watching them learn and grow has been one of the highlights of my life. My paternal grandmother grew up in poverty on the bayou in South Louisiana, with a smart mind and few choices. My mother grew up much like her own mother, just up the Mississippi River from New Orleans, in a culture entrenched in the past with no obvious path into the future. So my mother raised me to have what she did not: belief in myself and the courage to follow my dreams, even if they took me far away. And now here is the next generation in beautiful, inquisitive form. As I write, I look at their faces smiling from the picture on my desk and think, "I want to give you a better world, a better place." And ultimately, that is what historical work is all about: understanding the past so that we may understand the present and, hopefully, make better choices for the future.

Renée M. Sentilles
Cleveland Heights, Ohio
April 2002

Introduction

On Tuesday last, in the city of Paris, Adah Isaacs Menken, well known in this country as an actress of only meagre ability, died.

New York Herald, August 13, 1868[1]

The Menken is dead. The bare-faced, bare-limbed, reckless, erratic, ostracized, but gifted, kind-hearted, successful, yet ill-starred Menken is no more. . . .

Clipping from an unidentified newspaper[2]

The well-known equestrian actress, Adah Isaacs Menken, died of consumption on Monday afternoon. . . . She was born in New Orleans, in the spring of 1841. . . . At the commencement of the civil war she evinced strong southern sympathies, and on one occasion was arrested on a charge of rebellious conduct, and was imprisoned for 30 days. . . .

London Daily Telegraph, August 12, 1868[3]

Miss Adah Isaacs – for such was her maiden name – was born in Chicago about 1832. . . . Menken's success on the stage has been attributed to her fine figure, easy carriage, and thoroughly debonnaire deportment. . . . The more recent celebrities with whom her name has been associated in unenviable notoriety, were Alexander Dumas, the novelist, and the young English poet, Algernon Swinburne. . . .

New York Daily Tribune, August 12, 1868[4]

She died in London. Her name has been in the mouth of all men for the last half dozen years, and very seldom has she been mentioned with respect. . . . Her first name was Ada McCoard. She was born in Memphis. . . . Bad as was her course, there are worse women living than the dead Menken.

Galveston Bulletin, August 19, 1868[5]

She was a whole-hearted girl, magnificently beautiful, brave, muscular, with superbly developed limbs, high arched insteps, boldly marked hips; splendid in her virile loveliness; strong yet flexible tendons and a dare-devil brain to command them.

San Francisco Bulletin, September 12, 1868[6]

---

[1] "Adah Isaacs Menken," *New York Herald*, Aug. 13, 1868.

[2] Unidentified newspaper clipping, Adah Isaacs Menken clipping file, Harvard Theatre Collection (hereafter HTC), Houghton Library, Harvard University, Cambridge, Massachusetts.

[3] "Death of Adah Isaacs Menken," *London Daily Telegraph*, Aug. 12, 1868. Menken was not arrested in Pittsburgh, but she was briefly detained by Union officials in Baltimore; more on that subject in Chapter 5.

[4] "Obituary," *New York Daily Tribune*, Aug. 12, 1868, p. 5.

[5] "Death of Ada Menken," *Flake's Semi-Weekly Galveston Bulletin*, Aug. 19, 1868, p. 6, c. 3.

[6] *San Francisco Bulletin*, quoting the San Francisco *Evening Illustrated*, Sept. 12, 1868, noted in Nicholas Kovach collection, Special Collections, University of Minnesota, Minneapolis.

Cette pauvre Menken est morte!...Pauvre Menken! Folle joyeuse, amazone insensee!... C'etait une artiste pourtant! Au theatre elle avait la chance.

Clipping from an unknown French journal[7]

Miss Menken...was almost as well known in Europe as in this country....Miss Menken played principally in "Mazeppa"...and other pieces of a similar character, which require the principal performer to be very much undressed....She was generous to a fault, and in consequence will be regretted by many.

New York Times, August 12, 1868[8]

[Her] first name was Adelaide McCord....Her expressive features and talent as a pantomimist enabled her to present the character of Mazeppa in its most romantic and picturesque aspect....Her nerve and self-possession were put to severe test throughout the drama, and her command of the equestrian art was evident to the public.

Clipping from an unknown journal[9]

Obituaries of Adah Isaacs Menken published in newspapers throughout the United States and western Europe in the second week of August 1868 illustrate how she was viewed upon her death. Everyone had heard of her, but there was a wide range of opinions on how to describe, evaluate and categorize her. Was she from Memphis or New Orleans? There are discrepancies in her reported age, place of birth, cause of death, parental ethnicity, and birth name. Had she been talented or conniving? Was she worthy of mourning or scorning? Assessments of her character color even the briefest mention of her death and widely disagree: She was "generous to a fault," "kind hearted...yet ill-starred"; men paid her little respect, and she performed equestrian drama "undressed." Several sketches imply that Menken had been a "whore with a heart of gold," a bad girl with the best intentions. Others depict her as a confidence man in female form, beguiling the public into accepting corrupt behavior as exciting and fashionable. Women's rights advocates became her most surprising defenders, asserting (now that she was dead) that they could see that Menken had not been a villain but a victim, the product of a male-centered society.[10] Although neither journalists nor the American public could agree in their assessment, evaluating her was clearly important; in determining how society should view Menken, they could also define where society was headed in the aftermath of the Civil War. The discussion was about Menken, but it was also about social mores, class struggles, and gender roles. Despite her fame, Menken proved to be an unsolvable puzzle, and many soon saw the advantage of using her ambiguity to advance their own views.

---

[7] Clipping in J. S. G. Hagan, Records of the New York Stage, 1860–1870. Extended and illustrated for Augustin Daly by Augustin Toedteberg (New York: New York Dispatch, 18??), vol. II, n.p., HTC, TS 1529.291.

[8] "Adah Isaacs Menken," *New York Times,* Aug. 12, 1868, p. 4, c. 6.

[9] Clipping in Hagan, vol. 2, n.p.

[10] Elizabeth Cady Stanton, "Adah Isaacs Menken," Seneca *Revolution,* Oct. 1, 1868, pp. 201–202.

In the process of describing Menken, the obituaries reveal a deep concern with identifying her character, both as an individual and as a social participant. Journalists grasp at evidence of her "true" nature, such as her financial generosity or her propensity to marry. The subtext is frustration: How could such basic "facts" as ethnicity, religious identity, social class, and ancestry be so difficult to discern? Menken had mixed up contradictory cultural markers and yet she managed to make most of them plausible. What did this suggest about those cultural markers and categories? Social categories have two defining and paradoxical characteristics: They appear stable and reliable, which is why we use them to organize our views of society, while they are, in fact, fundamentally unstable. To function in changing societies, social categories *must* be malleable; they must constantly adjust to fit the community that creates them. On the other hand, to be of any use those social categories must also appear to be fixed. In many ways, changes wrought by the Civil War disrupted social relations to the point where the ideology of static social categories was revealed to be false. Menken made this social fluidity visible. She capitalized on it, mocked it, and used it, leaving her public with a discomforting sense that, despite all the press she had received, she remained an enigma.

Their readings of Menken reveal concern with larger social changes. She was a sex symbol who played male roles on stage; what did that say about connections between sex, sexuality, and gender? Menken geared her performances to both the working and middle classes, depending on the venue in which she performed. Did this mean the classes were merging? Was respectability still important? Was sensation trumping merit? Journalists agreed only on her most famous last name and the reason why her death should be noted: She was the Menken, a major celebrity.

This is the biography of "the Menken," the celebrity persona who became known to the western world during America's Civil War years. But it is less a narrative of her life than an investigation of Menken as a deliberate performance, a self-created celebrity who shaped her image to suit the times.[11] Thus, this examination of Menken addresses the development of mass culture and celebrity during the Civil War period – a national culture that was emerging as the nation itself was dividing. Menken's experiences imply that there are important continuities between her century and our own. Although a few celebrities existed in the antebellum period, the cult of celebrity – that is, a sort of media-driven social world woven around celebrities – developed during the war and has been expanding steadily since. This study of Menken's celebrity exposes the roots of that cultural phenomenon, demonstrates its connection to changes in cultural performances of social

---

[11] Judith Butler's writings on performance have greatly influenced this text. Butler suggests that identities are performed by questioning assumptions about those identities. See Judith Butler, *Gender Trouble: Feminism and the Subversion of Identity* (New York: Routledge, 1990), 16–25.

class, ethnicity, and gender, and reveals the importance of the mass media in shaping postbellum American culture. Because of Menken's success at manipulating signifiers of social identity, this is also a study of identity itself and why determining her identity mattered and continues to matter so much to Menken's public.

Because of her talent for public relations and reliance on newspapers and photography, Menken's life as a performer is well documented. However, an examination of primary source material on Menken – the numerable accounts of her life, reviews of performances, her letters to the public and personal friends, and the many reminiscences of friends and fans – quickly reveals a minefield. For the most part, Menken was an invented character; to write a biography of her as a person distinct from the images she created would be impossible and misleading.

Central to this study of Menken and the cultures surrounding her, therefore, is the verb "perform," and it deserves a note of interpretation. Other verbs appear often in this study of a woman who consciously shaped and reshaped her image and blurred distinctions between her private and public self: suggest, signify, exhibit, portray, project, and play. But none is so important as the verb perform, which I argue is all that we can knowingly say about Menken. Menken performed roles upon a stage but she also performed herself offstage and in print, which is to say that she performed a Menken identity that was all about constant change. If this sounds murky, then think of a contemporary entertainer, such as Madonna; despite her many changes, we know the image of Madonna, but who knows the person? Can we avoid confusing the person with the performance?

Similarly to Madonna, Menken affirmed and questioned cultural norms and transgressions in the process of performing aspects of gender, class, and ethnicity. She performed what many at the time believed were natural, immutable identities. My approach to Menken's cultural performance is rooted in the work of Judith Butler, who broke new ground with the book *Gender Trouble* by taking identity theory and applying it to gender. She refuted the argument that many elements of gender are "natural" and substantiated that gender is all performance. When trying to convey that concept, however, Wil Coleman provides the simplest, most concrete example by offering the scenario of a woman asking a man to hold her purse while she tries on clothes. Rather than slinging the strap over his shoulder, the man awkwardly holds the purse away from his body, as if to clarify to any observers "This is not mine. I am a guy." Even with a feminine accouterment, he performs masculinity.[12] Crucial to this scenario is the culture surrounding it. Gender, like race and class, is a historical, social, and

---

[12] Wil Coleman, "Doing Masculinity/Doing Theory," in *Men, Masculinities, and Social Theory*, ed. Jeff Hearn and David Morgan (London: Unwin Hyman, 1990), 196.

cultural construct that "cannot exist outside of time and space."[13] Karen Halttunen's study of middle-class American culture, *Confidence Men and Painted Women*, provides a wonderful example of studying social performances historically. She demonstrates that class distinctions were performed in response to surrounding fears, ideologies, and published material. While the concept of "performing sincerity" may sound oxymoronic, that is exactly what nineteenth-century middle-class Americans found themselves doing in an effort to fulfill their cultural ideals.

"Perform" is the central verb in this text because this study of Menken is all about our inability to say what "is" but rather only what "appears to be." Because cultural history explores human expression, which is always as much about constructions of the mind as about the exterior world, "appears to be" is the only unifying historical truth. Menken performed herself, gender, respectability, class origins, ethnicity, and, through her poetry and the legends that she largely constructed, she continues to perform for a public that constantly searches for different truths in her performances.

If we accept that celebrities are essentially commodities, then we must examine her within the context of commercialism and emerging mass culture. This study uses Menken as a means of exploring her time, to examine what was unsaid and unwritten but manifest in her successes and failures. She does not reflect her time so much as refract it, producing a spectrum of images to investigate and explore.

Celebrities were and are media creations; without the media they cannot exist. By sharing seemingly personal information, the media makes a public figure into a celebrity, that is, a distant social figure with whom spectators perceive themselves as sharing a personal relationship. In the 1830s, cheaper paper and more productive presses suddenly made reading material affordable to the masses. A larger reading public and less expensive production gave rise to the modern newspaper in the form of the penny press, newspapers hocked on the street rather than sold by expensive subscription. This form of sale meant creating papers for a mass audience, and determining what that mass audience wanted to read essentially meant creating the audience itself, putting a pattern to the concerns and desires of the larger reading public. Celebrities gave an intimate, personal feeling to a world that was suddenly expanding beyond comprehension. Menken came into being as a celebrity just as the machinery to create and maintain celebrity was being put into place.[14]

---

[13] Ira Berlin, *Many Thousands Gone: The First Two Centuries of Slavery in North America* (Cambridge: Harvard University Press, 1998), 1.

[14] Andie Tucher, *Froth and Scum: Truth, Beauty and the Ax Murderer in America's First Mass Medium* (Chapel Hill: University of North Carolina Press, 1994); Dan Schiller, *Objectivity and the News: The Public Rise and Fall of Commercial Journalism* (Philadelphia: University of Pennsylvania Press, 1981);

People did not just want to see Menken's stage performances, they wanted to know her; indeed, many wanted and tried to be her. Technically, Menken was most famous for bringing nudity to the stage, marrying too many times, and enjoying friendships with some of the greatest writers of her period. She lived large and died young, at the height of her international fame. When her book of poetry hit the stands two weeks after her death, the world mourned the sensitive woman they had been too insensitive to see. But Menken's identity as a celebrity went beyond obvious reasons for her fame, as many at the time recognized; there was something almost inexplicable about the public's interest in the Menken.

Today, in the early twenty-first century, we live in a world shaped in many ways by the media and infused with celebrity worship. Information on celebrities appears nearly everywhere one looks. One would think we might get tired of seeing their faces, hearing their stories on national news, and reading about their homes. And, in fact, many of us are weary of the celebrity buzz, but there is no denying our society's persistent fascination with them. Menken was at the forefront of that culture of celebrity; she was both creating and feeding a social hunger, and, while not the only one, she was one of very few and was singularly successful.

Celebrities quickly became important during the chaos and expansion of the Civil War era because they served a purpose. Clearly, they provide illusory personal relationships in an increasingly impersonal world; celebrities people a sensational fictional community accessible to all. But celebrities also function as a sort of social mirror. The public can look at them and say, "This is who we are" (fun, glamorous, sincere) or "This is who those people are" (sensational, exhibitionist, uncultivated). Who the public adores says much about that time period, and successful celebrities adjust to maintain public interest. They are both different from the audience in that they are glamorous, glowing in a bright world of beauty and privilege, and familiar because they seem to share their personal lives. They are distant and close, everywhere to be seen and yet rarely spotted in person. Through the media, they promote a sense of shared humanity that supersedes social class, suggesting that, despite their glamour or the viewer's own circumstance, they are on equal footing with their public.[15] Menken's phenomenal success suggests that she was an ideal celebrity, an ideal mirror, during a time of incredible social instability; she changed constantly before the public's eyes, giving the people what they wanted and what they believed or wished they were. But as a mirror, she was also incredibly frustrating, because while she flattered her public, whom among them she mirrored always remained unclear.

Michael Schudsen, *Discovering the News: A Social History of American Newspapers* (New York: Basic Books, 1978).

[15] Peter Buckley, "To the Opera House: Culture and Society in New York City, 1820–1860," Ph.D. dissertation, State University of New York at Stony Brook, 1984, p. 502.

Menken's first significant bid for attention came when she publicized her work as a Jewish poet and actress living in Cincinnati in 1858. Most Americans, however, did not hear of Menken until 1860 when she claimed marriage to a pugilist named John Heenan and became a hot topic in the national press. Her poetry began appearing in nationally distributed newspapers, and she finally won contracts to perform on the New York stage. This was the point at which Menken first became a celebrity, but the initial flush of fame quickly turned to infamy when Heenan himself denied the marriage and Menken was branded as both a bigamist and prostitute. Menken fought back, publishing pages of verse playing on romantic and sentimental stereotypes, suggesting that she was the victim, not the villain. These contradictory portrayals of Menken established her name and image. By 1861, she was well publicized in the mass media as an "adventuress," a sensationalist actress, the victim of love and unethical journalism, and, finally, as one of a self-selected group of New York literati, a bohemian.

A year later, in 1861, Menken starred in an equestrian play called *Mazeppa*, which she turned into an international career within four years. Menken's identity as Mazeppa, the undressed Tartar prince, soon rivaled her image as Heenan's possible wife. Although Menken did not begin performing Mazeppa as her principal role until 1863, this was the role that defined her in the public mind. *Mazeppa* involved faux nudity, war, and horse stunts, and Menken's version was the most exciting spectacle on the boards. Theater historians credit the popularity of Menken's *Mazeppa* for bringing burlesque and nudity to legitimate theaters.[16] Menken and *Mazeppa* were synonymous by 1865, both in the United States and Europe.

Menken also became famous for the men in her life, for both their number and their names. She married and divorced four times in her celebrity life, and spoke of earlier marriages. She also indulged in public affairs with famous men, among them French mulatto novelist Alexandre Dumas and British poet Algernon Charles Swinburne. Besides her many amorous relationships, she enjoyed the acquaintance, and in some instances real friendship, of many authors still celebrated today: Walt Whitman, Mark Twain, Bret Harte, and Charles Dickens, among others. In her own time, Americans would have paired her with other writers they saw as equally famous, such as playwright Gus Daly or novelist Charles Reade. By 1866, the attention she received by legitimate talent began to challenge the images of the Menken made famous by the Heenan scandal, the many marriages, and *Mazeppa*.

By the time of her death two years later, in 1868, Menken had earned wide-ranging assessments of her character because she played to many different audiences over several years of incredible cultural change. The obituaries

---

[16] Robert C. Allen, *Horrible Prettiness: Burlesque and American Culture* (Chapel Hill: University of North Carolina Press, 1991), 117.

gave contradictory information because Menken herself promoted conflict-ing stories of her past and her achievements. And as she became more celebrated, the press and public began confusing her life with those of other female celebrities, and there were many of them.

Menken was the reigning female celebrity actress of the Civil War period, but she was proceeded and followed closely by several others: Lola Montez, Fanny Elssler, Anna Cora Mowatt, Fanny Kemble, and Kate Bateman, among many others. And these were only the brightest stars; glancing through tomes such as Thomas Alston Brown's *History of the American Stage* suggests that numerous other female performers struggled to establish a similar measure of recognition. The term "female celebrity" had been in circulation since the 1830s and could be applied to any woman with a significant public following with whom the public felt they shared an in-timate relationship.[17] People wrote poems in their honor, collected their photographs, and wrote passionately about them in personal diaries and let-ters. Female celebrities could be lecturers, such as the politically oriented Frances Wright, singers such as Adelina Patti, or poets such as Phoebe and Alice Carey; wherever there were women publicly performing as individ-uals, whether on stage or on the printed page, there were celebrities. But this was also a time when images of the lady and the whore constituted the major categories of womanhood and served to define each other. The jour-ney to fame for all of these women was a tightrope walk between what the public considered daring (and therefore alluring) and what was seen as re-spectable (and therefore acceptable). Just as different social performances were expected of men and women in everyday life, celebrity performances also differed by gender. Menken is an especially compelling figure because the peak of her fame spanned the Civil War years; she was fearless in her manipulation of her own image and the media; and she proved to have an uncanny knack for measuring the social weather. She was to the mid-nineteenth-century what Madonna was to the late twentieth: a celebrity who captured and held the public's attention not by creating something new but by taking what was already present but marginal and putting it on center stage. Also Menken marked a larger phenomenon: She was not an isolated female celebrity but rather the reigning celebrity over a host of others who suddenly populated the pages of newspapers and magazines.

If we can see Menken as a cultural foremother to Madonna, than we must also give recognition to Lola Montez, who clearly broke the path for Menken. Montez was a lovely but mediocre dancer of the 1840s who gained some notoriety for her "spider dance," a slim excuse to wiggle suggestively on stage while she shook imaginary spiders from her clothing. But while the dance sparked attention, Montez became a celebrity because she was a good source of gossip: Her affairs and marriages with politically or culturally

---

[17] Buckley, "To the Opera House,"501–502.

powerful men made her adventures interesting to follow. Obviously hoping
to capitalize on Montez's established route to fame, Menken openly borrowed several identifying details from Montez, including family names and
Irish ancestry. Menken also played Montez on stage, adopted her habit of
making up false pasts, and became equally famous for romances with writers
and royalty. Menken so resembled Montez that some writers added events
from the latter's life into Menken's biographies as well. The strangest example may be the long-standing folklore that Menken contracted a morganatic
marriage (marriage between royalty and a commoner without transfer of
property or titles) with the King of Wurtemburg, which seems to stem
entirely from legends of Montez having a morganatic contract with King
Ludwig of Bavaria.[18] Menken borrowed so many details from Montez that
their stories became entangled.

The uncanny resemblance between the Menken and Montez adds to the
confusion about Menken; it can be difficult to determine where the two part
company, even though Montez was famous two decades before Menken,
and passed away just as Menken came into fame, in 1861. Indeed, their
connection suggests a line of celebrity foremothers that can be traced from
Montez to Menken and on through to reigning female celebrities of the
present. They were dangerous but beguiling, beautiful, mercurial in their
emotions, fearless, and arrogant; a combination of masculine freedoms and
feminine grace in a female body. Popular images of Montez and Menken
can be so interchangeable that if one does not see the name, it is not clear
which one is being described: "Her beauty was reputed to conceal a physical courage as great as any man's, and the cigarettes she constantly smoked
characterized her disdain for conventional femininity. She could ride like
an Amazon, was deadly with a pistol, and had horsewhipped more than
one man who dared impugn her character."[19] The above description is of
Montez, but similar ones would later be attached to Menken. Obviously,
such characteristics had appeal during the period, or Montez and Menken
would not have used them as signifiers, but it is equally important to recognize how thin the line was between some of these performances of celebrity.
Menken was merely one of the most successful entertainers to pick up on
images of Montez, and literally scores of now-forgotten actresses attempted
to do the same with Menken's image. Many of the stories of both Montez
and Menken imitators found their way into depictions of Menken as she
made her way across the United States and Europe.

Menken herself probably picked up on Montez's image for several reasons,
including the fact that it gave her a part to play offstage. But perhaps as

---

[18] Montez did not have a morganatic marriage with King Ludwig, but they did have an affair and he
did give her a title. King Wurtemburg merely attended Menken's performances and may have known
her socially. Bruce Seymour, *Lola Montez: A Life* (New Haven: Yale University Press, 1995), 95–242;
Elizabeth Brookes, *Prominent Women of Texas* (Akron: Werner, 1896), 158.

[19] Seymour, *Lola Montez*, 167.

important to an ambitious woman like Menken who did not have the benefit of connections or inherited wealth, Montez was entirely self-invented. She had determined her own path at a time when most women (including public performers) felt they had few choices. Montez, like the archetypal American hero (and wholly unlike the heroine), moved independently, engaging in various adventures, and inspiring others to celebrate her in song and story. Menken's own desire to play the hero can be read in her biographies that tend to read like popular fiction of the day, with a young Menken traveling alone or with a male servant/companion through untamed southwestern lands. And when Menken finally met with Montez at the end of her life, perhaps Montez expressed to Menken what she had said in her autobiography, that regardless of how one judged her, she had made an impact. She had "influenced the mind or manners of society, for good or evil."[20]

Menken did not witness the scorn Montez had faced during her youth, only the respect she received in her twilight years. In the final years of her life, Montez remade her image, traveling from the United States to England and back, giving humorous but thoughtful critiques on women's rights, American culture, slavery, and a host of other issues.[21] Menken undoubtedly saw Montez as proof that a woman could live an adventurous life and still gain social respect; she was a powerful, if somewhat misleading role model.[22]

Since actresses were public women, and perceived as related by occupation to prostitutes, it was much harder to cultivate an image of respectability than one of daring. Fanny Kemble, a British actress from a well-established theatrical family, forged a respectable image by publishing her *Journal* in 1835. Writing gave her a way to communicate with the public as a voice and mind and circumvent the complications of speaking from an inescapably female body.[23] Menken attempted to do the same with her own writing, but her stage persona veered in the opposite direction. Menken *wanted* to capitalize on her female body and wanted to do so in mainstream theaters. Such desires were inherently contradictory in the early part of the century, but they became more compatible by the late antebellum period, although it still took incredible skill at both reading the public and manipulating the press to realize such goals without destroying her career in the process.

[20] Montez, *Lectures of Lola Montez (Countess of Landsfeld), Including Her Autobiography* (New York: Rudd and Carleton, 1858), 12–13.

[21] Seymour, *Lola Montez*, 373.

[22] Menken, in fact, paid Montez a visit once in January 1861, because she said a "strange, irresistible attraction" had compelled her. She wrote to a friend, "I have been to see Lola Montez, to-day. I think she is happier than I am. She asks nothing more of the world, while I ask much. You know wherein dwells the better philosophy." Letter quoted in Robert H. Newell, "Adah Isaacs Menken," periodical unknown, pasted into "Biography of Adah Isaacs Menken. Extra Illustrated," Harris Rare Books, 76-M545x, Brown University Library, Providence, Rhode Island.

[23] Faye E. Dudden, *Women in American Theatre: Actresses and Audiences, 1790–1870* (New Haven: Yale University Press, 1994), 44–45.

People had opinions about Menken's character, and they wanted to know more about her. They wanted to know who she "really" was when not trying to win over her public.

But the Menken whom they saw was always trying to win over an audience, of course; what viewers took to be the "real" Menken or her "private" life were ones created for public consumption. Once famous, Menken did not sell tickets to plays but rather to see the Menken; her true talent lay less in her stage performance than in her advertising. The Menken was a commodity of her creation. Menken played with the midcentury notion that there are two principle forms of behavior: sincerity and duplicity. Although antebellum Americans acknowledged fears of confidence men and other social predators pretending to be sincere, they also tended to believe that the "real" performances were not something purposely put together, but rather the individual's unself-conscious response to a given situation. They operated on the assumption that informal or backstage behavior revealed the essential self.[24] Using the backstage language of intimacy allowed Menken to suggest she shared her true self, even when done in a public venue.

Menken went about this in many ways, most frequently by "exposing" (in truth, performing) her emotions, whether she spoke as an actress, a poet, an essayist, or correspondent. By constantly sharing stories of her childhood, she also suggested that her personal past was open for viewing. In interviews and personal letters from 1860 to 1868, she spoke easily of her late father. It was not until she had sustained national attention for several years that journalists began noticing that she frequently changed her father's name, ethnicity, and occupation. She claimed fathers from the margins of society, from groups most Americans considered not quite white; they were usually Jewish, Irish, or Spanish. Posthumous writings suggested that she also claimed African ancestry. She sparked the public's desire for information by creating several incredible stories that played on the tropes of popular fiction, and thus served to make her larger than life. She spoke of being a childhood star in Havana, and captured by Indians on the Texas frontier. Like Barnum, Menken left an abundance of material on her life that said a lot about the preconceptions and interests of her audience yet in the end revealed little about herself.[25]

Indeed, Menken, owed a tremendous debt to Barnum. If she learned her celebrity style from Montez, she copied promotional skills from Barnum, and profited from the entertainment world that he shaped. P. T. Barnum was the most successful showman of the nineteenth century and in many

---

[24] For a discussion of performance of sincerity, see Karen Halttunen, *Confidence Men and Painted Women* (New Haven: Yale University Press, 1982); for identity theory, see Erving Goffman, *The Presentation of the Self in Everyday Life* (Garden City, N. Y.: Doubleday, 1959), 75, 70, 128.

[25] Buckley, "To the Opera House," 471.

ways determined the foundations of America's entertainment culture. It was he who first convinced the masses that theater could be pure and pious by putting on *The Drunkard*, a temperance play, in his family-oriented New York museum. As important, Barnum made mainstream what James Cooke describes as "artful deception" and Barnum himself called "Humbug," a complex style of showmanship dependent on the public's desire to be challenged. Menken made herself into the object of controversy. She challenged the public to think and debate: Was she ingenious or devious? Artistic or opportunistic? Barnum's success revealed that Americans wanted to be provoked and that lies could be far more profitable than truth as long as they were more entertaining.[26]

With the incredibly successful tour of Jenny Lind in 1841, Barnum also destabilized the notion that women who performed in public were inherently disrespectable. It was a shift that would prove incredibly valuable to subsequent female celebrities. Before Lind, female celebrities were considered outside the bounds of good society because one could not be of the public world, female, and respectable; it was an impossible equation. Barnum broke that code by advertising the domestic qualities of Lind. He played up her femininity by downplaying her female body, because to be a female body on stage was to lose femininity. Instead, he presented her as saintly and self-effacing despite her celebrity. Her sublime image was heightened by the fact that she came to the stage plain in appearance and dress and unleashed a voice of surprising strength and sweetness. Menken and many others profited from changes wrought by Lind but rarely shared her self-effacing, genuinely altruistic qualities; female performers did not have to be like Lind to benefit from society's acceptance that female celebrities could be respectable. Simply by becoming famous without losing social status, Lind irrevocably changed public perceptions of female celebrity.

This was an incredibly important shift for performers such as Menken, who wanted to play for mainstream audiences. For if a female celebrity could prove herself respectable, then she could perform for middle-class audiences without endangering the reputation of her female spectators. Menken's fame would prove that even simply destablizing a notorious image could suggest enough respectability to win contracts in decent theaters. After all, Menken did not introduce nudity to the American stage; there was plenty of that going on in musical halls in cities nationwide. She introduced it to middle-class audiences. Respectable society's willingness to entertain her performance is what gave it cultural power.

Because later accounts of Menken's audiences tend to rely on newspaper reviews from her dismal 1865 performances in New York, they almost

---

[26] James W. Cooke, *The Arts of Deception: Playing with Fraud in the Age of Barnum* (Cambridge: Harvard University Press, 2001), 23; Neil Harris, *Humbug: The Art of P. T. Barnum* (Boston: Little, Brown, 1973), 105–108, 113–141.

uniformly assert that she performed for crass male audiences, but evidence suggests that the types of spectators one could find in Menken's audience varied greatly depending on time and place. When Menken first began performing in cities in the Deep South and Midwest, she played in theaters patronized primarily by men and those catering to the middle class. In New York City she first performed in places such as the Old Bowery Theater, for predominately working-class, male audiences. As she gained celebrity status, however, she again played for male and female spectators. Indeed, she began performing matinees in 1863, which were scheduled specifically so that respectable women and children to attend. Once out west her audience became mostly male because the population itself was mostly male, but records of Astley's theater in London suggest that her audiences again included women and children.[27] Most of her spectators were undoubtedly white, but she did perform in theaters with seating for people of color. *Mazeppa*, her most popular piece, relied on physical display and pantomime, so in places with extremely cosmopolitan populations, such as San Francisco or Virginia City, members could conceivably come from any region in the world; one did not have to speak English to enjoy the spectacle. Social class also shifted with the location and timing. Generally speaking, Menken's fame attracted middle-class as well as working-class spectators, and as more middle-class people attended and commented on her performances, she became more accepted as a sensation, if not as a person.

Nevertheless, many Americans continued to consider celebrities such as Menken culturally dangerous because of their financial success and growing acceptability. The success of such salacious performers made it clear that market forces were disrupting social hierarchies. As more Americans entered the middle class, particularly during the war years, definitions of respectability began changing. A sort of tug-of-war ensued between the antebellum middle class and the emerging middle class over what should be considered acceptable for mixed-gender audiences, and whether or not fashion should be on equal footing with respectability. The established taste makers, members of the antebellum middle class, tended to control the press with the exception of publications such as the *New York Herald*, which catered to the masses, but recent joiners of the middle class now had money for leisure and along with that came the power to challenge previous standards. In the United States, celebrities tended to emerge from the lower classes and their status clearly came not from established institutions but from a mercurial cultural marketplace.[28] Their existence signified that the larger public could be fooled by performance, and provoked fears in established

---

[27] Receipts from Astley's Theatre, London, England, for Oct. 19 through Nov. 26, 1867, Adah Isaacs Menken correspondence in ALS file (hereafter AIM ALS), HTC.

[28] Thomas N. Baker, *Sentiment and Celebrity: Nathaniel Parker Willis and the Trials of Literary Fame,* (New York: Oxford University Press, 1999), 8.

taste makers that as the larger public became more powerful, puffery and sensation would eclipse talent and sincerity. Speculation over a celebrity's "real" character were commonplace throughout the 1850s and 1860s and absolutely tied to struggles over cultural control. With her ability to perform contradictions, Menken provoked more debate than most.

While Menken's changing truths compelled public scrutiny, her tactics were part of a larger cultural phenomenon. As Andie Tucher pithily summarizes, "Antebellum America was a jamboree of ballyhoo, exaggeration, chicanery, sham, and flim-flam. . . . In fact, we cannot understand nineteenth-century culture, let alone nineteenth-century journalism, without understanding its complicated relationships with the truth. . . . the adventures of man and myth were completely indistinguishable and equally improbable." Menken had good company in her construction of false pasts; Barnum and author Ned Buntline, among others, wrote life stories equally riddled with hyperbole and falsehood both because more adventurous texts sold well and because exciting self-portrayals enhanced the market value of their other cultural productions. Menken apparently subscribed to Barnum's contention that "an untruth that does not deceive is not a lie. And a truth that does not satisfy is no better than a lie." Barnum argued that there was virtue in entertaining the masses, regardless of the level of veracity involved, and his self-portrayal was clearly part of the entertainment; in Menken's case, it was everything. Indeed, what Constance Roarke once suggested of Barnum could also be said of Menken, that perhaps he truly had no personal character because "he had no private life. . . . he lived in the public; at times it seemed he was the public."[29]

What is seen as a falsehood in our time was in hers a form of entertainment, and because "artful deception" was so common by midcentury, most of the public would have recognized the possibility that she, too, juggled truth and lies. Her various life stories, like all successful hoaxes, were a skillful blend of the believable and the extraordinary. She was emblematic of her time; even the penny press regularly padded its pages with hyperbolic stories, understanding that part of their job was to entertain. Newspapers rarely clarified when a story was fabricated because that was the beauty of the prank — that some readers would get it while others would swallow it with fascinated disbelief. They played to their audience to sell papers, and understood that the mid-nineteenth-century reader hungered to "expose," to uncover deceit by virtue of his or her own talents of deduction. Such marketing practices required constant deceit to promote the public's craving and constant debate to attract its attention. This kind of chicanery was useful for a woman striving to sell her image. Menken did not necessarily have a past that needed hiding; she may have acted on the same impulse as

[29] Tucher, *Froth and Scum*, 46–47, 55; Harris, *Humbug*, 79; Constance Roarke, *Trumpets of Jubilee* (New York: Harcourt Brace, 1927), 371.

Barnum, believing that "everything depended upon getting the people to think, and talk, and become curious and excited."[30]

Menken played upon the tensions in Victorian culture represented by the close link between Barnum, who was celebrated and successful, and the confidence man, who figured prominently in urban fiction and functioned as a social warning. Both practiced artful deception, but one was largely revered while the other was feared. Of course, their goals were quite different even if their methods were similar; Barnum established a new world of entertainment, while the fictional confidence man preyed on young men and women coming to the city, appearing helpful but ultimately leading them to ruin. Karen Haltunnen asserts that the confidence man of antebellum fiction personified hypocrisy, which was seen as an enormous threat to American society. Hypocrisy arose directly from a crisis of social identity faced by Americans on the move both socially and geographically. "In what was believed to be a fluid social world where no one occupied a fixed social position, the question 'Who am I?' loomed large; and in an urban social world where many of the people who met face-to-face each day were strangers, the question 'Who are you really?" assumed even greater significance."[31] Imbedded in the figure of the confidence man was the fear that people were passing for what they were not. And yet at the same time there was Barnum, practicing many of the same arts but for entertainment. But was entertainment a source of benign pleasure or was it socially destructive?

The idea that Menken was "fallen" was less important than her manipulation of her admirers. She was not the "painted lady," so much as the confidence man. And the confidence man, although portrayed as villainous, had an important social function: He clarified the uneasy relationship between stated ethics and tolerated practices.[32] What did it mean for a woman to play a role seen as inherently male? Menken occupied the link between the entrepreneurial entertainer and the confidence man. Many of the fears expressed about confidence men echo in criticisms of Menken, that she was passing for what she was not and making what was reprehensible appear benign.

Of course, if one were to ask most twenty-first-century Americans to describe their nineteenth-century counterparts, they would probably talk about repressed Victorians rather than Barnum and ballyhoo. But prudery and humbug were two sides of the same coin: The middle-class was obsessed with identifying and creating order, and therefore was equally concerned with anything that suggested the opposite – masking and chaos. As popular magazines became ever more specific about appropriate conduct, other

---

[30] Tucher, *Froth and Scum*, 52, 70; Harris, *Humbug*, 82.   [31] Halttunen, *Confidence Men*, xv.

[32] Gary Lindberg, *The Confidence Man in American Literature* (New York: Oxford University Press, 1982), 4.

forms of popular culture challenged propriety. Beginning in the late 1850s, burlesque entertainment, a form of comedy that did not yet involve nudity, became popular because it poked fun at and deliberately confused class and gender signifiers, and presented social order as intrinsically absurd. Menken could hardly pull off her humbug if she did not, like Barnum, project a resemblance to mainstream culture. Her poetry and essays reflect an ability to generate an incredible mix of sentimentalism, intellectualism, and sensationalism – three strands of expression that commingled freely in nineteenth-century popular culture.

To understand the public Menken wooed, one must also understand patterns of conduct that shaped the cultural cosmology of the population. Her story is clearly attached to a changing middle-class identity, with its characteristics reconfigured by the social, economic, and cultural changes unleashed by war. She wanted to play in the most profitable theaters, and by the late 1850s, that meant playing to the middle class rather than the working class. Cultivation of esthetic knowledge, respectability, and fashion signified middle-class identity, and people were not distinguishable by one characteristic alone. Respectability meant exhibiting a measure of moral superiority, while cultivation implied demonstrating an esthetic or intellectual sensibility. Fashion, not surprisingly, was more indeterminate; although on the surface it seemed to be about esthetic judgment, in truth it signaled inclusion in or exclusion from wealthy circles.[33] Although fashion became a middle-class signifier, by midcentury it simultaneously undermined both cultivation and respectability.

Menken was all about fashion, even if part of her fashion was performance of respectability and cultivation. Fashion is an illusion that must constantly change; it is founded on appearance rather than substance and is a way for people to change their self-performance.[34] In her early years in the limelight, Menken tried to capture respectability through her written voice, but that characteristic for the most part eluded her. Respectability, after all, was grounded in restraint and incompatible with commercialization, and thus, the Menken. Consumerism, which was certainly fueled by fashion, replaced restraint with self-indulgence by the turn of the century.[35] In the midst of this shift from respectability to fashion, Menken came into being, and so she pursued both characteristics. Being fashionable made her famous, but lack of respectability ultimately made her notorious.

Luckily for Menken, fashion overtook respectability in the marketplace during the Civil War years. Although the Civil War itself rarely intruded into her life, the cultural dislocations created by war were crucial to Menken's success. She played to audiences facing national crisis and she geared her

---

[33] Richard Butsch, *The Making of American Audiences: From Stage to Television, 1750–1990* (London: Cambridge, 2000), 61.

[34] Ibid., 68. [35] Ibid., 67.

performance toward their fears and desires. Families, friends, and towns were divided in their allegiance to the Confederacy or the Union, and the resulting fissures revealed layers of cultural and ideological differences. Americans abhorred the bloodshed but they most feared the destruction of mythologies and ideologies that had supposedly united a diverse people into a democratic nation. The war made it clear that Americans actually defined their national heritage quite differently. Most important in terms of understanding Menken's decisions, war further destabilized class identity, gender roles, and racial definition, which had already been brought into question by successful industrialization and urban growth. It also raised questions about national versus religious and ethnic affiliation, heightening the danger of difference. In the spring of 1861, when Menken first rode as Mazeppa, few Americans thought that the war would go on as long as it did, but the act of secession had already brought about the beginning of the end of the old nation.[36] In the Union states, particularly in cities driven by commerce, such as New York and Philadelphia, the war gave rise to an economic boom. Disruption released desires repressed during peace time, scrambled status signifiers and gender roles, and spurred industrialization that increased the amount of spare change needed to create a mass entertainment market.

Menken played with the questions raised, she performed gender on a spectrum that had women assessing her attraction as a man, and men speaking of her as "one of the boys."[37] Her aggressive claims of Jewish identity, her preference for stage roles hinting at Orientalism, and the hearsay about her ancestry combined to present her as exotic and mysterious. She played upon the nineteenth-century fear of anonymity by telling so many detailed and varied stories of her past and her parentage that the public could not sort them out. She claimed both Confederate and Union allegiance, but more importantly promoted herself as rebellious, regardless of her adversary. But perhaps Menken became most famous for taking what were essentially working-class forms of entertainment and making them just acceptable enough to play in legitimate theaters, yet so close to scandalous that they filled those theaters. She pushed the boundaries of identity and taste and thrilled audiences.

From 1861 to 1863, the first two years of war, Menken traveled throughout the Northeast and what we now call the Midwest, performing Mazeppa and other "breeches parts," the descriptive term for male roles performed by actresses. In 1863, she fled the war-torn East and earned a fortune performing for silver miners out west. In 1864 she decided to try her

---

[36] One of the best books I've found on Civil War and society is Catherine Clinton and Nina Silber, *Divided Houses: Gender and the Civil War* (New York: Oxford, 1992).

[37] Tess Ardenne, "Black-Eyed Susan," *Golden Era*, April 24, 1864, p. 5, c. 3; Walter Lemann, *Memories of an Old Actor* (San Francisco: A Roman, 1886), 301.

luck abroad, and sailed to London, where she performed *Mazeppa* for over a hundred nights. The attention Menken received from royalty and British literati had a serious impact back home. Suddenly, formerly skeptical Americans began to see that she might be more than a "shape actress," and while some admired her for her fame, others now saw her as a much more serious threat to public morality. She performed only once more in the United States, on Broadway in 1866, to venomous reviews.[38] She quickly recrossed the Atlantic to charm Parisian audiences and the French authors she had long admired. And finally, on the oppressively hot day of August 10, 1868, Menken died from a mysterious illness and was buried with a modest funeral in Paris. Two weeks later her book of poetry, *Infelicia*, was released to the public and motivated another debate over the true nature of her character.[39] Although reviewers became polarized over her poetry, some finding it drivel and others seeing true genius, *Infelicia* remained continuously in print until 1902, and is currently in print.[40]

Menken's skillful manipulation of the public suggests that she understood that sustaining an identity meant not only possessing the required attributes but also adhering to the group's standards of conduct and appearance.[41] Early in her career, Menken promoted herself as a "protean comic," meaning that she excelled at rapidly transforming into several characters over the course of a short play. In farces such as *Three Fast Women* and *Unprotected Female*, she performed as many as nine male or female parts, and often ended the evening with impersonations of famous public figures. Her talent lay in her ability to differentiate between several characters by playing with easy-identified stereotypes. Given her proclivity toward self-promotion and role changing, her performance of "Menken" as a figure of constant mutation is hardly surprising.

Some readers will be disturbed at the idea that Menken was entirely a performance, arguing that that would be impossible for anyone. It is not my intention to suggest that she did not express unconscious preferences or exhibit a few consistent traits. Menken clearly enjoyed food, understood horses, and liked dogs and children. Unlike most touring actors, she rarely complained about travel conditions. On a personal level, both men and women found her charismatic and charming. She drank, gambled, and

---

[38] Most notably, William Winter, "Theaters, Mazeppa at the Broadway Theatre," *New York Daily Tribune,* May 1, 1866, p. 5.

[39] The Latin word "infelicia" translates to "unhappiness" and corresponds with "Infelix," the masculine form meaning "the unhappy one," with which Menken began signing letters in 1866. See Adah Isaacs Menken correspondence in AIM ALS, HTC.

[40] Elizabeth Cady Stanton, "Adah Isaacs Menken," *SenecaRevolution,* Oct. 1, 1868; "Miss Menken's Poems," *Every Saturday,* Sept. 12, 1868; *New York Clipper* quoted in Wolf Mankowitz, *Mazeppa: The Lives, Loves and Legends of Adah Isaacs Menken* (New York: Stein and Day, 1982), 238.

[41] Erving Goffman, *The Presentation of Self in Everyday Life* (Garden City, N.Y.: Doubledaly, 1959), 75.

socialized with irreverent friends in every city she visited and was known for being generous, impulsive, and gregarious. In her letters she displays a keen wit, appreciation for the absurd, and an engagingly reckless approach to life. She expressed her opinions confidently and enjoyed intellectual relationships with men. She read widely, from popular fiction to scholarly work, and liked to discuss poetry, philosophy, and religion. A shrewd and gifted manipulator, she exercised those talents on virtually everyone around her, from her closest friends to the public at large. Once she could command a high salary, she extracted exorbitant promises from theater managers and then spent the money treating and supporting less successful writers and performers. Her letters reveal an extremely self-absorbed person, prone to depression, insomnia, and periods of intense anxiety. She was well aware that she had difficulty separating fantasy from reality. In 1860 she wrote to a friend, "It is so unfortunate, this imaginative nature; it is ever creating ideals and seeking to invest them in reality."[42] In many letters, Menken berates herself for being vain and impulsive, but Menken's moments of self-loathing were merely counterpoints to deep self-love. She fascinated others because she enthralled herself.[43] To say that the Menken was a performance is not to entirely divorce the persona from the person but rather to suggest that she was consistently self-conscious about how others perceived her and what she must do to maintain interest. Menken was the performance; who she was underneath that mask is difficult to define, and is ultimately unimportant when using her as a lens on her time period. How her performance was used by Menken and has been used by others, both then and now, proves far more historically illuminating.

She understood that "the Menken" was a public figure, and therefore a creation; she also knew this was something that the public did not understand. She was aware that her audiences mistook her confessional poetry and offstage performances as expressions of her "real self." She explained to a friend in 1861:

> I do not give all my heart out in my writings – I mean for publication. Let me confess that I sometimes affect to do so when writing of something I know nothing about. But public writing is like acting – to reach the hearts of others we must appear in earnest ourselves. We must convey the idea that we feel and suffer all that we portray. It would be absurd to say that an actor is a part of every part he represe nts; and the same of the poet. It is the art of each to portray the passions and emotions of the whole great human heart.

Still, she adds, "you must give me credit for not feeling *all* like an actress."[44] Despite her tag line – suggesting that there was an "authentic self" behind

---

[42] Newell, "Adah Isaacs Menken," n.p.
[43] The most comprehensive collection of Menken's letters are in the ALS file at HTC.
[44] Newell, "Adah Isaacs Menken," n.p.

Ambrotype Ada sent to Rosina in 1857. Menken was probably twenty-two years old. (Harvard Theatre Collection)

the images – Menken did not observe boundaries that would persuade onlookers to agree; Menken made little attempt to present a consistent self. Continuity is the defining criteria of identity, and it "entails being the same person today as yesterday or last year or next week."[45] However, as Menken continued to move from place to place, she did *not* have to be the same person that she had been before except within the confines of print, and even that was negotiable.

Intrinsic to the story of Menken is the fact that from the time she first entered the public eye up until the present, others have actively contributed to creating and recreating her image. Most of Menken's biographical claims came from the pen of another, even if she supposedly dictated the stories. Throughout the years of her stardom, particularly when she traversed the northeast from 1860 to 1863, journalists published short biographical notices, using material provided by Menken or one of her publicists. Immediately following her death, several sensational biographies made competing claims about various details of her life, from her ethnicity to her marriages.

---

[45] Roy Baumeister, *Identity: Cultural Change and the Struggle for Self* (New York: Oxford University Press, 1986), 18.

Other fans and friends recorded their reminiscences of this famous woman over the next few decades. These biographies eventually formed the basis of twentieth-century versions of her life as writers scrambled to find solid ground in Menken's fluid self-presentation. If one now searches the Internet for mentions of Adah Isaacs Menken, she appears under several different descriptions, including black, Jewish, lesbian, and bohemian. In the century and a half since her death, her identity has, if anything, become more confusing. And the subtext to contemporary depictions of Menken expresses the same frustration as journalists had century and a half before: Why is she so impossible to categorize? What evidence should we accept?

The years of Menken's public life, from roughly 1857 to 1868, were among the most tumultuous of the nineteenth century, and the Civil War period is conventionally seen as a watershed in American history, with the rivers flowing in opposite directions across the divide. The Civil War itself has generated its own industry in the shape of feature films and documentaries, textual histories, national parks, fiction, comic books, travel tours, and celebrity reenactors. *Performing Menken* traces the cultural and social changes often masked by emphasis on the war itself. Menken, a self-invented, self-made female celebrity, responded to the desires of a nation rife with contention. Ultimately, Menken's story makes it clear that whatever order we struggle to project on the chaos of the Civil War era, it was a complex time of contending views. Menken in all her many forms reflected a culture made up of many currents that, like all rivers, reshaped the terrain that held it.

Chapter 1

Playing Deborah

[The reporter has] taken several liberties with his knowledge of the facts, the most serious of which is that I embraced the Jewish religion. I was born in that faith and have adhered to it throughout my erratic career.

A. I. [Menken] Heenan to the *New York Illustrated News*, March 24, 1860

. . . as far as form and birth is concerned, [Mrs. Menken] is no Jewess, although she invariably calls the Hebrews "our people," and sympathizes altogether with them when she feels like sympathizing.

The Cincinnati *Israelite*, December 30, 1864

On March 1858, Ada Menken sat on a steamer just outside Baton Rouge, Louisiana, writing a letter to her sister-in-law, Rosina, whom she had yet to meet. Her script scrawled thin and skittish across the page. "My dear Sister," she began, "Do not think our long silence neglect, it cannot be that when we talk of you everyday and love you so dearly." At the moment she traveled alone, she explained, because "'our' dear Alex left Nashville two weeks before I did and has gone to Shreveport and made the arrangements for me to play there a few weeks." She added, "I was obliged to leave the [New Orleans] Gaiety Theatre in consequence of nonpayment where I am now going we can make more and be far more comfortable. I intended to be in Cincinnati by Passover but it is impossible, but depend on seeing us this summer as soon as the spring season is over we will come to you and all the dear ones at home."[1] Ada (she had yet to add the "h" to her name) had married Alexander Isaac Menken, Rosina's estranged half-brother, in Livingston, Texas, nearly two years before and had been corresponding with Alexander's four half-siblings, and Rosina's husband, Lewis, ever since. She had her motives: Menken was setting the stage for the arrival of herself as a Jewish wife, poet, and actress.

There is no record of what Menken told Alexander's family or members of the Reform community about her past other than the fact that she began claiming that her father had been a Jewish merchant in the New Orleans area. The only evidence of Menken's Jewish identity is her own claims. Indeed, all evidence suggests the opposite: that Menken was neither born Jewish nor converted to Judaism. Yet Jewish identity in Cincinnati was central to

---

[1] Adah Isaacs Menken (hereafter AIM) to Rosina [née Menken], March 8, 1858, "Biography of Adah Isaacs Menken. Extra Illustrated," Harris Rare Books, 76-M545x, Brown University Library, Providence, Rhode Island (hereafter Menken scrapbook).

Menken's initial success at crafting a public persona. How she capitalized on a marginal identity and how that identity enabled her to market herself is the subject of this chapter. In the process of exploring her Jewish life in Ohio, however, it is helpful to have some sense of who she was before she became Adah Isaacs Menken, which was not a story she chose to share truthfully.

Through her 1856 Texas marriage license to Alexander Isaac Menken we can connect Menken to her former name: Ada Bertha Theodore. As Theodore, the woman who would become Menken published poetry and performed on stage in East Texas but met with little success and landed no starring roles. Later, in 1860, Menken would once explain that she had originally eloped from New Orleans to Texas around 1853 for a short-lived marriage with a wealthy man's son. She decided to stay in Texas after the father had the marriage annulled, and most evidence suggests that she found work as an equestrienne for a traveling horse show, or hippodrome.[2]

Menken most consistently claimed to be a native of the New Orleans area, a city famous in the United States for being exotic, sinful, and Gallic. A century of racial intermingling also led to its reputation as a city rife with indeterminate ancestry, and this reputation combined with Menken's mysterious ways and the name Theodore later suggested to posthumous biographers that she may have had African ancestry. In 1868, just after her death, biographer George Barclay wrote that her father had been August Theodore, a free man of color. The free people of color made up a distinct racial caste in southern Louisiana; they were people with more white than African blood and deep ties to Louisiana's French Creole culture. Many of them could pass for white had they wished, and indeed, in the upheaval of the Civil War, many left the area to live elsewhere as whites. In 1938 a freelance writer named John Kendall proposed the same theory as Barclay: that Menken's father had been August Theodore. This time the theory took root and now, in the twenty-first century, Menken is often identified as African American.[3] But that was not an identity suggested in her own

---

[2] Lucille Fain, articles on AIM ran on the first page of the Sunday supplement, section D, from May 17 to July 19, 1981, in the Nacogdoches *Redland Herald*; "Adah Isaacs Menken, the Wife of John C. Heenan, the Benecia Boy," New York *Illustrated News* (hereafter *Illustrated News*), March 24, 1860; Kate Wilson Davis, "Adah Isaacs Menken – Her Life and Poetry in America," M.A. thesis, Southern Methodist University, 1944, pp. 20–23. Davis derives this information from nineteenth-century claims made by equestrian trainer and circus master Dan Rice and a biography by theater critic Fulton Oursler, *The World's Delight* (New York: Harper, 1929), 26. Hippodromes and small traveling circuses were popular in East Texas at the time, perhaps explaining where Menken acquired equestrienne skills. Menken's claims to have performed in Havana during this time are undermined by conflicting dates; see Wolf Mankowitz, *Mazeppa: The Lives, Loves and Legends of Adah Isaacs Menken* (New York: Stein and Day, 1982), and Gregory Eiselien, ed., *Infelicia and Other Writings* (Peterborough, Ontario: Broadview Literary Press, 2002).

[3] George Lippard Barclay, *The Life and Remarkable Career of Adah Isaacs Menken, the Celebrated Actress* (Philadelphia: Barclay, 1868), 25; John S. Kendall, " 'The World's Delight': The Story of Adah Isaacs

time; no one ever accused her of "passing" or claimed to have known her as a young black girl. Indeed, census records and city documents reveal that it was far more likely that Menken was a white Protestant from Memphis who moved to New Orleans when she was fifteen.[4] At this point in the story it is important to recognize that Menken concealed her past from the beginning and that concealment sparked curiosity. Questions about Menken's racial identity run throughout this story of her life, but the theory of African ancestry was not put forth publicly until after her death.

The Jewish and black identities have tantalized biographers since Menken's death and are accepted as fact by many, despite lack of evidence. They are identities essentially created by both Menken, in her evasiveness, and the public, in their compulsion to solve her mystery. The only truth reliable is that Menken never clearly or consistently explained who she had been before marrying Alexander Isaacs Menken, and that mystery, combined with the city she claimed as her birthplace, made her excitingly and dangerously ambiguous. At the time, such ambiguity tapped directly into basic fears among white Christians at a time of expanding mobility: What if one befriended her, hired her, fell for her, or married her and discovered that she was not white? Most of what can be asserted about her pre-Menken years comes from piecing together fragments from official documents, decaying newspapers, and her earliest extensive press release.

An 1854 Galveston marriage certificate tells us that before she married Menken, she had married W. H. Kneass, signing herself as "Adda Theodore." She later described "Nelson Kneass" as a musician from her stock company (which she did not name).[5] While Kneass continued to tour she remained in the small town of Washington (now Washington-on-the-Brazos) and began sending simple poetry to the *Liberty Gazette*, a weekly newspaper published in a nearby town. Signing her work as "Ada Bertha," she submitted several sentimental poems, including one dedicated to her "Brother Gus" and another to Josephine, possibly a younger sister. Menken later claimed having started the paper with managing editor Henry Shea, but the *Liberty Gazette* suggests otherwise, referring to her in 1855 as a "gifted correspondent."[6]

Menken," *Louisiana Historical Quarterly* 21 (July 1938): 850–52; Arna Bontemps and Jack Conroy, *They Seek a City* (Garden City, N.Y.: Doubleday, Doran, 1945), 98; Mankowitz, *Mazeppa*, 33.

[4] John Cofran, "The Identity of Adah Isaacs Menken: A Theatrical Mystery Solved," *Theatre Survey* (May 1990): 47–54.

[5] Facsimile of marriage certificate published in Mankowitz, *Mazeppa*, 41; *Illustrated News*, March 31, 1860. W. H. Kneass could have been the son of a number of Kneasses in New Orleans, as has also been suggested. See New Orleans City Directories and Louisiana Census Reports, New Orleans Public Library, New Orleans, Louisiana; Louisiana, vols. 9 and 13, R. G. Dun & Co. Collection, Baker Library, Harvard Business School, Cambridge, Massachusetts.

[6] Ada Bertha, "To my Brother Gus," *Liberty Gazette*, Oct. 8, 1855 (writer's date also Oct.), 2; "The Bright and the Beautiful; to Josephine, "*Liberty Gazette*, Nov. 12, 1855 (writer's date Oct.), 2; editorial note, *Liberty Gazette,* Nov. 5, 1855.

From the earliest known public records of Menken, she demonstrated an unconventional approach to marriage that suggests her unions were more a means than an end; they allowed her to pursue her desires, rather than hampering her freedom. On November 5, 1855, the *Liberty Gazette* published a poem she had written to her young husband in October, entitled "I am Thine – to W. H. K." But Menken later suggested her marriage to Kneass had merely been a means of escaping the unwanted advances of a married man. While still Kneass's wife, she fell in love with a Texas Ranger, last name Travis, stationed in Austin. Her writings in the *Liberty Gazette* support her story that while Kneass was touring, Ada invited Travis to "come and see her."[7] By November she had moved to Austin and felt unmarried enough to publish a flirtatious little ditty "New Advertisement!!! to R. M. T.****," that began "I'm young and free, the pride of girls,/ With hazel eyes and 'nut brown curls,'" and ended, "I've had full many a Beau Ideal,/Yet never – never – found one *real*/There must be one I know, somewhere, in all this circumambient air;/And I should dearly love to see him!/now what if *you* should chance to be him?"[8] This time she signed her "advertisement" "Ada Bertha T———e."

Despite her attraction to R. M. T.****, it was Alexander Isaac Menken whom she married four months later, in a brief ceremony on April 3, 1856, in Galveston, signing the marriage certificate "Ada Bertha Theodore."[9] It is doubtful that the marriage between the Menkens was entirely legal. There is no record of Ada Theodore divorcing W. H. Kneass, but if "Adda Theodore" was indeed a stage name, then her marriage to Kneass was never legal, either – making the legality of her marriage to Alexander Isaac Menken equally questionable. Also, if Theodore was her legal name and she was indeed born in New Orleans, then she may have been a free woman of color and therefore both marriages were illegal anyway (since marriage between whites and blacks was illegal). Marriage for Ada was clearly not a contract of "until death do we part"; she seemed to look upon it instead as license to live openly with a man and follow her ambitions.

Alexander Menken was a small-time musician from Cincinnati when he met and married Ada. They first tried to make their living as itinerant dance instructors, with Ada teaching and Alexander providing the music.[10]

[7] Ada Bertha, "I am Thine – to W. H. K." *Liberty Gazette*, Nov. 5, 1855 (writer's date Oct.), 2; *Illustrated News*, March 24, 1860.

[8] Ada Bertha T———e, "New Advertisement!!! To R. M. T.****," *Liberty Gazette*, Dec. 1855 (writer's date Nov. 23), 2. Austin is located in Travis County; Menken may have been trying to lay claim to a locally famous hero.

[9] Transcript of marriage license and certificate granted by Polk County deputy clerk L. S. McMicken, in the R. B. Black Collection, Nacogdoches Depository, Nacogdoches, Texas; facsimile of marriage certificate in Mankowitz, *Mazeppa*, 41.

[10] In the *Illustrated News* biography of March 31, 1860, Menken claims that they "formed a concert troupe" with Adah as both "prima donna" and "manageress" of the company, and that they traveled

Ada's only stage experience was as a member of a dance or equestrian troupe; she had not yet played a speaking part on stage and could not count on acting to provide income. In late 1856 the Menkens returned to New Orleans where, by her own account, they lived in "comparative poverty." Somehow – through connections, talent, or moxie – Ada managed to land a star position in the J. S. Charles company, based not far from the Texas border in Shreveport, Louisiana, in March 1857.[11] On the strength of reviews earned in Shreveport, she was able to secure a week starring at the Gaiety Theatre in New Orleans in late August. Her star finally began to rise.

Billing herself as Mrs. A. I. Menken, and supported by the amateur Crescent Dramatic Association, Ada won critical raves for playing respectable characters such as "Bianca" and "The Widow Cheerly," both staple roles for antebellum actresses. The New Orleans *Daily Delta* declared that "in her we have an actress of real excellence, and one whose dramatic genius will command the approbation of every lover of superior acting. With her fine natural abilities, her intensity, her clear, ringing, musical vocalization, and personal beauty," she surely could not fail to become a box-office star. By fall of 1857, Ada had become the couple's principal breadwinner. Staking their fortune on her newly discovered stage talent, they arranged for Ada to support theatrical stars such as Edwin Booth and James Murdoch in the Memphis and Nashville theatres of W. H. Crisp.[12]

Menken did not truly manage to cultivate a celebrity image until she and her husband made Cincinnati their home. There she finally developed her poetic voice and figured out how to craft a public persona that compelled attention. Within the city's thriving Reform Jewish community, Menken learned the art of cultivating an "authentic" offstage image of herself. Jewish identity gave her a role to play, and Deborah, a prophet of the Old Testament, provided her with a strong female model. Not only had Deborah successfully led an army into battle, but she had also constructed the telling of her story without sacrificing femininity. With Deborah, Menken discovered the part through which to bring together her various selves as a good Jewish wife, poet, and public performer. She apparently learned that playing contradictory images onstage and off gave her surprising freedom. And, as her offstage self became more cultivated and respectable, her onstage

all over Texas. I am more inclined to believe the less glamorous account from the diary of a woman in Livingston, Texas, who noted that the Menkens were "stopping at the Minter Hotel" and trying to raise enough students for dance classes, Mankowitz, *Mazeppa*, 41.

[11] *Illustrated News*, March 31, 1860.

[12] "The Performance at the Gaiety, " New Orleans *Daily Delta*, Sept. 6, 1857. The term "star" is used several ways beginning in this period: Star actresses were the ones who played the central female roles, but those who could draw audiences with their names were simply called "stars." To "star" in a play was to play a central role, but not necessarily to sell tickets with one's name. *Illustrated News*, March 31, 1860; James Murdoch, *The Stage; or, Recollections of Actors and Acting from an Experience of Fifty Years; A Series of Dramatic Sketches* (Philadelphia: J. M. Stoddart, 1880), 53–57.

roles became more sensational. In the constant struggle to land contracts to star in Midwestern theaters, Menken had discovered she had particular talent for breeches parts and comedy, neither of which had a good reputation but both of which were commercially viable. Eventually, the salacious theater roles would undermine Menken's relationship with her husband and the community, but the intellectual image of the poet endured.

She owed much of her success as a celebrity to the fact that the Reform Jewish community of Cincinnati was in the midst of determining its own boundaries and was at the time of her arrival particularly focused on fostering public roles for Jewish women. Within the poetry she published first in the Cincinnati *Israelite* and later in the *Jewish Messenger* (a New York weekly), Menken constructed herself as a modern parallel to Deborah and in so doing claimed a powerful role within the community.[13] Ethnic impersonation can lend the performer real power because it allows one to dwell in the liminal spaces of social and cultural categories, performing the otherness of social margins while knowing the desires of one's own group.[14] In Menken's case, assuming a Jewish identity allowed her to speak as someone else, to deliberately construct a self based on her understanding of both Jewish and non-Jewish audiences. But it is doubtful that she would have used the same tactics or been so successful in another place or time. Reform Judaism was still in the chrysalis and the community in Cincinnati was just beginning to bloom. Menken emerged on borrowed wings well chosen.

Money was undoubtedly the couple's primary motivation for reconnecting with the Menken family and moving to Cincinnati. In the spring of 1858, Ada expressed to Rosina the hope that their friendship might dispel the lingering rancor between Alexander and his half-brothers: "I cannot write to you as a stranger...let us all be friends, no matter who is wrong, we can be so very happy if all is unity and peace, if they are in the wrong, speak to them first, yours will be the triumph, for our dear father [meaning the late Solomon Menken] (God rest his soul) try to be at peace with his son and wife." Menken ended the letter by enclosing an ambrotype of herself taken in New Orleans in roughly 1851, explaining apologetically that the only picture of Alexander was held captive in a brooch she wore at her breast. "Your affectionate sister, Ada," she signed, without the sweeping flourishes of later signatures.[15]

Rosina Menken Ronkustirt was the most approachable member of Alexander's family because she did not partake in the family business along

---

[13] Eiselien deserves credit for discovering Menken's work in *The Jewish Messenger*. He also notes that within *The Israelite* and *Die Deborah*, she claimed to be working on a book called "Tales and Poems on Judaism." Eiselien, ed., *Infelicia*, 19.

[14] Laura Browder, *Slippery Characters: Ethnic Impersonators and American Identities* (Chapel Hill: University of North Carolina Press, 2000), 6–7.

[15] AIM to Rosina, March 8, 1858, Menken Scrapbook.

with her brothers and thus had little reason to protect herself from Alexander and his personable wife. While she may have been interested in Menken and Sons, the profitable dry-goods business left to her mother by their late father, Rosina did not play a role in its running. And she had no claim at all to her brothers' real estate investments in Kentucky and Ohio.[16] Alexander, the sole offspring from Solomon Menken's first marriage, had inherited nothing from the father who, on his deathbed in December 1853, stated that everything should go to Gallatha, his second wife.[17] Alexander left Cincinnati shortly afterward and spent the next three years working his way through the Texas frontier as an itinerant musician. By 1858, Rosina had not seen her older half-brother in at least five years. Had she sent him letters about the prosperity of the Menken business? Did her brothers brag about their success?

By 1860, the Menken brothers – Judah, Jacob, and Nathan – had earned a reputation in the Cincinnati business community for being "extravagant." In 1861, a R. G. Dunn & Co. credit reporter noted that it was impossible to assess the credibility of Alexander's brothers as "their bus[iness] is scattered around a good deal – one who knows them thinks they have 2$ for every 1."[18] Ada and Alexander probably figured that his siblings had enough to share. Alexander also may have assumed that he would inherit a substantial part of the Menken estate upon his stepmother's death: His father's will had clearly stated that should Gallatha remarry, the estate would go to Solomon's children – not "their" children, but "his" children, which included Alexander. Ada and Alexander could not foresee that the depression that exacted such a toll on northern industry in 1857 would ensure the bankruptcy of Menken and Sons by 1861, shortly after the death of Gallatha in 1860.[19] In 1858 Ada was seeking reconciliation with a family whose estate was worth a few million dollars.

Ada sought their friendship and trust not only through letters and poetry, but also by refashioning herself as Jewish by ancestry. Her writings suggest

[16] Rosina's married name is impossible to determine, as she shows up with different spellings in several different sources, such as married to "Lewis Rankstirt" in the *Restored Hamilton County Marriage Records, 1808–1849* (Cincinnati: Ohio Genealogical Society, 1998), 514; married to "Lewis Rosenstiel" in the *Cincinnati Daily Gazette*, Feb. 10, 1846; married to "Lewis S. Ronkustirt" in *Hamilton County Marriage Records*, vols. 14–15 and 16 (Cincinnati: Daughters of the American Revolution, 1941). Ohio, vol. 80, p. 49, R. G. Dunn & Co., Baker Library, Harvard Business School, Cambridge, Massachusetts.

[17] Will of Solomon Menken, signed Dec. 4, 1853, County Clerk's Office, Hamilton County, Cincinnati, Ohio. Solomon Menken wrote, "I bequeath and devise the whole of the residue of my Estate, real, personal and mixed of every kind and description to my beloved wife Gallatha Menken." If she was to marry, she was to pass the property "to my children to be by them received." He died 18 days later.

[18] Ohio, vol. 80, pp. 49, 53, R. G. Dun & Co. Collection, Baker Library, Harvard Business School, Cambridge, Mass.

[19] Will of Solomon Menken; Ohio, vol. 80, p. 53, R. G. Dun & Co. Collection, Baker Library, Harvard Business School, Cambridge, Mass.

that she did not begin studying Hebrew or writing on Jewish themes until she had been married to Alexander for over a year. Her poems, which so many biographers over the years have celebrated as displaying a superior understanding of Judiasm, were often plaigiarized from other poets. At least five of the poems she published in the *American Israelite* were lifted from Penina Moïse, a Charleston poet.[20]

Her interest in Judaism prior to coming to Cincinnati should not be attributed to Alexander, who left no evidence of having identified with his faith. She may have known Jews while growing up in New Orleans, as it had significant Sephardic and Ashkenazic communities. And while performing in Shreveport in 1857 and 1858 as a young Jewish wife, Menken undoubtedly found herself befriended by members of its substantial Jewish population, many of whom ran prominent businesses. Anti-Semitism ran high in Shreveport, which may also have sparked her interest.[21] Outrage with historical and contemporary prejudice against Jews certainly defines her writing of this period, plagiarized and not. But, given the shrewdness that Menken would often display over the next few years, it is most likely that Menken was laying the groundwork for wooing the Menken family.

In September 1857, as Mrs. A. I. Menken, she published her first essay on a Jewish theme, "Shylock," from Shakespeare's *Merchant of Venice*. Menken's "Shylock" first appeared in the New Orleans *Daily Delta*, and again a month later in the *Israelite*, the newspaper of the Reform Jewish community of Cincinnati.[22] Over the next few months she published several more poems in the *Israelite*, several addressed to her husband's family members.[23]

Shakespeare's character Shylock was the archetype for Jewish male identity among non-Jews, who made up the majority of the readership of the *Daily Delta*. The Jewish men of cheap paperback fiction, children's books, and religious tracts were of more or less the same basic outline as Shylock: male, miserly, and self-serving, with long, unkempt beards. But Shakespeare's Shylock had a human dimension not found in antebellum plays or prose. Menken centered her essay on the famous monologue when Shylock reminds his captors that he, too, is human, and momentarily transcends the cultural and racial perceptions of his enemies and the audience. "Hath not a

---

[20] Eiselien, ed., *Infelicia*, 31. The poems are "Queen of Nations," "The Sacrifice," "The Hebrew's Prayer," "The Sabbath," and "Passover."

[21] Louisiana, vol. 3, R. G. Dun & Co. Collection, Baker Library, Harvard Business School, Cambridge, Mass. Credit reporters are shockingly blunt about their anti-Semitism, suggesting that most Jewish businessmen were of a low social order and not to be trusted. Nevertheless, several Jewish men ran successful dry goods and general stores, creating a thriving Jewish enclave.

[22] Mrs. A. I. Menken, "Shylock," *Daily Delta*, Sept. 6, 1857; the Cincinnati *Israelite* (hereafter *Israelite*), Oct. 2, 1857. The *Israelite* was later renamed the *American Israelite*.

[23] AIM "Sinai" "Affectionately inscribed to brother Jacob," Sept. 25, 1857; "To Judah," Feb. 1858; "To Brother Nathan," June 25, 1858, *Israelite*.

Jew eyes?" Shylock cries, "Hath not a Jew hands, organ dimensions, senses, affections, passions? Fed with the same food, hurt with the same weapons, subject to the same diseases, healed by the same means, warmed and cooled by the same winter and summer as a Christian is? If you prick us, do we not bleed?"[24] If there was an ignoble Jew, Menken argued, he was created by a world that stunted his dreams and withheld the means of self-fulfillment. She made it clear that misguided Christianity was the problem, and in doing so indirectly challenged the claims of social reformers that Christianity could rid America of its vices.

By writing her piece on Shylock, Menken was also essentially staking her first claim to Jewish identity. She defended Jews and signed herself Menken; Jewish identity was implied. So how would Menken's non-Jewish New Orleans audience have viewed the author herself? Non-Jews took their image of Jewish women from popular culture, where they were rare but present in three principal forms: young women who defy their families and convert to Christianity, women who demonstrate the failings of Christianity, and exotic women who lure men as bees to flowers. The first can be found principally in Sunday school literature; always young and consumptive, these Jewish women converted to Christianity on their deathbeds, thereby inspiring their grieving fathers to do likewise.[25] In the popular play *Pauline* the heroine converts on her deathbed, and in *The Merchant of Venice* Shylock's daughter Jessica disobeys religious duty for the love of a Christian.

But Menken had more use for the other two images, which allowed her to assert respectability through an identification of faith while, at the same time, heightening her exoticism. The most enduring examples of these two nineteenth-century Jewish heroines are Rebecca of *Ivanhoe*, first appearing in 1820, and Miriam, of Nathaniel Hawthorne's novel *The Marble Faun*, published in 1860. *Ivanhoe* proved immensely popular throughout the nineteenth century as both a book and a play, and Rebecca was the most beloved character. Menken herself performed the part several times over the next few years. Literary critic Ian Duncan asserts that Rebecca was "one of the sublime heroines of nineteenth-century fiction" because she, "in particular, represents the Jews as figures far more potent than scapegoats. . . . They command[ed] purity of faith." By the end of the novel, Rebecca makes it clear that Jews are more morally Christian than the Christians themselves, "who are united in nothing but their anti-semitism."[26] This version of the Jewess worked well for Menken, who was, at this point, determined to establish respectability alongside celebrity.

---

[24] Mrs. A. I. Menken, "Shylock," New Orleans *Sunday Delta*, Sept. 1857.

[25] E.g., see N. A., *The Dying Jewess* (New York: Mahlon Day & Co., 1839); *The Converted Jewess: A Memoir of Maria* ―― (New York: G. Lane & P. P. Sanford for the Sunday School Union of the Methodist Episcopal Church, 1843).

[26] Ian Duncan, "Introduction" to Sir Walter Scott's *Ivanhoe* (New York: Oxford University Press, 1996), xxiii, xxvi.

Rebecca's Jewishness serves to mask her innate Christianity, which is to say that she performed what non-Jewish readers defined as Christian morality even if she claimed Judiasm. The sublime image of Rebecca was compelling in part because she was the very opposite of the Jewish male stereotype. Was she as pure as she appeared? Hawthorne added a sinister edge to the virtuous Jewess by creating Miriam, an autonomous and unusually gifted woman, who wore a mask of Christianity over her Jewishness. Miriam has many virtues, but she is not virtuous. Mysterious and otherworldly, she is a predator so extraordinarily beautiful that she would get "into your consciousness and memory and could never afterwards be shut out, but [haunt] your dreams, for pleasure or for pain; holding your inner realm as a conquered territory."[27] She is dangerous because she inspires too much admiration and does not assert control over her desires. In the climax of the book, devotion to Miriam so compromises an admirer that her telling gaze compels him to murder on her behalf. But Miriam is complicated; she mourns her own depravity and struggles unsuccessfully to rise above it. She is all the more frightening because she is sympathetic while being monstrous. Hawthorne connects her beauty and deceit to a Jewish ancestry that she does not claim but he suggests is clearly written on her body in the darkness of her hair and eyes and in the tint of her skin. The contradictory yet parallel figures of Rebecca and Miriam suggest that Jewish female identity carried connotations of purity, mystery, beauty, and corruption in nineteenth-century popular culture.[28] Together, they suggested a fascinating Jewish female identity that provoked many questions and returned few answers.

The predatory, sexualized characteristics of Miriam might also be gleaned from modern readings of the term "Jewess," used throughout the nineteenth century and sometimes applied to Menken. Twenty-first-century readers might note that Jewess, like Negress, suggests a sort of anthropological view of Jewish women as racial other. Yet, without exception, the Jewess was portrayed as refined, not bestial, like depictions of the Negress. She was foreign but not alien. She commanded respect as well as desire, and thus dwelt on the border of gentile and Jewish society. But because Jewish men were depicted as not quite masculine, the Jewess was by implication not quite feminine, which meant her sexuality was on a looser leash. The provocative question was, how loose? Dangerous, desirable, admirable, exotic, and mysterious, the Jewess defied narrow categories of gender and ethnicity.[29]

---

[27] Nathaniel Hawthorne, *The Marble Faun*, republished in *The Works of Hawthorne* (New York: Modern Library, 1937), 617.

[28] *The Marble Faun* was published in 1860, but it is not likely that Hawthorne had yet heard of Menken. At the time he would have been writing the story she was famous only in the Midwest.

[29] Amy-Jill Levine, "A Jewess, More and/or Less," in *Judaism since Gender*, eds. Miriam Peskowitz and Laura Levitt (London: Routledge, 1997), 150–151; Sander L. Gilman, *Inscribing the Racial Other* (Lincoln: University of Nebraska Press, 1991, 22–23.

And if Menken needed proof of the advantages of a Jewish identity she had only to turn her eyes to the international world of entertainment where Rachel had until recently taken center stage. To claim to be a Jewish actress was to invite comparison with the most famous Jewess of the early nineteenth-century stage: Rachel, the French tragedienne, who also projected a complex personality that seemed to defy traditional definitions of class, race, and gender. Rachel was famous throughout the western world for her thespian talent and her intrigues with the intellectuals and aristocrats of Europe. She was also self-made; she had begun her career as a little girl singing for pennies to support her family and quickly moved to the world stage by virtue of talent and intelligence. Americans had heard of her for twenty years before she finally came to the United States in 1855. Unwilling to use sensationalist advertising, her tour was a financial failure but she brought her name into American culture. Americans could claim to have witnessed the great Rachel, the actress needing only one name. With that name came intellectual grandeur; she was friends with the Parisians Menken would later attempt to win over: Alexandre Dumas (both father and son), Théophile Gautier, and George Sand, among others. Unlike Menken, Rachel never married and had two children out of wedlock, so to equate oneself with her was not without social danger, but in the United States Rachel's Jewish and French identity might explain and perhaps even excuse her scandalous behavior. Menken had no talent for tragedy, but she knew a marketable identity when she saw one and probably realized that Rachel's Jewishness contributed to the moral latitude she was given by American spectators. Rachel died of consumption in 1858, making association with her image more marketable than ever.[30]

Ada and Alexander lived up to their promise of being in Cincinnati by the end of the spring dramatic season in Louisiana, arriving in June 1858. After traveling by train along the Mississippi from New Orleans to Louisville, they boarded a steamer up the Ohio.[31] One can imagine them arriving hot and dirty from the cramped, sooty quarters of the trains and the sticky humidity of a midwestern summer, wearing traveling clothes and carrying their possessions in carpet bags and trunks. Since actresses were expected to provide their own costumes, Ada probably arrived with considerably more baggage than Alexander.[32] Still, trains and steamers were a vast improvement over the stage coaches and canvas-walled wagons of East Texas and Louisiana, and the couple may have been relatively cheerful. No doubt Ada greeted Alexander's family with warmth and

---

[30] Bernard Falk, *Rachel the Immortal, Stage Queen: Grand Amoureuse, Street Urchin: Fine Lady* (New York: Appleton, 1936).

[31] James E. Vance, Jr., *The North American Railroad: Its Origin, Evolution, and Geography* (Baltimore: Johns Hopkins University Press, 1995), 102, 114.

[32] Tracy C. Davis, *Actresses as Working Women: Their Social Identity in Victorian Culture* (London: Routledge, 1991), 19–20.

charm, in an effort to successfully launch the reunion of Alexander and his family.

The Menkens stepped off the riverboat into a prosperous city of commerce and trade. Cincinnati, built on the bluffs of the Ohio River, benefited from its location between four tributaries that facilitated transport of goods in all directions. And because of its position at the terminus of the canal system, Cincinnati functioned as the primary connection between New York City and New Orleans, and thus between the Atlantic and Gulf of Mexico.[33] By midcentury Cincinnati had grown into the fourth largest city in the United States and earned the sobriquet "Queen City of the West."[34] Although many considered New Orleans a major site of theater and opera, Cincinnati enjoyed geographic advantages that gave its theaters name recognition beyond the Ohio Valley. In addition, Cincinnati acted as the center of western publishing, which meant more avenues to the public outside the city.[35] For Menken, moving to Cincinnati offered opportunities to reach wider audiences, and to travel from city to city quickly and easily, by nineteenth-century standards.

The Menkens undoubtedly knew that the Ohio Valley was becoming an important site for theatrical work. By the late 1850s, Cincinnati had established itself as a center for performing arts, both high and low, principally because of its large German immigrant population.[36] By 1840 the Ohio census noted that 45 percent of the population had been born abroad and most prominent among them were the German bourgeoisie, who considered cultivation of music and the arts essential.[37] By the time Ada arrived in 1858, the city boasted two major theaters and an opera house, as well as several smaller theaters and concert halls. Perhaps just as valuable to Menken, Cincinnati enjoyed easy access to other cities, such as Louisville and Nashville, which housed equally impressive numbers of theaters.[38]

Religion provided another version of entertainment, as several zealous religious groups competed for members and economic resources. As early

---

[33] Alan I. Marcus, *Plague of Strangers: Social Groups and Origins of City Services in Cincinnati, 1819–1870* (Columbus: Ohio State University Press, 1991), 1.

[34] Carl W. Condit, *The Railroad and the City: A Technological and Urbanistic History of Cincinnati* (Columbus: Ohio State University Press, 1977), 5.

[35] Bridget Ford, research talk on the "Western Book Trade," American Antiquarian Society, Nov. 1998.

[36] Bruce Levine, "Community Divided: German Immigrants, Social Class, and Political Conflict in Antebellum Cincinnati," in *Ethnic Diversity and Civic Identity: Patterns of Conflict and Cohesion in Cincinnati since 1820,* ed. Jonathan Sarna (Urbana: University of Illinois Press, 1992), 48.

[37] Marcus, *Plague of Strangers*; 64; Levine, "Community Divided," 48.

[38] As one of America's most promising new cities, it was a prime habitat for charlatans as well as entertainers. In 1859, Ada could pay a dollar to have her fortune told by thirteen-year-old Tennessee McClaflin, who advertised consultations in the *Cincinnati Daily Commercial.* McClaflin would later surpass Menken in infamy as a scandalous woman when she and her sister, Victoria Woodhull, became vocal proponents of "free love" in the 1870s. See advertisement in the *Cincinnati Daily Commercial,* Aug. 19, 1859, p. 3.

as 1820, ten different Protestant denominations shared the city with a sizable population of Catholics. In 1824 a traditional Jewish congregation quietly formed.[39] The Christians did not seem to notice, as they were absorbed in Protestant-Catholic struggles for dominance.

On this first visit to Cincinnati, Ada and Alexander stayed for several months, recovering from their journeys and visiting with the Menken family. Relying on Alexander's family probably alleviated their most pressing financial concerns, freeing Ada to pursue her writing. She performed for one week in June at Wood's Theatre, Cincinnati's principal home of variety and drama, but then turned her attention to establishing herself as a member of the Reform Jewish community and exploring her newly claimed Jewish identity. Alexander's brother Nathan undoubtedly introduced Menken at the offices of the *Israelite*, where she would regularly join a social circle of young Jewish intellectuals. There, they smoked cigarettes and discussed history and politics for hours at a time.[40] Respectable women did not smoke publicly, so Ada's cigarettes acted as a signal fire, marking her as reckless and bold. Yet Menken apparently toned down her personality when with the rest of Alexander's family, presenting herself as a sweet and generous sister and daughter-in-law.[41]

Early in her Cincinnati sojourn, Ada began telling Alexander's family that her deceased father had been Jewish. Since religious identity is matrilineal in Jewish culture, such claims gave her an ancestral tie that also explained her need for formal conversion. In later newspaper biographies she would say that she had been "born Jewish," but while in Cincinnati she expressed a fervent desire to convert.[42]

Menken also changed the spelling of her first name – a change that some Jewish scholars would later see as a key to establishing her Jewish identity. She added an "h" to Ada, making herself Adah. But the "h" may have had more to do with a passion for Byron than Judaism. "Adah" is the sister and wife of Cain, and described by the poet as "[m]ore beautiful than beauteous things remote."[43] Tellingly, at times of great

---

[39] With the advent of Reform Judaism, traditional Ashekenazic Judaism would come to be defined as "Orthodox." In the late nineteenth century, Conservative Judaism would evolve as a middle ground between Orthodox and Reform.

[40]

[41] Leo Wise, "Israelite Personalities: People Who Wrote for the Israelite and Other Things of Interest in Connection Therewith," *American Israelite*, supplement, July 24, 1924, p. 32; Allen Lesser, *Enchanting Rebel: The Secret of Adah Isaacs Menken* (New York: Beechurst Press, 1947), 31–32. Lesser claims to have spoken with descendents of the Menken family.

[42] Menken declares, "I was born in that faith [Judaism] and have adhered to it all my erratic career" in letter to editor J. W. Campbell of the New York *Illustrated News*, March 24, 1860. Rabbi Wise himself wrote in the *Israelite*, Dec. 30, 1864, p. 212, that Menken "wanted the senior editor [Wise] of the Israelite to accept her into the covenant of Israel, which he did not do; hence, that as far as the form and birth is concerned, she is no Jewess."

[43] Davis, *Actresses as Working Women*, 13.

distress in later years, Menken sometimes lapsed and signed "Ada" to her letters.

The most reliable source for refuting Menken's Judaism comes from Isaac Mayer Wise, the rabbi of the Menken's synagogue.[44] She made a powerful alliance when she sought out Dr. Wise, who was not only the leader of the Reform community of Cincinnati but also the nationally recognized founder of Reform Judaism. Menken began cultivating an intellectual relationship with Wise while she and Alexander were still in Louisiana by submitting work to the *Israelite*. The newspaper was one of Wise's most important contributions to the Reform Jewish community. In 1855, he founded the *Israelite* as the main mouthpiece of Reform Judaism, but it also served to tie together the immediate community within Cincinnati. Wise also edited and produced *Die Deborah*, a German language newspaper targeted primarily at the Jewish women of Cincinnati. Significantly, stories of Menken surfaced in the *Israelite* but rarely in *Die Deborah*. The German paper focused on women's domestic issues, and Menken was neither German nor domestically inclined.

As managing editor of the *Israelite*, Wise published Ada's essay on Shylock and her Jewish poetry and introduced Menken to the Reform community as an essayist and poet. It was not until Ada anticipated moving to Cincinnati that she forwarded reviews of her theater work. On April 8, 1858, Wise publicly hailed her arrival as "our favorite and ingenious poetess . . . who comes to us from the south, crowned with the brilliant success, genius and talent always meet."[45] The efforts of Menken and the endorsement of Wise made her into a community-based celebrity before she lived there; the Reform community knew something about her before ever seeing her. More important, Menken's work in the *Israelite* established her as a woman of sensitivity and intellect who took great pride in being Jewish.

Reform Judaism had developed in the United States only within the decade of Menken's arrival in Cincinnati. Reform leaders were in the midst of experimenting with the overlapping parameters of American and Jewish identities, and were clearly sensitive to outside views of their community. Like their brethren in Germany, American Reform Jews maintained several traditional characteristics: They lived in close proximity with other Jews, went into commercial occupations, and maintained a conscious "otherness" despite acculturation. Like Protestants, they also began to treat their faith as a religion, rather than as a way of life. Within the temples, they officially changed the basic service and eliminated such ideas as the impending arrival of the Messiah and the reestablishment of Zion as the Jewish kingdom, dismissed *Halakah* (Jewish law) as embodied in the *Talmud*, and turned to the Old Testament as the fundamental source of Judaism. Many

---

[44] *Illustrated News*, March 31, 1860.   [45] Lesser, *Enchanting Rebel*, 31–32.

of these mid-nineteenth-century Reform Jews strove to reflect American culture by "stripping Judaism of all that made it alien, including the concept of a peoplehood, and dismissing the belief that Israel and its Torah are one."[46]

Menken had entered a situation that had the promise of allowing her great freedom, if she could find the appropriate means. Cincinnati was the center of Reform Judiasm, but, like the doctrine, how one performed that religion in a cultural sense remained ambiguous. Reform under the leadership of Isaac Mayer Wise and Max Lillienthal, the two most prominent leaders of American Reform Judaism, established Cincinnati as the center of Jewish American life in the 1850s. Wise, Lillienthal, and their followers encouraged the perception that Jews could pursue a Jewish version of the American dream in Cincinnati.[47] From 1848 to 1860, nearly two million Ashkenazi Jews emigrated to the United States, thousands of whom traveled inland to the Queen City and transformed it into "the economic, religious, and cultural focal point of German Jewish settlement" west of the eastern seaboard.[48] Although the Cincinnati Jewish population never attained the wealth found in New York or Philadelphia, the young city allowed Jews to interact on an equal basis with their non-Jewish neighbors." Until the Civil War, Jews and Christians intermingled in the city's social organizations, including the Cincinnati Country Club. A number of Jews intermarried with Christians, and many more interacted with gentiles in their homes.[49] The Reform Jews of Cincinnati were conscious of the need to "develop a new kind of Judaism in Cincinnati, one better suited than traditional Judaism to the new American milieu."[50] By the time Menken arrived in 1858, Cincinnati Jews (Reform and traditional) had formed a tightly knit community with nearly half of the Jewish population of the city living within a thirty-square block area.[51]

These Jews also did their best to assimilate to American (Protestant) ways of life, ostensibly without betraying their Hebrew heritage. Just as Menken created a Jewish identity based on her recent studies of Hebrew, the Reform Jews attempted to adopt what they understood to be American culture based predominately on depictions found in American periodicals and literature. This adaptation was the latest version of respectable identity sought by the

---

[46] Hasia R. Diner, *A Time for Gathering: The Second Migration, 1820–1880* (Baltimore: Johns Hopkins University Press, 1992), 118–119, 169.

[47] Jonathan D. Sarna and Nancy H. Klein, *The Jews of Cincinnati* (Cincinnati: Center for the Study of American Jewish Experience, 1989), 1.

[48] Robert Friedenberg, *"Hear O Israel": The History of American Jewish Preaching, 1654–1970* (Tuscaloosa: University of Alabama Press, 1989), 41; Stephen G. Mostov, "A 'Jerusalem' on the Ohio: The Social and Economic History of Cincinnati's Jewish Community, 1840–1875," Ph.D. dissertation, Brandeis University, 1981, p. 2.

[49] Jonathan Sarna, "A Sort of Paradise for Jews": The Lofty Vision of Cincinnati Jews," in Sarna, ed., *Ethnic Diversity*, 134, 142–143.

[50] Sarna and Klein, *The Jews of Cincinnati*, 4.   [51] Mostov, "Jerusalem on the Ohio," 192.

German Ashkenazi Jews, many of whom came to the United States already rooted in a tradition of assimilation.

Reform Judaism essentially sought to Americanize bourgeois cultural values and practices already formed in Germany. In 1781, German Jews began the ninety-year trek down a narrow corridor toward emancipation from the legal constrictions that banned them from professions, denied them rights of citizenship, and consigned them to ghettos. Although Jews began to prosper in Germany, they remained socially isolated from the gentiles, creating a Jewish bourgeoisie that strove to adapt to its surroundings but internally preserved Jewish traditions. Many Jewish leaders advocated a "regeneration" of Jewish society based on liberal ideals and bourgeois customs.[52] The more German law makers questioned whether Jews were German enough for full emancipation, the more Jews themselves tried to appear more "German" by upholding bourgeois social values. In 1848, when the liberal revolutions across Europe failed to bring about significant change, many German Jews packed their belongings and left for the nation that had already written republican ideology into its constitution: the United States.

Thus, in many ways, the Reform Jewish community was in the midst of self-conscious performance much like Menken herself; its members projected American identity based on their understanding of what it meant to be American. For the most part, transition was not difficult; the bourgeois cultural characteristics developed in Germany appeared to translate easily into American middle-class culture. The Jewish immigrants saw that the drive for respectability mediated most aspects of urban life, as it had in Germany, elevating the importance of upward mobility and self-control.[53] But there was a telling difference: In German cultures, cultivation led to respectability, while respectability among Americans had more to do with public performance of morality. Thus they cultivated a broadly appreciative esthetic that celebrated literature, theater, and music at a level hard to find outside New York (the nation's metropolis) or New Orleans (a foreign city despite its domestic location).

Menken chose to make herself into a Jewish poet just as the leaders of Reform Judaism, feeling the pressures of assimilation, were seeking to create a public role for women akin to that enjoyed by Protestant women in their churches. The culture of Reform Judaism meshed well with the larger Protestant culture, and allowed Jews to embrace many of the ideals promoted by American politicians and periodicals. But religious leaders ran into difficulty when trying to determine acceptable public and private roles

[52] Monika Richarz, *Jewish Life in Germany: Memories from Three Centuries*, trans. Stella P. and Sidney Rosenfeld (Bloomington: University of Indiana Press, 1991), 1–2; David Sorkin, *The Transformation of German Jewry, 1780–1840* (New York: Oxford University Press, 1987), 4–5.

[53] George Mosse, "Jewish Emancipation: Between *Bildung* and Respectability," in *The Jewish Response to German Culture,* eds. Jehuda Reinharz and Walter Schatzberg (Hanover: University Press of New England, 1985), 4.

for women. At about the time that Menken arrived in Cincinnati, Isaac
Mayer Wise began pursuing an impossible goal: He wanted to transform
gender roles without tampering with gender relations.

Born in Bohemia, Wise was perhaps the only true Bohemian Menken
would ever know. He later remarked that his readings in English and
American literature – particularly, the novels of James Fenimore Cooper –
had made him "a naturalized American in the interior of Bohemia." He
arrived in New York in 1846, fully convinced of the need to free Jews
from the traditional Judaism that had kept them from embracing modern liberties.[54] He moved to Cincinnati in 1854, and was a charismatic
man of thirty-six when Menken joined his congregation, B'ne Yeshurun,
in 1858.

Like Menken, Wise had a natural inclination for public relations. He
was intensely aware of how Ashekenazi Jews differed externally from their
American neighbors, and fundamentally believed that "if we wish to know
the political and moral condition of a state, we must ask what rank women
hold in it."[55] He indicated that the success or failure of Reform Judaism
hinged on the treatment of women. Like Reform leaders in Germany, Wise
advocated instructing girls in religion, empowering women as trustees and
members of temple school boards, ordaining female rabbis, allowing women
to initiate divorce, and employing a double-ring marriage ceremony.[56] In
1854, Wise dismissed the traditional argument that women's voices were
"a potential source of sexual excitement for men," and asserted that the
judgments of the ancient Talmudists should have no bearing on present-day
worship.[57] Wise's radical suggestion posed the question of where Reform
should begin and end: If the Reform Jews disregarded the Talmud, what
else might they discard? If Jews became too American, what would make
them Jewish? All of these changes destabilized the Jewish community for a
short time, as members struggled to determine where the boundaries lay.
Did the changing role of women in the temple indicate that it was now
respectable for women to take on public roles? Did the waning emphasis
on household duties mean that a woman like Menken no longer had to
perform the traditional rituals to prove her piety?

For two years, Wise and Menken enjoyed compatible goals: Wise wanted
Jewish women to be more publicly involved, and Menken wanted public attention. She submitted poems advocating that Jews celebrate their heritage,

---

[54] Max B. May, *Isaac Mayer Wise: The Founder of American Judaism: A Biography* (New York: G. P. Putnam's
Sons, 1916), 22–43.

[55] Isaac M. Wise, "The Influence of Women," *Israelite*, Jan. 25, 1856.

[56] Charlotte Baum, Paula Hyman, and Sonya Michel, *The Jewish Woman in America* (New York: Dial
Press, 1976), 27.

[57] Karla Ann Goldman, "Beyond the Gallery: The Place of Women in the Development of American
Judaism," Ph.D. dissertation, Harvard University, 1993, pp. 129, 141. Goldman bases this argument
on an article by Wise in the *Israelite*, Aug. 17, 1855.

and Wise published them in the *Israelite*. Menken's early submissions were primarily sentimental in language and imagery, but as time wore on, they began expressing outrage. Many of the more militant poems of this period she plagiarized from the Charleston poet Penina Moise, but it is significant that Menken chose them as part of her performance as a Jewish woman. She challenged the concept of women as intellectually subordinate. And like the prophet Deborah, she did so by appointing herself as a leader of her chosen people, and calling men to arms in poems such as "To the Sons of Israel."

Changes in Menken's poetic voice at this time made sense given her unusual role as a female public figure in the community. Despite Wise's desire to see Jewish women taking a more visible role, most Jewish women continued to express their faith primarily through household rituals. Menken was not a domestic woman, however, and she and Alexander did not maintain a household but rather lived with family or in hotels. Menken performed religious devotion through intellectual work, which essentially meant crossing a traditional gender line. Other women of the community submitted sentimental poetry to the *Israelite;* Menken veered significantly off the feminine path by commenting on political issues.

The elevated position of female poets in the Jewish Reform community may explain why Menken first found her voice as a Jewish woman. Well before her work appeared in Cincinnati newspapers, an 1857 article in *Die Deborah*, "Die Zionstochter oder das Weib in Israel" (Daughter of Zion or Woman of Israel), stressed the renewed importance of Jewish women poets. The anonymous author expressed concern that outsiders would misconstrue the lowly position of women in the synagogue, "an unworthy, unJewish one," as indicative of women's role in Jewish society. To prove Judaism's "compatibility with Christianity" (suggesting that Christianity allowed women more freedom), the author turned to female poets, claiming that they played an important role by "igno[ring] vice and shortcomings and turn[ing] to the beautiful and noble, the great and glorious in people."[58] The description aptly suited Menken's verse, although Menken did tend to emphasize the "vice and shortcomings" of Jewish adversaries. Most of Menken's work dealt with overtly religious themes, as she constantly evoked the saga of the chosen people in covenant with God, and she also addressed Jewish women's private role by speaking to her husband through the pages of the *Israelite*. Despite her frequent contradictions to emerging Reform ideas – such as insisting upon a coming Messiah – Wise continued publishing Menken's poetry until she left Alexander and Cincinnati in 1859.

[58] Kirsten Otto, "The Image of Women in Isaac Mayer Wise's *Die Deborah* between 1855 and 1874," M.A. thesis, University of Cincinnati, 1993, pp. 41–42. Otto translates "Die Zionstochter oder das Weib in Israel," *Die Deborah*, v. 2 (March 6, 1857).

Menken first cultivated the persona of a contemporary Deborah in her poetry, and then claimed the identity outright in her publicity.[59] On September 3, 1858, the *Israelite* published Menken's essay, "A Jew in Parliament," in which she defended Baron Lionel de Rothschild's right to sit in British Parliament and explored the principles of allowing Jews to participate in government generally. Menken later claimed that Rothschild responded to her work by calling her "the inspired Deborah of our people," but no evidence exists to support that claim.[60] The phrase most likely was devised by Menken herself and indicates the importance of Deborah in her self-creation.

In Deborah, Menken saw a valuable image already familiar to her public. Amid women of the Old Testament who martyred themselves for their families, Deborah stands apart as a judge, military leader, and poet.[61] Chapters four and five of *Judges* recounts "The Judgeship of Deborah," a prophet the Israelites noted for " her inflammatory speeches and warlike spirit." In *Judges* 4, Deborah summons a warrior, Barak, to lead the Israelites into battle against their Canaanite oppressors, but he refuses to go into battle unless she accompanies him. She agrees but warns that by complying she will also steal his glory, "for the Lord will give Sisera over into the hand of a woman." Deborah leads the troops and inspires them in battle from her perch on the hilltop. But she does not kill Sisera; that is the act of another woman, Jael, who gives Sisera refuge and impales his head with a nail while he sleeps in her tent.

Judges 5 is Deborah's song, or poem, recounting the oppression of her people and their deliverance by the hand of God. Among biblical and literary scholars, her composition is seen as a literary masterpiece.[62] As Menken would do in her own poetry, Deborah assumes an almost masculine position of aggression and importance, uses her authority to construct the narrative, and praises the act of another woman, Jael, within her song. Yet she retains her femininity as "a mother in Israel."[63]

Deborah was the most powerful female symbol in the Cincinnati community, as is suggested by the title of the women's newspaper, *Die Deborah*. She

[59] Deborah stands apart from most other women in the Hebrew Bible as a positive example of female leadership and strength, but she does not stand alone. Three other women – Miriam, Huldah and Noadiah – are also named as prophets in the Old Testament. Jephthah's daughter and Samson's mother also receive attention. But the two most prominent among women of the Old Testament are Hannah and Ruth. Theologians consider Hannah, of the *Book of Kings*, important because she defines the act of prayer. Ruth, also living during the period of Judges, is the only woman of the Hebrew Bible with a book in her name. Menken also later identified with Judith, the subject of an apocryphal text, who took an even more active role than Deborah, and actually slayed the enemy, Holofernes.

[60] Lesser, *Enchanting Rebel*, 37; Mankowitz, *Mazeppa*, 57.

[61] Rachel Adler, "The Jew Who Wasn't There: Halakhah and the Jewish Woman," in *On Being a Jewish Feminist: A Reader*, ed. Susannah Heschel (New York: Schocken Books, 1983), 14.

[62] Reverend A. Cohen, editor and translator, "The Judgeship of Deborah," *Joshua Judges: Hebrew Text and English Translation with Introductions and Commentary* (London: Soncino Press, 1976), 4.1–5.31.

[63] *Illustrated Dictionary and Concordance of the Bible* (New York: Macmillan, 1986), 274.

probably held particular appeal for Wise and other Reform Jewish leaders because both she and her time period provided a suitable parallel to what they were trying to accomplish in America. The Hebrew Bible identifies the period of *Judges* as a time when women *could* take an active part in social, political, religious, and even military affairs despite subordinate legal status, although few actually did. Deborah also signified a relatively open phase of Israelite society, when Israel functioned as a republic of twelve tribes.[64] Menken was able to capitalize on the symbolic importance of Deborah on several different cultural levels.

Like the ancient prophet, the ideal American woman that the Reform Jews sought to emulate also commanded unprecedented power in the public realm. Deborah proved to be a rather contradictory symbol for Reform Jews bent on assimilation, however, since she was far more aggressive than the American ideal. By the late 1850s, many Protestant Americans took it for granted that virtuous women were so innately moral that public ills would compel them to work toward societal reform. But the public influence of American middle-class women began and ended with their role as moral caretakers; American women could be aggressively redemptive, but true ladies turned away from public fame. This complex rendering of women's roles as both aggressive and self-effacing made it difficult for Reform Jews to grasp which parts of the public realm should be open or closed to women.

The clearest instance of Menken "playing" Deborah can be seen in her poem "To the Sons of Israel," published in January 1859, and based on the highly publicized case of Edgar Mortara. In June 1858, authorities under the orders of Archbishop Michele Viale Prèla seized the six-year-old Mortara from his parents' home in Bologna, Italy. Five years earlier, during what had appeared to be a terminal illness, a Roman Catholic nurse had secretly had the Jewish infant baptized. Because Italian law decreed that Christian children could not live with non-Christians, when the deathbed act became known by authorities, they took the child from his parents and placed him in a convent orphanage. Eventually, Mortara's father was granted permission to visit his son, but not to reclaim him. The Mortara case sparked outrage in Europe and the United States among both Protestants and Jews. Most newspapers in the United States published blistering criticism of the Roman Church, and urged President Franklin Pierce to intervene, to no avail.[65] The Mortara case created a temporary alliance of American Protestants and Jews.

Menken joined the fray by calling young Jewish men to take up arms against Catholic oppressors. Like Deborah, she calls the men to battle: "Awake! ye souls of Israel's land,/Your drowsy slumbers break." She depicts "the barbarous fiends of priest-hood" gathering to destroy the "sacred

---

[64] Ibid., 1034.

[65] Morris U. Schappes, ed. *A Documentary History of Jews in the United States, 1654–1875* (New York: Schocken Books, 1971), 385–392.

home" and crush "loving hearts." Menken prods the men to protect their homes and reminds them of the sanctity of the maternal bond: "A dying mother's heart-shrieks,/Are sweeping o'er the wave — /How can ye sleep, with that haunting cry/Praying for her child to save?" The images she paints of priests and cathedrals resonate with evil: "Heed not the dark cathedral walls/That frown above ye there — /Nor priestly showers of hissing threats,/ that fill the venomed air." Finally, she challenges passive Jews: "curses rest upon ye all/If when that flag's on high/Ye are not with the glorious brave,/To struggle or to die!"[66] Sharply drawn images, such as "priestly showers of hissing threats," convey the kind of grotesque grandeur found in popular fiction.

Menken also developed the less-celebrated aspect of Deborah as a chosen, rather than self-selected, leader. Deborah had agreed to accompany Barak only because he demanded it; she was reluctant to steal the glory of victory from a man. Menken vividly described her own martyrdom as the poet of her people in "Light for the Soul." As the narrator, she begs God to give her the spiritual vision she needs to do his work and suggests that without it she will have no goal and wander hopelessly: "Almighty Father! mine eyes unseal — /Let them grow/Quick to discern whate'er Thou dost reveal;/That I may be, in mercy, spared that woe, Blindly to stray/Through hopeless night, while all around is day."[67] When she becomes a visionary in poems such as "Queen of Nations," she suggests such prayers were answered.[68] At the very time that Reform Jews emphasized peace and assimilation, Menken peddled images of death, cultural loss, and resilience. She portrayed the nation of Israel as a weeping woman, strewn with blood and ashes: "The glory of the earth were thou,/Thy beauty is no more;/For dust defiles thy royal brow,/Thy garments trail in gore."[69] Entwined with her images of pain and despair is also the promise of the coming messiah. Occasionally, as in "Voice of Israel," Menken goes so far as to portray herself as that Messiah.[70]

The Reform Jewish community left no clues as to how they viewed Menken's poetic persona. She suited their public recognition of women's strength, but not their desire to emulate American women. With the benefit of hindsight, the Reform Jewish community's failed attempts to create a parallel version of the middle-class woman demonstrates that domesticity was an explicitly Christian (and implicitly Protestant) ideology that did not easily translate across cultures. Reform Jews could not simply adopt the ideology without dramatically restructuring gender roles. Subscribing

---

[66] AIM, "To the Sons of Israel,"*Israelite*, Jan. 28, 1859.

[67] AIM, "Light for the Soul," *Israelite,* July 23, 1858.

[68] Menken plagiarized this poem from Penina Moise, but Menken's use of it works toward her performance of herself as Deborah. The poetry is not hers, but her use of it shapes her image. For specific information on Menken's poetic thievery, see Eiselien, ed., *Infelicia,* 31.

[69] AIM, "Queen of the Nations," Israelite, Dec. 31, 1858.

[70] AIM, "Voice of Israel," Israelite, Nov. 12, 1858.

to domesticity meant assuming a subordinate yet revered station within the home, which sounded easily adaptable, except that domesticity insisted on triumph through submission, a very Christian ideal. Also, the domestic reformers of Protestant America found their notions supported by men in the highest public station: Ministers, preaching to a predominantly female laity, actively supported and shaped this new American woman.[71] From within their churches, they formed organizations and associations that shaped American public life. The social activism of Deborah would seem to mesh with such ideals, except that Deborah (and Menken) gained notoriety through action, not submission.

The activism Menken prompted was at odds with appropriate female behavior in the Jewish community; only alliance with Deborah kept it from being labeled masculine. Unlike the Protestant women, who played a significant role in the activities of their churches, Jewish women had no significant role in temple life and were not required to attend services. Male laity controlled the synagogue, which stood in direct contrast to Protestant churches. Just as Christian women ran church picnics and decorations, Jewish men decorated temples and organized social functions.[72] This made assimilation with domesticity problematic. Jewish leaders wanted to demonstrate that Jewish women enjoyed the same rights and privileges as Christian women, but religious practice made that impossible. The figure of Deborah provided Jewish women with a past that seemed to connect with the present, as Menken clearly recognized.

In other poetry that focused on Jewish oppression, Menken also attempted to conflate her Deborah persona with that of redemptive womanhood. In "What an Angel Said to Me," published in December 1858, she adopted not only the sentimental overtones of the larger Victorian culture but also its Christian imagery. The narrator speaks in first person, suggesting gender neutrality belied by the feminine connotation of sentimental language. She describes endlessly walking with a lovely female angel hovering alongside as her "worn feet tread sadly, day by day/ Longing in vain for rest." The angel clearly embodies ideals of Victorian womanhood "with pale, sweet face, and eyes cast meekly down." A bittersweet coronation at the hands of the angel sets the poet apart from the rest of mankind: "with iron bands, and flowerless stalks,/She weaves my fitting crown."

Menken would return to the imagery of the iron crown for years to come, particularly in 1860, when she described her "crucifixion" at the hands of callous men. No "iron crown" exists in the Bible, but the image obviously signifies on Christ's crown of thorns, particularly when coupled with allusions to crucifixion. When Menken published this poem in the

---

[71] Ann Douglas, *The Feminization of American Culture* (New York: Knopf, 1977).

[72] Karla Goldman, "Beyond the Galley: The Place of Women in the Development of American Judaism," Ph.D. dissertation, Harvard University, 1993, p. 211.

Israelite in 1858, she had not yet depicted herself as crucified, but rather as one set apart by God – a prophet or messiah. The overtly Christian images of crucifixion, often central to her later New York poetry, extended from this imagery she first introduced as a Jewish poet in Cincinnati.

In the poem's final stanza, she suggests her martyred patience, "Angel! behold, I wait/Wearing the iron crown through all life's hours – /Waiting till thy hand shall ope the eternal gate,/And change the iron to flowers." The juxtaposition of iron, gates, flowers, and triumphant martyrdom foreshadows the sentimental style she would begin employing shortly in New York. "What an Angel Said to Me" implies that God has set Menken apart. Yet it is the angel, not Menken, who plays the "true woman" in the poem; Menken merely submits to the angel's feminine sway. Despite the sentimental tone of the poem, the poet remains a strong figure, enduring but not submissive.[73]

Menken's theatrical identity also began clashing with the personality she displayed as a Jewish poet. A particularly sensational evening in Dayton ultimately led to the ending of her marriage and her tenure in the Cincinnati community. At the end of July 1858, she performed one of her first male roles, Jack Sheppard, in the well-known, rather disreputable play *Sixteen-String Jack*, that would become one of her staples. The still boyishly slim Menken cavorted about the stage with an abandonment that thrilled the Dayton audience. A gathering of young men cheered as she sang a minstrel song, "Comin' thro' the Rye" at intermission and performed a Spanish dance that the Dayton *Empire* termed "fascinating."[74] Although the shift to the more profitable and lowbrow "breeches" part of Jack Sheppard indicated a fundamental change in Menken's approach to theater, the backlash she soon faced had little to do with her performance onstage.

A volunteer militia calling themselves "the Dayton Light Guards" greeted Menken after the show. Escorted by all seventy-five members, Menken joined them for dinner at a local hotel and sat through elaborate speeches in her honor.[75] There she proudly accepted the title, "Captain of the Dayton Light Guards." The next day, the *Empire* reported that she had drunk seventy-five glasses of champagne, and the story circulated far beyond the Ohio Valley.[76] Menken apparently appreciated the publicity, since she marketed herself as "Captain Menken" for several years afterward, but the incident seems to have undermined her image as a good Jewish wife.

Until the Dayton incident in August 1858, Menken the actress had remained largely out of sight in Cincinnati. Wise seldom mentioned her upcoming performances in the Jewish newspapers and Menken usually performed outside the city, in Nashville, Dayton, or Louisville. She tended to

---

73 AIM, "What an Angel Said to Me," *Israelite*, Dec. 10, 1858.　74 Mankowitz, *Mazeppa*, 55.
75 Lesser, *Enchanting Rebel*, 33–34.　76 *Illustrated News*, March 31, 1860, p. 311.

play "serious" heroines in pieces such as *The Soldier's Daughter and Macbeth.* Although she performed poorly in such roles, reviews suggest that she had startling charisma. While playing Lady Macbeth opposite James Murdoch in Nashville, for example, she upstaged the famous tragedian despite knowing only half her lines. Murdoch vowed never to repeat the experience.[77] It is doubtful that Wise and other members of the community attended many of Menken's plays since she seldom performed in Cincinnati, and then she played only in English-speaking theaters. According to *Die Deborah,* Cincinnati Jews tended to frequent the German theaters.

For several months after the Dayton incident, Menken attempted to shore up her image as a devoted and devout wife and published several poems on domestic themes. On September 3, 1858, she published a poem that suggests Alexander may have been threatening to break off the marriage. In "Karazah to Karl" she begins with the plea: "Come back to me! The stars will be/ Silent witnesses of our bliss,/And all the past shall seem to thee/But a sweet dream to herald this!"[78] With this poem pledging submissive love, Menken supposedly displayed her private side.

In "Wife's Prayer," Menken assured the Reform community that her wifely role remained paramount. Seeking strength to remain "a great blessing and comfort" to her husband and "amiable forever in his eyes," not given to "ungentleness and ill-humor," the ambitious Adah asked God to make her "humble and obedient, useful and observant." Finally, she wove these Victorian sentiments together with a fervent call to "our God of Israel." Like advocates of Reform Judaism, Menken attempted to place a concept of the Jewish wife within the overlapping curves of Victorian ideology and Israelite identity.

In her last poem to Alexander, "A Heart Wail," Menken asserts that her role as wife took precedence over other ambitions. Published in February 1859, the poem also suggests that her marriage was ending against Menken's will. She aligns herself with sentimental poets by portraying herself as fragile: "I know that I am faint and weak,/Scarce fit for the long strife,/Of those who would with honor fill/The stern demands of life." She suggests that, despite her public ambition, her private life is sacred: "Ye may send that riches, fame nor power,/Ne'er at my bidding come,/But spare, oh God! in its purity,/My peace and love at home." Despite her declarations of love and faith, the marriage continued to disintegrate.

Yet on February 21, 1859, in a letter written to Rosina on the road between engagements, Adah portrayed her marriage to Alexander as happy. She affectionately referred to her husband as "Allie," commenting that they had celebrated his birthday the day before. Menken also

---

[77] James Murdoch, *The Stage; or, Recollections of Actors and Acting from an Experience of Fifty Years; A Series of Dramatic Sketches* (Philadelphia: J. M. Stoddart, 1880), 53–57.

[78] AIM, "Karazah to Karl," in *Infelicia* (Philadelphia: Lippincott, 1873), 97.

apologized to her sister-in-law for failing to visit during her previous engagement in Cincinnati, where she had performed *The Jewess* at the New National Theatre.[79] She added that she might "go to New York to play" but that she was "not certain yet."[80]

In performing *The Jewess* on stage, Menken played with her offstage Jewish performance. *The Jewess; or, The Council of Trent*, by W. T. Moncrief, added layers of meaning to Menken's offstage performance by focusing on the fate of a young Jewish woman, Rachel, who is seduced by a man who she later discovers is married, Christian, and the prince. Through her own desire for vengeance, she becomes a pawn in a game between two other men: Lazarus, the bitter Jewish man whom she believes is her father, and the Catholic cardinal, who, upon hearing Rachel's accusations, sentences Rachel, her lover, and her father to death. Just as soldiers push Rachel into a cauldron of boiling water, Lazarus reveals that the cardinal is Rachel's true father.[81] Audiences surely wondered about parallels between Rachel and Menken. In Cincinnati, Menken tantalized curious fans by suggesting that a Jewess herself might not know her own true identity, and that of her father. Rachel's Judaism becomes false when Lazarus reveals that her biological father is not Jewish – confirming Menken's tendency to anchor her own identity in that of her (fictive) father. Later audiences may have focused more on the heroine's betrayal at the hands of her lover, as that would also prove to be one of Menken's favorite themes in the years to come.

Despite Menken's increasing audacity onstage, the *Israelite* continued to publish her poems, which is somewhat surprising since articles in *Die Deborah* continued to emphasize that women in the arts should be celebrated only if they continued to find their greatest worth in the home. But by 1859, it was becoming clear that the two papers held somewhat contradictory views, and the women of Reform Judaism were in a paradoxical position. Female poets and artists could speak, but only within a space severely circumscribed by gendered propriety. At the same time, Reform Jewish women faced pressure to leave behind the traditional forms of religious observation that had given them an important and active role in the home. In many ways, the situation of Jewish women appeared to resemble that of Protestant women, but the differences were telling. Jewish women were *losing* power in the home by adopting Christian "domesticity," since the home had traditionally functioned as their religious space. Nor could they use religious involvement in the synagogue to leverage influence because their means of participation remained restricted. By coopting the figure of an ancient female prophet, Menken had found a singular means of cutting

---

[79] "Amusements," *Cincinnati Daily Commercial*, Dec. 27, 1858, p. 2.

[80] AIM to Rosina, Feb. 21, 1859, Menken scrapbook.

[81] W. T. Moncrief, *The Jewess; or the Council of Trent* (n.p., n.d.), prompt book in Harvard Theatre Collection, Houghton Library, Harvard University, Cambridge, Massachusetts.

through societal strictures to empower her voice and vision. She succeeded until September 1859, when she and Alexander parted company. When her marriage fell apart, Menken ceased to appear in the Jewish Reform newspaper, and her voice in the community became silent.

Four and a half years passed before Menken's name again appeared in the *Israelite*, when, on December 30, 1864, the paper publicly denied her claims to Judaism. Although Menken "wrote several excellent poems for the Israelite," Wise had supposedly refused to accept her into the covenant of Israel, and "hence, that as far as the form and birth is concerned, she is no Jewess, although she invariably calls the Hebrews 'our people,' and sympathizes altogether with them when she feels like sympathizing."[82] At that moment, Wise probably chose to disavow Menken's Jewish identity because of the stigma widely associated with her "naked lady." But sixty years later, when Menken was no longer threatening but had become instead a beloved cultural memory, his son, Leo Wise, reiterated the rabbi's claims: "Menken . . . was not a Jewess, but she most ardently desired to become one, and often requested Dr. Wise to receive her into the fold, going so far at one time as to implore him on her knees . . . to accept her as a convert. For some reason unknown to me he steadfastly refused to do this."[83] Adah Menken, however, did as she pleased. She decided she was Jewish enough in her heart to claim Judaism, and in so doing implicitly rejected conventional understanding of that identity. For contemporary scholars to endorse Menken's Jewish heritage ignores the claims of Jewish Reform leaders during her own time.

In 1924, Leo Wise raised questions about the definition of Jewish identity when he stated diplomatically that "while she did not have a drop of 'Semitic' blood in her veins, she was in faith and ideals an ardent Jewess."[84] Menken continued to observe Judaism after she left Cincinnati by refusing to perform on Jewish holidays, claiming Jewish identity up to 1866, and requesting a Jewish burial.[85] But aside from her brief sojourn in Cincinnati, Menken never again lived in a Jewish community, and later entered two Christian marriages. This is not to say that Menken was not devoted to Judaism, only that she was neither born nor raised Jewish and that she practiced Judaism much the same way she did everything else: in her own way, paying attention to rules or customs only when it worked to her advantage. Whether or not anyone believed Adah's claim to Jewish ancestry when she first came to Cincinnati, the fact that Rabbi Wise endorsed her work rendered her part of the community for nearly two years.

---

[82] Israelite, Dec. 30, 1864, p. 212.

[83] Leo Wise, "Israelite Personalities: People Who Wrote for the Israelite and Other Things of Interest in Connection Therewith," *Israelite*, supplement, July 24, 1924, pp. 31–32.

[84] Ibid.

[85] Jacob R. Marcus, *American Jewish Women, 1654–1980* (New York: KTAV Publishing House, 1981), 33.

Menken in a breeches role in 1859. Her dress in this photograph is closer
fitting than what she would wear in breeches roles from 1860 to 1864. (Harvard
Theatre Collection)

Menken's ability alternately to assume and doff Jewish identity was perhaps more idiosyncratic and extreme than the practices of most Americans
at midcentury, but it was at most an exaggerated version of more subtle
patterns. In a nation of immigrants, many citizens must actively choose
which ethnicity to embrace as their own. Besides strengthening ties with
Alexander's wealthy family, there were obvious advantages to Menken claiming membership in such a strong community on the verge of great change.
The *Israelite* gave her access to the media, so that she might shape public
perceptions of her. The struggles over gender boundaries and definition
gave her great freedoms to create her celebrity image. And once she left the
Reform Jewish community, Jewish identity would allow her to cultivate her
image as an artistic outsider and capitalize on mass culture's understanding
of Jewish women as mysterious, brilliant, and beautiful.

When Menken left her husband and Cincinnati she took with her a
few valuable lessons in crafting her own celebrity. She had learned that she
needed to get her name in the media if she wanted to get contracts and
fill theaters, and that there were two quick routes to fame: direct contact
and scandal. The Dayton incident, while it had damaged her personal life,

gave her wider name recognition and ultimately taught her that scandalous publicity could make an unknown actress known. At the same time, literary expression lent her respectability regardless of her reputation because it allowed her to speak directly to the public. She was able to live two lives: one that made money and one that inspired admiration. Adapting the role of Deborah to perform offstage as herself had taught her lessons in self-fashioning, creating herself as a recognizable persona. Cincinnati, with its easy access to the world and the Reform Jewish community as an intimate safe haven, had been an ideal place to create local celebrity. In September 1859 Menken left to take up residency in New York City and put her new skills to work at the national level.

Chapter 2

Playing the Pugilist's Wife: 1859–1860

The Empire City, into whose bosom pour the luxury and the crime of the Old World and the New. Upon her bay the ships of every sea; within her streets the people of every tongue, behold her, as she throbs with a million lives, throbs beneath that cloud made luminous by her glare, the Empire City clad in purples and in rags, splendid with countless wealth, festering with countless crimes....

George Lippard, *The Empire City, or New York by Night and Day* (1850)

It took Menken only five months to put herself in the national spotlight after moving to New York City. A virtual unknown in September 1859, by February 1860 newspaper readers from the East Coast to San Francisco knew her name. Scandal, the quickest route to fame or infamy, put Menken in the public eye. The term "scandal" implies a dissolution of public and private boundaries; it exposes a person's private actions to be judged on the public stage. Given all we know about Victorian emphasis on respectability, one would think that a major scandal should have destroyed Menken, but it did not. In many ways the scandal *made* Menken: It initially put her name before the public, won her contracts, and gave her an excuse to "share" her personal story, creating the illusion of intimacy necessary for celebrity. Menken also put some of the tricks she learned in Cincinnati to good use, such as publishing poetry that "revealed" her true self and suggested that she was the victim of male infidelity and nasty journalism. Under the guise of defense, she was able to speak directly to the public. For a short time she appeared to succeed at crafting herself as a sentimental victim while at the same time performing sensational theater and profiting from name recognition. But eventually the events of the scandal became too extreme and she ultimately failed to convince the public of her right to their sympathy. Still, in the long run, lack of respect did not diminish her later success. She became known to the public, and once known, she could not be ignored.

In January 1860, Menken claimed she was married to pugilist John Carmel Heenan, which seemed to come as a surprise to just about everyone. When the story broke, Heenan himself was on a steamer bound for Liverpool, en route to fight in the first World Heavyweight Championship, scheduled to take place in London in April. In late December, newspapers across the country had begun featuring a gentlemanly portrait of Heenan, wearing a somber expression and a dashing moustache, and comparing his various statistics with those of opponent Tom Sayers. As a result, hundreds of fans flocked to see him board the steamer for Liverpool on January 5. Twenty days later, a brief line in the "amusements" section of the New York *Tribune* stated that Heenan's wife, actress and poet Adah Isaacs Menken, "was exceedingly anxious to accompany her husband in his professional trip across the water, but he objected to it for various reasons." George Wilkes, editor of *Wilkes' Spirit of the Times,* a popular newspaper geared toward male leisure, commented three days later, "This is incorrect. Heenan is not married."[1] The news items were small – two short sentences in newspapers intended for different audiences – but they led to a scandal that entertained the nation for weeks to come, and irrevocably shaped Menken's public image.

Menken immediately sent Wilkes a blistering response. After commenting that he had never heard of her but (possibly believing he faced charges of libel) that the "lady's word...must be taken as sufficient," he printed her letter.[2] Given the close connections between the theater world, pugilism, and newspapers, it is difficult to believe that Wilkes had neither heard of nor met Menken. But if in fact he *did* know her, and the announcement began as a lark or as a means of winning publicity, it quickly backfired and Menken, Heenan, and Wilkes were all wounded in the ensuing conflagration. Menken wrote:

> In your last issue, bearing date Saturday, Jan. 28, there is an article copied from the N. Y. Tribune, stating the well-known fact of my being the wife of John C. Heenan. Of this I have nothing to complain; on the contrary, I am proud and happy to be known as the wife of the bravest man in the world! But you or your "Itemizer" took the unauthorized liberty of adding "This is incorrect. Heenan is not married."
>
> I have no right to suppose, nor do I wish to, that *malice* prompted these words, as daggers to stab the reputation of the wife of a man for whom you have repeatedly expressed the warmest and most disinterested friendship. I can only suppose, and hope, it to be a *mistake,* perhaps a "slight mistake" to you, but a bitter heartrending one to her whose earnest, toiling life looks up to the Good and True to bless that inner life – the conscience – and to be worthy of the brave and noble man whose name she bears.
>
> Remember that woman's reputation is like the camellia, "wound it with a single touch, and you can never recall its bloom."
>
> Now, for the sake of your mother and sisters – and for your own sake God send that you have both for through their purity and gentle influence we look for the grand and noble results of all that is good in man's nature – for their

[1] *New York Tribune,* Jan. 25, 1860; editorial, *Wilkes' Spirit of the Times* (hereafter *WST*), Jan. 28, 1860, p. 336.
[2] Wilkes admits fear of libel suit, *WST,* Feb. 18, 1860, p. 384.

sakes, I beg that you will do me and John C. Heenan the justice to correct this grievous mistake, which has caused me the deepest trouble.[3]

In effect, Menken pointed out that Wilkes had acted both erroneously and thoughtlessly and jeopardized her reputation in the process. Using the sentimental language popular in women's magazines and novels, Menken emphasized her fragile femininity and likened a woman's reputation to a delicate flower. She asserted that Wilkes's unchivalrous acts had proven that he, not Menken, was morally lacking. Despite the blantantly manipulative edge to her note, readers knew that Menken was justified in her sensitivity. The fluidity of the antebellum social world had heightened the precarious nature of female reputation to the point of making Wilkes's assertions dangerous to her, professionally as well as personally.

But Wilkes had good reason to believe he was an authority on Heenan: He and Frank Queen, editor of the *Clipper*, had virtually created Heenan as a celebrity. Although sparring for money remained illegal, Wilkes and Queen used their newspapers actively to promote both the sport and its combatants. Heenan combined boxing talent with good looks, but Queen and Wilkes were responsible for crafting the Heenan's celebrity image. Wilkes owned and edited the most well established of the "sporting newspapers," inexpensive papers that reported primarily on sports, theater, and gambling. Wilkes used his influence to facilitate pugilism's first world championship match and Heenan was his protegé. In every issue for three months prior to the match, his paper had included detailed accounts of Heenan's background, past triumphs, and vital statistics.[4]

Menken, meanwhile, was a virtual unknown in the Northeast, although not for long. Her letter to Wilkes pricked public interest, and other papers quickly picked up the story and pressed for more information about Menken herself (who now called herself Mrs. John Heenan). Newspapers across the country portrayed her in two notably different ways: as an actress (hard, manipulative, tawdry) or as a poet (gifted, refined, sincere). They were images from the opposite ends of the cultural spectrum and Menken capitalized on both of them. Over the next several months, she deliberately played the two images against each other – first to profit from the notoriety and later to survive the scandal. Much of the public considered marriage between an actress and pugilist as one of equals – as the joining of performers with questionable morals. The union of a poet and pugilist, however, suggested

---

[3] "Letter from Adah Isaacs Menken, claiming to be the wife of John C. Heenan," *WST*, Feb. 4, 1860, p. 352.

[4] There are many different opinions about what constitutes a "sporting paper." I am using the broader definition, which does not limit the term to pornographic papers, but includes all papers that celebrate a working-class style of masculinity and target an exclusively male audience. Donald W. Klinko, "Antebellum American Sporting Magazines and the Development of a Sportsman's Ethic," Ph.D. dissertation, Washington State University, 1986, p. 5; Sam G. Riley, ed., *American Magazine Journalists, 1850–1900, Dictionary of Literary Biography*, vol. 79 (Detroit: Gale Research, 1989), 304.

a contradiction and increased the public's attraction to the story. Her first publicity photos, taken that fall, show a slim-hipped, athletic Menken with short dark curls, who challenged the camera's eye with her gaze. Menken knew she was bright, talented, and beautiful; if fame could be won, then why not by her?

But Menken, while not backing down from claiming marriage to Heenan, did not always play the outraged wife. She was already making it difficult for spectators to define her. When rumor suggested she had been the wife of salacious author Ned Buntline, among others, she responded to the insult with good humor, saying:

> Now, as I never have had the pleasure (?) of knowing those gentlemen, my marriage with them must have been extremely poetic and spiritual. You will please say that I never was married to James Buchanan . . . neither am I the daughter of Prince Albert by a former marriage. . . . But my present honorable relation to John C. Heenan is a source of greater pride for me than any of these could bring. If I have committed an error in marrying him, time will convince me of my error, and not the press.[5]

Menken was daring, stylish, and witty, but, more important, she was constantly in motion. She routinely turned different sides to the public, soon creating a brilliant kaleidoscope of Menkens.

The debate over the Menken–Heenan marriage soon found its way into newspapers as far away as San Francisco.[6] Indeed, the story may have had more appeal far away, where readers could only imagine the great metropolis. Americans both within and without the city routinely devoured fiction that portrayed New York as dangerously immoral. Many popular novels portrayed New York theater districts as sights of unfettered hedonism. Despite the fact that the New York publishing industry played a central role in disseminating middle-class ideologies, many Americans saw the city as a center of vice – not the culturally exotic, safely distant vice depicted in stories of New Orleans and Texas, but the vice of Anglo-Americans lost to their own ambitions and desires.

Menken had taken up residence in a city as rich in contrasts as herself, and the sheer number of residents and their contradictions and cultural differences would work to her advantage over the next few months. New York was in the middle of a phenomenal growth spurt and building the infrastructure to facilitate further growth. Its residents enjoyed communication systems unrivaled in the United States, making it an ideal setting for aspiring celebrities. It also boasted living standards unheard of in most of the nation, as the

[5] *San Francisco Call*, April 1, 1860, p. 1, quoting letter from Menken to an unnamed New York paper, dated March 1, 1860.
[6] *San Francisco Call*, April 1, 1860, p. 1.

municipal government experimented with pavement, sewage, and waste disposal, and began piping gas into private dwellings as well as businesses. By 1859 most New Yorkers depended on reservoirs outside the city for fresh water and sent their waste swirling down great underground pipes that emptied into the Hudson. Menken could walk or take a horse-drawn hack cab or omnibus to any part of the city, although she would have traveled over a variety of surfaces, from noisy cobblestones to splintering wooden planks to granite slabs that sent the horses' feet sliding. Or she could easily visit friends in outlying neighborhoods, as over 142 miles of streetcar track linked New York's smaller streets with its principal thoroughfares. Meanwhile, twenty-five ferries connected New York with surrounding cities and towns, allowing farmers to commute into the city to sell their wares, mechanics and other laborers to live in low-rent towns such as Hoboken, and the elite to enjoy the peace of country life without sacrificing business advantages. By Menken's time, New Yorkers had become accustomed to mailing letters and packages by express, knowing that their items would be delivered by horse, train, or steamer to their final destinations in the United States or abroad.[7] Menken often took advantage of the messengers who delivered missives around the city, much as late nineteenth-century urbanites would make a phone call to invite friends over or cancel a luncheon date.[8] Connected by iron pipes, streets that turned from mud to pavement, and tracks that created both separation and unity, by 1859 New York was already emerging as the city that would shape American popular culture of the industrial age.

For as little as two cents, city dwellers could choose among a selection of dailies to find their own views expressed – or to be instructed in what their views should be. By the 1850s, New York City's lively and well-established print culture had evolved into an ongoing public forum. Unsurprisingly, much of the discussion in 1860 focused on the possibility that the southern states would pull out of the union. Because so much of the South owed a fortune in credit to New York businesses, Mayor Fernando Wood went so far as to proclaim, "The City of New York belongs almost as much to the South as to the North."[9] Newspapers, sensational pamphlets, Christian

---

[7] Philip Wallys, *About New York: An Account of What a Boy Saw in His Visit to the City* (New York: Dix, Edward, 1857), 59, 63; Junius Henri Browne, *The Great Metropolis; A Mirror of New York* (Hartford, 1869), 463, 100–102; Mary C. Henderson, *The City and the Theatre: The History of New York Playhouses – A 235 Year Journey from Bowling Green to Times Square* (Clifton: James T. White, 1973), 100; *City Sights for Country Eyes* (Philadelphia: American Sunday School Union, 1857).

[8] Several of Menken's "letters" in various collections are really short messages inviting a visit, thanking someone for a gesture, or canceling an appointment.

[9] For discussion on the links between gender and America's Civil War, see Catherine Clinton and Nina Silber, eds, *Divided Houses: Gender and the Civil War* (New York: Oxford University Press, 1992). For analysis of gender and war in general, see Miriam Cooke and Angela Woollacott, eds., *Gendering War Talk* (Princeton: Princeton University Press, 1993), introductory references to war as challenging previous gender roles, xii; Ernest McKay, *The Civil War and New York City* (Syracuse: Syracuse University Press, 1990), 15–16.

publications, magazines, and popular fiction spoke to one another, defining
and redefining urban culture in print.[10]

From the beginning Menken had her defenders as well as accusers, and
journalists bickered back and forth. Horace Greeley's New York *Tribune*
placed its faith in Menken, and the New York *Sunday Mercury*, where she
regularly contributed poems, defended her outright. According to these
papers, Menken was the victim of sensation-seeking journalists, and later of
Heenan himself. Two men who would remain friendly with her throughout
her life, Gus Daly of the *Sunday Courier* and Frank Queen of the *Clipper*,
chastised the public for vilifying her.

Many other papers made the most of the scandal by opening Menken's
closets and dragging her dirty linen through the streets of the national press.
Wilkes gleefully reprinted jabs from other papers, many of which alluded to
the incident with the Dayton Light Guards. Wilkes included the *New York
Leader's* opinion:

> A very pretty dispute is going the rounds of the papers, as to whether Captain
> Adah Isaacs Menken is or is not the wife of the Benicia Boy. *The Tribune* says
> that she is; *Wilkes Spirit* denies the fact; the lady asserts it under her own hand,
> and everybody either does or does not know something about the affair. We
> believe we are the first to ask the important question in connection with it:
> Who Cares?[11]

The definitive answer came from Alexander Isaac Menken himself, the
day after Menken's letter appeared. He addressed his blistering condemnation of Adah to George Wilkes via the *Cincinnati Commercial* – clearly
assuming that Wilkes would reprint it in the next week's edition. He wrote:

> I see by the last number of your paper that you have published a letter signed by
> a woman calling herself Adah Isaacs Menken Heenan. In justice to myself and
> friends, I cannot permit this very delicate effusion to pass unnoticed. Allow me
> to inform you, my dear sir, that you were perfectly correct when you stated to
> your correspondent that John C. Heenan was not married to this individual –
> at least, not legally married, unless it be lawful in your State for a woman to
> have two husbands at one and the same time. The effrontery and *nonchalance*
> with which this woman sentimentalizes in her letter to you, in reference to
> your damaging *her reputation*, and the manner in which she tries to enlist your
> sympathies in her behalf, by alluding to your position as a son and brother,
> would be very amusing to me were I not so deeply interested in the matter.
>
>   And now, my dear sir, let me briefly state the facts in this case as they really
> exist.

[10] McKay, *Civil War*; Edward K. Spann, *The New Metropolis: New York City, 1840–1857* (New York:
Columbia University Press, 1981).
[11] *WST*, Feb. 11, 1860, 368.

On the third day of April, 1856, in the town of Livingston, in the County of Polk, and the State of Texas, I had the misfortune to be married, by a Justice of the peace, to this adventuress, since which time I have never been divorced from her; on the contrary, have lived with her up to last July. . . .

I would say, in this connection, that I have instituted proceedings in the proper courts which will rid me of this incubus and disgrace, and that this public expose of private matters has not been sought by me – that I have borne disgrace for this woman, through the medium of the press and otherwise, "til forbearance has ceased to be a virtue." Even now I would not notice her, but her superlative impudence and brazenness, as evinced by her late letter to you, in attempting to impose upon you, and through you on the public, in the most conspicuous way possible, renders her unworthy of my further charitable silence. In conclusion, permit me to say that I do not regret the phase matters have taken, as far as regards the separation of this person with myself, but I must remark, that as long as she is married to John Heenan, I would much prefer she would make use of his name and discontinue mine, as I think, from recent developments, I would be "more honored in the breach than in the observance."[12]

Very respectfully, A. I. Menken[13]

Alexander's letter must have shocked the public, both because of the message and because he made little effort to temper his hostility. It was clearly a letter intended to publicly destroy his wife. If Wilkes and Adah had been friendly before, then they certainly were no longer; he had reprinted a letter that not only branded Adah an adventuress but also accused her of bigamy, a serious legal and social crime. The charge of bigamy carried images of lawlessness popularly associated with the Far West and the infamous Ned Buntline, whose biography of deceit had recently entertained the public. Cultural critic Junius Henri Browne later wrote a chapter devoted to identifying an "adventuress" in *The Great Metropolis* (1868), stating that she "earns all her success by seeming to be what she is not; by an adroit assumption of virtue she can hardly remember to have had."[14] His description fits Menken so well that one wonders if it was shaped by Menken's career. Alexander's need to publicly clarify his position is understandable: Adah's marriage to another man implicated him because they were still legally bound. But he went further than mere self-protection when he crudely mocked her use of sentimental language and implied that she deserved to be treated as an abomination of womanhood.[15]

Wilkes reprinted sharp snippets from other city papers beneath Alexander's letter. For example, the Dayton *Empire* viciously mocked a poem that Adah had dedicated to Heenan, provocatively stating that the

---

[12] The quote is from William Shakespeare's *Hamlet.*
[13] A. J. Menken to Wilkes, *WST*, Feb. 18, 1860, p. 384.   [14] Browne, *Great Metropolis*, 197.
[15] Papers around the nation summarized the letter, see, e.g., *San Francisco Call*, April 1, 1860, p. 1.

poem entitled "Come to Me" was truly "to anybody, as a general invitation to 'go in!'" Over the next few months Americans would submit parodies of Menken's poem to several papers, usually giving Heenan's imagined answer.[16] The Dayton *Enquirer* alluded to other current events when it remarked that Menken could not be married to Heenan, "[p]olygamy being unlawful." Polygamy was an inflammatory charge, as the *Enquirer* well knew; the United States Army was in the midst of launching a war against Mormons in Salt Lake City, supposedly because their church continued to advocate polygamy.[17] George Wilkes reminded the public of Menken's original statement, asking, "What motive induced Mrs. Menken to write the letter in question we are at a loss to conjecture, unless for the purpose of obtaining notoriety."[18]

The speed with which the story unfolded indicated the growing sophistication of news networks. Although that sophistication initially proved harmful to Menken, it would soon play a crucial role in her ascendancy as a national (and eventually international) celebrity. Communication technology allowed the Menken–Heenan scandal to develop as naturally as a conversation. The papers fanned the flames as best they could because a good scandal increased their sales. By 1860, newspapers across the country had become adept in using comments in other papers to spice up their own. The invention of the telegraph in 1845 had revolutionized news gathering, but because each newspaper was limited to only fifteen minutes of telegraph use a day, New York newspaper owners pooled their resources and created the New York Associated Press in 1848. Until the transatlantic cable was laid and working in 1866, the association also chartered a steamer to travel to and from Halifax to bring news from European and British ships before they had time to reach America. To help fund such expensive ventures, the Associated Press began selling their stories to out-of-city papers, creating an empire of news gathering that largely originated from New York.[19] The problem with this structure is that it made many papers look just like their competition; opinion pieces and sensationalist stories were needed to spike the punch.

---

[16] "The Benecia Boy's Reply," *WST* (reprinting from *Boston Post*), Feb. 11, 1860, p. 368; "Heenan's Answer to His Wife's 'Come Back to Me,'" *WST* (reprinting from *Racing Times*), March 31, 1860, p. 59; "Scene after the Fight," *WST* (reprinting from *Cincinnati Herald*), April 21, 1860, p. 108.

[17] There are many excellent sources on the "Mormon War," and most suggest that polygamy was the popular issue but not necessarily the central reason for the war. For a short summary, see Richard White, *It's Your Misfortune and None of My Own: A New History of the American West* (Norman: University of Oklahoma Press, 1991).

[18] *WST*, Feb. 11, 1860, p. 368.

[19] Dan Schiller, *Objectivity and the News: The Public Rise and Fall of Commercial Journalism* (Philadelphia: University of Pennsylvania Press, 1981), 48; Michael Schudsen, *Discovering the News: A Social History of American Newspapers* (New York: Basic Books, 1978), 23; Andie Tucher, *Froth and Scum: Truth, Beauty and the Ax Murderer in America's First Mass Medium* (Chapel Hill: University of North Carolina Press, 1994), 48; James L. Crouthamel, *Bennett's New York Herald and the Rise of the Popular Press* (New York: Syracuse University Press, 1989), 17, 24.

Focusing on a juicy celebrity scandal in 1860 probably held particular appeal. Tensions over sectional differences ran high, and it was an election year; the daily papers were filled with dense type and complicated political reporting. Sensation created a diversion for, as William Wordsworth once suggested, it fed the public's craving for excitement while at the same time keeping them out of danger.[20] Sensational scandal was clearly linked with the celebrity phenomenon; just as celebrities allowed the public to enjoy intimacy without risking rejection, sensation gave the public thrills without danger, and scandal provided an easy link between them. Readers and journalists alike seemed to understand that Menken and Heenan were public property, and therefore their personal lives, which would normally be labeled private, were also public property. Menken and her personal affairs particularly interested the public because they were debatable as well as scandalous, and could thus be drawn out for weeks.

The papers never managed to establish whether or not a marriage had taken place, but records suggest that Menken had valid reasons for believing she was married to Heenan. She had probably met him while still living with Alexander, on Christmas night of 1858 when she starred as Rebecca in *Ivanhoe* at the National Theatre in Cincinnati. Twenty-three-year-old Heenan was scheduled to box a short demonstration match after the play. Tall, broad-shouldered, and dashing, Heenan would have been hard to forget even without the fame attached to his name. Menken later told a reporter that she and Heenan had met a second time in New Orleans, in the summer of 1859. There are no records to establish Menken's whereabouts that summer, so there is no way to verify whether she took the trip she claimed.[21] In any case, all accounts agree that at the end of that summer of 1859 she met Heenan in Frank Queen's office at the New York *Clipper*, where she had gone to peddle her poetry – or perhaps to meet up with Heenan.

A ceremony of some sort took place between Menken and Heenan a month later, on September 3, 1859, at Rockaway Cottage on Bloomingdale Road. Despite the fact that Heenan later denied the marriage, witnesses in later trials would substantiate the time and place, and confirm that for several months that autumn Heenan and Menken had lived as husband and wife at Westchester House, a hotel.[22] It is possible, however, that the marriage

[20] Karen Halttunen, *Murder Most Foul: The Killer and the American Gothic Imagination* (Cambridge: Harvard University Press, 1998), 67.

[21] New York *Illustrated News*, April 14, 1860. Menken's next husband, Robert Newell, later said that she had been institutionalized for "melancholia," or depression, that summer. See Robert H. Newell, "Adah Isaacs Menken," publication unknown, pasted into "Biography of Adah Isaacs Menken. Extra Illustrated," Harris Rare Books, 76-M545x, Brown University Library, Providence, Rhode Island. According to a letter from a woman claiming to be Heenan's "true wife," Adah began corresponding with Heenan soon after their first meeting in 1858, and frequently mentioned her unhappy marriage while declaring sisterly friendship with Heenan. See Josephine Heenan to Alexander Menken printed in *WST*, April 14, 1860.

[22] *Illustrated News*, April 14, 1860; "The Petition of Adah Isaacs Menken for Divorce from John C.

was ceremonial rather than legal. The location of "Bloomingdale Road" held specific connotations for New Yorkers: It had long been a picturesque lane that rambled northward out of the city, lined with small cottages and rustic inns. By the 1850s Bloomingdale Road had become a popular place for young dandies to race their horses and engage in romantic trysts with unchaperoned young women. Nor would a quaint title like "Rockaway Cottage" fool those who knew the area. As early as 1852, M. M. Huet's popular city mystery, *Silver and Pewter: A Tale of High Life and Low Life in New York*, depicted a picturesque cottage with the appearance of graceful retirement. "But the Bower Cottage at Bloomingdale . . . was no seat where virtue or good ever came to see pure enjoyment; but it was a pest house, beautiful without but foul within, where lust and passion held their high revels and committed fiendish deeds, in the face of the very smile and sacred repose of nature."[23] New Yorkers would have seen the address of the marriage place much the way later Americans would think of Vegas – the place where fast people marry in haste to repent in leisure.

So why did Menken decide to claim the marriage in January 1860 when Heenan was conveniently out at sea? He was famous, so she could capitalize on his name. He had the potential to earn a lot of money, so perhaps she was looking ahead. But she may have been motivated by something else as well: By January 1860 Menken was several months' pregnant. Although abortion was an option, she may have disregarded it because she considered herself married or because a baby could bind Heenan to her. And despite the strong tone of her letter, Menken was faltering badly. Worn out by pregnancy and a demanding travel schedule, as well as unrelenting public scrutiny, Menken found it increasingly difficult to perform. Although "Annie Josephs," whom Menken referred to as her sister, assisted on stage in late January, her drawing power as a star appeared to be weakening.[24] New York papers complained of bitter cold and impassable streets during those winter months, and Menken took an uncharacteristic break from performing that February.[25]

Upon reaching England that January of 1860 Heenan must have heard of the commotion over his marriage to Menken, but he did not address the subject for several months. The *Clipper* and *Wilkes' Spirit* spoke at length about the upcoming fight, but chose not to mention Menken. Meanwhile,

Heenan," *New York Herald*, Oct. 31, 1861; letter from Clerk of Circuit Court, McHenry County, Illinois, to Allen Lesser, citing date of divorce as April 3, 1861, in Allen Lesser Collection, American Jewish Archives, Cincinnati, Ohio (hereafter ALC). "For Women Only," *The Last Sensation*, vol. 1 (May 2, 1868), 294; transcript in the Nicholas A. Kovach collection, Special Collections, University of Minnesota, Minneapolis (hereafter Kovach).

[23] M. M. Huet, *Silver and Pewter: A Tale of High Life and Low Life in New York* (New York: H. Long and Brother, 1852), 60.

[24] New Gayety Theatre playbill, Albany, Jan. 25, 1860. It is impossible to determine whether Annie Josephs was actually Menken's sister, as she frequently "adopted" friends as family members, and there are no public records of Annie Josephs in known existence.

[25] *Sunday Mercury*, Feb. 5, 1860; *New York Evening Post*, Feb. 4, 1860.

Menken wrote to one of Heenan's friends, Mr. Robbins of Boston, on February 19, 1860: "I have had *three* letters from my dear husband since he arrived in England. The last I received yesterday from his training quarters. He gives me a full description of the place, and says everything that should make me contented and happy. But I only worry and fret the more in my present and isolated situation I only miss him the more." She expressed the fear that Heenan's name would be dragged through the mud before ruminating at length about her own deplorable situation.[26] A week later she again wrote to Robbins, reminding him of her "constant and energetic exertions to support [her]self independently since the departure" of her husband, adding:

> My Buffalo engagement proved the worst I ever had the misfortune to ex-
> perience, and by the falsehood and duplicity of the managers there, I am left
> entirely penniless. I returned last night to this city for the purpose of seeking
> some employment and also to dispose of my theatrical wardrobe if possible.
> My present state of health does not admit my continuing on the stage and I
> am more over completely disgusted with its toils and trials. But withal I can
> work. I hate idleness. But I can only write for paper or books, or teach in a
> school. I can not sew as many women. I could read or lecture in public, at
> least I could do something and I intend to. Now will you advise me? Yours
> Truly, Mrs. Heenan[27]

The letter is a plea for assistance that exposes Menken's artful manipulation; by impressing Robbins with her honor and sincerity she meant to convince him to send her money, not advice. Her "state of health" probably referred to her pregnancy by his friend, Heenan, but we know from theater records that she was back on the boards by March and worked without rest until May. It is hard to imagine a pregnant actress being allowed to perform onstage, suggesting that Menken either found some means of concealing her figure or was not as far along in her pregnancy as the baby's June arrival would suggest. She may have worked out of necessity, but she was not too ill to earn her own keep. She implies that economic independence is a point of honor for women as well as men, lest Robbins consider her as a fortune-hunter and see through her ploy. To win his sympathy she emphasizes how tightly her employment options were restricted by gender norms and prejudice against actresses, and cites her failed attempts to secure a teaching position. This last claim rings particularly false, as anyone would have known that an actress (let alone a pregnant one) would not be welcome in the classroom. But regardless of her motivation, her letter indicates the seriousness of her situation.

---

[26] Adah Isaacs Menken (AIM) to Mr. Robbins, Feb. 19, 1860, Adah Isaacs Menken Correspondence in
       ALS file (hereafter AIM ALS), Harvard Theatre Collection, Houghton Library, Harvard University,
       Cambridge, Massachusetts (hereafter HTC). I have been unable to identify Mr. Robbins any further.
[27] Letter from AIM to Robbins, Feb. 26, 1860, AIM ALS HTC.

At roughly the same time, Menken sent an artful letter to George Wilkes that managed to slow the negative effects of the scandal yet feed the public's desire for information. This time Menken tapped into temperance sympathies by suggesting that Alexander's drinking problems forced her to provide for both of them during their marriage. True or not, it was convenient that her allegations fit the temperance stereotype so nicely. Strangely, she stated, "if the alleged marriage of [Alexander] Menken and myself was legal (which he had repeatedly denied), the divorce granted upon his application and by him shown me, should be my protection."[28] Suddenly it was no longer clear whether she and Alexander were ever legally married, much less divorced. Had she been duped into a false marriage? It was pure theater, and once again Menken's situation became debatable. Even as Menken lived out the role of the painted woman she suggested that Alexander was a living version of the confidence man; he had preyed upon her innocent affection, leading her into a dissolute profession out of necessity.[29] She likens him to a "viper," the serpent in the garden who strikes "his fangs into [an innocent woman's] life's current." Implicitly, she warns the public not to be fooled, like herself, by the serpent.[30]

After establishing the image of herself as a victim, Menken asks for compassion, requesting protection from attacks by the press. It was an easy target; newspapers had already earned a reputation for inflating scandal. Popular novelist George Lippard may have put it best when he parodied New York papers, describing "*The Assassin Daily*, which ransacks the gutters of society for new calumnies, and keeps whole legions of household spies in pay, so that it may blast reputation with a hint, and damn purity with a slur."[31] The public knew that since scandal sold newspapers, journalists could be untrustworthy. The artfulness of Menken's second letter suggests that she knew the situation had gone too far; she was dangerously close to public censure.[32] Whether or not the scandal was justified, Menken transgressed genteel morality simply by being caught with her private life exposed, and her (ex?) husband's letter nearly put her beyond the pale. She presented herself as a victimized woman because it was the only viable way to defend herself.

Although papers began reporting that Heenan denied the marriage, he did not make a public statement to that effect until the following fall. Menken habitually read as many newspapers as she could find, and therefore must have seen the articles suggesting that Heenan would not claim her.[33] She

---

[28] "Letter from Mrs. John C. Heenan to George Wilkes," *WST*, March 3, 1860, p. 413.

[29] Karen Halttunen, *Confidence Men and Painted Women: A Study of Middle-Class Culture in America, 1830–1870* (New Haven: Yale University Press, 1982).

[30] Mrs. Heenan to Wilkes, *WST*, March 3, 1860, p. 413.

[31] George Lippard, *The Empire City; or, New York by Night and Day* (New York: Stringer and Townsend, 1850), 53.

[32] AIM to George Wilkes, *WST*, March 31, 1860, p. 413.

[33] Evidence of Menken's reading habits abound in AIM letters to Ed James, AIM ALS HTC.

disregarded the reports, however, and continued to proclaim her affection for Heenan and told friends that he wrote regularly.[34]

Two weeks after Menken's heartfelt defense, Wilkes published a letter from a woman calling herself Josephine Heenan, saying here "is another 'wife' writing letters to the papers to assert her claims to Heenan." Oddly enough, the letter contains several convincing elements. The writer gives concrete details of both her marriage to Heenan in 1859 and Menken's acquaintance with Heenan. Most damaging to anyone familiar with Menken's style, Josephine quotes Menken as saying she wrote as "'a loving sister might write a beloved brother.'"[35] Menken would write those same sentiments several times to another friend in later years.[36] Josephine also reported that Menken had told Heenan she was unhappily married and planned to apply for divorce."[37] In Josephine's version of the story, Menken essentially stalked Heenan and claimed marriage to him as soon as he left the Atlantic shore.

Josephine's letter briefly served to keep the scandal alive. The letter is dated nearly two months before its publication, so publishing it was undoubtedly a calculated move by Wilkes. Yet the subject of Josephine Heenan never surfaced again after this letter and her allegations did not lead to a scandal for Heenan.[38] There is no record of her marriage to John C. Heenan or her residence in New Orleans. Yet whoever she was and whatever her relationship with Heenan, both the quotations from the letters and Menken's described style of pursuit were entirely characteristic of Menken. It is as impossible to know the truth now as it was then, illustrating why the scandal continued to hold such fascination for the public: How did one distinguish fiction from reality? Whom should the public defend and whom should they vilify? The scandal effectively touched on social fears as well as curiosity.

As an actress, the timing of the scandal worked to Menken's advantage. She became a household name during a period of significant change in American theater. At an earlier point, middle-class Americans would have endangered their reputations to see her perform, despite their curiosity. Throughout the antebellum period the notion of respectability actively shaped public entertainment, social interaction, and use of leisure time. But as the numbers of Americans with leisure time and money increased, being fashionable – exhibiting knowledge of what was in style and what was not – became more important and definitions of respectability broadened along with demographics.[39] Even the design of theaters changed to accommodate demographic shifts. Those changes, as well as Menken's reception, illustrate

---

[34] Newell, "Adah Isaacs Menken."

[35] Josephine Heenan, "Another Claimant for Heenan," *WST*, April 14, 1860, p. 90.

[36] AIM to Edwin James, Dec. 1862, Baltimore, AIM ALS HTC.

[37] "Another Claimant for Heenan," *WST*, April 14, 1860, p. 90.

[38] It should be noted here that there was a good chance that Menken had a sister named Josephine, and the similarity of names may indicate a connection between the two women.

[39] Richard Bushman, *The Refinement of America: Person, Houses, Cities* (New York: Knopf, 1992), xiii.

a blurring of class signifiers in the entertainment world during and after the Civil War period.

Until the scandal, Menken did not have the clout to win a starring role on the Bowery, let alone Broadway. Broadway was already widely known as New York's great thoroughfare. As an 1857 children's book informed young readers: "from the Battery to the Reservoir it is four miles long, and on both sides are warehouses and shops (with a few dwelling houses, and hotels, and theatres) through its whole length. The street is filled from morning to night with omnibuses, carriages and people: and one would think that it is a perpetual holiday there." But although Broadway theaters had the better reputation, few Americans managed to star on its boards until the advent of war, when British actors became scarce. Meanwhile, pawnshops and lottery dealers marked the Bowery, which ran parallel to Broadway, from Chatham Square to Eighth Street. Respectable uptowners supposedly "viewed the Bowery with a mixture of fascination, amusement, and concern." That was where the American actors performed.

The two theater districts developed as opposites due to the sucess of Thomas Hamblin, who established sensational drama at the Bowery Theatre, and Lesser Wallack, whose morally saturated dramas attracted the pocket money of families on Broadway. By 1859 a theater did not even have to be located on the street to be labeled "of the Bowery"; by then the designation had more to do with the image of the theater and its clientele than its precise geographical location.[40]

Yet despite the persistence of past images, by the 1860s the theatrical fare of the two districts had actually begun to overlap a bit. Theater critics of both districts had begun praising "the natural style" that suggested performance from the heart, rather than the calculating head. It proved versatile in its appeal to both sentimentality – a genteel cultural form that gave preference to emotionally driven artistry – and to rebellion against gentility's requirements of social etiquette and self-control. This made it an ideal mode for Menken, of course, and she became widely known for her "gay and dashing" style of performance. Acting style, so class-oriented in earlier decades, had become insignificant.[41]

Theater was gaining popularity, but many still considered it dangerously hedonistic; indeed, that was part of the attraction. Morally infused literature presented the theater as viciously seductive, suggesting that "every young man well knows . . . that vice in its most fascinating garb riots in the

[40] Wallys, *About New York*, 59; James C. Burge, *Lines of Business: Casting Practice and Policy in the American Theatre, 1752–1899* (New York: Peter Lang, 1986), 113; McKay, *Civil War*, 10; Spann, *New Metropolis*, 345; Peter George Buckley, "To the Opera House: Culture and Society in New York City, 1820–1860," Ph.D. dissertation, State University of New York at Stony Brook, 1984, p. 44.

[41] Mary M. Turner, *Forgotten Leading Ladies of the American Theatre* (Jefferson, N.C.: McFarland, 1990), 61; "Amusements," *Missouri Republican*, Nov. 1, 1861; Bruce A. McConachie, *Melodramatic Formations: American Theatre and Society* (Iowa City: University of Iowa Press, 1992), chs. 4, 6, and 7.

atmosphere of the theatre; that when the senses are dazzled and the warm heart is under the strong dominion of animal excitement, then is the wine-cup offered to his lip, and his hand is seized by 'her whose steps go down to death.'" Some went so far as to trace urban social ills to the existence of theaters: "[I]t was found that a large portion of the boys began their course of crime by stealing money to buy tickets for the theatre." Even the more open-minded moralists recommended that one use caution when experimenting with the theater, because of its ability to "dazzle and bewilder" and gain control despite the viewer's best intentions.[42] Some sensational novels presented theater as an alluring vice, whetting the appetite for adventure at the same time they "warned" against its danger.

Meanwhile, the class assumptions of antebellum theater managers and entertainers shaped their approach to the public; they succeeded when they accurately gauged the desires of their audiences. Theater owners looked for proven means to highlight the respectability of their establishments and latched on to the attendance of middle-class women as the clearest indicator. Regardless of how well the formula actually worked, they began operating on the assumption that if the theater was chaste enough for women, then by implication it must be morally sound. In 1860 a theater manager remarked that last season "he ran his theatre to please, not the men, but the ladies. If the latter were satisfied with his performance he cared not whether the coarser sex liked it or not. 'You see...if the women like a play the men may despise its sentiments or its style as much as they please; they can't help coming to see it. Women rule this world, and where they go the men will either follow or be meekly led.'"[43] While the manager's reasoning was myopic, given that women at the time had little legal, economic, or political power, he no doubt expressed a common wisdom: Successful theaters must please female audiences.

This post-1850 emphasis on female attendance marked a significant change in the business of theater. Thirty years before, many urban Americans had considered theater a bastion of masculinity. City theaters of the early nineteenth century had developed as part of street culture – a male-dominated world of fluid class dimensions – and thus street behavior prevailed in theaters well into the 1850s. Theaters, like local militias, volunteer fire departments, and the marketplace itself, functioned as a crucial site of male social networking in New York City.[44] However, by the 1840s New York's middle class emerged as a significant source of patronage and began

---

[42] Spann, *New Metropolis*, 345; Helen Knight, *Reuben Kent's First Winter in the City* (1845; Philadelphia: American Sunday School Union, 1860), 88; Rev. Daniel Smith, *Anecdotes for the Young; or, Principles Illustrated by Facts* (New York: Carlton and Phillips, 1854), 224; William Makepeace Thayer, *The Bobbin Boy; or, How Nat Got His Learning: An Example for Youth* (Boston: J. E. Tilton, 1860), 221.

[43] "Who Makes Dramatic Taste?," clipping from 1860 newspaper, in Actors' & Actress's Portraits & Biographies in New York Newspapers, 1859–1879, box 22, item 168, HTC.

[44] Buckley, "To the Opera House," 118, 345.

reshaping theaters. Theater owners began searching for fare that would fill the house with a respectable audience.

The most visible change was the physical restructuring of theaters. By the 1860s, Menken was performing in theaters that had replaced the elite theater boxes and proletariat pit with more equitable seating. Although many audiences still actively participated in performances – heckling the players, calling out jokes, and verbally responding to events on stage – they could no longer mill and visit.[45] Perhaps most telling, "the family circle" replaced the notorious third tier, which had functioned as a site of prostitution, alcohol drinking, and male socializing since the colonial period. In the late 1850s, theaters also began offering matinees, which allowed respectable women to attend performances without male escorts and without inviting speculation on their virtue.[46] Menken performed many matinees over the years, suggesting that contrary to popular hearsay, she played to audiences dominated by women nearly as often as she performed for principally male audiences. The daughter of a respected minister later remembered attending a matinee of *The Black Crook,* a scandalous leg show, as part of a child's birthday party in the late 1860s.[47] Clearly, in terms of respectability, the conditions surrounding the performance were now more important than the actual subject.

Nineteenth-century Americans' active shaping of the entertainment industry reveals the inherent contradictions in class definitions that Menken used to her advantage as she attempted to woo as many spectators as possible. American theatrical traditions came out of street culture, but by the 1860s most theaters had been gentrified. Theaters increasingly pandered to middle-class audiences because they were supported by those audiences. Yet at the same time, because theater is enjoyed by a group, it is innately democratic, and despite differences in seating, viewers hold equal power. It is not surprising that theater would appeal to those who, like Menken, strove to keep themselves both below the elite yet above the laboring poor. Conventionally, most plays catered directly to such contradictions by celebrating the underdog struggling in settings defined by wealth and power, in a king's court, for example, or a sheik's harem. In other words, they frequently blended glamorous wealth with righteousness individualism.[48]

By at least the 1840s, rebellion against genteel strictures had become intrinsic to nineteenth-century middle-class culture. It was this characteristic that made Menken attractive to many Americans; as long as she partook in middle-class print culture, her marriage to Heenan and her career as an actress could be seen as rebellion. Significant numbers of Americans

---

[45] McConachie, *Melodramatic Formations,* 200–203.   [46] Ibid., 158, 164.

[47] Richard Butsch, "Bowery B'hoys and Matinee Ladies: The Re-Gendering of Nineteenth-Century American Theater Audiences," *American Quarterly* 46 (Sept. 1994): 375–391; Mabel Osgood Wright, *My New York* (New York: Macmillan, 1926).

[48] I have come to this conclusion after reading several plays that come up frequently in newspaper advertisements. Outside of a few comedies, Menken's favorite plays fit this profile.

began openly challenging various aspects of genteel life promoted by popular literature even as they embraced other middle-class behaviors. It is important to recognize that the rebellion came not from the working class, which by the late 1840s had little influence in the world of print culture, but from the middle class itself. It was a middle-class privilege to question rigid notions of appropriate behavior; the more comfortable one's position in the system, the greater one's security and ability to challenge.

And America's ever-widening middle class was ready to spend its discretionary income on something besides reading material. Economic prosperity for the masses meant that notions of culture could no longer be controlled by elites; as northeastern cities profited from the war, cultural control would begin to shift from top down to bottom up. Just because a person moved up the economic ladder did not mean he or she left behind familiar pleasures. Social fluidity led to repackaging traditionally working-class forms of entertainment for middle-class enjoyment. Wilkes and Queen set out to do this with pugilism and John Heenan. In her use of comedy, melodrama, and variety, Menken also brought elements of the lowly concert hall to her performances in theaters frequented by the middle class. Of course the working poor actively celebrated and took part in many of the same forms of entertainment and rebellion, but their participation did not carry the same cultural weight in terms of print culture and its dissemination. It took the efforts of middle-class participants to make the rowdiness of bachelor culture threatening to cultural elites; their financial and ideological promotion of rowdy masculine behavior openly challenged the genteel emphasis on self and social improvement. It was a two-way rebellion, with the latter group deliberately counterbalancing a celebration of male freedoms by reinforcing the need for behaviors suitable to the family parlor. Genteel Americans advocated clear parameters of social etiquette; they were the ones writing, selling, and buying the conduct guides and other social prescriptions. While the bachelors backed pugilists on the Bowery, the purchasing power of genteel Americans enabled them to attend performances at Wallack's Theatre, where the wealthy women wore diamonds in their hair and middle-class viewers sat in seats just like theirs.[49] Menken crossed these boundaries, suggesting that they could be crossed by her viewers as well.

Menken rose in the world of theater just as Americans were looking for relief from lives increasingly restricted by industrial jobs and the development of a class-based social etiquette. After the war the social hierarchy would become more rigid in response to the democratizing power of mass culture

[49] Edwin Burrows and Mike Wallace in *Gotham: A History of New York City* (New York: Oxford, 1999), dismiss the "genteel men who followed" pugilism in print, because pugilism played a more tangibly important role in working-class culture – that is, "it could be the ticket out of poverty into the middle-class realm" (756). I would argue that one does not necessarily reflect upon the other, and that a sport that received so much attention by middle-class men cannot be dismissed as limited to a working-class audience. Furthermore, in print pugilism was defined by the middle class.

unleashed by war, technology, and the media. Etiquette and social hierarchy would become more restricted because they were in truth breaking
down. The established middle class of the antebellum period was losing
its control over what constituted American culture not because it was losing social power, but because its composition was broadening. Menken's
self-constructions demonstrated the inherent weakness of a social structure
based on categories; she made it clear that no absolute boundaries between
categories existed.

Although some Americans still considered theater sinful and saw actresses
as prostitutes in another guise, such notions were radically changing. In 1860
a journalist noted that "a prominent New York manager" had said that "he
would not engage an actress in his company next season against whom there
existed a breath of suspicion." Although the journalist agreed that "it is a duty
managers owe the public not to engage in their companies women who are
notoriously unchaste," he also cautioned, "There is a wide margin, however,
between women who make of the stage only a stepping-stone on their road
to ill gotten finery and ill-gotten gains, and those against whom there may be
a 'breath of suspicion.'"[50] The reporter's attitude suggests that although the
respectability of many actresses should be questioned, their position as public
performers made them particularly vulnerable to gossip, and therefore paying
too much attention to 'a breath of suspicion' was both unrealistic and unfair.
Plays such as *The Drunkard*, produced by Barnum in 1844, and *Uncle Tom's
Cabin*, a decade later, had convinced many Americans that theater could
provide moral instruction. While ministers such as Henry Ward Beecher
continued to rail against theaters as a source of social corruption, by 1859
he and the rest of the American clergy were somewhat coopted by their
own need to capture an audience through performance, and Americans
seemed to form their own opinions.[51] Furthermore, several long-standing
theater families, such as the Kembles, Davenports, and Booths, had achieved
respectability by the 1850s. When Fanny Kemble, daughter of British actor
Charles Kemble, entered the profession in the 1830s, she profoundly elevated
the social position of other actresses and effected a lasting transformation of
public opinion.[52] The phenomenal popularity of female vocalists, such as
Jenny Lind and Adelina Patti, and the successes of theater owner/manager
Laura Keene, further contributed to public recognition that women could
succeed financially on stage without forfeiting virtue.[53]

---

[50] Clipping dated 1860, Actors' and Actresses,' Scrapbook Collection, HTC.

[51] Henry Ward Beecher, "Popular Amusements," in *Lectures to Young Men, on Various Important Subjects*
(Salem, Mass.: John P. Jewett, 1846), 236–237; Edward Magdol, *Owen Lovejoy: Abolitionists in Congress*
(New Brunswick: Rutgers University Press, 1967), 170; Claudia Johnson, *American Actress: Perspective
on the Nineteenth Century* (Chicago: Nelson Hall, 1984), 7–10.

[52] Johnson, *American Actress*, 9–12.

[53] Tracy Davis, *Actresses as Working Women: Their Social Identity in Victorian Culture* (London: Routledge,
1991), 76–77; Johnson, *American Actress*, 63–66.

Less-gifted actresses often tried to prove their virtue by sharing their private lives for public judgment – an approach that frequently backfired.[54] Menken used this tactic when she exposed her emotions through poetry and spoke directly to the public about her distress over the Heenan scandal. But although they played up their femininity, in truth the prevailing definitions of femininity, which were clearly rooted in domesticity, did not suit nineteenth-century female entertainers. Actresses earned wages from working on the public stage with men, and rarely for something more valuable than simple entertainment. It is significant that the antebellum ideology of redemptive womanhood, which advocated that women act in the public realm for the betterment of society, allowed actresses to use stage privileges to address social concerns – something that they increasingly did in the face of sectionalism and war.[55] In proclaiming a stake in social causes, they lay claim to middle-class status, but it was at best an act. American actresses played with the social roles assigned to women, but such roles fit poorly in a world where women and men worked together as equals on a daily basis. Thus actresses and female entertainers functioned as anomalies in American society. In many ways they lived like men, behaving autonomously and earning their own money, sometimes earning more than their husbands, and frequently more than their spectators. In these and other ways, actresses seemed similar to prostitutes, but acting did not carry the same degree of social stigma as prostitution. Because of an ongoing need to maintain certain levels of respectability, actresses did not live "openly" so much as perform private lives for public consumption.

Menken took more risks than most actresses. Of course, many of Menken's actions might be attributed to her personality; she had already demonstrated tremendous ambition and an unconventional understanding of marriage, to say the least. Of course it is possible that her initial handling of the bigamy scandal stemmed from her inexperience with the New York press. Before coming to the Empire City, she had largely benefited from the media exposure. But mass media had the power to both create and destroy. If newspapers could help her break into the New York entertainment world, they could also expose her past – at least as far back as the two previous years in Cincinnati – and potentially ruin her. Once Menken entered the national media, controlling her own image became an ongoing struggle.

Menken became a celebrity by connection but sustained the nation's attention through her own talents at self-promotion. She performed herself to be both respectable and scandalous. She entered the transcendent world constructed by the media, a fantasy realm that did not tangibly exist and yet was as real and familiar to readers as the world outside of newspapers. It was

---

[54] Davis, *Actresses as Working Women*, 69.

[55] Newspapers abound with stories of actors and actresses taking a public stance for or against the Confederacy. For a good example, see the New York *Sunday Mercury*, May 11, 1861, p. 1.

a place where all peoples could come together, and the class, gender, race, or ethnicity of the reader did not predetermine his or her relationship with the subject. It was also a world that existed separate and apart from geography and war, that could maintain a semblance of normalcy even as the real nation was falling apart. Menken became part of the fiction that the pleasures of life could continue despite the horror of war.

Yet to many New Yorkers, as well as Americans living outside the city, until her performance of *Mazeppa* in 1861, Menken was primarily a poet rather than an actress. Beginning in March 1860 she addressed readers almost weekly in the New York *Sunday Mercury*, a widely circulating paper filled with sentimental short stories, celebrity biographies, and editorial opinion.[56] Geared toward an educated but not intellectual audience, it was a paper meant to entertain rather than inform. Speaking through essays that adroitly conveyed her intelligence and poetry so personal that it seemed to expose her soul, Menken played with markers from several conflicting stereotypes. As the poet, she appeared most often as a sentimental narrator — tragic, sincere, and utterly feminine in her vulnerability. But her essays suggested a woman who thought as well as felt. Menken's printed persona as an educated and sensitive writer complicated the image of her as the pugilist's wife. As long as Menken appeared sincere and pathetic in print, she could push the parameters of respectability on stage. Gifted, vilified, and lonely, Menken went against the stereotype of the painted woman; at worst, she appeared to be the product of a neglected childhood, at best, a victim of heartless men and mercenary journalists. The events in Menken's most productive year as a writer, 1860, were shaped by the Heenan scandal, and her eruption of poetry would later form the basis of *Infelicia*, her posthumously published collection. Menken's written work resonates with the pain of a woman betrayed and embraces the elevation of women as mothers and moral arbiters. She frequently explores the divisions between reality and imagination, and suggests that public success hides private pain.

We have no record of how Menken regarded her own work, and stylistic categories such as "sentimental" are always questionable, since poets do not write to suit historians and literary scholars. Yet Menken's use of markers from popular writing clarifies the patterns easily recognized by midcentury. Menken capitalized on well-entrenched styles by incorporating particular symbols, diction, phrasing and meter into her poetry, and she compelled

---

[56] The *Sunday Mercury* described itself on Jan. 3, 1860, as "having the largest circulation of any Sunday Newspaper in America, without exception. . . ." It published three editions every weekend: The first one was mailed to the West and South, the second to the eastern and middle states, and the third was printed every hour on Sunday morning and sold on the streets of New York for four cents. It stated that "each edition contains the latest news up to the moment of going to press, thus affording to the public, in all parts of the Union, the latest and most reliable news, and the freshest miscellany and gossip, for the Sunday morning Breakfast table."

attention by mixing signifiers in provocative ways. Antebellum sentimental poetry most frequently portrayed images of death, sorrow, angels, nature, motherhood, and innocence. The sentimental poets strove to elicit the reader's sympathy, focusing on "the pleasure of despair."[57] In the United States, by the 1840s, the sentimental tradition had become identified with femininity and middle-class domesticity. The romantics, meanwhile, saw themselves in opposition to the moralizing and instructional intent of the sentimentalists. Like them, romantics emphasized the importance of feelings, but expressed emotions philosophically or in the domain of high culture.[58] Although some romantic publications proved lucrative, romantic poets did not write "popular poetry." And Romanticism, like sentimentalism, was gendered; the romantics were generally male and focused on individualism. Menken's use of sentimental symbols and language mixed with romantic themes and styles once again placed her between genders. In other words, Menken exhibited yet more contradiction through poetry.

Besides its ability to make her appear feminine, sentimentalism probably appealed to Menken because it was suitably melodramatic, and by the 1850s the best of the sentimental poets were cloaking socio-political questions in seemly innocuous verse. Sentimental poetry developed in nineteenth-century America as a means for women to "bare their hearts gracefully and without making an unseemly spectacle of themselves."[59] Although the designation first came into popular usage in the late eighteenth-century England as a term of approval for "the appeal to emotions, especially pity, as a means of moral distinction and moral persuasion," it developed as a genteel tradition in the United States in the 1830s and 1840s during the rise of industrialism and the separation of public and private lives.[60] The emergence of sentimental poetry coincided with the rise of women's magazines; from 1830 to 1860 sixty-four women's magazines entered the market, most of them profitably.[61] Most of the anthologized poets published their work in periodicals targeted at the aspiring middle class, such as *Godey's Ladies Book* or *Graham's*. Although sentimentality first developed as the favored style of writers portraying the "domestic sphere," the innocuous reputation of sentimental literature eventually rendered the style ideal for questioning and pushing social issues. By the 1850s several prominent sentimental poets, such as Maria Brooks, Elizabeth Oakes-Smith, and Lydia Sigourney, addressed

[57] Cheryl Walker, *The Nightingale's Burden: Women Poets and American Culture before 1900* (Bloomington: University of Indiana Press, 1982), 41.

[58] Suzanne Clark, *Sentimental Modernism: Women Writers and the Revolution of the Word* (Bloomington: University of Indiana Press, 1991), 28.

[59] Alicia Suskin Ostriker, *Stealing the Language: The Emergence of Women's Poetry in America* (Boston: Beacon Press, 1986), 31.

[60] Clark, *Sentimental Modernism*, 20–21.

[61] John Tebbel and Mary Ellen Zuckerman, *The Magazine in America: 1741–1990* (New York: Oxford University Press, 1991), 31.

and sought to rectify the deterioration of women's status that had resulted from middle-class women's isolation in the home.

Unlike the most celebrated sentimental poets, Menken never published her work in one of the women's magazines. Instead, she submitted poems to newspapers – the same forum that held her up to public scrutiny and advertised her theatrical performances. She was hardly alone: Both men and women published poetry in the papers, but publishing in newspapers meant speaking to a different audience than to the women reading *Godey's Ladies Book*. It meant placing poetry amid talk of politics and economics rather than surrounded by colored fashion plates and advice on health and decorum. The newspaper format allowed Menken to reach a larger, more heterogenous community than simply readers of women's magazines. Finally, publishing in newspapers gave her the advantage of having male as well as female readers; the readers most likely to see Menken perform on stage could imagine her internal complexities, as well as view her physical self.

While in New York, she began publishing her work in the *Sunday Mercury* with the most stereotypical of sentimental poems: a eulogy to orator Rufus Choate. By 1859 the *Mercury* was a well-established entertainment newspaper, although many genteel citizens objected to its inclusion of stories of lust and greed. Journalist Junius Henri Browne placed the *Mercury* in the same category as the *National Police Gazette*, saying "they reprint all the sensational facts and gossip they can find in the country press, or exhume from the licentious haunts of the City. They are widely read . . . [and] profitable. . . . The better class of the community do not read them, unless they happen to contain something extraordinary race [sic] and wanton, then curiosity overcomes the scruples of conscience and decorum."[62] Browne's "better class" must not have been very large, or they regularly overcame their scruples, because by 1860 the *Mercury* was one of the most popular and widely distributed papers in the country. Thousands of Americans depended on the *Mercury* for entertaining news and literature, as well as theater reviews and sports commentary.

Four overtly sentimental poems quickly followed her eulogy to Choate. "The Dark Hour," published March 25, 1860, exemplifies Menken's sentimental work in its language, but it also focuses on one of Menken's favorite subjects: visibility and obscurity. It begins with an emotionally charged description of dusk:

> Hast thou e'er marked, just when the day was closing,
> How all west-heaven seemed hung with vapors white;
> Red mingled hills, and yellow lakes reposing,
> A wreathy billow here, and there a light

---

[62] Browne, *Great Metropolis*, 314.

> Gleaming up, golden mountain clouds disclosing
>   Folded o'er with white wings of seraphs bright?
> Have ye ne'er watched them, too, minutely fade
> And all give place to black and sullen shade?

Such sensitivity to the vicissitudes of nature and her ability to see Christian symbolism in cloud formations marked Menken as a sentimentalist. The romantics saw Christianity in nature and called it sublime, but the sentimentalists portrayed a pastoral nature rimmed with pain and frequently populated by angels. Like most sentimental poems, "The Dark Hour" dwells more on despair than transcendent nature. Menken alluded to her own painful situation in the final four verses. Promises of joy tease and then flee her. "And Pleasure, if I seek her, seems to fly me/Or, caught, proves barren of her native grace;/Though if I spurn her, and to distance hie me,/A thousand joys pursue in elfin chase." She ends with tragic conviction: "Leave me! I'll battle on amid the crowd./Girded with patience, like an iron shroud."[63] She is a martyr of patience, although it is unclear if she is for Heenan or social absolution. Throughout "The Dark Hour," Menken employs sentimental imagery, plays up the stereotypical themes of secret sorrow and painful resignation, and uses fixed rhyme and meter. And, like most sentimental poetry, "The Dark Hour" appears to be autobiographical.

When Menken described herself in poetry she portrayed a beautiful woman with creamy white skin, golden hair and blue eyes rather than as her dark-eyed, dark-haired self. But lest the reader think she wrote as an alter-ego, she frequently alluded to events in her own life. At some level, she meant to convince her audience that she was the central character of such pathetic verses, the brave and vulnerable woman behind the public scandal. Again, Menken was performing – dancing the dance of the seven veils, allowing one to slip and reveal a shadow of herself behind yet another veil.

The haste of Menken's writing also allied her with the sentimentalists. Spontaneity supposedly made sentimental writing sincere; many saw the act of spouting lines without revision as suggestive of sincerity and sensitivity, while rewriting meant imposing reason. Menken wholeheartedly embraced this methodology, seldom revising her work to any significant extent. Her poems tend to begin with poignant lines that quickly muddle into messes of metaphor and allusion. Even when republished in *Infelicia*, her poems remained as one critic described her acting: "like the gold in quartz veins – all in the rough."[64] By antebellum standards, however, the lack of polish validated the emotions expressed.

---

[63] AIM, "The Dark Hour," *Sunday Mercury*, March 25, 1860, p. 1.

[64] *New York Tribune*, March 3, 1859, p. 7. Menken's poems as they appear in the newspapers and, later, *Infelicia* demonstrate that she revised her poems very little, with the exception of changing their titles.

Menken broke from the sentimental format in June 1860 when she published one of her most self-revealing poems, "My Heritage." She supposedly
wrote the poem in answer to an admirer who questioned her persistent sad-
ness, urging her to "Forget the world – laugh at poverty. Be glad and Happy
with your heritage of genius." Menken essentially snapped out a bitter response. In directly answering a letter written to her the narrator of this
poem is clearly meant to be Menken, not her blond alter ego. She is still
a victimized woman, but she comes across as furious rather than pathetic.
The first stanza reads like a howl of rage:

> "My heritage!" It is to live within
>   the marts of Pleasure and Gain, yet be
> No willing worshiper at either shrine;
> To think, and speak, and act, not for my pleasure,
> But others'. The veriest slave of time
> And circumstance. Fortune's toy!
> To hear of fraud, injustice, and oppression,
> And feel who is the unshielded victim.[65]

The free-verse structure and declamation of the poem is reminiscent of
Whitman, but unlike him, she dwells on personal pain, which was more
symptomatic of sentimental and romantic verse. Menken presents herself as
selfless and vulnerable to public desires: "To think, and speak, and act, not for
my pleasure,/But others'. . . ." The line suggests rage that she is somehow
trapped by the celebrity role that, in truth, she crafted and aggressively
pursued. "My Heritage" dwells on the narrator's sense of injustice, but
she never truly defines why this situation has become "her heritage" – an
unchosen reality that traps her. Was her "heritage" shaped by her gender
or a stigmatized minority identity? Was the impossibility of her situation
determined by her participation in a profession both celebrated and vilified?
Was it her awareness, her "genius," that made the hypocrisies of her life
particularly painful? "[M]arts of Pleasure and Gain" suggests a slave market
where human beings become commodities; a horrible place of exploitation
where the poet exists against her will. She can live in but not be of "marts
of Pleasure and Gain"; they are her means of livelihood but she remains
intellectually and emotionally repelled by the hypocrisy around her. Buffeted
by fame and circumstance, she is the victim of "cold friends" who hurt her
without reason, and her dangerous emotions erupt, "lava-like," destroying
her in the process. But her "high free spirit" does not break in the grasp of
poverty, whether emotional or financial. By the end, she makes it clear that
she will overcome poverty through force of will, and escape the influences
of greed and lust. It is the poem of a fighter, not a sweet, sentimental plea
for pity, but a demand for compassion. At the same time, it is also the song

---

[65] AIM Heenan, "My Heritage," *Sunday Mercury*, June 3, 1860.

of a martyr, one who transcends the situation by superficially capitulating, and leaving her body.

Although she signed her work as Menken, by the spring of 1860 she was billing herself as "Mrs. John Heenan." Economically, it was a brilliant move. By March, Heenan had become a national hero to whom the public clung, in large part because of national unrest. Sectional tensions motivated intense longings for national unity, and a dashing young athlete fighting for the first "world championship" title provided a welcome rallying point.[66] With both newspapers and the grapevine buzzing about the upcoming match, using Heenan's name guaranteed an increase in Menken's own market value.

As Mrs. John C. Heenan she filled the National Theatre in Boston for six nights in March 1860. Immediately afterward, she performed one night at the Old Bowery Theater with tremendous success. Her performance was not by "contract," but a one-night chance to prove herself worthy in the nation's entertainment capital. This performance marked the first time Menken obtained a booking in the city itself, and her star began to rise with positive reviews in several papers, including the *Clipper*, which heralded her as "one of the most beautiful women now upon the boards."[67] Even *Wilkes' Spirit* praised her stage ability. As Mrs. Heenan, Menken won consistent bookings in mid-sized theaters such as the National Theater in Boston and similar houses in Somerville, Baltimore, Providence, and Philadelphia. Cities of their size could not afford to support two theater districts, as in New York, so while theaters such as the Old Museum in Baltimore frequently featured spectacles, they also catered to middle-class families as well, unlike the Old Bowery. Clearly, theater managers understood that her appeal had less to do with her ability than her fame. To the delight of the Providence audience, Menken was willing to make fun of her situation if it meant revenue. In April she put on a farce, written by William English, called *Heenan Has Come!*[68]

Mrs. Heenan's fortune increased when descriptions of the fight filtered back from England in April 1860. The fight had an appropriately fantastic finish: Heenan and Tom Sayers fought forty-two grisly rounds, despite Heenan fracturing his right hand on a post in the sixth round. In the thirty-seventh round, Heenan attempted to strangle Sayers against the ropes, motivating an unknown person to cut the ropes. Still the fight continued, with fans pouring into the ring itself. Finally, the judges called a draw and both men were later presented with identical championship belts; they were joint champions, and became heroes in their respective countries.[69] Despite the fact that the sport would remain illegal, pugilism became a national

[66] Elliot J. Gorn, *The Manly Art: Bare-Knuckle Prize-Fighting in America* (Ithaca: Cornell University Press, 1986), 157. It was called a "world championship," but only the United States and England competed.

[67] New York *Clipper*, March 20, 1860.

[68] "Amusements," *Sunday Mercury*, April 15, 1860, p. 4. I could not find a description or review of this piece, and it appears to be no longer in existence.

[69] Gorn, *Manly Art*, 154–56.

obsession for the next few years. Newspapers elaborately described past fights and upcoming stars. During the initial months of Heenan's stardom, Menken hauled herself up on his pedestal and created her own fortune from his image – and became increasingly anxious about his return.[70]

Claiming marriage to the pugilist put Menken in the public eye, but it was a move that could have easily killed any chances she had to win a contract in a mainstream theater. Pugilism was the sport of the "bachelor culture," a fashionable social hybrid of young middle-class men and gritty working-class cultural forms.[71] The image of bachelor culture was based more on male fantasies of independence than on social reality, and despite its label, married as well as unmarried men participated. Bare-knuckles boxing became the sport of bachelor culture because it defied social control and celebrated machismo. Bachelor culture was antieffeminate rather than antifeminine, but from its supporters' emphasis on Jacksonian democracy to their contempt for middle-class forms of masculinity, pugilism also excluded women as cultural contributors. Menken's decision to publicize her marriage to Heenan had an element of danger.

Menken may have relied on the fact that by the 1850s many supporters of pugilism counted themselves among the middle class, and the middle class was broadening. The American middle class was, of course, the product of industrialism and shaped by its position between labor and elite, the two traditional classes. Because it was a relatively new social class, supposedly based on individual capability rather than on inherited position, and expanding by the day, those who considered themselves middle-class found themselves compelled to establish some form of definition. Inexpensive publishing provided the means; middle-class Americans controlled most publishing in the United States and throughout the nineteenth-century relied heavily on proscriptive literature to define their social norms against which all should be measured. Menken, like all participants in the entertainment world, was trying to determine how to win the attention of such a wide and contradictory audience. In hindsight, it is clear that the antebellum middle class defined itself most clearly through its fluidity and mobility. By the end of the antebellum period the most distinguishing characteristic of middle-class identity was its ability to move in and out of the classes above and below, crossing boundaries and flagging territories of behavior as its own.[72]

---

[70] E.g., see AIM to Mr. Robbins, Buffalo, Feb. 19, 1860, AIM ALS HTC.

[71] Timothy Gilfoyle talks about the roots of bachelor culture in *City of Eros: New York City, Prostitution, and the Commercialization of Sex, 1790–1920* (New York: W. W. Norton, 1992), 105–107, and the increasing celebration of it, 115–116.

[72] Gorn, *Manly Art*, 107. For interpretations of middle-class identity, I am indebted to Brian Roberts and Paul Erickson; see Brian Roberts, *American Alchemy: California Gold Rush and the Emergence of Middle-Class Culture* (Chapel Hill: University of North Carolina Press, 2000); see Paul Erickson, "Welcome to Sodom: The Cultural Work of the American City-Mysteries Novel, 1840–1860," Ph.D.

By the spring of 1860, Menken appeared to understand that the middle class had the ability to support less respectable forms of entertainment if repackaged properly. She learned a great lesson in the art of bringing low forms of entertainment into the mainstream. Pugilism provided a wonderful example. Pugilism may have begun as working-class, but the layout, price, and subject matter of sporting papers such as *Wilke's Spirit of the Times* suggest that many middle-class men were embracing it as a sort of rebellion against the increasing emphasis on feminine values in American culture. Couldn't Menken tap into the same cultural rebellion if she managed to convince middle-class theater owners that she would fill seats without risking reputations?

Summer put things on hold for a while. The heat forced most theaters to close from June through August, perhaps increasing the scarcity of Menken's bookings, but her lack of professional activity may also have had to do with the birth of her child. The *San Francisco Evening Bulletin* reported that her son was born on July 3, but there are no other reports or records indicating the child's birth date or sex.[73] Indeed, few comments indicate the child's existence at all. At the end of August, Menken wrote of the infant to Robert Newell, saying that Heenan's father "assists me by caring for his grandchild, my baby. He . . . regards it a privilege to do anything for his son's child. I might have a home in his house; but I could not live dependent on any human creature."[74] According to New York death records, the infant may have died shortly afterward from erysipelas, an illness caused by streptococcus in the bloodstream. If indeed it was Menken's baby, he was a boy named James – a name she commonly claimed for her father.[75] However, a letter from a reporter suggests that Menken and Heenan's child was still alive as late as October 20, 1860, describing the child as "a fine boy who is now three or four months old."[76] His observation suggests that Menken's son may not have died at all; she may have given him up or abandoned him in the next few months. No further mention was made of the child after that October. That fall Menken began including maudlin references to mothers and dead or dying children in her poetry, but she never discussed the baby directly. Even years later, when she wrote of Heenan reentering her life, she never mentioned having had his child.

dissertation, University of Texas at Austin, forthcoming. See also John Kasson, *Rudeness and Gentility: Manners in Nineteenth-Century Urban America* (New York: Hill & Wang, 1991), Anthony Giddons, *The Class Structure of Advanced Societies* (New York: Harper & Row, 1973), and Richard Butsch, *The Making of American Audiences, from Stage to Television, 1750–1990* (New York: Cambridge University Press, 2000).

73 "Letter from New York Dated October 20: The Benicia Boy and Adah Isaacs Menken," *San Francisco Evening Bulletin*, Nov. 7, 1860, Kovach.

74 Newell, "Adah Isaacs Menken."

75 New York Board of Deaths, Aug. 15, 1860, ALC; City of New York Board of Health, Bureau of Records, letter to Nicholas Kovach dated May 20, 1938, Kovach.

76 "The Benicia Boy and Adah Isaacs Menken," *San Francisco Evening Bulletin*, Nov. 7, 1860.

Such silences become a pattern apparent throughout the rest of her life. As a celebrity Menken had created a private life for public consumption, but there were a few instances when she did not make personal information available. Perhaps to maintain control over genuinely personal information, she gave the public no information on her child's existence or fate. Other than her note to Mr. Robbins we have no evidence of Menken mentioning her child, suggesting that if she did write about him, she did so infrequently and not for public consumption. Whoever Menken was as a mother, or before she became a celebrity, was simply not part of the image she sold.

When John Heenan returned to the United States in August he did not acknowledge Menken, and when she showed up at his welcoming reception he pointedly ignored her. Spying Menken, a reporter from the *Illustrated News* nastily remarked that Menken would "doubtless write another chapter in the scriptural style on this grand apotheosis to individual daring and endurance."[77] Nor did Heenan approach her in the weeks following the reception. The *Charleston Mercury* noted, "We will now test the truth of the gossip respecting the marriage of the Benicia Boy. Thus far he has held back and sought no interview with his Adah. . . . Heenan takes the matter as a good joke on a bad subject."[78] If indeed married to Menken, perhaps Heenan justified his treatment of her because he faced significant pressure to control his public image. Menken had used their relationship for self-promotion, and some of his advisers scorned her as a woman who had sold her reputation to fill theater seats. They may also have convinced Heenan that part of his appeal lay in his identity as a handsome, young bachelor. His single status suggested that he was not domesticated; regardless of their own personal situations, male spectators could identify with Heenan as hypermasculine, evading the wiles of women yet attracting them like flies. And finally, there was money at stake. Heenan's earnings for the Sayer's fight and resulting tours came to roughly $25,000, according to newspapers at the time.[79]

Menken publicly ignored the journalistic barbs until she found herself charged for lodgings at Westchester House, the family-oriented hotel near the Bowery where she had lived with Heenan and afterward until giving birth to their child and moving to a Broome Street boarding-house on July 3.[80] According to the press report, she had been unable to pay her rent for the months she had been ill (pregnant). Menken responded by renting a local auditorium called Hope Chapel, and placed an ads in several New York papers stating that she would be giving readings in poetry and Shakespeare on August 20.[81]

[77] *Illustrated News*, Aug. 25, 1860, 216.

[78] *Charleston Mercury* quoted in *New York Illustrated News*, Aug. 25, 1860, p. 243.

[79] Allen Lesser quotes a New York newspaper dated Sept. 2, 1860, ALC.

[80] "Letter from New York Dated October 20," *San Francisco Evening Bulletin*, Nov. 7, 1860, Kovach.

[81] *Sunday Mercury*, Aug. 19, 1860; *New York Tribune*, Aug. 19, 1860.

The public address that Menken called her "self-defense" makes it clear that Menken's greatest role and greatest invention was already Menken herself. The *Clipper* reviewed only her readings, stating "she has genius," but the *Tribune* presented an altogether different image of the evening.[82] On August 21, the latter published a lengthy critique of Menken's opening remarks, asserting that the readings were merely a ruse for presenting her grievances: "few suspected that under the pleasant guise of an 'Evening with Poets,' Miss Adah Isaacs Menken proposed martyrdom, seasoned, albeit, with magnanimity." According to the journalist, Menken asserted "that woman is an immemorial martyr to the base passions of man; that at all periods she has been wantonly deprived of every right bestowed upon her by impartial Heaven – even the right of speech; that society has set a face of stone against her, and that she has universally been left out in the cold." She introduced her subject: "I read and write for those men and women who do not reject religion – that sole sanctifier of man – and who do not turn away from the light of goodness wherever it may be found, and for those who honor a woman for her purity of motives, her aspirations, and her sufferings, wherever she may be found." Menken's audience applauded every utterance, "as some dreadful beasts are said to salivate and soften their prey before tearing to pieces and devouring it." With a brilliant display of male chauvinism, the reporter wished that she had kept her dark comments to herself and stuck to entertaining: "For Miss Menken has clever and entertaining qualities. Her person, when arrayed in simple and girlish white, is an agreeable object of contemplation." The irony here, of course, is that Menken *was* entertaining. The writer suggests that she might earn the respect she desired by abandoning "the rude habit acquired in the Bowery" and taking on the "graceful unconsciousness of the drawing room lady," but his insulting tone makes such a change sound impossible. The reporter addressed Menken and "other female apologists" when he stated that she could not demand respect she had not earned.[83]

The *Tribune* article, although insulting, implies that the moral constraints may have been loosening before the Civil War rather than tightening, despite the concurrent proliferation of conduct guides and advice on social etiquette. Menken's boldness in renting a public space and discussing her private life made a mockery of the notion of an impenetrable veil of domesticity. When the reporter called Menken yet "another female apologist," he confirmed that there were quite a few women challenging the double standards that penalized women for freedoms enjoyed by men. Menken's behavior, while neither common nor acceptable in her time, was also not anachronistic. Of

---

[82] *Clipper*, Sept. 1, 1860. The *Clipper* was a weekly, so its review appeared later than the one in the *Tribune*, and was probably written in response to the *Tribune* review.

[83] "An Evening with the Poets: the Position of Miss Adah Isaacs Menken," *New York Daily Tribune*, Aug. 21, 1860, p. 8.

course, Menken was hardly naive; she actively manipulated gender norms when she wore a costume of "girlish white" to delineate her innocence and suggest herself as a victim.[84]

Menken read the review of her performance at Hope Chapel, as she read all reviews of her work, and protested the authority of the press in representing her. She asked Newell, "Is it all true? Is that, indeed, my 'position'?... Can I never be anything more than what the Tribune represents?" Menken bemoaned her naivete – or gave a performance of naiveté – saying: "I am so sorry that I appeared at Hope Chapel, and presumed to be anything more than the vampires of the press would have me – a miserable outcast.... Where shall I bury my soul? Where shall I hide my impugned sensibility, pride, womanhood?... How can I try anything again?"[85]

In early September 1860, Menken published her most critically acclaimed poem, "The End," later renamed "Judith," alluding to the heroine of the apocryphal *Book of Judith*, and suggesting similarities to her own situation. Most Americans were familiar with Judith through popular engravings of her standing tall, with a long, stained sword in one raised hand and the other gripping the hair of an open-mouthed, decapitated head, flourishing the ghastly object with triumphant pride that suggested unity with her spectators. It was an unforgettable and complex image: the beautiful woman reveling in her own savage act, holding a head with such a monstrous expression that it seems to justify her brutality. The juxtaposition of beautiful, scantily dressed Judith and horrific, beheaded Holofernes also served as a frightening confirmation of the power of female sexuality. Lithographs of the image turn up in a variety of nineteenth-century texts, such as the *Boudoir Annual* of 1846, where it appeared between a short story and song.[86]

Who knows whether Menken's audience first thought of the famous image or the actual *Book of Judith* when they read her poem? Neither Jewish scholars nor Protestant churches accepted the *Book of Judith* as biblical, but the story has remained popular as an apocryphal tale of one woman's valor and cunning.[87] It confirms what many already believe, that sexuality is a means of attaining power – a concept that both attracts and frightens onlookers.

The *Book of Judith* begins with King Nebuchadnezzar deciding to punish his vassal states that refused to supply troops for war. Military chief Holofernes encounters no difficulty in destroying villages until he reaches the small town of Bethulia, inhabited by Jews, a devout people of whom he's never heard. Heeding the warning that any overt attack on such sinless

[84] Ibid. [85] Newell, "Adah Isaacs Menken."

[86] E. Bruce Kirkham and John W. Fink, comp., *Indices to American Literary Annuals and Gift Books, 1825–1865* (New Haven: Research Publications, 1975), 48.

[87] George Arthur Buttrick, ed., *The Interpreter's Dictionary of the Bible*, vol. II (New York: Abingdon Press, 1962), 1023–1026.

people will bring down the wrath of God, Holofernes instead cuts off their water and supplies, thinking that starvation will cause a moral collapse. After a month of deprivation, Judith, a beautiful, pious widow, realizes that her people are indeed weakening in their despair, and may soon compromise their religious devotion. She dresses in festival garments "in order to entice any man she might meet" and goes with her maid to the army camp, carrying a cloth bag of food. Overcome with her beauty, guards bring her to their leader's tent, where, similarly impressed, Holofernes invites her to remain as his guest. She stays for three days, being careful to make a show of her piety: saying her prayers, eating only of her own food, and taking customary ritualistic baths. On the fourth day, Holofernes invites her to a banquet in his tent, and her beauty, wit, and finery soon make her the center of attention. When the others finally leave, Holofernes falls into an alcohol-induced slumber, and Judith, seeing her chance, seizes his sword and cuts off his head. The maid carries the head in the food bag, and the two women exit the camp without attracting notice. Once in Bethulia, she displays her gruesome trophy, inspiring her townsmen to find the courage to launch an offensive. The significantly larger but leaderless army flees from their attack, and when the Jews return to Bethulia, Judith sings a song of praise to the Lord.[88]

With the poem "Judith" Menken moved from her earlier emulation of the warrior Deborah to the more cunning and independent figure of Judith. In many ways the story of Judith reads like a conflation of Deborah and Jael, of the *Book of Judges*. Judith is like Deborah in that she inspires her people to battle and sings the victory song, but she also performs Jael's role of soothing the enemy into a state of false security and then murdering him while he sleeps. Judith differs significantly in that she is a widow, and therefore not chaste, and she acts on her own counsel. Judith essentially prostituted herself to save her people. Despite the implicit generosity of such an act, it also renders her threatening; she has a beauty that disarms even the most powerful men. To a mid-nineteenth-century reader, Judith was clearly more dangerous than Deborah because she appeared so deceptively vulnerable. She was a pious woman with an impeccable reputation: beautiful, widowed, and gracious. But Judith demonstrates that her soothing exterior hides an incredible power that only she controls. If men dominate her, it is only through her own compliance. She uses her sex and beauty to achieve what male armies had failed, and in the context of the war, she is an alarming character *because* she is so pious and feminine.

On September 2, 1860, Menken voiced her rage through the figure of Judith. Considered her greatest work, "Judith" clarifies why readers could not easily dismiss Menken as simply an adventuress with a good figure and

---

[88] Ibid., 1023–24.

the audacity to show it.[89] The first stanza gives an air of romantic authenticity to the poem, as Menken grounds the story in the geography of ancient lands with exotic names.[90] In the apocryphal tale, Judith was not a prophet, but Menken makes her one by focusing on the power soon to be unleashed by Judith's sword:

> I have slept in the darkness –
> But the seventh angel woke me, and giving me a sword
> of flame, points to the blood-ribbed cloud, that lifts his
> reeking head above the mountain.
> Thus am I the prophet.
> I see the dawn that heralds to my waiting soul the advent of
> power.

In the second stanza, Menken creates herself as a parallel to Judith by addressing the public which has so criticized and vilified her, crying:

> Stand back, ye Philistines!
> Practice what ye preach to me;
> I heed ye not, for I know ye all.
> Ye are living burning lies, and profanation to the
> garments which with stately steps ye sweep your marble
> palaces.

She alludes to the hypocrisy of the press and public complicit in her debasement: "Your palaces of Sin, around which the damning/evidence of guilt hangs like a reeking vapor." By proclaiming their guilt Menken points out the profit and pleasure they had gained from Menken's trials. Interpreted more broadly, she makes it clear that those with money promoted the existence of actresses, prize fighters, prostitutes, and others who provided service to those who often vilified them. But Menken suggests she will be powerful in her own right, and those who scorn her now will fear her:

> A place in the ranks awaits me.
> I know that ye are hedged on the borders of my path.
> Lie and tremble, for ye well know that I hold with iron
> grasp the battle axe.
> Creep back to your dark tents in the valley.
> Slouch back to your haunts of crime.

[89] "Judith" was published as "The End" in the *Sunday Mercury*, Sept. 2, 1860. Menken renamed the poem "Judith" for inclusion in *Infelicia*, but changed only one word of the original text: "a" to "your" in the second line of the third stanza. Any other changes appear to have been geographical names misspelled in the original (e.g., "Gaza" was "Laza"). I have used the version from *Infelicia*, as it has the fewest such errors. No one has yet found evidence that this poem was plagiarized or reworked from another poet.

[90] Biblical scholars have been unable to locate the setting of the story; Menken made up the details. Buttrick, *Interpreter's Dictionary*, 1023–1026.

The end of the second stanza hints at the violence of the third, when she warns that her attackers have gone too far. Again portraying herself as having a personal self unknown to an unjust world, she states that she will wreak vengeance on those who have harmed her. She likens them to serpents, the biblical embodiment of evil:

> Ye do not know me, neither do ye see me.
> But the sword of the mouth is unsealed, and ye coil
> yourselves in slime and bitterness at my feet.
> I mix your jeweled heads, and your gleaming eyes, and
> your hissing tongues with the dust.
> My garments shall bear no mark of ye.
> When I shall return this sword to the angel, your foul
> blood will not stain its edge.
> It will glimmer with the light of truth, and the strong
> arm shall rest.

The final stanza flows with passionate outrage. It is too late for their pity and pathetic attempts at apology. "I am no Magdelene waiting to kiss the hem of your garment," she scoffs, mocking others' attempts to elevate themselves into Christ-like figures and force her into a false position as a guilt-stricken prostitute. The poem becomes graphically violent as it turns to the image of Judith holding the head of Holofernes. Lines resonate with sado-masochistic joy:

> Ere the last tremble of the conscious death-agony shall
> have shuddered, I will show it to ye with the long black
> hair clinging to the glazed eyes, and the great mouth
> opened in search of voice, and the strong throat all hot
> and reeking with blood, that will thrill me with wild un-
> speakable joy as it courses down my bare body and dab-
> bles my cold feet!
> My sensuous soul will quake with the burden of so
> much bliss.

Her poetic cunning comes through when she weaves together the biblical images and creates a scene of seductive and terrifying anger: "Oh, what wild passionate kisses will I draw up from that bleeding mouth!/I will strangle this pallid throat of mine on the sweet blood!/I will revel in my passion." The need, like the pious Judith, to become a killer in order to save herself turns the poet into a beast, consuming the flesh of her enemies in bitter isolation: "At midnight I will feast on it in the darkness." Lest the reader be repulsed by her violence, she makes it clear that she was brought to this act out of self-preservation: "For it was that which thrilled its crimson tides of reck-/less passion through the blue veins of my life, and made/them leap up in the wild sweetness of Love and agony of/Revenge!"

She is hungry for vengeance: "I am starving for this feast." And the final two lines are a clear warning to her enemies: "Oh forget not that I am Judith!/And I know where sleeps Holofernes." The symbolism of Judith suited Menken perfectly, as Judith, for all her independence and brutality, retained an outer image of beauty and wisdom. She fought for a righteous cause.

"The End" undoubtedly shocked and impressed readers with its force and violent imagery. Menken could not simply be dismissed as a shallow gold-digger. She expressed too much sensitivity, intelligence, and education to be seen as merely an actress, in fact. Many of the papers reviewing her stage performances began commenting on the shame of such a brilliant woman wasting her intellectual talent in pursuit of fame. No one gave recognition to the fact that acting, not poetry, gave Menken the money to live autonomously.

Menken's decision to confront public prejudice is particularly startling if indeed her mother died about this time, as Menken claimed. Menken and "sister" Annie Campbell Josephs traded poetry on the subject of their mother's death back and forth in the pages of the New York *Sunday Mercury* at the end of September 1860. Was this merely a ruse to gain more public sympathy? Since Menken left no concrete information about her mother, it is impossible to confirm whether she died that summer. In fact, it is impossible to prove that Annie Josephs was Menken's sister, since no records of her exist in New Orleans or any other possible childhood home. Whether Menken's mother actually died or not, Menken exhibited distress in her letters to Newell, writing, "[Y]ou do not know how black and cold this world has been to me; there is so little light left to me. The death of my dear mother seemed to shatter the last link to life. With her went out hope, ambition, goodness, and everything that makes the world beautiful and pure."[91] Unlike the death of her child, Menken packaged her mother's death for public consumption, expressing her loss in a sentimental poem entitled "Our Mother," printed on September 23, 1860.

But just as Menken began to succeed in arousing public sympathy, the scandal crashed down on her again in October, when she could not pay the bill for her lodgings from the previous winter. The boarding-house sued Heenan for her unpaid balance, saying that they had registered as a married couple. The New York *Herald* gave a detailed account of the proceedings, noting that Heenan did not attend the trial, and thus "the fair Adah, his wife, became the center of attraction." A journalist transcribed the case verbatim, stating the charge that Heenan owed the money to Westchester House for "board and lodging furnished to Mrs. Ada I. M. Heenan, as the wife of the defendant, at his and her instance [sic] and request, between

---

[91] Newell, "Adah Isaacs Menken."

the months of December 1859, and July 1860." The defense's tactic was to destroy Menken's character and prove that she had no legal claim on Heenan's money. The defense counsel's words appeared for the nation to read:

> I will prove that other men, with this same lady, entered her own name at this same house (Westchester) as John Doe and Lady, and that they occupied a room; probably the same as Mr. Heenan is alleged to have occupied. I will prove the character of this frail, fair woman, and that she had her name entered upon the books of this and other houses as the lady of John Doe or Richard Roe, or any who might have money enough to pay for that particular purpose. . . .

It was a damning and vicious defense. Heenan's attorney publicly accused Menken not only of prostitution but of turning tricks in the room she had formerly occupied with Heenan, whom many still considered her husband. The judge declared the attorney's insinuations irrelevant to the case, but the damage was done. Soon afterward the attorneys settled the dispute out of court, robbing Menken of the opportunity to defend herself.[92] A year later Menken was able to prove the marriage in order to obtain a legal divorce, but by then the Menken – Heenan scandal had already shaped her image.[93]

Menken's position became truly desperate after the trial as theater managers refused to book her in fear of a public boycott, but she still managed to garner a measure of public support from those who saw Heenan's lawyers as having transgressed acceptable boundaries of behavior. On October 27, 1860, the *Illustrated News* unequivocally criticized Heenan's actions, particularly citing his abandonment of mother and child. The paper accused Heenan of living up to the "charge fixed on his profession – total indifference to the finest ties which bind society and crush scandal."[94] The paper raised the question of who exactly was at fault when a man fathered a child and deserted the mother; did the legality of their marriage really make a moral difference?

But the damage done to Menken's reputation at first seemed unendurable and irreparable. Menken wrote to fellow entertainer Stephen Massett, with whom she briefly shared a romance: "Since Heenan declares me to be the most dangerous woman in the world, whenever a woman's husband neglects her she fancies that I have charmed him, body and soul." She described how two "frantic deserted wives came to demand the return of their lords, one early in the morning just as I was going to write you, the other as late as twelve. I had them locked up."[95] Menken clearly scorned the idea that

---

[92] *New York Herald*, Oct. 17 and 20, 1860, p. 5; "Self Defense," *New York Times*, Sept. 6, 1868, p. 3; "Letter from New York, November 6, 1860," *San Francisco Evening Bulletin*, Nov. 27, 1860, Kovach.
[93] Petition for divorce, *New York Herald*, Oct. 31, 1861.　　[94] *Illustrated News*, Oct. 27, 1860.
[95] AIM to Steve Masset, n.d., ALC.

she posed such a danger, yet her wording – "frantic deserted wives" –
indicates that she understood (even if she did not sympathize with) their
desperation. She was also boasting and promoting the image of Menken the
siren.

It would not be the last attack by an angry wife. From October 20
to November 10, Americans across the country were treated to news of
yet another Menken escapade when a reporter's jealous wife walked into
Menken's boarding house and attacked her. According to the *San Francisco
Evening Bulletin*, the *Herald* reporter had gone to Menken's room to conduct
an interview when his wife suddenly burst in upon them. When the reporter
denied knowing his wife, Menken ordered her out and moved as if to strike.
Enraged, the wife jumped on Menken and held her down by the hair until
Menken's cries roused the street police, as well as a crowd of onlookers. In
the end, Menken dropped all charges against the reporter and his wife, but
the incident further tarnished her image.[96] Several reporters glorified the
wife in question, making her sound like a hero fighting off the advances of a
dangerous woman on her "truent" husband.[97] Menken was clearly perceived
as a threat to marriage and married women despite her outspoken sympathy
for working women and the downtrodden.

While Menken continued to publish overtly sentimental pieces such as
the essay "The Affinity of Poetry and Religion" (October 1860) and poems
such as "Conscience" and "Lost Love" (November 1860), she also began
submitting more daring work more often. In November 1860, about the
time she wrote to Masset about her desperate situation, she also published
"Passion." It was a frank poem designed to tantalize an audience whom she
presumed wanted to hear more about her relationship with Heenan. Within
the poem, she constructs herself as initially innocent and romantic:

> When I believed thee true, my love
>   Was pure as virtue could impart –
> Pure as the feeling parents prove
>   For the dear nurslings of their heart

Now that Heenan has proven himself to be unworthy, her love is dissolving
to mere lust; once love is gone, the heart is debased, because she still cannot
bring herself to hate him.

> But, though, since all thy ways I know,
>   Thy heart is worthless in my eyes;
> Yet warmer still my passions glow,
>   I love thee more than I despise.

[96] "Letter from New York, October 22, 1860," *San Francisco Evening Bulletin*, Nov. 10, 1860,
Kovach.
[97] "Letter from St. Louis, dated October 26, 1860," *San Francisco Bulletin*, Nov. 3, 1860, Kovach.

Shockingly, Menken lays claim to her continued attraction to Heenan, stating that now that love was destroyed, she could no longer control her urges:

> But now that all respect is dead,
> I bid my pulse unbridled beat;
> From me, the soul of love has fled,
> And passion triumphs in its seat.[98]

A subtitle suggested that she found her inspiration in the work of Catullus, the lyric poet of ancient Rome. She (probably knowingly) picked at a scab; many middle-class Americans were not quite sure what to make of Catallus. After all, scholars considered his work central to the classical education, and since the Revolution, educators had stressed classical learning as essential to sustaining a truly democratic republic. Thus, Catullus's work remained a part of the literary canon studied by middle-class children, even though many nineteenth-century Americans considered his work distasteful because of its emphasis on physical passion.[99] Catullus was most famous for a body of poems written about a woman he called "Lesbia," referring to the island of Lesbos, which began passionately with love and evolved into disillusionment, lust, and anger. Catullus was also responsible for translating the work of Sappho into Latin, making her poetry accessible to later scholars.[100] Menken's mention of Catullus was crucial to the presentation of the poem; it suggested that classical poetry inspired her daring verse. She could write about such a dangerous topic because she found her muse in a widely celebrated (yet suspicious) source. If someone scorned the licentious tone of the verse, a prudent observer would be bound to point out that the inspiration came from having a good education, and not necessarily Menken's own life experiences.

It may seem surprising that such a frank admission of lust would be published in a nineteenth-century Sunday newspaper, but in fact Menken's work was well situated in an evolving literary style. Indeed, by the 1850s, many sentimental female poets addressed the topic of female desire, often through veiled references.[101] In that sense, Menken remained within the sentimental tradition with this poem, even if her veiling was transparent. In "Passion," she suggests that her lover's betrayal, not merely seduction, made her give in to baser instincts. However, she remains in control, saying, "I bid my pulse unbridled beat," not giving him responsibility for choices she has

---

[98] AIM, "Passion," *Sunday Mercury*, Nov. 18, 1860.

[99] The 1853 Encyclopedia Americana states, "A weighty objection, however, as to most of his writings, is their licentiousness and indelicacy." "Agius Valerius Catallus," *Encyclopedia Americana. A Popular Dictionary of Arts, Sciences, Literature, history, Politics and Biography* (Boston: B. B. Mussey, 1853), 8. Catullus writes about various expressions of sexuality.

[100] "Catullus, Agius Valerius," *Encyclopedia Britannica*, 11th ed.(1911),541–545.

[101] Paula Bernat Bennett, *Nineteenth-Century American* Women Poets: An Anthology (Malden, Mass.: Blackwell, 1998).

made. Did she mean to suggest to readers that she was the corrupt harlot depicted in the press? If so, then she was also a victim. Respect and love had maintained her virtuous resolution, until his betrayal destroyed them, allowing passion to triumph "in its seat."[102]

Clearly, the Menken who spoke nearly every week through the *Mercury* was very different from the bigamist chronicled in the 1860 scandal. Even in her most radical poetry and essays, Menken often relied on the images and devices found in sentimental literature, a style most frequently used by women. The propriety of most of her poetry was at odds with her image as a celebrity actress, and may explain why Menken was able to get away with as much as she did. She maintained a semblance of propriety, giving a nod toward etiquette. She constantly overstepped the boundaries of what the middle-class deemed appropriate, but she did so while using acceptable language and familiar scripts. She played off major signifiers of gentility and rowdiness, somehow managing to avoid definitive labeling.

Still, the charge of Heenan's lawyers that Menken had engaged in prostitution made Menken unfit for legitimate theater for several months. Queen used his contacts to secure her an engagement at the Stadt Theater, a large Bowery playhouse catering to German immigrants.[103] But Menken sounded utterly depressed, and loath to perform onstage, writing to Masset on November 11,

> I am almost despairing today. I have been out trying to get music, etc. . . . for my dances tomorrow night and have failed in everything. I am very sorry that I undertook the engagement at all, for I am sure that I will not be able to go on with it. I have no wardrobe – nothing to make an appearance in. What is the use of trying to do anything? I am more unhappy than ever.[104]

Oddly, she neglected the adopted spelling of her name, signing the note "Ada." A conscious ploy or not, using her real name suggested that she was letting down her guard with Masset, making her appear vulnerable and in need of his protection.

At this point, her depression became palpable in her writing, and it only grew worse when her three-week engagement at the Stadt Theatre ended and she accepted an engagement at a concert hall. A friend at the *Sunday Mercury* (probably Newell) did his best to make the Canterbury Concert Hall sound reputable. He remarked, "Knowing as we do, that a majority of concerns known as 'Concert Saloons,' etc, are nothing more than vestibules of gambling hells and worse places, we have frequently warned the unwary to

---

[102] AIM, "Passion," *Sunday Mercury*, Nov. 18, 1860.

[103] Edwin Burrows and Mike Wallace, *Gotham: A History of New York City* (New York: Oxford University Press, 1999), 757.

[104] AIM to Steve Masset, Nov. 11, 1860, ALC. A letter from AIM to Masset dated June 18, 1860, makes it clear that Menken and Masset had something more than a platonic relationship; see ALC. A romantic relationship is also suggested in the *Illustrated News*, Sept. 8, 1860.

beware of them." The Canterbury proved the exception, however: "Ladies form an important feature of its audience (a plain proof of its respectability) and notwithstanding the insignificant price of admission, the entertainments offered are first class in particular."[105] Unfortunately for Menken, the Canterbury itself advertised as one of its chief attractions "pretty waiter girls," a euphemism for full or part-time prostitutes. The wife of comedian Sam Cowells, who performed there at the same time as Menken, described as the Hall as "gaudily ornamented and . . . very dirty." Savvy New Yorkers knew that smaller theaters such as the Canterbury made little attempt to keep prostitutes out of the mingling crowd.[106] In effect, by performing at the Canterbury, Menken publicly crossed the very line she had been accused of crossing before.

The *Mercury*, still under the aegis of Newell, felt it necessary to clarify the situation, lest anyone misunderstand: "she only accepted the engagement at the suggestion of her friends, the theaters having made all their engagements for the year, and her own good sense teaching her that employment, even at a partial sacrifice of her *amour propre*, was more honorable than idleness."[107] But other players at the Canterbury saw her as beneath their company. Mrs. Cowell felt justified in confiding to her diary that Menken "is hissed, nightly. I was foolish enough to be a little afraid of her fascination over Sam *before he saw her*, but – though she declares that "the gentleman shines through him" and is generally gushing . . . Sam's heart has proven impregnable."[108] The audience may have hissed at Menken because of her notoriety, but they may also have been motivated by Menken's lackluster performance. Letters suggest that she was deeply depressed.[109]

Menken cut short her engagement at the Canterbury, and on December 29 she took the Cortlandt Ferry to Jersey City where she sat up in her hotel room, composing a letter "to the Public." In her customary large, slanting script she began: "I feel called upon to make an explanation of the rash step I have taken in defiance of all law, human or divine, because I know that many things will be said of me, some good and very bad, and perhaps blame attached to those who are innocent." She was contemplating the news in the next mornings' papers that she had died by suicide. While there is no evidence that she went so far as to injure herself (or was even truly suicidal), it is telling that the letter survived the hectic years of her life to eventually find safekeeping in the

[105] *Sunday Mercury*, Dec. 16, 1860, p. 3.

[106] Burrows and Wallace have an informative section on concert halls, *Gotham*, 805; Emilie Marguerite Cowells, *The Cowells in America: Being the Diary of Mrs. Sam Cowell During Her Husband's Concert Tour in the Years 1860–61*, Willson Disher, ed. (London: Oxford University Press, 1934), 237; Timothy Gilfoyle, *City of Eros: New York City, Prostitution, and the Commercialization of Sex, 1790–1920* (New York: W. W. Norton, 1992), 112.

[107] "Amusements," *Sunday Mercury*, Jan. 6, 1861, p. 4.   [108] Cowells, *Cowells in America*, 225.

[109] E.g., see Menken to Steve Massett, Nov. 19, 1860, AIM ALS HTC.

Harvard Theatre Collection. Did she carry the letter with her during her travels, or leave it with a friend? Menken traveled so frequently during those last few years of her life that she did not even own copies of most of her poems. In fact, when she decided to compile her poetry for publication in 1865, she had to rely on a friend to locate back issues of newspapers.[110]

The letter held significance for Menken because, although she did not take her life that December night, she apparently decided to kill off one of her personae. Years later, when she succumbed to illness in Paris, and her book of poetry found its way into the hands of genteel readers, they would mourn the loss of that Menken as well. They would bemoan not the passing of a popular actress, but rather of the poet who wrote "To the Public" with sentimental melodrama:

> *God* forgive those who *hate* me, and bless all who have one kind thought left for a poor reckless *loving* woman who cast her soul out upon the broad ocean of human love, where it was the sport of the happy waves for a few short hours, and then was left to drift helpless against the cold rocks, until she learned to love *death* better than *life*.
>
> Because I am homeless, poor and friendless, and so *unloved*, I leave this world.
>
> Because I have forgotten to look up to the *God* of my childhood prayers, and ceased to remember the counsel of my dear old mother – and because one of *God's* grandest handiworks – one of His glorious creatures lifted up my poor weary soul to see the light of his love, and the greatness of his brave heart, until his sweet words of truth and promise, drank out *all* my life – absorbed all of good and beauty, and left me alone, desolate to die. I am not afraid to die. I have suffered so much, that there can not be any more for me.
>
> I go prayerless, therefore *pity* and not condemn me.
>
> My worthless life has long since left me and gone to dwell in the breast of the man, who by foul suspicion of my love and truth for him, has thus ushered me up to the bar of the Almighty, where I shall pray his forgiveness for the cruel and wrong he has done the weak and defenseless being whose sin is her love for him, as my death proves. *God bless him*, and pity me.[111]

The Menken in the suicide letter matches the poignant figure of loss many Americans had met in her poetry since 1859. The poet Menken, unlike Menken the actress, was not a siren but rather a woman betrayed by love. She resembled the tragic heroines of sentimental fiction who suffered a similar fate, paying with their lives for follies of the heart while unjust society allows their corrupters go free. Someone did die that night in the Jersey City hotel room: the feminine victim that Menken had created through

[110] AIM letters to Ed James, 1865–67, AIM ALS HTC.
[111] AIM to "The Public," Dec. 29, 1860, AIM ALS HTC.

Menken fully dressed as Mazeppa, the Tartar Prince. Photograph by Sarony, 1866. By this point her Mazeppa was looking remarkably feminine and his costume had become quite ornate. (Harvard Theatre Collection)

poetry. From that point onward, Menken made few attempts to capitalize on the power of powerlessness found in her earlier work. She wrote less poetry, but what she did publish tended to focus on the slippage between reality and imagination.

By the end of 1860, Menken was most famous simply for being famous. Her poetry and stage performances effected the outlines of her identity, but most Americans still principally knew Menken as the possible wife of John C. Heenan. For several months, it looked as if Menken would go down as simply another player in yet another scandal that briefly lit up popular culture. The trick was to turn that residual fame into something more lasting, and for a time it seemed that notoriety would make that impossible. And then she found *Mazeppa*, a role even more scandalous than her past.

Chapter 3

Performing Mazeppa

On June 6, 1861, spectators filled Albany's Green Street Theatre to capacity. Flickering gaslights cast a golden glow throughout the evening, allowing spectators to greet friends and mingle. When the curtain lifted, a row of calcium lights – flames of nitrogen gas reflecting off sheets of lime – outlined the stage with a bright blaze of white light. Young men – mechanics, clerks, journalists, tradesmen – and a few women crowded the pit while others sat on low-backed wooden benches in the gallery behind them. Peanut shells crunched under the feet of the patrons, and the smell of freshly roasted nuts penetrated the warm, sticky air, briefly masking competing odors of beer, tobacco, and unwashed bodies. The number of people attending that night forced some spectators to seek refuge along the edges of the auditorium, behind the seating, and against the back wall of the balcony, despite the anticipated three-hour length of the performance.

They came to see Menken perform the title character: Mazeppa, the rebel prince whom they had never seen played by a woman.[1] Many of them had probably seen *Mazeppa; or, The Wild Horse of Tartary* before; the play had proven itself to be a crowd-pleaser over the past thirty years with its sword fights, battle scenes, and horse tricks. But this time advertisements claimed that Menken would do what no actor had attempted: At the end of the first act she would allow herself to be tied to the back of a horse and sent up a mountain of scaffolding that rose from the stage floor into the rafters. The stunt was so dangerous that former Mazeppas had allowed a dummy to ride in their stead, even though it was the central event of the play. Rumors (probably begun by Menken herself) further suggested that she would play the rest of the role *just like a man*. Since most of the audience knew the story of *Mazeppa*, they understood this meant that soldiers would strip the hero on stage before lashing him to the horse. If Menken played the role as men before her, wouldn't she also be stripped of her clothing? The event promised sex and danger to an audience hungry for diversion.[2]

The play opened smoothly: Menken entered as the dashing adolescent page Cassimer, a Tartar found in his infancy on the battlefields and adopted

---

[1] Menken was not the first woman to play the part. Charlotte Cushman and Charlotte Crampton both played the role before her, but without the stripping and horse ride. Elizabeth Reitz Mullenix, *Wearing the Breeches: Gender on the Antebellum Stage* (New York: St. Martin's Press, 2000), 62.

[2] "Amusements," *Albany Standard*, June 7, 1861.

into the court of a Polish count. With her expressive eyes and short dark curls, Menken was a beautiful boy, cavorting about the stage with athletic abandon. As he, she evoked the sighs of servant women in the play, won a sword fight, and shared vows of undying love with the already-betrothed countess Olinska.

The normally social audience undoubtedly paid unusual attention as the final scene approached: Cassimer stood captive in the hands of Polish soldiers while Olinska lay prostrate at the feet of her father, begging for Cassimer's life.[3] The Count, seeing Cassimer's attack on Olinska's fiancé as treasonous, ignored his daughter's pleas. He called for soldiers to bring in the "untamed steed" – a black mare that looked askance as the soldiers prodded her into rearing.[4] With a gesture from the Count, the soldiers began roughly stripping the struggling Cassimer of his clothing: black velvet cape, ornate trousers, plumed helmet – until Cassimer faced the audience in a woman's body, clothed in seemingly nothing but a white shirt that bared a pale curve of shoulder and ended at mid-thigh. The soldiers lashed the boy Cassimer to the back of the snorting horse, facing up, with his/her spread legs gleaming white against the black hide and his/her face turned to the audience. A sharp slap sent the horse cantering up the wood-and-canvas mountain at the back of the stage – up and up and up the horse ran, over forty feet above the stage. The eyes of audience fastened on the pale body disappearing over the top of the mountain, and her dark eyes watching them, watching her.[5]

The crowd went wild, standing and cheering, and calling for Cassimer's return – probably yelling "bring her back" or "bring him back" depending on how they perceived the figure on the horse. They received their wish: The entire second act of the play consisted of the half-dressed Cassimer still tied helplessly to the "untamed steed," giving monologues on his pain and agony. Behind him, a moving panorama suggested that they passed over fields and rivers, and through wild country lashed by lightning, thunder, hail, and rain. A giant hovering vulture and packs of hungry wolves inspired the weary Tartar to declare: "Welcome, eternal rest!"[6]

But of course, Cassimer did not die, and in the next scene awoke to find himself among his native countrymen. Naturally, the King of the Tartars quickly recognized Cassimer as his long lost son, Mazeppa, and there was great rejoicing (the language barrier did not pose a problem as the Poles and Tartars alike spoke English). In the final act of the play, Mazeppa returned to Poland to fight for his true love. In leaving his boyhood (and, in this case,

[3] "Amusements," *Albany Standard*, June 8, 1861.

[4] Many of the "untamed steeds" over the next few years would be well-trained geldings as well as mares.

[5] H. M. Milner, *Mazeppa; or, The Wild Horse of Tartary* (Samuel French, n.d.), housed in Prompt Books, Harvard Theatre Collection, Houghton Library, Harvard University, Cambridge, Massachusetts (hereafter HTC); lithographs of Menken on the horse, Adah Isaacs Menken Collection, Billy Rose Theatre Collection, New York Public Library, New York City.

[6] Milner, *Mazeppa*, act II, scene I.

womanhood as well), he also left behind his Polish name and position as a servant, and riding the now-tamed black steed, Mazeppa the prince returned to fight as a man for his woman. He returned to seek vengeance on those who had raised him from infancy yet kept him in servitude, and now faced him as an enemy. The final curtain came down on a triumphant Mazeppa with his arms around the fair Olinska, surrounded by the battlefields of the devastated Poles.[7]

Within five years, Menken would ride that wild horse of Tartary to national and international fame. Menken brought to *Mazeppa* sex and danger, and *Mazeppa* gave Menken a rebel image uniquely suited to the Civil War period. Audiences thrilled to the violent stripping, the sexually suggestive, death-defying horse ride, and the illusion of nudity. Menken's daring to play the role destroyed any remaining vestiges of respectability still clinging to her name, but it was a good time to be a rebel, with a lowercase "r." Onstage, Menken played the underdog who triumphs over a self-important aristocrat, a role that worked regardless of one's loyalty in America's Civil War, and the exoticism of the setting allowed audiences to think about war within a safely alien setting. There were also several elements to this rebel that made her as him appealing for contextual reasons. Menken played a boy who, in his nudity, becomes a woman before returning as a fully clothed man. Although there is no denying that appreciation for the female form made that particular leap of imagination possible, the act assumed new dimensions at a time when cross-dressing itself was undergoing a transformation and becoming ubiquitous offstage as well as on. There was also an element of interracial conflict, if spectators took the time to think about the implications (and there is no evidence that they did); the Tartars were considered "Oriental" by nineteenth-century standards. Did the fact that the hero was Oriental have any impact on the play's reception? Did it matter that he fell in love with a European woman and destroyed her people to be with her?

But, of course, the nudity was central and the decision to place nudity in a mainstream theater was also entirely contextual. War was closing theaters, and managers were desperate to stay open; Menken's *Mazeppa* sold tickets. Historians have credited Menken with bringing nudity to the American stage, but in fact what she did was move it into middle-class theaters. She was able to do so because of the literary pretensions of the piece, the element of spectacle already acceptable to middle-class audiences, and because war was destabilizing class structures and their performance. What Menken did was pull together several elements that should have put her act beyond the pale – sex, nudity, danger, and an interracial affair – that instead made her an overnight sensation. Her secret was timing: The war had broken out two months before, and war made all the difference.

[7] Ibid., act III, scene III.

Without rumors of Menken's audacity circulating the town, the play would not have filled the Green Street Theatre that June evening. Since the twelfth of April, when South Carolina first fired on Union-occupied Fort Sumter, theater audiences nationwide had dwindled to nothing, forcing theaters across America to close their doors.[8] Even the nation's entertainment capital, New York City, had only two theaters operating by June of that year.[9] The people of Albany came that night because curiosity broke through their focus on the national crisis, and for the rest of that summer, newspapers noted that Menken brought in the first full houses since the beginning of the war. Only P. T. Barnum's museum in New York fared so well.[10]

Audiences of the Civil War period apparently loved *Mazeppa* and attended many different renditions, including parodies and burlesques of the original, and paid to see it performed with mules or hobby horses in frontier towns. In Louisville alone, the play appeared sixty-five times between 1858 and 1866.[11] Once Menken shifted interpretation of the play, *Mazeppa* would become one of the most popular plays of the century, and a favorite role for actresses as well as actors. Over the next two years, from 1861 to 1863, she traveled extensively, performing Mazeppa and various other male or "breeches" roles as far south as St. Louis and Washington, D.C., and as far West as Milwaukee. Because Menken was the first to combine sex and danger in the familiar play, by losing her trousers and riding up the canvas mountain, she enjoyed credit for the role even when not performing. It became *Mazeppa* à la Menken, regardless of the person on the horse. In fact, Menken's version of *Mazeppa* became so popular that men began to parody her, with a male actor cross-dressed as Menken cross-dressed as a man.[12]

The historical and literary basis for the sensational play gave it cultural weight and an illusion of erudition. The play was based on the real-life rise to power by Isaac Mazeppa in the seventeenth century, a Ukrainian folk hero whose military skill enabled him to emerge from peasantry to become a legendary Hetman of the Ukraine. Mazeppa secured a place in the western imagination when his lover's aristocratic husband had him tied naked to a horse and sent off into the Siberian Steppes to die. According to folklore, peasants saved Mazeppa and he eventually led them in war

[8] "A Theatre in Hard Times...," New York *Sunday Mercury*, July 7, 1861, p. 1, c. 1.

[9] The New York *Clipper*, 1861; Richard Barksdale Harwell, "Brief Candle: The Confederate Theatre," *Proceedings of the American Antiquarian Society* (April 1971): 44–48.

[10] *Sunday Mercury*, June 9, July 7, and Aug. 4, 1861.

[11] Margaret G. Watson, *Silver Theatre: Amusements of the Mining Frontier in Early Nevada, 1850 to 1864* (Glendale, Calif.: Arthur H. Clark, 1964), 251–252; John Jacob Weisert, *A Large and Fashionable Audience: A Check List of Performances at the Louisville Theatre, 1846–1866* (Louisville: John Jacob Weisert, 1955), 186.

[12] See advertisements for burlesques of *Mazeppa* in period newspapers of San Francisco, New York, and London.

against the Russian Czar. In eastern European legend, Mazeppa continues to be portrayed as either a hero to the people or a traitor to Russia.[13] The American public, however, heard of *Mazeppa* through the poem by George Gordon Byron and the 1831 stage adaptation by Henry Milner. Byron (and thus, Milner) left behind political conflict in favor of romantic love, portraying Mazeppa as a boy who becomes a man by first being stripped of everything – identity, clothing, love, family – and then recovering all of those things on his own terms with deliberate aggression.

Linking the play to Byron further colored the public's perceptions of the play itself and, by extension, Menken's performance. As the bold, bad boy of British Romanticism, Byron appalled and thrilled readers with his emotional sensuality, and he himself projected an androgynous image that contributed to his appeal. Throughout the early nineteenth century, "Byronism" held the nation in thrall, as women and men read his poetry together in daring courtship. They affected his dress style of delicate ruffles suggestively unbound at the throat, and bought lithographs, sheet music, and dinner sets illustrated with portraits of Byron as a young man with large liquid eyes and feminine beauty. Dozens of biographies appeared during his lifetime, rendering him still more enticing with hints of a wicked, erotic past. With his sudden death during the war for Greek Independence in 1824, Byron solidified his masculinity. He was "respectable and scandalous all at once," as was the play based upon his work, and Menken herself.[14] His blurring of gender definition was part of his personal image, and the heroes of his poetry had similar attributes: They were independent, aggressive men with emotional depth. The Oriental identity of his heroes allowed them to project mystery and exoticism that wooed the reading audience as well as the fictional heroines. The parallel to Menken's personal image should be obvious, with her mysterious, ethnically tinged identities. Once she became famous as Mazeppa, she often styled her appearance to resemble Byron, with the same short curls swept toward the face and ruffled shirts left daringly open at the throat. Menken clearly played up the links between Byron, Mazeppa, and herself, suggesting that Byron's connection to the play was an important element of its appeal.

While Menken's performance of the physically demanding and revealing role was unusual enough to fill theaters when little else would, most Americans did not see it as socially reprehensible. What Menken did was sensational, titillating, and unconventional, but she did not alienate the

[13] Herbert L. Babinski, *The Mazeppa Legend in European Romanticism* (New York: Columbia University Press, 1974), 1–4.

[14] Andrew Elfenbien, *Byron and the Victorians* (New York: Cambridge University Press, 1995), 206, 48; Peter W. Graham, *Lord Byron* (New York: Twayne, 1998), 9, 86; James Soderholm, *Fantasy, Forgery, and the Byron Legend* (Lexington: University of Kentucky Press, 1996), 13. Menken was scandalous in *Mazeppa*, but as the Menken she wrote sentimental poetry and worked hard to destabilize her notoriety.

public even if she shocked it. If the prurient quality of the performance sounds out of place in mid-nineteenth-century America, with the Victorian focus on respectability and self-control, then we clearly need to change our image of that time. When one considers the flourishing of opposites in mid-century American culture – the success of humbug in the midst of a didactic culture of sincerity, the blossoming of reform societies and prostitution in the same urban areas, or the seemingly discordant strains of sentimental and iconoclastic literature – the period was defined by social and cultural tension, by a taut balance between social and cultural opposites. It is no wonder that the public responded fiercely (both positively and negatively) to Menken's performance as Mazeppa: It reflected the competing images of the surrounding world. It could appeal to a wide range of viewers because the play in cross-dress resonated with the disruption caused by war. Men could focus on war as Mazeppa's rite of passage, for example, even as they saw her as a sexual object when revealed on the horse. Women might identify with a female hero, even as they responded heterosexually (in their minds) to her attraction as a man.[15]

Cross-dressing was standard theater fare by the time Menken first revealed herself as Mazeppa in 1861, but her audiences' understandings of gender were changing under the impact of secession and war. We can see changing notions of gender in the proliferation of cross-dressing beyond the boundaries of the stage. While Menken was traveling around the Union from 1861 to 1864, the number of novels and biographies of women cross-dressing increased significantly. Americans read the popular biographies of cross-dressing spies and soldiers. Newspapers carried snippets of information about women caught in men's clothing or wearing it boldly.[16] A children's book published in 1859, *Little Miss Consequence*, threatened hoydenish girls that acting too much like boys could result in becoming one. Fictional tomboys – those prepubescent female characters who dressed like girls but claimed many of the same freedoms and desires as boys – increased in popularity during the 1860s as well.[17] Women's participation in public life increased during the Civil War era, from the rumblings of war in the 1850s onward. Changing ideas of women's roles found expression in entertainment, although the messages were mixed and rarely straightforward. Cross-dressing had long been used in the theater to reveal women's figures

[15] We have few examples of women reviewing Menken's performance, but those available make note of her attraction as a man. See Tess Ardenne, "Black-Eyed Susan," San Francisco *Golden Era*, April 24, 1864, p. 5, c. 3 and Florence Fane, "About Poor Cassimer," San Francisco *Golden Era*, Sept. 27, 1863, p. 1, c. 2.

[16] There are many examples available, such as "A Woman in Male Attire Chases a False Lover," *New York Evening Post*, Jan. 21, 1860, p. 1, c. 3; "A Woman and a Heroine," New York *Home Journal*, June 20, 1866.

[17] Alfred Haebegger, *Gender, Fantasy, and Realism and American Literature* (New York: Columbia, 1982), 172–173.

under the guise of drama, but now cross-dressing was assuming different dimensions, as it became something women were doing in venues other than the stage. Those different images of cross-dressing in turn effected gender play onstage, and the way Menken's act would be received.[18]

By 1861, Menken's audience was already quite familiar with cross-dressing on stage and in print, and many expected it to happen on the battlefields.[19] "Cross-dressing" is a complex blend of signifiers that works in a variety of ways. At its most basic, cross-dressing is when a man or woman dresses in the clothes and performs the gender behaviors normally assigned to the other sex. It can mean someone cross-dressing so convincingly that the "true" sex of the player is secondary, but it just as often involves a tacit understanding that the viewer will remember that the sex of the performer is the opposite of what is visible. Conversely, the term can describe a woman dressing as a man to highlight her femininity, creating a disjuncture that focuses the viewers' eyes on the physical differences between male and female bodies. Androgynous cross-dressing means exhibiting behavior that suggests the performer is no more male than female, but a seamless blend of both. For example, an androgynous cross-dresser might be dressed to look male and fight battles, but lack facial hair and express feminine emotion. Androgynous cross-dressers appeal to the widest variety of viewers, because although androgyny is gender-neutral, it embodies the full spectrum of gender positions, and is often sexually charged. Clearly, cross-dressing can be a disguise or masquerade that reveals as well as conceals, and although it was sometimes performed across racial lines – in minstrel shows, for example – the "cross" invariably refers to gender. Cross-dressing appeared on the nineteenth-century stage in all of these forms.

Cross-dressing during Menken's period of fame differed significantly from others in that there was a veritable explosion of female cross-dressing both onstage and off, and during the early years of the war, depictions of gender shifted away from exaggeration of the female body as androgyny

[18] Mullenix provides the most recent and thorough examination of cross-dressing on stage in this period. She draws on other excellent work, such as Faye Dudden's *Women in American Theatre: Actresses and Audiences, 1790–1870* (New Haven: Yale University Press, 1994), and articles in compilations such as *Crossing the Stage: Controversies in Cross-Dressing*, ed. Lesley Ferris (London: Routledge, 1993), and *Passing Performances: Queer Readings of Leading Players in American Theatre History*, eds. Robert Schanke and Kim Marra (Ann Arbor: University of Michigan Press, 1998). Julie Wheelwright's *Amazons and Military Maids: Women Who Dressed as Men in the Pursuit of Life, Liberty and Happiness* (London: Pandora, 1989) is a useful examination of women on the battlefields in literature and biography. Judith Butler's pathbreaking *Gender Trouble: Feminism and the Subversion of Identity* (London: Routledge, 1990) has assisted scholars by providing the theoretical tools to dismantle and examine cross-dressing regardless of venue. Butler's ideas heavily influence my perspective, even when I am not intentionally drawing on her text.

[19] Lyde Cullen Sizer, "Acting Her Part: Narratives of Union Women Spies," in *Divided Houses: Gender and the Civil War*, eds. Catherine Clinton and Nina Silber (New York: Oxford University Press, 1992), 115–117; Wheelwright, *Amazons*, 27.

briefly regained popularity. The timing of such popularity and society's preoccupation with female soldiers makes it clear that the war itself fostered in interest in cross-dressing, but the reasons for this phenomenon are open to speculation.

Wartime exaggeration of sex roles in terms of combatants (men) versus noncombatants (women) undoubtedly gave rise to a fascination with gender transgression. Popular magazines and newspapers publicized war as a masculine pursuit despite the obvious fact that war did not merely allow women access to a male world, but in fact often forced them to enter it. Women cross-dressing, whether on stage or in writing, thus provided an entertaining illustration of gender tensions exacerbated by war. Women's participation in the war was essential to both sides, whether they supported troops, ran hospitals, or collected funds. As able-bodied men enlisted in the fight, women ran the nation's economy, taking on distinctly male roles even as they dressed as women and acted feminine. Furthermore, news stories of women actively engaged in spying and defense, on the battlefields and behind enemy lines, undoubtedly provoked women who were *not* engaged in warfare themselves to consider how they might also act. The notion that real men were fearless and eager to enlist made masculinity dangerous to perform. Yet, at the same time, the notion that soldiering was a male pursuit was being challenged by evidence that women were in fact fighting as well. The advertising of genders, and the wartime rhetoric that supported it, did not mesh with the roles men and women found themselves in, *or imagined themselves* playing, and that tension found expression in popular culture through a celebration of cross-dressing.

At least as far back as the seventeenth century, cross-dressed figures appeared in virtually every form of cultural expression, from stage productions to folk songs and tales, paintings and prints, diaries, legends, and literature.[20] Cross-dressing was in fact a central theme in the development of British drama, and since antebellum America inherited its theater culture from the British, such traditions directly shaped gender play on the American stage. Not only do many of Shakespeare's comedies, such as *A Midsummer Night's Dream*, center on complicated acts of cross-dressing, but he wrote knowing that it was illegal for women to appear onstage, and therefore young men would perform the female roles. Thus, from the origins of British theater, cross-dressing involved multiple layers of meaning – with boys playing girls who cross-dressed as boys, and who then were sometimes forced to cross-dress yet again. Oddly enough, as soon as women were allowed to perform on the British stage, they also immediately began cross-dressing. One estimate suggests that out of 300 plays performed in London from

[20] For a concise rundown of examples in British theater, see Rudolf M. Dekker and Lotte C. Van de Pole, *The Tradition of Female Transvestism in Early Modern Europe* (New York: St. Martins, 1989), for American theater, see Mullenix, *Wearing the Breeches*, ch. 1.

1660 to 1700, eighty-nine contained roles in which actresses wore men's clothing.[21]

By the nineteenth century, the sex of the performer usually determined the nature of the cross-dressing. Male performers usually cross-dressed in jest, performing wildly exaggerated versions of femininity to make the audience laugh; this would change very little during the Civil War years. Female performance of masculine roles, however, developed along different lines. Cross-dressed actresses became extremely popular in the United States beginning in the 1830s. At that point, many Americans (including most of the audience) still considered actresses only slightly more reputable than prostitutes in part because of the public nature of their work. Early female cross-dressers appeared particularly salacious, *not* because they convincingly performed masculinity and threatened social order (as one might argue later), but because male garments revealed the shape of their legs. Voluminous skirts had fetishized legs to the point where simply disclosing their existence made a statement, and breeches parts gave actresses a reasonable excuse for displaying their shape. Given American assumptions of French promiscuity, it is hardly surprising that French actress and dancer Madame Celeste was the first to successfully capitalize on cross-dressing on a large scale, when she toured the United States in the mid-1830s.[22] Madame Celeste's version of manhood was intended to titillate and beguile, not fool the audience into a state of suspended disbelief. Her success unleashed a host of imitators, and suggestive cross-dressing became a theater staple.

Female interpretation of male roles gained artistic legitimacy in the 1840s with the success of Charlotte Cushman, considered one of the greatest talents of the nineteenth-century stage. Cushman achieved international acclaim for her renditions of Hamlet and Romeo, and brought female performance of masculinity to a new level. Indeed, Cushman performed male roles so well that many viewers claimed to forget she was female, and thus she won acclaim as an artist rather than as a "shape actress." Cushman first took on the roles of Hamlet and Romeo because female roles proved too limiting. Respectable female characters in early nineteenth-century plays were often nothing more than foils for the hero, and left little scope for imagination. Cushman found her creativity further hampered by the fact that if she rendered disreputable female characters complex, she ran the risk of offending the audiences and harming her reputation.[23] Cross-dressing opened up interesting roles and challenged her ability. Furthermore, star actresses such as Cushman invariably played the romantic leads, rather than supporting male characters, and thus were able to bask in heroic splendor unlike anything

---

[21] Wheelwright, *Amazons*, 7.

[22] Robert C. Allen, *Horrible Prettiness: Burlesque and American Culture* (Chapel Hill: University of North Carolina Press, 1991), 89–90.

[23] Dudden, *Women in American Theatre*, 93.

afforded most heroines. Even though many Americans undoubtedly still objected to the display of her body in male clothing, public recognition of her talent marked a change in the way other actresses began performing male roles, at least through the early 1860s.[24]

Cushman's successful portrayals revealed a peculiar advantage for cross-dressed actresses: because mid-nineteenth century society considered female homosociality more acceptable than public displays of heterosexual desire, women could perform the romantic hero with more freedom than male actors. Historian Fay Dudden has shown that female cross-dressers found themselves in a bizarre position of privilege completely at odds with the restrictive mores women faced offstage. One reviewer remarked of Cushman's Romeo that his fencing skills and amorous manners were "of so erotic a character that no man would have dared indulge in them."[25] A male actor performing so suggestively with an actress would have grossly trespassed propriety. Had Cushman worn female attire, an open expression of eroticism would have damaged her reputation. Ironically, male cross-dressers could not enjoy the same freedom; in the era of men cross-dressing almost strictly in jest, a male cross-dresser could not seriously express passion toward another man. Thus the cross-dressing actress, due to mid-nineteenth-century America's notions of propriety, respectability, gender, and sexuality, found herself able to express the otherwise inexpressible. A woman convincingly dressed as a man had more freedoms that any other actress or actor. She could with impunity make love to female characters on the stage – and she did.[26] Menken sweet-talked women to prove her manhood in several plays, and in *The French Spy*, one of the period's most popular sensation plays, shared a quick kiss with another woman.[27] By the 1850s, actresses invariably played the hero with aggressive passion, and audiences responded by making breeches parts the most financially successful roles available to women throughout the antebellum period.[28]

What is especially unique about cross-dressing during the Civil War era, however, is how much it began to surface in printed forms, some drawn from the imagination but just as many from life. From roughly 1855 through

[24] Mullenix, *Wearing the Breeches*, 59–66; Dudden, *Women in American Theatre*, 93–94; Mary M. Turner, *Forgotten Leading Ladies of the American Theatre* (Jefferson, N.C.: McFarland, 1990), 66–69. Mullenix and Dudden both suggest that Cushman's popularity overseas had an impact on her acceptance in the United States, and that acceptance challenged previous dismissal of cross-dressing as merely exhibitionist.

[25] Dudden, *Women in American Theatre*, 92.

[26] Kristina Straub, "The Guilty Pleasures of Female Theatrical Cross-Dressing and the Autobiography of Charlotte Chark," in *Body Guards: The Cultural Politics of Gender Ambiguity*, eds. Julia Epstein and Kristina Straub (New York: Routledge, 1991), 142.

[27] J. T. Haines, *The French Spy; or, The Siege of Constantine* (New York: Samuel French, n.d.), act 1, scene 1.

[28] Dudden, *Women in American Theatre*, 93.

1869, cross-dressed characters, particularly women, began appearing more frequently in the pages of newspapers, biographies, and fiction. The shift should not be overstated; cross-dressed female characters had appeared in written works sporadically throughout the antebellum period. Cheap short novels, such as *A Narrative of the Life of Mrs. K. White* (1809), *The Female Marine* (1816), or *The Female Wanderer* (1826), entertained the public with tales of women dressed as men. The first women cross-dressing in popular fiction appeared as early as 1845, with the adventures of Maturin M. Ballou's female pirate captain, Fanny Campbell.[29] It was not until the height of the sectional crisis, however, that written stories of cross-dressing women gained popularity parallel to stage performances.

The increased frequency of cross-dressing in print and offstage appears to be directly connected with the wartime experience. Cross-dressing onstage had long been quasiacceptable; it could be dismissed as merely entertaining, and therefore socially threatening only if one took it too seriously. During the 1850s and '60s, cross-dressing became more ubiquitous and often even celebratory. Cross-dressing gained legitimacy with convincing performances of masculinity onstage, and, in the late 1850s and 1860s, offstage, as women prepared to fight alongside the men. And despite their differences, 'fact' and 'fiction' came in forms that were often entangled. Many biographies and novels had nearly interchangeable story lines.

In fiction, images of female characters cross-dressing for short periods of time began appearing in serialized literature, a form of publishing particularly popular in middle-class periodicals and newspapers. Two of the most popular novels of the nineteenth century, Harriet Beecher Stowe's *Uncle Tom's Cabin* (serialized in 1851) and E.D.E.N. Southworth's *The Hidden Hand* (first serialized in 1859), portrayed heroic women dressing as men out of necessity. In the first novel, the exemplary mother Eliza disguised herself in men's clothes, and dressed her son Harry as a girl, to escape from slavery. Readers initially meet the young heroine of the *Hidden Hand*, Capitola Black, as a male street urchin. Capitola apologetically defends her choice to pass as a boy by explaining that it was the only way to survive on the streets, implying that her cross-dressing was virtuous because it kept her out of prostitution.[30] Novels and newspaper articles suggest that most Americans deemed it acceptable for females to dress in male costume as a measure of self-protection, if only for a limited amount of time, because an abundance of written material suggested that women were particularly vulnerable in the urbanized modern world. Characters such as Eliza and Capitola dressed

---

[29] Henry Nash Smith, *Virgin Land: The American West as Symbol and Myth* (Cambridge: Harvard University Press, 1973), 112.

[30] Harriet Beecher Stowe, *Uncle Tom's Cabin; or, Life among the Lowly* (first serialized in 1851; New York: Bantam Classics, 1983); E.D.E.N. Southworth, *The Hidden Hand; or, Capitola the Madcap* (first serialized in 1859; Rutgers: Rutgers University Press, 1988).

The drawing of Menken as Mazeppa with one breast bared became typical after
1864. In every case the breast is bare but there is no nipple, perhaps to make
the drawing less pornographic. (Harvard Theatre Collection)

as male because they were clever and good; the barbarism of their situation
had forced them to don male garments as a means of self-protection.

As the war drew closer, celebratory portrayals of women disguised as
male soldiers became common. Of course, stories of women dressing as
soldiers were not far-fetched in a nation where ladies now plowed fields,
hauled crops, and ran businesses. In fact, stories of women going off to
fight played directly into the fantasies of many American women, who
would gladly have left the unrewarded responsibilities of home to take a
more visibly active role. Accounts of Deborah Sampson enlisting as a male
soldier in the American Revolutionary War, originally published in 1797,
were republished in 1850 and again in 1866.[31] In 1865, the public read about
the adventures of S. Emma Edmonds in her autobiography, *Nurse and Spy in
the Union Army*. Strangely, Edmonds does not bother to tell the reader that

[31] Herman Mann, *The Female Review* (1797); John Adams Vinton, *The Female Review: Life of Deborah
Sampson, The Female Soldier in the War of the Revolution* (Boston: J. K. Wiggin and Wm. Parsons Lunt,
1850; reprint, 1866).

she cross-dressed, even though illustrations make it clear that she fought as a male soldier. The only time she gives details of her dress are when she is assigned to spy on the enemy while disguised as a male slave.[32] Loreta Janeta Velazquez gives more satisfactory details about the difficulties of disguising oneself as male in *The Woman in Battle*, which she openly proclaims she wrote for money. Velazquez begins by describing her life-long desire to be male, and boasts of her successful seduction (without consummation) of women as evidence of her masculinity. She suggests that in fact she became male psychically, saying, "I began to pride myself as much upon being a successful lady's man as upon being a valiant soldier."[33] Perhaps because Valezquez's book was a northern publication about a Confederate cross-dresser, it could afford to be far less noble than the biographies of Sampson and Edmonds. Such publications address the public's ongoing curiosity about how many women were fighting. At one point, Valezquez confirms that she met many cross-dressed female soldiers while on the battlefields, suggesting that the phenomenon was not only common, but that her reading public had long suspected as much.[34]

Menken in her many breeches roles, but particularly as the warrior Mazeppa, played against this backdrop of female soldiering. As a female playing a male hero, she represented onstage what was already happening in the world around her. The war valorized the concept of women not only dressing but even acting as men, up to a point. There was a blurry sort of line of propriety that a female soldier must not cross, of course; for example, it was acceptable for a cross-dressed soldier behave as one of the boys to avoid detection, but she must not express enjoyment in her situation. She dressed as a soldier to do a duty, and that was heroic. If she stepped beyond that point, into acting as a male soldier because it gave her access to another world, then she had discarded virtue in favor of opportunity. The problem was that whether the woman was seen as patriotic or opportunistic was really a matter of opinion, there was little proof either way; it was the same dilemma as that presented by the confidence man all over again. Given this, in the context of war, breeches roles gained another dimension: They could be seen a celebration of patriotism, and not merely an excuse to exhibit an actress's legs. It is especially telling that Mazeppa, the role that won Menken so much attention, required athletic agility as well as lack of inhibition. Mazeppa was a daring, independent, resilient warrior in a society hungering for those qualities in its soldiers, male and female.

---

[32] S. Emma Edmonds, *Nurse and Spy in the Union Army: Comprising the Adventures and Experiences in Hospitals, Camps and Battle-fields* (Hartford, Conn.: W. S. Williams, 1865).

[33] Loreta Janeta Velazquez, *The Woman in Battle: A Narrative of the Exploits, Adventures, and Travels of MLJV, Otherwise Known as Lieutenant Harry T. Buford, Confederate States Army* (Hartford: T. Belknap, 1876), 5–6, 48, 109.

[34] Ibid., 110.

It should not be surprising that androgyny suddenly became appealing. Again, this should not be overstated; there were fictional accounts of female soldiers who were too feminine to convince a reader they fooled anyone into thinking they were male. At one extreme were characters such as the cross-dressed heroine Remy St. Remy, who was fantastically beautiful with "beardless lips like cut coral over his pearly teeth."[35] Remy disguised as "the boy in blue" sounds so effeminate that the most surprising aspect of the story is that s/he did not get trounced by her comrades. But far more common, the cross-dressed heroines in popular fiction appeared beautifully androgynous when dressed in uniform, and their righteous reasons for donning male dress serve heighten their sex appeal. Courage (often fueled by love for a man) allowed them to transcend the confines of womanhood to become beautifully masculine in terms of courage and agility while remaining feminine in sensibility. Heroines such as Madeline Moore, who follows her husband into battle, or Castine, who dresses as a soldier to avenge her sister's death, were presented as the perfect pairing of the best of both genders.[36]

In fiction and biography, cross-dressing as a soldier meant successfully exhibiting the highest standards of masculinity and femininity. For the woman to be acceptable as a male soldier, she had to be a good woman; she could not lose her female sense of virtue, only her feminine distaste for rough work. She had to rise above the supposed inferiority of her body to march all day, dig ditches, and endure difficult conditions without complaint. In literature, the proof of a woman's successful androgyny came when she faced the enemy with a gun in her hand. Then she revealed her masculine courage and rationality by recognizing that killing the enemy was morally justified, and did so without feminine remorse. Significantly, novels and other tales of female soldiers usually include at least one incident of the woman killing an enemy soldier.[37] The killing both complicated the prevailing image of women as naturally maternal and nurturing and served to justify wartime acts of violence.[38] If a woman – the moral pillar of the sacred home – was forced to shoot and kill the enemy to save herself, her family, or her comrades, then surely killing the enemy was a just cause. Such actions infused the brutalities war with righteousness.

The androgynous female cross-dresser was an ideal character during these times of unrest because she proved an acceptable vehicle for fantasy regardless of the viewer's sex or sexual preferences. A man watching a female

[35] Mrs. C. H. Gildersleeve [Rachel Longstreet], *Remy St. Remy; or, The Boy in Blue* (New York: James Okane, 1865), 36.

[36] Madeline Moore, *The Lady Lieutenant; or, The Strange and Thrilling Adventures of Miss Madeline Moore* (Philadelphia: Barclay, 1862); Edward Edgeville, *Castine* (Raleigh: William B. Smith, 1865).

[37] E.g., see Edmonds, *Nurse and Spy*, 94; Valazquez, *Woman in Battle*, 107.

[38] Barbara Cutter gives an excellent discussion of this phenomenon in "Devils in Disguise, Angels on the Battlefields: American Womanhood, 1800–1865," Ph.D. dissertation, Rutgers University, 1998.

Menken as the French spy. The photograph was probably taken between 1860 and 1863 at the height of the Civil War. Note the military dress and sexually charged androgyny of this photograph. She crosses her arms in masculine fashion but her face and body are beautifully neutral of gender. Photographer unknown. (Harvard Theatre Collection)

cross-dresser onstage, for example, could see her as a sexually available woman or man. To put a woman into men's clothing was to take her out of the domestic world that defined her as a mother and a homemaker. To dress her in men's clothing was to sexualize her – to remove all signifiers of piety, purity, and domesticity, leaving only the essential difference of the sexual body beneath the clothing. Men were not held to the same sexual restrictions as women, and a woman in male clothing suggested that she enjoyed those same sexual freedoms. But women also fantasized about cross-dressed women, whether they saw them as an ideal man or woman. In San Francisco, for example, columnist Florence Fane accused Menken in cross-dress of "bewitching" young ladies and inspiring infatuation.[39]

The revelation or knowledge of the character's physical sex was often central to the appeal. In most popular novels of cross-dressed heroines, the central scene involves a man accidentally discovering his friend was female – usually by trying to save his life and encountering breasts. In *Virginia Graham,*

---

[39] Florence Fane, "About Poor Cassimer," San Francisco *Golden Era*, Sept. 27, 1863, p. 1.

the Spy of the Grand Army, when the male narrator goes to assist a fallen soldier on the battlefield he describes a slow stripping of male layers to reveal "a fairer and more symmetrical neck and bosom [than ever] delighted the eyes of a sculptor."[40] These pages of protracted undress no doubt showed the marks of many fingers, as readers returned to savor the scene, imagining themselves as either or both characters. The performer was open for viewing, and mixed signifiers left interpretation in the hands of the spectator. The act of revealing the sexual body became a shared experience between spectator and the actress or fictional heroine; the eroticism of knowing and mentally possessing that figure pulled the spectator into the story.

This period was also awash in depictions of men dressed in women's clothes, but to the opposite effect; if female soldiers were courageous, men dressed in women's clothes were simply absurd. Salacious novels portrayed men dressed as women either to escape or, as in the case of George Thompson's *The Outlaw*, to infiltrate the private parlors of unsuspecting women and seduce them.[41] Political cartoons particularly abounded with images of male public figures in women's clothing. The 1860 Currier and Ives print *The Great Exhibition of 1860*, for example, satirized the antislavery orientation of the Republican platform by depicting William H. Seward dressed in a skirt and playing mammy to a wailing black infant. In 1861 another Currier and Ives print portrayed Missouri secessionist governor Claiborne F. Jackson dressed as a frontierswoman, barely eluding a lion with the head of Union commander Nathaniel Lyon. However, the number of such images scarcely compares with the proliferation of cartoons of a cross-dressed Jefferson Davis after Union soldiers captured him in 1865 supposedly disguised in female clothing.[42] The cartoon image of Davis in female dress was meant to underline the subjugation of the South. Davis as the South was emasculated, not merely defeated, by the North. This kind of cross-dressing did not hint at a need to reconsider gender, but rather reinforced gender stereotypes by mocking the masculinity of public figures.

So while this image of America fascinated by cross-dressing complicates the conventional understanding of nineteenth-century America as a time of strictly binary gender roles, it does not contradict it. Restriction and rebellion form a powerful dialectic in American culture, both then and now, and increasingly stringent ideas of dress undoubtedly gave rise to cross-dressing as a form of rebellion – and perhaps vice-versa. Print culture in the form of conduct guides, newspaper articles, and even women's novels gave the middle class a forum in which they could analyze and suggest

---

[40] Harry Hazel [Justin Jones], *Virginia Graham: The Spy of the Grand Army* (New York: American News, 1867), 12.

[41] George Thompson, *The Outlaw; or, The Felon's Fortunes* (New York: Frederick A. Brady, n.d.)

[42] Bernard F. Reilly, Jr., *American Political Prints, 1766–1876: A Catalog of the Collections in the Library of Congress* (Boston: G. K. Hall, 1991), 441, 476, 560–561.

appropriate behavior. Many Americans were eager to learn what was appropriate, but just as many others undoubtedly found such prescriptions overbearing. Burlesquing Victorian gender norms through cross-dressing was one way of lightening the atmosphere. But regardless of what lay behind it, the midcentury predilection for cross-dressing suggests that ordinary men and women, and not simply cultural rebels, recognized that the binary gender order could be shifted at will.

The heroism of all of these cross-dressed characters allowed for increased cross-dressing on stage, as they guaranteed a middle-class audience to theater managers already walking a fine line between thrilling and offending their patrons. Cross-dressing on stage differed significantly from literature, of course, by allowing spectators to see actual bodies in ways they could not offstage. Even at the height of androgynous cross-dressing (roughly 1858–63), cross-dressed performances were sexually charged simply by the fact that they *revealed*. What exactly they revealed depended on what the viewer chose to see.

Whether fully dressed as the boy Cassimer or the manly Mazeppa, Menken displayed a woman's body without corsets and able to move freely. Ironically, even though Menken revealed her legs by wearing trousers, her body was actually less defined onstage than off. During this period, voluminous crinoline petticoats that could extend as far as twelve feet in circumference obscured women's legs, but women's bodies were fully outlined above the waist. Tightly laced corsets reshaped women's torsos, creating an exaggerated hourglass above the sweep of skirts. Constricting corsets and ungovernable hoops constrained women's movements, forcing them to move slowly. By contrast, women dressed as men were able to pose in positions seldom seen in the age of corsets. A woman out of her corsets and skirts was truly a woman set free of constrictions, both socially and physically. So if the male costume made the female body easier to see, it was also a body that had less shape. The most popular cross-dressers in the early late 1850s, including Menken, tended to be less voluptuous than the performers of the midwar years, further emphasizing the differences between the fully dressed woman and the actress playing a man.[43]

Texts indicate that Menken's agility was a major aspect of her appeal. Reviewers throughout the 1860s, regardless of geographic location, raved about Menken's athleticism. The fact that the second most popular woman to play Mazeppa was Leo Hudson suggests that physical ability was a significant variable in this equation. Hudson, who began playing the role shortly after Menken, was the least physically attractive of all of Menken's imitators. Although androgynously built, Hudson had none of the "beautiful boy" so

---

[43] Menken becomes known as volumptuous beginning in 1863, after she had put on weight and began emphasizing her female shape while in male dress. See photographs of Adah Isaacs Menken in HTC.

celebrated in Menken, and reviewers consistently cited Hudson's athletic grace as central to her success.[44] Menken, and Hudson after her, captivated the audience with a show of the female body in motion as one rarely saw it off the stage. Admiration for Menken's athleticism undoubtedly had an element of sexual connotation, but that included the novelty of seeing a woman's agility when unhampered by clothing and inhibition.

The vacillating passivity and aggression of Mazeppa rendered Menken's faux nudity paradoxically acceptable, threatening, and thrilling. Audiences had become accustomed to immobile nudity in the form of statues and tableaux vivant, or live reenactments of classic nude paintings. Historian Joy Kasson examined the popularity of female nude statues from 1830 through the 1880s, and found that the imaginative stories created by viewers were crucial to the sculpture's overall success and acceptance. She notes, "The narratives told the story of the female body as their authors understood it – vulnerable, dangerous and endangered, representing beauty and shame, attractive in its self-absorption but threatening to overwhelm the viewer."[45] Perhaps most fascinating were the number of viewers who claimed that the chaste expression of *The Greek Slave* clothed its nude form, suggesting an exposed body could be cloaked by purity of thought.[46] By contrast, Menken as Mazeppa was an active nude – not standing still in her vulnerability, but fighting or tied on the back of a moving horse – a victim, a defrocked and feminized hero, absolutely powerless and yet able to seize control of the viewer. Like *The Greek Slave*, the nude figure (suspended between identity as Cassimer/the boy page and Mazeppa/the manly prince) on the horse was pathetic, simultaneously arousing empathy, sympathy, and desire.

The disruption of expected patterns came when Menken allowed herself to be disrobed, tied to the horse, and sent up the dangerous mountain of scaffolding. At that point no audience member could ignore that the page's clothes had hidden a woman's body. The disclosure came with violence: Cassimer was forcibly stripped, suggestive of rape, with the audience complicit as spectators. Soldiers tied the visibly female figure in spread-eagle fashion to the horse, highlighting her sexual vulnerability, before forcing her to ride over forty feet above the stage, seemingly unable to steer the horse or escape should the horse fall. The last part was an illusion – Menken could let go of the horse and fall clear, and was forced to do so at least three times in her career. So there existed not only a case of simulated nudity, but also the threat of danger to not only the character (in the form of assault and death) but even the actress herself.

---

[44] E.g., see Jan. 1865, George C. D. Odell, *Annals of the New York Stage* (New York: Columbia University Press, 1931).

[45] Joy Kasson, *Marble Queens and Captives: Women in Nineteenth-Century American Sculpture* (New Haven: Yale University Press, 1990), 72.

[46] Ibid., 65.

Mazeppa, both poem and play, also expressed the western world's fascination with Orientalism. The Orientalist images so titillating to western viewers came not from the Islamic Asian world they supposedly depicted, but rather from the minds of western Europeans and Americans. And the imagined Oriental world was a provocative opposite of the western world. Resplendent with highly colored silks, filled with lushly populated harems, and set in a landscape of languid golden warmth and the slim bodies of naked slaves, the Orient was decadent, exotic, and debauched. Never mind that few of these images were based in fact, because they were everywhere in western culture; in their ubiquity, the distant imagined land became real. Ambiguities present in Orientalist images seem to add to their appeal; they could be interpreted in a variety of ways by a variety of people. Many paintings suggested a land of extremes, of wealthy merchants and filthy slaves, beautiful women smudged with dirt and ragged beggars squatting in palaces elaborate with tile. And the gender distinctions were particularly confusing. On the one hand, Oriental cultures had harems, but on the other, similarities in clothing seemed to blur sexual differences.[47]

The Orientalist aspects of *Mazeppa* heightened the gender ambiguities Menken already brought to the role. Certainly, the part was already loaded: Mazeppa was a Tartar and therefore of the Islamic Oriental world. His lover was Polish; the daughter of a white Duke. *Mazeppa* is essentially an interracial romance. While there is no written evidence to indicate that the audience paused to consider the interracial dimensions of the play, the fantasy of a love affair between a middle-eastern hero and white woman was clearly enjoyed. Audiences thrilled to the romance just as they had to Byron's Orientalist poetry, and as they would sixty years later to the image of Rudolph Valentino in *The Sheik*. Perhaps through the white female character white audiences could surrender themselves to the seduction of the forbidden, the exotic. And with a woman playing the male role, the gender ambiguities already present in Oriental images became more pronounced. Even when Mazeppa returns from his perilous ride fully dressed once more as a man, he has become distinctly foreign. He has, in a literal sense, gone over to the dark side, the unknown, the ethnically and racially different. As Cassimer, he wore European clothing, but now he is of the Oriental world. In this costume he resembles the white women who wore bloomers in the 1850s, with his Turkish trousers, turban, and jewelry. Yet he must be a man, because he wins the battle and the woman. The Orientalist aspects of the play already gave it deliciously subversive nuances, and Menken as Mazeppa further emphasized the ambiguities already embedded in the play. All of this could be dismissed as merely entertaining, and yet the social danger suggested by the play was also what excited the audiences and drew them in.

---

[47] Edward W. Said, *Orientalism* (New York: Vintage Books, 1978), introduction.

Orientalism was celebrated throughout the nineteenth century; indeed, it was a defining trait of the western world, if not truly descriptive of what lay to the east. The Zouaves, a touring militia of the late 1850s, popularized the concept of combining military and Orientalist images. From 1860 through 1861 enlistment fever coincided with the celebration of the Zouave militia, and it was no accident that Menken's *Mazeppa* of 1861 featured the Tartar Prince dressed as a Zouave. During the Crimean War of the mid-1850s, special regiments of the French Army, named Zouaves after the Algerian warriors who trained them, received international attention for their valor and skill. Key to their performance were their loose-fitting Turkish trousers and blouson shirts (again reminiscent of the bloomer costume) that allowed freedom of movement. In late 1859 a volunteer militia from Chicago named "The United States Zouave Cadets," trained by Elmer Ellsworth, began traveling around the Northeast performing drills and marching in parades. Their display of skills earned the Zouaves celebration in the national press, and enormous crowds gathered to watch their rather flamboyant drills. Soon other volunteer militias began copying the Zouaves, particularly adopting their uniforms of Turkish trousers, brilliant red shirts, and jaunty blue caps.[48] By 1860, a young Cincinnati actress, Clara Morris, noted "everything was military," and it became common practice for American theaters to feature drill teams of young girls in Zouave costume, performing with rifles.[49]

The heroism of the Zouaves was secured when Ellsworth, now a personal friend of President Lincoln, became the first official casualty of the Civil War on May 24, 1861 – a scant two weeks before Menken opened with *Mazeppa* in Albany. There was no battle; the proprietor of an inn in Alexandria, Virginia, shot and killed Ellsworth when he tried to remove a Confederate flag from the roof. Ellsworth became a Union hero overnight, and "Remember Ellsworth!" endured as a popular Union battle cry.[50] In the antebellum period, actors were responsible for their own costumes, and Menken chose to capitalize on the popularity of the Zouaves by dressing Mazeppa in a lush version of their famous uniform.[51] Later versions of her Mazeppa retained the trousers, but became more ornate with jewelry and symbols of Oriental identity, such as the Islamic crescent moon. As a military play, *Mazeppa* appealed to Americans when enlistment fever was at its peak, and Menken's costume as Mazeppa on his way to battle capitalized on the heroism of a recently slain public hero, Elmer Ellsworth.

---

[48] Meredith M. Dytch, "Remember Ellsworth! Chicago's First Hero of the American Civil War," *Chicago History* 11 (Spring 1982): 17–21.

[49] Clara Morris, *Life on the Stage: My Personal Experiences and Recollections* (New York: McClure, Phillips, 1901), 20–21.

[50] Dytch, "Remember Ellsworth," 23–25.

[51] See cartes de visite of Menken in Mazeppa costume, Adah Isaacs Menken photographs, HTC, Billy Rose Theatre Collection (New York Public Library), California State Archives, and American Jewish Archives.

The war may also have influenced the way some spectators perceived the disrobing. In Menken's version of *Mazeppa*, the character is a boy until he becomes physically vulnerable to his enemy, and thus becomes a woman. Perhaps the violent scene of stripping and binding graphically illustrated fears in the hearts of the onlookers. But if so, the play also worked as a hopeful metaphor, because in the end, not only has the hero regained his masculinity but the experience has transformed him into a man. Now a man-prince, rather than a boy-servant, he returns to the scene of his humiliation, leading armed troops to vanquish his enemy (his former family) and win the ultimate symbol of manhood, the desirable woman.

One of the most salient features of *Mazeppa*, and of all of Menken's cross-dressing roles, is that it contained multiple layers of identity that went beyond her merely dressing (and undressing) as a man. In transforming from Cassimer to Mazeppa, the character went from boyhood to manhood and, in so doing, was forced to reconstruct his former enemy as his true family, and his former family as his enemy. The disconcerting image of a female Menken appearing in the evolution from boyhood to manhood served to reinforce the trauma of the act. Was a man without control over his own destiny the same as a woman? In *The French Spy*, on the other hand, Menken played a mute female character who disguises herself as a male soldier, who disguises himself as an "Arab boy," and is forcibly made female by being dressed in a harem costume and threatened with rape. The easy shifting from woman to man to boy to girl, from wife to soldier to servant to slave, created a dizzy mix of signals meant to entertain by befuddling the audience. Menken's cross-dressed heroes were by their very nature confusing, suggesting a topsy-turvy world that particularly resonated with Civil War era audiences.

Central to the spectacle of *Mazeppa*, and all of the cross-dressed roles Menken played, was the understanding that perception could be misleading, again picking up on the same source of anxiety aroused by the stories of confidence men. Americans were fairly obsessed with the concept of empirical knowledge. Science and pseudoscience, such as phrenology, insisted that the interior could be discerned from exterior evidence, yet stories of confidence men and fallen women suggested that wolves lurked about in sheep's clothing. Barnum made a fortune because of Americans' penchant for solving puzzles, and James Gordon Bennett created a newspaper empire from reporting conflicting stories that invited the audience to debate.

One of the most interesting illustrations of cross-dressing intersecting with the phenomenon of disclosure is the story of Ella Zoyara, an British trick rider who captivated American audiences in 1860. Menken must have witnessed the spectacle up close, as the hoax unraveled in New York just as she was about to enter the national spotlight with the Heenan scandal. On January 22, the *New York Sunday Mercury* reviewed the performance of the visiting equestrian troupe playing at Niblo's Garden, and noted of its star Zoyara, "Her *savoir-faire* in the domestic circle cannot excel her well bred ease in the *pedestrian saddle* . . . she is the queen of all equestriennes we can remember." Five days later the *New York Tribune* began questioning her sex, stating, "She dresses and acts with the grace of a woman, and her face has nothing masculine in its expression; it is, in fact, a most feminine and gentle face. But she has the springy agility of a man." Questions regarding Zoyara's sex were probably promoted by the troupe itself, as it soon became clear that this was a marketing device. By January 28, advertisements for the troupe included long quotes from the *Tribune*, unmasking Zoyara as a man. According to the *Tribune*, a circus proprietor had raised Zoyara as a girl to "enhance the child's attractions" as a trick rider. Zoyara supposedly "grew up in womanly graces, was constantly dressed as a girl, taught as a girl, made a sensation in the ring, was greatly admired for her beauty and grace, and became the recipient of a good many valuable presents in the shape of jewelry from her admirers." When Zoyara reached her teens, she threatened to "leave off crinoline and put on trowsers," but in the end struck a deal with the manager, who "allowed [Zoyara] the privilege of putting on male attire, except when performing in the ring."[52] In fact, Ella Zoyara was a married man named Otto Kingsley, who dressed in feminine costume for performances as a gimmick. Long before the *Tribune* broke the story, his billing had teased, "Is she a boy or a girl?"[53]

The story of Ella Zoyara vividly suggests one of the main reasons nineteenth-century Americans delighted in acts of cross-dressing and why even the most sombre cross-dressed pieces (such as Cushman's Hamlet) were innately sensational: The mental act of unmasking, or uncrossing, was central to the performance itself. This was yet another version of America's preoccupation with seeing "behind the veil," which can be found in cultural expression throughout the century, particularly in urban fiction. Menken's undressing in the famous scene of *Mazeppa* was in this sense about more than showing off her body. Seeing an uncorseted woman barely clothed and splayed suggestively on a speeding horse was certainly exciting enough, but the concepts of both masking and unmasking were integral to its appeal.

The most important and unpredictable component of theatrical cross-dressing was, of course, the audience, as Menken well knew. Theatergoers paid for cross-dressing, so they dictated its popularity. Men in their twenties continued to make up the majority of the audience, but female attendance in the theaters increased dramatically from the 1830s through the 1870s. By Menken's period, enough women apparently enjoyed her performances to create a demand for matinees. Comments on cross-dressing make it clear that the sex of the viewer was critical to the way the performer was perceived;

[52] *New York Tribune*, Jan. 27, 1860; *New York Evening Post*, Jan. 28, 1860.
[53] Laurence Senelick, "Boys and Girls Together: Subcultural Origins of Glamour Drag and Male Impersonation on the Nineteenth Century Stage," in Ferris, ed., *Crossing the Stage*, 84.

sharing the sex of the cross-dresser seems to have determined whether or not the viewer identified with the performer and performance. Men could identify with men performing caricatures of female behavior in ways that female audience members probably could not.

A diary entry from a viewer in 1835, for example, suggests that in the eyes of some Americans, the transgression lay not only in the performer but also in the audience. Benjamin Brown French commented in his diary after attending a cross-dressing performance by Madame Celeste: "I would never see a female upon the stage in male attire, could I avoid it, and it is only pardonable under circumstances where in actual life such disguise would seem to be necessary" for a "female in breeches, through play after play, and character after character, though it shocks not my delicacy, for I never carry any with me to a theatre – still it lowers the female character in my estimation, especially when I see the most respectable female audiences gazing on with much apparent satisfaction."[54] According to French, even a cross-dresser as blatantly feminine as Madame Celeste appealed to female viewers as a transgressive figure. Indeed, the gaze of those female audience members seemed to anger him more than Celeste. He concluded, "Celeste is handsome and dances elegantly." One can only imagine how he might have reacted to women enjoying the sight of an undressed Menken or, just as bad, a sword-fighting male Menken.

Clearly, Menken's success as Mazeppa held implications for the midcentury audiences that went beyond nudity, violence, danger, and transgression of gender or race. When the Count's soldiers stripped Menken and tied her to the black mare, audiences saw a comely woman in a sexually suggestive position, but may also have seen far more, as the laying bare of Menken's body exposed layers of cultural meaning. Caught up in the moment, they undoubtedly enjoyed the rush of desire and adrenaline, but the content of the play within the context of war gave *Mazeppa* particular brilliance. Although the male clothing and faux nudity was certainly a large part of its appeal, *Mazeppa's* success cannot be explained as merely the novelty of an attractive woman exposing her body.

After June 1861, Menken was able to make a substantial living because she presented a public image that most women and men found compelling, even if they would not dare assume it themselves. Part of Menken's great attraction was her novelty as an unconventional woman, yet she did not transgress social mores to the point where middle-class theaters refused to book her. Why would they? If they took apart the play, it was hard to figure out why Menken brought it so much appeal. The play itself was worn out by the time Menken took the role; after thirty years of being on the boards, many considered it a tired old horse opera by 1861. Audiences of women, men, and even children

[54] Benjamin Brown French, *Witness to the Young Republic: A Yankee's Journal* (Hanover, N.H.: University Press of New England, 1989), 58.

were accustomed to seeing cross-dressing; it was practically everywhere one looked during the war. The stunt with the horse was incredible, but stunts had also become standard theatrical fare. Orientalism, the seductive idea that an opposite culture existed to the east, already dominated nineteenth-century western culture. None of these elements was foreign to middle-class audiences, but all held an element of delicious danger. The act of undressing was a bit more salacious, but faux nudity was not unheard of in middle-class theaters, and was absolutely commonplace in the working-class world of entertainment. Menken's radical act was in combining all of these elements, creating a piece of entertainment dizzy with suggestive ambiguity, brazen in its physicality, intoxicating in its daring. *Mazeppa* with Menken as the hero was potent because it reflected so many of the desires and fears of its audiences, and it distracted them at the time they most needed distracting.

Chapter 4

Performing Menken

Mrs. Heenan's maiden name must have been Campbell, for she is the daughter of the late Dr. Josiah Campbell, of New Orleans, in which city she was born, January 1839.

New York Illustrated News, 1860

Marie was married in New-Orleans, where her first and best beloved child, Marie Rachel Adelaide de Vere Spenser [Menken] was born, December 11, 1839.

New York Times, 1868 (written 1862)

Dolores Adah Isaacs Menken ... was born in New Orleans, Louisiana, in the year of 1840, of French and Spanish parentage, of the Jewish religion. . . . Her father, of whom we can learn but that he was exiled from France for political offenses, died during [Menken's] early infancy.

London Age, 1864.

Miss Adah Isaacs Menken est née en 1841, à la Nouvelle-Orléans, de parents franco-américains appartenant à la religion israélite qu'elle a toujours aimée et chaleureusement défendue.

Notice Biographique sur Miss Adah Isaacs Menken Artiste Américaine, Paris, 1867

She was born in New Orleans in the spring of 1841. Her father, Ricardo Fiertos, a Spanish Jew, was a merchant in that city, and her mother was a native of Bordeaux.

London Daily Telegraph, 1868

Her first name was Adah McCoard. She was born in Memphis.

Galveston Bulletin, 1868

On the 15th of June, 1835, in a little village a few miles from New Orleans, a babe of the feminine gender was born ... christened Adelaide McCord. . . .

Folly's Queen, 1868[1]

From the moment Adah Isaacs Menken first caught the public's attention in 1860 as the reputed wife of John C. Heenan, reporters, fans, and friends began asking questions about her past: "Who are you?" "Where

---

[1] "Ada Isaacs Menken, the Wife of John C. Heenan," New York *Illustrated News*, March 17, 1860; "Adah Isaacs Menken: Some Notes of Her Life in Her Own Hand," (hereafter "Notes") *New York Times*, Sept. 6, 1868, p. 3, c. 2; "Adah Isaacs Menken," *London Age: Theatrical, Musical, and Sporting* (Sept. 17, 1864), clipping in Joseph Norton Ireland, Records of the New York Stage from 1750 to 1860, extended and extra-illustrated for Augustin Daly by Augustus Toedeberg (New York: T. H. Morell, 1867), vol. 3, Harvard Theatre Collection (hereafter HTC), Houghton Library, Harvard University, Cambridge, Massachusetts, TS 939.5.4; "*Notice Biographique sur Miss Adah Isaacs Menken Artiste Américaine*," Théâtre de la Gaité (Paris: Morris et Compagnie, 1867), 5; "Death of Adah Isaacs Menken," *London Daily Telegraph*, Aug. 12, 1866; "Death of Ada Menken," *Flake's Semi-Weekly, Galveston Bulletin*, Aug. 19, 1868, p. 6; "The Misfortunes of a Lawless Genius," *Folly's Queen* (n.d.), from Adah Isaacs Menken clippings files, HTC.

Menken in a sweet pose set by Napoleon Sarony in 1866. Note the naturalness of her smile, revealing dimples, the daring of her shirt open at the throat, a military style jacket echoing fashion trends of the period, and the hairbrush that signifies the privacy of the moment. The photograph is clearly meant to suggest both intimacy with the viewer and the sweetness of the "real Menken" behind the notorious image. (Harvard Theatre Collection)

do you come from?" "Who are your parents?" They wanted to put things in order, to make sense of Menken's appearance, behavior, and motivations by fitting them into already established sociocultural patterns. To understand Menken, they yearned for her biography. And since designations such as social class, ethnic background, regional origins, and religious faith usually satisfy such questions, Menken answered along those lines. But she responded creatively and provocatively by playing with social assumptions and fabricating pasts that held particular connotations in her present time and place. Her dissembling enhanced her market value. In a culture defined by opposites and pulled taut by contending forces, Menken's determination to willfully roam the spectrum captured and held her audience's attention. Her constant shifting also suggested the instability of the viewer, for the subtext of the question "Who are you?" was "Are we the same?" Menken's answers were such a complicated layering of fantasy and mundane detail that viewers found themselves in a maze of liminal categories, with boundary lines brought into question by her graceful disregard.

This chapter examines how Menken portrayed herself in published personal narratives, and reveals how her explanations, though seemingly questionable, instead demonstrate how well she understood her public. Menken creatively constructed her past at the same time that she shrewdly crafted herself into a celebrity. Again, to be a celebrity one must be relatively famous (and therefore distant) yet still convey intimacy and equality with the spectator. Menken's varied performances of identity were thus about evoking appropriate responses from the public. If we examine Menken's self-presentations in the context of the wider surrounding popular culture, it becomes clear that she drew upon formulas and conventions already established in print culture.

Menken was clearly establishing herself as a celebrity, which was still a relatively new concept in the 1850s. One of the first women labeled as such by the American media was Fanny Elssler, a Viennese dancer who titillated Americans by exposing the shape of her legs on stage when she toured from 1840 to 1842. But while her legs received attention, she became a celebrity because of rumored love affairs; it was her personal story that captivated the public.[2] Like most celebrities, Elssler could also be called a star, which at the time meant that she toured from city to city, performing with available stock companies and drawing crowds to the box office. "Stars" signed contracts with theater managers and usually earned all their money on the last night of their run, called "benefit night," when they took all the box-office earnings. Stars had drawing power; they pulled in ticket money. Celebrity was a different concept altogether; it enhanced a star's drawing power and was connected with having a public presence, but it was a distinctly different public identity. Elssler, for example, was a celebrity because the public's fascination with her went beyond her stage work; people wanted to know *her*, the person behind the performance. Elssler, and by extension Menken, was a person with whom the larger public felt they had a personal relationship. That social claim of intimacy also seemed to supersede other social categories that might have divided Elssler, a foreigner in the United States, from her American audience.[3] In the context of the emerging celebrity-fan relationship of the nineteenth century, status as an outsider appeared to add to her appeal because it made her exciting yet still accessible and excused her behavior to some degree. Her "indiscretions" could be blamed on her cultural background.

Likewise, affinity for an enigmatic Menken allowed fans to partake in her mystery. In March and April 1860, Demorest's *New York Illustrated News*

---

[2] Peter George Buckley, "To the Opera House: Culture and Society in New York City, 1820–1860," Ph.D. dissertation., State University of New York at Stony Brook, 1984, pp. 501–502.

[3] Ibid., 502.

published "Ada Isaacs Menken, the Wife of John C. Heenan," Menken's
first biographical account. The *Illustrated News*, with "illustrations on all live
subjects and a national & family newspaper in its most comprehensive sense,"
declared itself "devoted to the diffusion of the Useful and Entertaining
and Universal intelligence."[4] Crammed with small print around large steel
engravings, the *Illustrated News* published biographies of entertainers and
athletes alongside tales of mystery and romance. As a weekly tabloid, it
focused on leisure activities, such as sports and theater, before news of the war
took over its pages in 1861. It was marketed to a wide audience that clearly
included women and children as well as men and was probably intended for
the lower rungs of the middle class.

The engraving of Menken was notably unflattering, the artist having
tossed her wildly curling hair and widened her nose so that she appeared
disheveled and coarse. The heaviness of her features alluded to Menken's
identity as a notorious woman, picking up on fictional portrayals of fallen
women as large and swarthy.[5] At that point Menken was best known as
the self-proclaimed wife of John Heenan. The article itself provides a useful
demonstration of how Menken and/or the media chose to portray their
marriage. Menken is introduced as a "novelty," with the reporter adding
that "commonplace people and commonplace events are out of the fashion." Interestingly, he downplayed Menken's acting career, choosing instead
to focus on her as a poet so as to portray the marriage as "a contradiction of the laws of affinity." Pugilists and actresses did not make strange
bedfellows, but a poet and a pugilist challenged the conventional order of
high and low culture. Of Menken's many biographies, this one holds up
best to scrutiny – not because it is largely factual, but because its facts and
fictions are easily separated. In it, Menken gives specific names and events
easily verified by public records. It was Menken's first major write-up, and
she was noticeably less artful in the first of the four installments than the
last.

In this version of Menken's life, her father died when she was a child,
leaving the family in poverty. Menken's mother moved them to Memphis,
where young Adah began her lifelong association with the press by finding her unambitious brother, Augustus, employment as a paper carrier for
the *Memphis Daily Enquirer*. A few years later, the family returned to New
Orleans and the enterprising Adah found employment for her brother and
herself at the Olympic Theatre, where they played fairies for the J. S. Charles
Company. The reporter notes that Menken's childhood career ended when
her mother "recovered property of her late husband's" and no longer needed

---

[4] *Illustrated News*, March 17, 1860.
[5] Such images can be found throughout formula literature, such as westerns and city mysteries. E.g.,
see, Ned Buntline, *Mysteries and Miseries of New York* (New York: Berford, 1848); Osgood Bradbury,
The Belle of the Bowery (Boston: H. L. Williams, 1846); Mary Andrews Denison, *Edna Etheril; or, The
Boston Seamstress* (New York: Burgess, Stringer, 1847).

the extra income. The reporter declined to give dates for most events of her life, so the story is set in the past without demarcation.[6]

Compared with later biographies, Menken shared a surprising amount of factual information, including material designed to win sympathetic leniency. She mentions growing up in poverty, for example, supporting her family while still a child and traveling alone as a young girl in East Texas – adventures that suggest a life bereft of sensibility and moral teachings. The implication was that her deprived childhood might explain, if not wholly excuse, her adult lapses. Even so, it is surprising that, given her present situation, she mentioned having several husbands *before* she married Alexander Isaac Menken. Where might she have seen similar images and why might they have seemed advantageous? Present-day portrayals of nineteenth-century culture often reinforce the assumption that women experienced no advantage in transgressing conventions, despite evidence that some did so quite profitably. The commercial success of Menken, and her predecessors, such as Lola Montez, suggest that as the entertainment industry blossomed in America, it revered rebellious women as well as men. At the same time, it appears to have been important that these rebellious women all grew out of neglected girls, so that they were not reprehensible so much as misled. The idea of "neglected girls" resonated with a middle-class culture that was circulating images of "unprotected" girls and debating the causes of prostitution with a far more sympathetic eye toward the women than ever before. Unlike Montez, Menken deliberately played the opposing sides of virtue and vice, apparently out of the desire to woo a larger audience; the middle class itself was changing composition, but part of playing to that larger audience was maintaining a semblance of balance between virtue and intrigue.

Once again, Menken did not create an image, but rather put it on stage. Popular fiction forged the image of female entertainers as corruptive yet vulnerable long before Menken. Beginning in the late 1840s, cheap novels abound with images of actresses as both practiced seducers and sympathetic victims of their own talent. A remarkable number of them sound suspiciously like Menken, suggesting that she was fully aware of the convention she drew upon. Newton M. Curtis was one of many authors who churned out dozens of cheap trade novels in a year, and, like Menken, his profession compelled him to pay attention to contemporary values. In *The Matricide's Daughter: A Tale of Life in the Great Metropolis* (1847), Curtis's hero, Claude Syneham, falls in love with actress Fanny Hemans. One day he notes a flattering announcement of her upcoming performance at the Park Theatre (then the most celebrated theater in New York City) that states she is not only a great actress but also beautiful and accomplished. Fanny answers wryly, "'Yes, it is flattering indeed. The heart that dictated that paragraph,

---

[6] "*Illustrated News*, March 17, 1860.

would probably be the last to be seen publicly conversing even for a moment, with the 'most accomplished woman of the day.' Ah! Claude, ours is indeed a bitter lot." Caught up in his admiration for the theater, Claude fails to understand her implication. "'I mean,'" Fanny explains, "'it is most humiliating, to be applauded and despised by the same persons. Perhaps not despised, but scorned, and looked upon as the mere puppets of passion, worthy only the privilege of whiling away time for the rich, the proud, and ignorant." She explains that this is the principal fate of female performers and begs his protection: "'On the stage they are admired and applauded; off the stage they are shunned and neglected, except perhaps by the vile and abandoned. You must guard my honor, Claude.'"[7] Fanny remains the heroine of the tale, winning the sympathy of readers as an innately good woman placed in a horrible position by hypocritical audiences and journalists. Such heroines were precursors to the still widely celebrated "whore with a heart of gold" that has come to characterize formula westerns; like the good-hearted prostitute, the actress in these tales is forced to suffer disrespect at the hands of those who financially support her. The frequency of characters such as Fanny Hemans suggests that Americans not only could imagine the trials suffered by actresses who were both celebrated and vilified, but in fact did not have to go through the trouble, as such characters were already common in popular fiction.

Menken resembled the fictional actresses in other ways as well. Menken's friends and acquaintances would later describe Menken's character much the way Claude saw Fanny Hemans: "So bold, yet so modest; so free and unrestrained in her intercourse . . . yet so chaste in language and action, and so truthful in the affection that she did not seek to disguise."[8] She was a living version of the bewitching Therese in George Thompson's *The Mysteries of Bond Street*, described as "very beautiful, scarcely twenty-three years of age. Her form was rounded to a miracle of perfection, while her dark hair fell in beautiful ringlets down a neck as white as the purest alabaster. She was an accomplished singer, and a perfect actress in the versatile range of drama."[9] Menken resembled the beguiling heroines who bewitched men as naturally as breathing, conveniently suggesting that neither Menken nor the men she enchanted could be held entirely responsible for falling prey to such powerful passions. But Menken and her literary parallels were also subtly threatening, as their romanticized images destabilized prescriptive notions of ideal womanhood. Although historians have focused primarily on sentimental fiction, particularly, popular novels such E.D.E.N. Southworth's *St. Elmo* or Susan Warner's *Wide, Wide World*, those images of pious and

---

[7] Newton M. Curtis, *The Matricide's Daughter: A Tale of Life in the Great Metropolis* (New York: W. F. Burgess, 1847), 47.

[8] Ibid.

[9] George Thompson, *The Mysteries of Bond Street; or, The Seraglios of Upper Tendom* (New York, 1857), 50.

passive heroines were counterbalanced by a significant coterie of less proper, more compassionate protagonists of cheap fiction.

Menken increasingly fashioned herself to resemble the heroines of formula fiction as she developed the daredevil celebrity persona that would determine her professional niche. Menken's decision to use Heenan's name professionally indicated a change in her self-presentation as she moved from aspiring actress, defined by artistry, to American celebrity, measured by popularity or infamy. While on the Texas and Louisiana frontier, and later performing on the midwestern theater circuit, Menken had predominantly chosen respectable dramatic roles. Now she focused on becoming a well-known personality, performing primarily comedic, suggestive, and sensational parts. The New York press, with its ability to make as well as reflect public taste, demanded that every actor or actress develop a marketable public persona. Menken's was clearly outrageous and courageous, and she displayed a beguiling mix of innocence and experience. By the mid-1850s, it was clear that celebrities such as Menken and Heenan sold as well as those with more substantial talent.

Menken became a national celebrity in 1860 as the wife of Heenan because of the commercial rewards of exploiting scandal and the blossoming of mass media. Scandal was her most efficient means of reaching celebrity status, because it meant achieving fame while appearing to shatter the barriers fame created, exposing what the public assumed to be her private self. Then and now, a harrowing scandal highlights the humanity and vulnerability of a celebrity who is otherwise cloaked in the impenetrable glamour created by an exalted unavailability. With the scandal, she gained a certain market status that required she manage her public life to maintain popularity.

As a successful mimic, Menken operated on the assumption that identity is always performative and that identities themselves are organized and defined by context.[10] Her ability to imitate and quickly change character – sometimes playing over half a dozen characters within a one-act farce – suggests that she had a keen awareness of stereotypes and how to evoke them through telling characteristics. Her early experiences as an itinerant performer had taught her that one could efficiently suggest an identity by donning or demonstrating cultural markers already established in popular culture through the repetition of stock characters.[11] Just as she excelled at rapidly transforming into several characters on stage, Menken shifted deftly from one performance of self to another. Like a chameleon, she sought to become part of her environment, but at the same time emphasized characteristics that set her apart. It is not surprising that with her talent for

---

[10] Roy Baumeister, *Identity: Cultural Change and the Struggle for Self* (New York: Oxford University Press, 1986), 7.

[11] Erving Goffman, *Presentation of the Self in Everyday Life* (Garden City: Doubleday, 1959), 75.

role-changing and self promotion, she could perform "Menken" as a figure of constant transformation.

The biography in the *Illustrated News* reinforced Menken's identity as a mysterious woman who embraced masculine freedoms without losing femininity – a woman so far outside the realm of most people's experiences that she should be held to a different standard altogether. References to adventures on the Texas frontier, complete with Indians and Rangers, and later travels to Cuba and Mexico, marked her as an exciting woman fit for legends, not censure.[12] The reporter portrayed Menken's moral lapses as symptomatic of her disadvantaged upbringing – a story line already made popular in cheap fiction and reformist literature, and one that Menken would use frequently.[13]

One year after the *Illustrated News* story, and shortly before she became a major attraction with *Mazeppa*, Menken compiled biographical notes for Thomas Allston Brown, a theater critic who later published an enormous two-volume set of biographical sketches of actors, called *History of the American Stage*. Menken happily responded to Brown's request for her life story, assuring him that "all contained in the notes is strictly *true*, of course I have left out a great many of my adventures in Cuba and Texas, but as it is I fear you will find more matter than you can work up for that sketch."[14] According to the biographical sketch later written by Brown, she told him that she was born in a small town outside New Orleans on June 15, 1835. She repeated the earlier story that her father had died when she was seven years old, in 1842, leaving destitute her mother, brother, sister, and self. Out of desperation, Menken's mother found her daughters positions at the New Orleans Opera House. He also asserted that Menken was not born Jewish, but embraced the Jewish faith in her adult life.[15]

Brown's biographical sketch of Menken became the one most widely accepted in the nineteenth century, with a few adjustments here and there. It also formed the basis of the introduction in Menken's book of poetry, *Infelicia*, from 1888 to 1902. However, the introduction to *Infelicia* added three pieces of information that Menken also commonly claimed: that her maiden name was Adelaide McCord, that her father James McCord had been a New Orleans merchant, and that she and her sister used the "Theodore Sisters" as their stage name.[16] Most of Menken's American friends and fans would later assert that her "true name" was "Ada McCord."

Menken clearly understood that she created "Menken" as a public figure, but she was also aware that the public did not understand that she was

[12] *Illustrated News*, March 17, 24, 31, and April 14, 1860.

[13] *Illustrated News*, March 31, 1860.

[14] Letter from AIM to Colonel [Thomas Allston] Brown, May 2, 1861, Adah Isaacs Menken Correspondance in ALS file [hereafter AIM ALS], HTC.

[15] Thomas Allston Brown, *History of the American Stage* (New York: Benjamin Blom, 1969), 243–244.

[16] "Introduction" to *Infelicia* (Philadelphia: J. B. Lippincott, 1902), iii–iv.

performing an identity offstage, as a person, poet, and actress. The Romantic movement of the early nineteenth century had taught readers to see poetry as self-expressive, rather than as a literary form used by writers to elicit particular responses. Readers responded to the works of Byron, to cite the clearest example, because he conveyed emotional parity with his readers, and his public image suggested that his poetic protagonists were shadows of himself.[17] Menken's poetry was similarly emotional, and she understood that her audience took her confessional tone and offstage performances as expressions of her "real self." But Menken made little effort to actually present a consistent personal self. As long as Menken moved from place to place, and no one read old newspapers, she did not have to be the same person that she had been last year or last week.

Menken also got caught in something that many other public figures had begun to experience as well: As the media blossomed and communication systems snaked out across even the most remote country, a performer's different personae would eventually catch up with each other. We all understand that people create different personae to speak to different audiences, but the development of the media changed the game. If one stayed out of the media, one could change one's self-performance to fit one's environment and appeal to more audiences, but paradoxically, the only way to national fame was through the media, which by its very nature made those performances permanent. Individual portrayals became fixed on the printed page, but communication and transportation meant that those pages could be distributed across the nation. When Menken was portraying herself as Deborah in Cincinnati in 1858, she could be relatively confident that her playful verse of Liberty, Texas, would not surface to challenge that image. By 1861, fame and improved transportation and communication systems changed all of that; Menken's transformations began to follow her. And as commercial process commodified culture and language, objects and images were removed from their original contexts, to become spectacles open for definition.[18] Until she gained entrance to the national public stage, Menken had made decisions suited to her local and situation; with a national identity, she had to make decisions that would also serve her in the eyes an audience far removed from her immediate context. With Menken's experiences we can see how the publicity game changed with the evolution of communication systems.

As a celebrity, Menken performed a private life for public consumption, even as she published essays, such as "The Real and the Ideal," and several poems, such as "Images of Beauty," that cautioned the public to remember that projected images often hid unromantic truths. Menken used "informal

---

[17] Andrew Elfenbein, *Byron and the Victorians* (New York: Cambridge University Press, 1995), 4, 47–48.

[18] Jonathan Rutherford, "A Place Called Home Identity and the Cultural Politics of Difference," in *Identity: Community, Culture, Difference*, ed. Rutherford (London: Lawrence and Wishart, 1990), 11.

or backstage" language to suggest that what her readers saw was her "real, sincere and honest" self, and her responses were "an unintentional product" of her unself-conscious response to her situation.[19] Despite the public nature of her performance, the intimacy of language created the effect of her exposing or revealing a nonpublic self. By constantly sharing stories of her childhood, she suggested that her personal past was open for viewing. Yet she shaped those stories for the public she addressed at the time, and as she became a frequent fixture in the press, journalists and readers began to notice that the facts of her story frequently changed. It took a while for the public to notice, for example, that Menken consistently changed her father's name, ethnicity, and occupation, describing him as Jewish, Irish, Spanish, English, and possibly mulatto. Menken's stories were not about Menken; they were about portraying a woman her audience would find compelling, whether that meant projecting a provocative or a pathetic image.

Menken gave many different versions of her life to publicists and journalists, but we have evidence of her crafting only three of those stories directly: the interview for the *New-York Illustrated News*, the McCord story she sent to Thomas Alston Brown, and a highly colored memoir she wrote over several years. In 1862 she began writing the story of her girlhood as Marie Rachel Adelaide de Vere Spenser, daughter of a Louisiana planter named Richard Spenser and a French woman, Marie Josephine de Vere Laliette, and finally mailed it to Gus Daly three years later.[20] Daly, a longtime supporter of Menken and a celebrated playwright by 1865, published the revised "Adah Isaacs Menken: Some Notes of Her Life in Her Own Hand " in the *New York Times* less than a month after her death, in 1868. He prefaced them by saying that when she wrote this autobiography, Menken was "enjoying the first rosy flush of notoriety, and... everybody was asking 'Who were you *before*?' The reckless girl was not averse to paying the penalty and gratifying this curiosity, but with a shrewd sense of justice, she was determined the public should pay for this knowledge." In other words, Menken decided to work up a good tale. Daly stresses that Menken designed her autobiography for the public and that its only reliable element is Menken's "honest revelation of her own feelings." He framed "Notes" with his own biography of Menken, insisting that her name was Adelaide McCord and that she was not Jewish.[21]

"Notes" stands out because it is the only biography in which Menken claimed a privileged childhood. She describes her girlhood self as a spoiled child who grew up as the ward of a European uncle, in "mixed society, all rather fast."[22] Again, whatever Menken hoped to achieve with this portrayal

---

[19] Goffman, *Presentation of Self*, 70, 128.

[20] In a letter to Augustus Daly, Menken indicates that she was just beginning to write the notes; AIM to Daly, July 18, 1862, AIM ALS HTC. Daly claims she began writing them in 1862; Daly, "Introductory" to "Notes."

[21] "Notes."   [22] Ibid.

of her past, the public did not see this autobiography until after her death in 1868 – and when they did, Daly stole her thunder by suggesting that the story should be read as indicative of Menken's imagination. Consequently, the Spenser story, one of Menken's most elaborate attempts at autobiography, did not play much of a role in shaping the Menken image. The story may indicate the adult Menken's desire to elevate her present class status while still explaining her unconventional sense of propriety. Perhaps she hoped to escape the hardship of her childhood by constructing a past that denied it. However, every other biography portrays her family as impoverished by her father's death.

Ed James, a British attorney who practiced in New York as well as in England and considered Menken a close personal friend, further perpetuated the story that Adah Isaacs Menken had been born Ada McCord in Milneburg, a small town outside of New Orleans that had since conveniently disappeared. James gathered most of his information through years of correspondence with Menken. However, it is important to understand what James chose to ignore: Menken told her closest friends and peers the same hyperbolic stories that she told the public. In personal letters, Menken frequently declared that she was about to reveal "her true self," but the truths she told soon thereafter appeared in her publicity. Apparently, Menken used her friends as sounding boards for the next creative spin on her life. In his biography, James acknowledges Menken's many paternal claims, but, like Daly, he insists that she grew up Christian. He adds that her sister's name was Josephine, her father died in 1842, and her mother "subsequently married J. C. Campbell, an army surgeon." He states that the death of their stepfather in 1855 forced the two sisters to earn money as dancers for the French Opera House in New Orleans. For the most part, his story works in tandem with the introduction to *Infelicia*. Yet despite the many personal letters documenting his close friendship with Menken, we cannot accept James's story as factual. For one thing, he uses several dates and events that newspapers and public records easily refute, such as asserting that Adah Theodore performed in New Orleans in 1858 *before* marrying Alexander Isaac Menken in 1859.[23] Records show that Adah married Alexander in 1856 and did not perform as Mrs. A. I. Menken until late in 1858.[24]

The Adelaide McCord story gained support in Texas after Menken's death, when one of Menken's contemporaries, Thomas Ochiltree, claimed he had grown up with her in Nacogdoches, a town just west of the Louisiana border. An absolute dearth of McCords living in nineteenth-century Nacogdoches easily refutes Ochiltree's story; it is the persistence

[23] Ed James, *Biography of Adah Isaacs Menken* (New York: Ed James, 1869), 3.
[24] Photocopy of marriage certificate, Nicholas Kovach Collection, University of Minnesota, Minneapolis (hereafter Kovach).

of the Texas biography makes it intriguing.[25] Despite a complete lack evidence, the story of her girlhood in Texas has found a remarkable number of willing pens, ears, and tongues. In the Texas version of Menken's biography, Adelaide McCord grew up with her "illiterate and unenterprising father and her hauntingly beautiful, educated mother in a log cabin."[26] Thus in Texas lore, at least, Menken joined an illustrious cohort of legendary American heroes who transcended the modesty of their log cabin origins.

During her initial flush as a London star in 1865, Menken changed the larger patterns of her life story again, confessing to friends and reporters that she was really Dolores Adios Los Fiertes, daughter of a Spanish Jew. She publicized this identity until her death, three years later, and even signed personal letters "Dolores" or "Dolo."[27] It was the wide acceptance of this story in Europe that resulted in Père-Lachaise cemetery originally interring her body under the name Dolores Los Fantos Barkley (the latter being her latest married name).[28] It is possible that Dolores was a name from her past; she told Newell as early as 1862, "My father called me Dolores, after his mother; but, in the course of time, and because I had spirit and soul enough to work for my mother, the proud relatives of my father refused to own me. I would no longer be called Dolores. Adah is indeed my name."[29] In the second half of "Adah Isaacs Menken: Some Notes of Her Life in Her Own Hand," published by Daly, Menken refers to herself in the third person as alternately Dolores or Adah.[30] American scholars and biographers tend to shrug off the Dolores identity without pausing, probably because it came at the end of a long line of biographical claims. However, many of Menken's friends abroad thought of her as Dolores. Although she continued to bill herself as Adah Isaacs Menken, one could say that when Menken went to Europe her private self became Dolores. They began to serve as opposite sides of a coin: Adah Isaacs Menken was gregarious and sensational while Dolores was intellectual and melancholic.

Whether she called her father McCord, Theodore, or Los Fuertes, Menken's focus on her paternity implies that when Americans asked who she was, she saw the answer as laying principally in the identity of her father. She was ostensibly trying to satisfy a nineteenth-century cultural

[25] Lucille Fain, series of articles in *Redland Herald*, the Sunday supplement to *the Sentinel of Nacogdoches*, May–July 1981.

[26] Frances Edward Abernathy, *Legendary Ladies of Texas* (Dallas: E-Heart Press, 1981), 86.

[27] Allen F. Lesser, *Enchanting Rebel: The Secret of Adah Isaacs Menken* (New York: Beechurst Press, 1947), 246–247; AIM to Gus Daly, n.d., AIM ALS HTC; AIM to Ed James, Aug. 15, 1865, AIM ALS HTC; there are several more letters during this period signed "Dolores."

[28] Certificate of burial, photocopy in Kovach.

[29] AIM to Newell, quoted in Newell, "Adah Isaacs Menken," publication unknown, pasted into "Biography of Adah Isaacs Menken. Extra Illustrated," Harris Rare Books, 76-M545x, Brown University Library, Providence, Rhode Island.

[30] "Notes."

anxiety – the need to identify strangers – which, of course, her changing answers served only to reinforce. Urban and industrial growth had left many Americans with a deep-seated fear of the power of "strangers" to mislead them. Without the means of knowing a person's past, a listener would have to rely on his or her own judgment.[31] Actually, when Menken first began making her claims in 1860, her mother was probably still alive in New Orleans; had a reporter or fan *really* wanted to know Menken's past, they could have hired someone in New Orleans to investigate the matter. Perhaps significantly, Menken did not introduce the subject of her mother until her mother's death, when she published a poetic tribute in the *New York Sunday Mercury*.

The mid-nineteenth century was an age of puffery, and Menken blatantly catered to her public. They wanted entertainment and she responded by freely mixing details about her parents with outlandish tales of her girlhood. She teased the public, charming and beguiling her audience with stories that invited them to dream with her and leave truth for another time. The construction of her most fanciful tales seemed to come from a child's imagination, as if she rendered her youthful daydreams into autobiography. Tales of her triumph as a ballerina in the glittering city of Havana echo tales of triumph by other female entertainers.[32] Her supposed adventures on the "wild frontier" of Texas and Mexico seem straight out of one of the inexpensive formula novels so popular since the 1830s.[33] Stories of her genius were equally hyperbolic; Menken frequently portrayed herself as a child prodigy who spoke several languages and translated the *Iliad* into English when she was less than twelve. Such overblown claims demand that they be recognized as creative fiction, yet many people went on to retell and reprint them as fact. The public seemed to accept (perhaps a subconscious level) that Menken was public property, and thus open to their projections and fabrications. Just as Davy Crockett went from a colorfully dressed senator to a backcountry legend, and riverboat driver Mike Fink grew an alligator tale, the adult Menken became ever smarter and richer, and her childhood more exciting. Menken produced humbug and her public responded by adding a bit of their own.

---

[31] Karen Halttunen, *Confidence Men and Painted Women: A Study of Middle-Class Culture in America, 1830–1870* (New Haven: Yale University Press, 1982), xv.

[32] Triumph in Havana was a popular theme because it was a major stop on the entertainment circuit in the early antebellum period, particularly for opera troupes. One can find examples throughout papers such as the New York *Illustrated News* and the New Orleans *Daily Delta*, and also in biographical sketches included in Brown, *History of the American Stage*. There is no credible evidence that Menken ever performed in Havana, but there are odd conflicts to the story. See Wolf Mankowitz, *Mazeppa: The Lives, Loves and Legends of Adah Isaacs Menken* (New York: Stein and Day, 1982), 31–33; Gregory Eiselien, ed., *Infelicia and Other Writings* (Peterborough, Ontario: Broadview Literary Press, 2002), 18.

[33] See Henry Nash Smith, *Virgin Land: The American West as Myth and Symbol* (Cambridge: Harvard University Press, 1973).

From Menken's first biography, in the 1860 *Illustrated News*, she cast herself as the prototypical American hero (not heroine).[34] In it, she assumes heroic identity cautiously, entering the story in girlish form and slowly gaining masculine attributes. She first presents herself as a gifted young dancer traveling with a troupe through Mexico. At this point, she is the quintessential romantic heroine: young and alone, vulnerable to corruption. She describes her triumphant reign at the Tacon Theatre in Havana, before a "respectable and wealthy old Cuban offered her his fatherly protection." Obviously in need of parental guidance, she accepted and "became his adopted child." The old man soon died, leaving her little money but "large estates in Texas."[35] In other words, Menken won the wealth and security that the heroine usually wins by the end of the story but without entering marriage or having sex – without taking the nineteenth-century woman's most accessible routes to money and power. Nor could she claim her inheritance passively, but by necessity had to push on to Texas, a place most northeastern Americans saw as lawless and synonymous with danger.

Then the story turns and Menken's character adopts a few male prerogatives, such as traveling unchaperoned with her male slave, Lorenzo, and hunting for sport. There is something provocative about the image of a lovely, young (and therefore vulnerable) Menken traveling unchaperoned with the romantically named male slave. The very image of the fragile Menken and manly Lorenzo suggests a dangerously seductive intimacy between master and slave. Oddly enough, in Menken's story, the image leads not to her becoming more distant and ladylike, but evolving into a young man herself. Once in Texas she says she bought horses and hounds "and scarcely a day passed but she bore home some trophies of the chase." She also formed friendships with "several Mexican girls . . . living in the neighborhood, and to two of them Adah became ardently attached." The idea that Menken, the hunter, went down into the village and formed an attachment with two Mexican girls sounds suspiciously like a romantic tale of a feudal lord – it becomes difficult to remember that in this case the *siegneur* is a woman and she is presumably not exploiting the girls sexually.[36]

The duality of Menken's gender increases as the story progresses, until she is captured by Indians and returns briefly to female identity. In this version of the story, she and the village girls go "camping and hunting" and stop for a snack of *"pate de fois gras."* "While they were seated on the ground, munching and swallowing the dainty meal, and wiping their pretty little mouths with embroidered napkins" a shot whistled through the thicket and

---

[34] Nina Baym, *Feminism and American Literary History: Essays* (Rutgers: Rutgers University Press, 1992).

[35] *Illustrated News*, March 17, 1860. Mankowitz researched Menken's presence in Texas, Cuba, and Mexico but could not find evidence of her under any of her known names until she shows up as in Galveston, Texas, as Ada Theodore married to W. H. Kneass in February 1855; Mankowitz, *Mazeppa*, 331–33.

[36] *Illustrated News*, March 17, 1860.

"a party of Indians" entered the clearing and "advanced toward the *pate de fois gras.*" While attempting to save her horses (not her friends), Menken is captured by the chief who decides to take her as another "squaw." For a short time, Menken is once again vulnerable, and fights back with the spitting fury of a conventional heroine. One of the chief's wives objects to his plan to marry Menken, demonstrating the innate morality of her sex. She protects Menken from the chief's advances – deferring Menken's loss of virginity once again. Menken lives with the Indians for another week before being rescued by the Texas Rangers. Oddly enough, at the Rangers' headquarters she is given "a suit of boy's clothes" so that she can "roam about at will." She becomes "like a little brother to the old General" and learns equestrian arts.[37]

In 1868 George Barclay printed another version of the Indian story, supposedly dictated by Menken to Barclay's friend, William Wallace, with whom Menken may have been acquainted in Paris. This version of the story suggests the importance of exoticism in Menken's appeal as she embraces emotional affinity with a Native American woman who serves as a parallel to herself. This time Menken called herself Bertha Theodore and said that she was actually hunting with a party of ladies and gentlemen when the Indians attacked and carried her off. The heart of the story is again female unity as a bulwark against male aggression, but this more romantic version centers not on Menken but on a Native American named Laulerack, a young woman without "refined beauty" but possessing a "grand" mien. Menken instantly forms a strong attachment to her and introduces herself to Laulerack by saying, "[A]lthough I have seen you but once before, I already love you." To which Laulerack replies, "My white sister has my pity." Menken turns this apparent rejection to her favor, paraphrasing a line from Shakespeare's *As You Like It*: "[P]ity in a woman . . . amounts to, or soon turns to love."[38] Shortly later, Laulerack agrees that yes, she loves Menken in return. This odd little dance of words places Menken in the role of the romantic aggressor and casts Laulerack as the accepting female.

Many historians have argued that nineteenth-century Americans celebrated deeply felt affection toward the same sex during Menken's time; sometimes these feelings found expression in sexual passion, and sometimes they did not.[39] Whether or not Menken meant to cast herself as the lover of Laulerack, she gave herself the masculine role in the romantic equation. At the end of the story, Laulerack sacrifices herself to save Menken's life, like Pocahontas to Menken's John Smith. Thus Laulerack becomes the martyr,

---

[37] Ibid., March 24, 1860.

[38] George Lippard Barclay, *The Life and Remarkable Career of Adah Isaacs Menken, the Celebrated Actress* (Philadelphia: Barclay, 1868), 23.

[39] Carroll Smith-Rosenberg, "The Female World of Love and Ritual," *Disorderly Conduct: Visions of Gender in America* (New York: Knopf, 1985); David Reynolds, *Walt Whitman's America: A Cultural Biography* (New York: Vintage Books, 1996), 198–199.

typically the only role available to the heroine, and Menken plays the griev-ing lover. When Laulerack gasps that she is dying from the bullet of a Texas Ranger, Menken attempts to quiet her: "You will get well and then we will never leave each other."[40] In this version of the story Menken is heroic, but her image is complicated: She enters as a sophisticated lady, the member of a hunting party, but emerges as a grieving "sister" who sounds more like a lover. Menken went on to write a poem entitled "Laulerack" that ends on a somber note of unrequited love: "Too late we met, the burning brain,/The aching heart alone can tell,/How filled our souls of death and pain,/When came the last sad word, *Farewell!*"[41] Menken favored the poem enough to publish it in 1860 as "A Memory," and included it in *Infelicia*. Laulerack may or may not have existed, but her image held a powerful appeal for Menken.

The story of Laulerack demonstrates the importance of exoticism in Menken's celebrity. Readers of Menken's story would have recognized Laulerack as a familiar figure who appeared in many forms of popular cul-ture, usually as romantic foil to white heroines. White and Native American women can be found paired in many stories and paintings set in the western frontier. In popular novels such as Osgood Bradbury's *Therese; – or – the Iroquois Maiden. A Tale of New York City and of Forest Life* (1852) and stage pro-ductions such as J. B. Buckstone's *Green Bushes* (1844), the Native American woman embodied feminine nobility in its natural form, reinforcing popular images of women as inherently nurturing and moral.[42] In James Fenimore Cooper's *The Deerslayer*, published in 1841, a white woman consumed by religion, Hetty, becomes the soul sister of Hist, an Indian maiden of the same age. In 1857 Thompkins H. Matteson painted *The Meeting of Hetty and Hist*, emphasizing the sisterly relationship of the two women by paint-ing them with similar faces and figures but showing their difference with the dark skin and clothing of Hist contrasting against the light coloring of Hetty. Both women resemble madonnas or saints in their peaceful pose of loving friendship.[43] One can only imagine the impact such a compelling image might have had on the public, and therefore why Menken would see it as useful. Even if Menken missed Cooper's immensely popular book and Matteson's painting, she could scarcely have ignored the plethora of captivity narratives produced in the eighteenth and nineteenth centuries. The story of Pocahontas saving John Smith, for example, particularly resonated with the nineteenth-century American public. John Brougham's play *Pocahontas*,

---

[40] Barclay, *Life and Remarkable Career*, 28.

[41] Ibid., 51. Menken revised "Laulerack" and published it as "A Memory" in the *New York Sunday Mercury*, June 24, 1860. She included another slight revision of "A Memory" in *Infelicia*.

[42] Osgood Bradbury, *Therese, the Iroquois Maiden: A Tale of City and of Forest Life* (New York: Samuel French, 1852); J. B. Buckstone, *Green Bushes* (New York: 1844).

[43] William H. Truettner, ed., *The West as America: Reinterpreting Images of the Frontier, 1820–1920* (Washington: Smithsonian Institute, 1991), 180–181.

one of the greatest theatrical successes of the 1860s, was in production at rival theaters several times during Menken's early career.[44] Throughout the nineteenth century, white artists and writers created and honed images of the Native American, and thus Menken's depiction of the affinity she shared with Laulerack emerged from a well-developed popular genre. There is no record that Menken ever claimed Native American heritage, or even implied it, but she played with the idea of a spiritual sisterhood between Native American and Euro-American women and the exoticism of Laulerack colored Menken.

And yet, within this story, Menken also emphasized an white identity, thereby marking herself as respectable. To be exotic was to be interesting, but outside good society; to be white was to be accepted, but not necessarily interesting. With Laulerack, Menken found a way to be both white (respectable) and a friend to the Indians (exotic). One of the most interesting aspects to the Laulerack story is how Menken used the tale to play up her own whiteness, something she also emphasized in several other first-person poems, such as "Battle of the Stars," "Myself," and "Drifts That Bar My Door." Like the poem about Laulerack, Menken created personal settings for these poems, suggesting that they were a sincere expression of her innerself. Thus, it is all the more striking that Menken focuses her description upon her own white bosom, golden hair, and blue eyes – perhaps because Menken herself was racially indefinite, with dark eyes, curls, and soft features suggesting a New World mélange of ancestors.

Menken's representation of herself as fair is an interesting departure from her other, often more well-known claims to marginal identities. It certainly leads directly to two ethnic identities that contemporary scholars find most compelling: Menken as Jewish or as a free woman of color from New Orleans.[45] Menken claimed to be Jewish yet also created stories emphasizing her whiteness. After she died, rumors surfaced into "biographies" suggesting that she was actually a free woman of color. Menken's growing determination to emphasize her whiteness and even create an Anglo identity in the "Notes" suggest that she had a need to destabilize the exotic identity she had cultivated. Did she do this only to increase her mystery or did she have something to hide? Was she "passing" as white or Jewish? Or was "passing" itself the problem? Perhaps she did not know her own ancestry, in which case, no matter what definition she chose to highlight, she was passing in some way. Perhaps her identity was mixed – a Jewish father and Christian mother, a black father and white mother, an unknown father and a known

---

[44] Rayna Green, "Pocahontas Perplex: The Image of Indian Women in American Culture," *Massachusetts Reviewed* 16 (Autumn 1975): 698–714.

[45] No one has suggested the possibility of Menken being both, although the New Orleans community of Free People of Color did produce at least one influential Jewish philanthropist. See Rudolph Desdunes, *Our People and Our History*, trans. Dorothy Olga McCants (Baton Rouge: Louisiana State University Press, 1973).

mother – and it all came down to which side she chose to highlight. In any case, Menken began to cultivate a white past and identity alongside a marginalized ethnic one.

In the 1850s, Americans were sitting on a powder keg and the need to maintain control, or repress, promoted a simultaneous need to express. Certainly, within the imagined world, to work from the margins is to be a rebel – to challenge conventional social and cultural hierarchies simply by being. In the binary culture of antebellum America, those at the center projected upon the margins all that they saw as opposite, so that, in effect, the marginal world came to mirror and represent what was deeply familiar to the center, but projected outside itself. Those at the margins were, in many ways, disenfranchised, but surviving outside traditional avenues to power also meant that the margins could function as a site of resistance. Asserting the existence of the margins threatened to expose the cultural structures of knowledge that made up the subjectivities, discourses, and institutions of the larger middle-class culture.[46] As long as Menken remained both an outsider within her environment yet paradoxically a member based on other performed characteristics, her claims to marginality added to her allure as a figure of resistance without diminishing her cultural power.

As discussed in the first chapter, Menken first began claiming Jewish heritage while residing with her husband's Jewish family in Cincinnati, and kept that identity long after she left Ohio. Responding indignantly to the first installment of the *Illustrated News* biography in 1860, Menken protested that the reporter had "taken several liberties with his knowledge of the facts," and his greatest offense was suggesting that she merely "embraced" Judaism. She used her practice of Judaism to claim some point of stability, asserting, "I was born in that faith, and have adhered to it through all my erratic career."[47] From that point on, newspapers identify Menken as Jewish, but her American friends uniformly denied her Jewish identity long after her death. Of course, their rejection of her Jewish identity may have had more to do with their own Christian limits than personal knowledge; at a time when Protestant culture overwhelmingly defined American identity, many Americans probably could not conceive of a celebrity having an identity so unlike their own.[48] Oddly, in private correspondence, Menken herself undermined her claim to Judaism in 1861: "[M]y religion is the Great and Almighty God, creator of all in Heaven and Earth. What do you believe in more or less than that? The forms and dogmas of no church cling to me. . . ."[49]

---

[46] Rutherford, ed., *Identity*, 11–22.

[47] A. I. M. Heenan to the editor, *Illustrated News*, March 24, 1860.

[48] There were a few Jewish performers (not celebrities) in the 1850s and 1860s, most notably, pianist Louis Gottschalk and actress Rose Eytinge, but none claimed Jewish identity as insistently as Menken.

[49] Newell, "Adah Isaacs Menken."

In any case, public claims of Jewish identity could have worked to Menken's advantage even after she left the Reform Jewish community of Cincinnati, because of both images in popular culture and misunderstanding among non-Jews. While the stereotype of the nasty, greedy old Jewish man, with his hooked nose and thick Germanic accent, shows up often in antebellum children's stories and popular fiction, the more rarely seen Jewish women are portrayed as beautiful and gifted.[50] Indeed, most are tragic heroines who fall victim to male duplicity and prove their own innate morality. Meanwhile, nonfiction portrayals of Jewish women ignored their presence in North America and placed them in the Bible Lands, as otherworldly women who dress similarly to their men.[51] Just as the young, white, Protestant heroine in *Hebrew Customs* (1839) excuses the eastern custom of women wearing "jewels in their noses" because of cultural differences, Menken's claims to Judaism probably meant that society granted her slightly more freedom – at least until her success made her appear to be a real threat to morality in the mid-1860s.[52]

Clearly, in popular culture, Jewish women were not seen as the gendered equals of Jewish men, but rather as victims of their culture or as virtuous women misguided by respect for male relatives. So to claim to be a Jewish woman was to adopt a rather ambiguous identity, one that made Menken's actions questionable but difficult to condemn outright. And it was also an identity that explained Menken's dark coloring; although Ashkenazi Jews are often quite fair, the Jew of stereotype had dark hair and eyes like Menken.

Menken's emphasis on whiteness does speak to the subject of mid-nineteenth-century constructions of color. Just as we can say that race and gender are culturally constructed, color is also constructed, and Menken clearly played with that idea. In a chapter on her self-presentations, it is important to emphasize that we have no evidence of Menken *ever* claiming African ancestry. And yet with August Theodore as a possible father and all Menken's contortions over ethnicity and color, the smoke on the horizon suggests that a fire burned somewhere. But what kind of fire? In the decade before the Civil War, Americans nationwide began expressing a preoccupation with color – especially the idea that one could look white and be black. It was the confidence game all over again: Was the stranger what he or she appeared to be? Could one trust one's own judgment? This concern came through in dozens of stories of tragic quadroon girls, born

---

[50] This figure appears frequently in many genres. One of the most offensive examples I found was a children's story, called "The Jew in the Bush," in *Bo-Peep Story Books* (New York: Leavitt & Allen, 1852).

[51] Two good examples of this type may be found at the American Antiquarian Society: *Hebrew Customs; or, The Missionary's Return* (Philadelphia: Sunday-School Union, 1839); John W. Nevins, *A Summary of Biblical Antiquities: Compiled for the Use of Sunday School Teachers, and for the Benefit of Families* (Philadelphia: Sunday-School Union, 1829).

[52] *Hebrew Customs*, 14–15.

supposedly white to wealthy planters, and cast into slavery upon the deaths of their fathers. But it was an older story in places like Menken's hometown of New Orleans, where constructions of color versus ethnic identity created a hierarchical social scaffolding so complex that outsiders could seldom sort it out. Playing with constructions of color spoke to a current preoccupation with deep and tangled roots.

Menken's play on coloring can most clearly be seen in the "Notes," in which she commented on her maternal ancestry for the first and only time. She portrayed her mother as one of two beautiful twin sisters, "one a delicate blond, the other a Spanish-looking brunette," who had exactly the same name: Marie Josephine Rachel de Vere de Laliette. Not far into the story, the dark twin dies in a boating accident, causing the fair one to nearly die of grief before meeting Richard Irving Spencer, "a young American student," and giving birth to Menken, or "Marie Rachel Adelaide de Vere Spenser" as she was originally named. The story implies that Menken's dark coloring could be traced to her mother's sister, while asserting that her own parents were fair.[53]

Menken's preoccupation with fairness and darkness is significant in light of posthumous (and unproven) accounts that Menken believed herself to be the daughter of a free man of color.[54] If, in fact, Menken believed that she was legally black, the symbolism of the twin sisters and Laulerack suggests that Menken strove to hide any taint of darker blood and promote her own whiteness. The story of Menken's remarkably blond mother having a dark *twin* sister disposed of the notion of a quadroon mother at the same time that it suggested a white paternal heritage. Likewise, the character of Laulerack served to emphasize Menken's whiteness. Laulerack repeatedly calls Menken "white" or "fair," and like Hetty in Matteson's painting, Menken glows brighter against the shadowy backdrop.

Barclay's 1868 biography probably articulated speculation already alive in public culture. In the eyes of many, Menken's determination to keep her past mysterious suggested that she had something to hide. She performed lowbrow theater and openly claimed several marriages; what else was left to disclose but shameful origins? Besides evoking sympathy, the preponderance of tragic quadroon heroines had also informed the northeastern public that black women might appear white, and thus could mingle among other whites unbeknownst to them. Other southern women of mystery, such as Arabella Huntington, the second wife of mid-nineteenth-century railroad tycoon Collis P. Huntington, faced similar speculation about their racial origins.[55] By claiming New Orleans as her birthplace, Menken would

[53] "Notes."

[54] John S. Kendall, "'The World's Delight': The Story of Adah Isaacs Menken," *Louisiana Historical Quarterly* 21 (July 1938): 850–52; Arna Bontemps and Jack Conroy, *They Seek a City* (Garden City, N.Y.: Doubleday, Doran, 1945), 98; Barclay, *Life and Remarkable Career*, 25; Mankowitz, *Mazeppa*, 33.

[55] Files on Arabella Huntington, Mariner's Museum, Newport News, Virginia.

have added to grapevine conversations that she was passing as white on the American stage. The racially ambiguous New Orleans area had long appalled and fascinated Anglo-Americans. At least as early as the 1830s, Americans began suggesting that the French-speaking Louisiana Creoles, a population to which Menken sometimes claimed membership, were in fact partially African.[56] The fact that no one actually wrote of Menken as being black until after her death does not refute the notion that Americans may have speculated about her racial identity during her lifetime.

Since white Americans commonly believed that African American women were innately promiscuous, Menken's racial identity might have affected perceptions of her performance of *Mazeppa*. Would the rumor that Menken passed have undermined the force of her sexually charged act by suggesting that she was not transgressing norms but doing what came "naturally"? Perhaps, but such notions could also have freed the audience to enjoy her display since, in their minds, she no longer devalued white womanhood.

An 1868 article from the rather salacious *Boston Illustrated News* suggests that even if Menken was not seen as black, her sexually suggestive performance put her in the same category as a true quadroon.[57] In "A Dusky Beauty – Menken Outstripped," the writer begins with a statement already well disproven by history: "[B]eauty beneath a dusky skin is seldom found of sufficient merit to absolutely fascinate a man of Caucasian blood." However, he adds, "one of the leading women of the demi-monde in Paris is a beautiful quadroon girl from Savannah. . . . Although she undoubtedly has African blood in her veins, she is as lovely as a full-blooded Spanish girl; and has a form which is as luscious as ever sculptor dreamed of for a Venus." Menken, of course, also looked stereotypically Spanish and was also frequently compared with Venus. But the true blow came at the end of the article, when the writer suggested a comparison between Menken and the quadroon girl, cattily remarking: "It is said that at the private theatre of the Duke de P – , she won a bet by out-vieing and out-stripping la Menken in *Mazeppa*; and it is whispered by those who were present, that her personal beauty is as far superior to Menken as were her dash and abandon."[58]

Menken's adoption of exotic and ill-defined minority identities suggest a fluidity of ethnic identity that paralleled that of class and gender. As with those other social categories, many Americans worked hard to

---

[56] Virginia R. Domìnguez, *White by Definition: Social Classification in Creole Louisiana* (New Jersey: Rutgers University Press, 1986), 140; Grace King, *New Orleans: The Place and the People* (New York: Negro Universities Press, 1968), 273–282.

[57] Outside of cities with viable free colored communities, Americans used the terms "quadroon" and "octoroon" interchangeably to indicate a person who looked white but was legally black. In southern ports such as Charleston and New Orleans, "octoroon" meant having one black great-grandparent, and "quadroon" one black grandparent.

[58] "A Dusky Beauty – Menken Outstripped," Boston *Illustrated News*, July 14, 1868, p. 11, c. 1.

The poet Menken, taken by Napoleon Sarony in 1866. The photograph depicts the intellectual Menken who publishes poetry and is friends with great writers. It gives the illusion of privacy, suggesting that the viewer is in a privileged position of intimacy. (Harvard Theatre Collection)

establish stable definitions and parameters in print, but they worked against a larger culture cut free from its moorings by the upheaval of war and its aftermath. Regardless of the facts behind Menken's presentations of biography and self, the images she chose reveal complex cultural patterns. As a celebrity, she chose images that evoked a response that made her both larger than life yet did not threaten the intimacy she maintained with her public. Since social categories were in greater fluctuation than during times of peace, the patterns revealed are not clear, but rather a colorful suggestion of the cultural confusion that enabled her to manipulate images to her advantage.

After 1861, she began to shape her celebrity identity to the image of Mazeppa: an undeniable hero of ambiguous gender and ethnic origins who challenged and triumphed over established hierarchies of class and power. She seemed to gather strength as a culture force as the war itself gained momentum. As she transformed her daring as Mazeppa into a personal fortune, she continually sorted through which images to promote. She effected off-stage dress that hinted at masculinity, such as donning a man's jacket over her billowing skirts, even as she flaunted her female body on stage. She was one of the boys who constantly asserted her rights to be treated as a lady; that is, she strove to claim the benefits of femininity with none of its constraints.

In midst of the War of Rebellion, she promoted the joys of social rebellion while she also continued to build her image as an intellectual and began cultivating connections with great men of literature. As the war flamed into a full-scale conflagration from 1862 through 1863, and the North finally began winning some battles, she took her act on an extended tour, shaping her public self within mass media.

Chapter 5

Among the Bohemians

I think that just in proportion as others reveal their true selves to us, by accident as it were, just as they involuntarily impart, and we instinctively understand the secret of the genuine mechanism lying hidden below their visible lives, just so much are they veritably ours. Beyond that they are but fancies to us.

Menken to Robert Newell, summer of 1861[1]

Midway through the year of the Heenan scandal, Menken began crafting the image of a private self that existed beyond the celebrity image. Within her poetry she explored the idea of "seeming" and "being" and reflected on her confusion, disillusion, and pain at being unable to pull the two apart. Indeed, she made the conflict between performance and reality central to her celebrity. On February 10, 1861, she published the poem "Now and Then" as if to finally reveal the woman behind the masks of gaiety and scandal. The poem remained one of Menken's favorites, and years later she retitled it "Myself" and included it in *Infelicia*.[2] Her multiplicity of self is clearly visible in this poem: She is both the external Menken (constructed as the false self), and the internal Menken (the authentic self). The first two lines suggest that she has never had a strong hold on reality or understood her own identity: "Away down into the shadowy depths of the Real I once lived./ I thought that to seem was to be." She expresses loneliness and a sense of betrayal by the world at large:

I waited, and hoped, and prayed; Counting the heart-throbs and the tears that answered them.
Through my earnest pleadings for the True, I learned that the mildest mercy of life was a smiling sneer;
And that the business of the world was to lash with vengeance all who dared to be what their God had made them.
Smother back tears to the red blood of the heart!
Crush out things called souls!
No room for them here!

[1] Adah Isaacs Menken (hereafter AIM) to Robert Henry Newell, quoted in Robert Newell, "Adah Isaacs Menken," publication unknown, pasted into "Biography of Adah Isaacs Menken. Extra Illustrated," Harris Rare Books, 76-M545x, Brown University Library, Providence, Rhode Island.
[2] AIM, "Now and Then," New York *Sunday Mercury*, Feb. 10, 1861, published as "Myself," in *Infelicia*, reprinted in *Collected Black Women's Poetry*, vol. 1 (New York: Oxford University Press, 1988), 47–50.

From that point on, life became a masquerade. Speaking through the poem, Menken suggests that she is not what the world assumes; the Menken is merely an act. She ravages her deliberately created public image when she says:

> Now I gloss my pale face with laughter, and sail my voice on with
> the tide.
> Decked in jewels and lace, I laugh beneath the gaslight's glare,
> and quaff the purple wine.
> But the minor-keyed soul is standing naked and hungry upon one
> of heaven's high hills of light.

Menken appeals to the sympathy of readers, prompting them to see beyond her act of gaiety and extend kindness and understanding. She is,

> Starving for one poor word!
> Waiting for God to launch out some beacon on the boundless
> shores of this Night.
> Shivering for the uprising of some soft wing under which it may
> creep, lizard like, to warmth and rest.

Menken compares herself to Christ, binding her "aching brow with a jeweled crown, that none shall see the iron one beneath." The poem reads autobiographically and she clearly suggests that, as with Christ, death and salvation will expose her true self: "[W]hen these mortal mists shall unclothe the world, then shall I be known as I am." And yet at the same time she struggles with the idea that there is no reality, only a performance: "After all, living is but to play a part!/The poorest worm would be a jewel-headed snake if she could." She can perform herself to greatness, but at best it means projecting a dazzling and cruel image over a self that is vulnerable in its softness and ultimately repugnant.

With its images of roses, snakes, wings, tears, and secret sorrow, the poem wears a cloak of sentimentality and follows that tradition in its autobiographical quality, but strays from sentimental tradition in its format and style. Its tone is strident, even bitter, without the sweetness of sentimental martyrdom. Menken adopted a style that suggested she was marching about a stage, defending herself to a crowd of spectators. Nor is the subject matter sentimental, as she heroically denies her need for sympathy, stating that God will allow her the voice that society has stolen. She evokes the power of the powerless – the strength of refusing spiritual victimization regardless of assault.

In truth it had become necessary to the survival of her celebrity that Menken create another offstage self to replace the image of sentimental victim. Throughout 1860, the Heenan scandal reshaped her public image, so that her claims to sympathy began to wear thin. She needed another part to play as Menken, and she found it in Pfaff's tavern off Bleeker Street, the meeting place of the self-proclaimed American bohemians. The bohemians formed the roots of a nascent counterculture of the 1850s and early 1860s. Within nationally circulating magazines and newspapers, they questioned and defied notions of respectability and challenged conventions of gender and sexuality. Their public image was one of intellectual dissent and bonhomie, male bonding and pleasure, arrogance and experimentation. They validated rebellion against bourgeois cultural strictures by coming out of the middle class itself and speaking a language Victorians understood. The war would make their movement short-lived, but for a time they presented a legitimate challenge to social conventions. They provided the perfect image for Menken to embody as she moved away from her sentimental victimization. With bohemianism, Menken's public life began to influence her private one as she found new models on which to build a personal identity.

The cerebral bohemian image suggested there was more to Menken and her scandalous behavior than met the eye. The bohemians of the 1850s centered their identity on the conviction that the drive for respectability was stifling personal freedoms, and they treated transgressions of class, sex, and gender as welcome means of cracking the false veneer to reveal authenticity. Although outside skeptics might say that bohemianism was all about spectacle, they did not explicitly embrace spectacle because it was part of the commercial world they largely rejected, but their rejection of conformity suggested that trangression could have a legitimate intellectual basis. To say that Menken recognized that a bohemian identity could give depth to her scandalous and sensational theater persona is not to say that she was not genuinely attracted to bohemian culture. It had the power to bring together her many selves: the poet, the actress, the intellectual, and, perhaps most important, the transgressive. Bohemian identity legitimated her experimentation with social forms and gave them an intellectual cast. It was an identity that blended middle-class signifiers of cultivation and fashion yet allowed her to challenge bourgeois notions of respectability.

Alliance with the bohemians marked the point at which Menken began implying that an intellectual "real" self existed behind the staged Menken. While the flamboyant Menken established herself through action onstage, the private self found expression in poetry and intellectual prose. Performance of a private self was a necessary part of celebrity; there had to be a private self worth knowing, or the public would lose interest. The tragic Menken image that had emerged during the Heenan scandal was never quite successful and by the nature of its birth had a short life-span. In a sense, shortly before she killed off her image as a victimized woman, she began revamping her image as a literary intellectual. Menken played with alternative constructions of herself throughout the year of 1860 (the year of the Heenan scandal), and firmly shifted gears by 1861 to become identified with the bohemians rather than the sentimentalists. Bohemianism allowed Menken to create a more enduring private self that was both at odds with her sensational image and yet connected by a similarly irreverent attitude toward gender roles and sexuality.

As the Jewish poet and pugilist's wife, Menken had attempted to shape her celebrity identity by portraying her private self in revealing poetry. Now the influence of the public moved in reverse, and with bohemianism, Menken's public image began to influence her private life. As her public persona began to openly challenge conventions of gender and sexuality, she also began to experiment with them in her personal life. Indeed, her private explorations were ideally suited to bohemianism, situated as it was between rebellion and convention, as her experimentation soon gave way to embracing middle-class forms. She had a brief and unfulfilled foray into same-sex relations before entering the most staid marriage of her public life.

Menken began joining the bohemians at Pfaff's Tavern while still publishing copious sentimental poetry in response to the scandal with Heenan, in mid-1860. Located at 653 Broadway, Pfaff's benefited from an influx of both New Yorkers and tourists, and its close proximity to Bleecker Street. Bleecker Street held particular appeal as a sort of safe zone for social dissent. One contemporary said of Bleecker, "The freedom there of every sort is absolute; and if you seek to be independent of opinion, above scandal, preserved from criticism, become a dweller in its confines."[3] Charlie Pfaff encouraged the bohemian gatherings by providing them with a large table while other patrons sat at small square tables scattered about the large room. A regular for several years, travel writer Bayard Taylor later depicted Pfaff's as a shadowy intellectual oasis in the midst of an industrialized, mechanized society, saying, "mild potations of beer and the dreamy breath of cigars delayed the nervous fidgety, clattering-footed American hours."[4] Although a rather exclusive group of literati and entertainers, the bohemians publicized their philosophy effectively through print. By 1860, the bohemian gatherings had become so well known that one writer listed Pfaff's as a tourist attraction, along with Tammany Hall and Barnum's Museum.[5]

Henry Clapp, Jr., a seasoned journalist, was responsible for organizing the gatherings and publicizing their philosophies. As if he was himself a living illustration of the connection between American bohemianism and middle-class idealism, Clapp began his public life as a adamant temperance advocate before a sojourn in Paris entirely reversed his convictions. While staying in the Latin Quarter he became enamored with the impoverished artists and writers who presented themselves as morally and intellectually

[3] Junius Henri Browne, *The Great Metropolis: A Mirror of New York* (1868; Hartford: American Publishing, 1869), 379.

[4] Albert Parry, *Garrets and Pretenders: A History of Bohemianism in America* (New York: Corici, Friede, 1933), 21–22.

[5] Browne, *Great Metropolis*, 379.

superior to the capitalistic bourgeoisie.[6] In 1854, he returned to the United States and initiated the gatherings at Pfaff's, determined to foster the spirit of the Latin Quarter in Manhattan. Indeed, he and his followers began calling themselves "bohemians" to identify themselves with the French intellectuals of the 1830s. Outside views were not so complimentary; many Americans saw their gatherings as more about bacchanalian pleasure than intellectual conviction. One contemporary later described them as writers who were as clever and "careless; who lived in to-day, and despised tomorrow; who preferred the pleasure and the triumph of the hour to the ease of prosperity and the assurance of abiding fame."[7]

But they were productive, regardless of their decadence. In 1858, Clapp founded a weekly literary magazine called the *Saturday Press* that enjoyed spectacular critical success if chronic financial failure. Clapp deliberately cultivated both the *Saturday Press* and the bohemian circle as an intellectual alternative to middle-class pap, and most of the bohemians published or aspired to publish work in the magazine. Given Menken's audacity and skill at publicity, she probably submitted work to the *Saturday Press*, but her work never appeared there. The *Saturday Press* went in and out of business three times before folding at the end of the war, in 1865, in part because the bohemians had lost their spirit for gathering.[8]

Regulars made up the heart of the bohemian circle, and for the most part, they were formidably talented writers, such as novelist Richard Henry Stoddard, humorist Artemus Ward, and theater critic William Winter, who had significant impact on the reading culture of New York and therefore around the nation. Regulars also included the writers of mass media such as Ned Wilkins of the *Herald*; Edward House and Franklin J. Ottarson of the *Tribune*; humorist Mortimer (Doesticks) Thompson; travel writer Bayard Taylor; poet and stockbroker E. C. Stedman; *Vanity Fair* contributors Harry Neal and Frank Wood; playwright Charles Gayler; John Du Solle of the Sunday *Times*; George Arnold, who freelanced poetry and prose; William North, a failed writer whose suicide in 1854 cast a tragic glow over the bohemian group from its inception, but had the happy result of finally winning him a book contract; and story writer Fitz James O'Brien, who died from tetanus on the battlefields. Walt Whitman showed up nightly, but he was not so much a member of the group as the object of their admiration.[9] The bohemians defied conventionality from positions of cultural authority and made up a predominantly male group, in part by definition. A few women showed up regularly to the gatherings, such as stock actresses Getty Gay, Jenny Danforth, Mary Fox, Dora Shaw and Annie Deland, but the only two women whom the men seemed to accept as part of the circle were the

---

[6] Tice Miller, *Bohemians and Critics: American Theatre Criticism in the Nineteenth Century* (Metuchen, N.J.: Scarecrow Press, 1981), 15–16, 22–23.

[7] Browne, *Great Metropolis*, 150.   [8] Parry, *Garrets and Pretenders*, 24.   [9] Ibid., 39.

ones with the greatest literary talent: satirical essayist Ada Clare and novelist Elizabeth Barstow Stoddard (married to R. H. Stoddard).[10] Still, despite the male-centered nature of the group, it promoted more mixing of men and women in an intellectual setting than one might find in most of middle-class America. Ada Clare appears to have become Menken's friend around 1860, giving her a legitimate reason to be with the bohemians if not one of them (as she claimed in her publicity bios when visiting other cities).

The bohemians found plenty of followers because they were only one manifestation of backlash against prescriptive standards of behavior. For example, they touted the work of the French bohemians George Sand, Honoré de Balzac, Theophile Gautier, and Charles Baudelaire, among others, raising questions about the liminalities of sexuality.[11] This was in direct contrast to the more pervasive message that sexual passions should be controlled for the good of individuals, marriages, and society. But as Menken's later triumphs would suggest, the sexual atmosphere before and during the Civil War was increasingly varied and unrestricted.[12] Indeed, Americans actively participated in the growth of commercialized sex, expressing their values with money if not words. Prostitution grew at a phenomenal rate. In 1858, New York physician William Sanger estimated that nearly 6,000 women worked full-time and 2,000 part-time in prostitution, and New York developed its first red-light district between 1850 and 1870.[13] Of course, growth of the sexual marketplace and social efforts to control sexual activity were connected. By advocating less sex in the home, moralists contributed to the argument that men should find ways to exercise their carnal passions so as not to sully their wives' purer natures. The bohemians openly scoffed at such "rationalization" or control of human nature.

The overt intention among bohemians to live in opposition to genteel culture generated a certain amount of posturing and image making, which suited Menken quite well. While in hindsight, one scholar summarizes Clapp as "lashing out at everything, but standing for little besides a love of fine coffee, strong liquor, and lively repartee," those tastes were charged with social and political meaning at the time. Americans who admired or embraced bohemianism undoubtedly saw its participants as cultural rebels striving to keep alive a participatory spirit disappearing in an increasingly commercialized society.[14] But that participatory spirit was narrowly defined by the midcentury bohemians. They celebrated the democracy and

---

[10] Browne, Great Metropolis, 15; Miller, *Bohemians and Critics*, 16.

[11] Miller, *Bohemians and Critics*, 9–10, 16.

[12] David Reynolds, *Walt Whitman's America: A Cultural Biography* (New York: Alfred A. Knopf, 1995), 155; Timothy Gilfoyle, *City of Eros: New York City, Prostitution, and the Commercialization of Sex, 1790–1920* (New York: W. W. Norton, 1992), 119–142.

[13] Edward K. Spann, *The New Metropolis: New York City, 1840–1857* (New York: Columbia University Press, 1981), 251; Gilfoyle, *City of Eros*, 119–20.

[14] Reynolds, *Whitman's America*, 376.

masculinity of the Jacksonian age without the embracing of ethnic difference and gender equality that would characterize later American bohemian movements.[15] Although the bohemians were all about dissent against social convention, their image had deep roots in American culture. Indeed, one might say that they served their public by providing easy access to social rebellion. Once bohemianism was a trend acknowledged by the press, Americans could signify their bohemian sympathies without actually dropping in at Pfaff's or struggling with French literature. They could simply discuss works of transgressive poets, such as Byron and Walt Whitman, subtly alter their dress to defy convention, or buy tickets to daring plays put on by performers such as Menken.

Yet despite all of the posturing, the bohemian gatherings played a significant role in American print culture. *Saturday Press* focused on publishing original work by American authors and brought attention to emerging writing styles. Most Americans first heard of Mark Twain and his famous jumping frog in the *Saturday Press*, for example. And again, most of the regulars at Pfaff's enjoyed access to the national print forum through magazines such as *Vanity Fair* or penny press papers. The bohemians' celebration of individualism, as well as the extremes of melancholy and bacchanalian joy that colored their writing, reflected Menken's own ongoing self-production. She began publishing more thoughtful pieces as if to emphasize that the gay public mask hid a true intellectual.

Bohemianism both in France and elsewhere gained its romantic glow and literary clout through the writings of Henri Murger, a young writer who rescued himself from starvation in the Paris streets by rendering his life into fiction. From 1845 to 1846, Murger published a series of short stories portraying bohemianism in a whimsical, humorous light, despite the fact that a couple of his peers had literally starved to death in Paris. The stories proved so popular that he recrafted them into an enormously successful musical, *La Vie de Boheme* (1849), which later became the basis for Puccini's opera, *La Boheme*. It was Murger who first popularized bohemianism by cloaking its poverty and desperation in joyful nonconformity, and it was this bohemianism that so enamored Clapp. The New York bohemianism Clapp and his followers perpetuated stemmed not from brutal social conditions but from Murger's romantic portrayal of talented young rebels living an unconventional life of creativity.[16]

Social rebellion was at the heart of both French and American bohemianism, as well as the core of Menken's public image by 1861. Like most

---

[15] For a discussion of turn-of-the-century bohemianism, see Christine Stansell, *American Moderns: Bohemian New York and the Creation of a New Century* (New York: Henry Holt, 2000).

[16] Murger coined the term "bohemian," because he erroneously believed that gypsies originated in Bohemia, a region of Czechoslovakia. The gypsies in fact originated in India. See Jerrold Siegal, *Bohemian Paris: Culture, Politics, and the Boundaries of Bourgeois Life, 1830–1930* (New York: Viking Press, 1986), 17.

educated Americans, she had probably heard of the French bohemians a decade before the gatherings began at Pfaff's. The two bohemian groups were significantly different because of their different cultural contexts, but it is doubtful that neither Menken nor most of the American participants understood why. Parisian bohemianism of the 1830s, the model upon which the American version was built, emerged from grinding poverty in absolute rejection of bourgeois cultural values. American bohemianism, by contrast, arose from the heart of middle-class culture; it was rebellion within a social class, not between two social classes.[17] As the American middle class developed during the antebellum period, it demanded new limits be placed to protect society from the vulgarities of personal freedoms. The American bohemians questioned where such limits should be drawn, asking at which point personal cultivation ceased to be beneficial or acceptable to the social class that sponsored it.[18] It was the *image* of rebellion than excited the Americans about the Parisian bohemians, not the political intricacies of their conflict. Bohemianism in the United States was essentially a conventional American ideal, social rebellion, masquerading in French couture.

But the element of class conflict made bohemian rebellion mesh well with Menken's performances, which essentially brought working-class entertainment into middle-class forums. Also, bohemianism in the United States defined itself through celebration of the underdog, something that Menken both explored and exploited with her public personae. American bohemianism arose in protest to increasingly rigid concepts of middle-class identity, and nothing challenged middle-class prudery like the financial success of a celebrity who found a way to sell sensational fare in their theaters. And here the middle-class origins of American bohemianism worked to Menken's advantage. As a bohemian, she could both defy the middle class and suggest herself as one of its members.

The bohemians made the most of the French connection since it provided useful freedoms, as Menken herself had discovered by claiming New Orleans as her birthplace. Since Americans on the whole tended to both revere French culture as cultivated yet vilify it as debauched, it fell into a gray, middle ground that defied containment. France and America had enjoyed strong cultural connections since the colonial period through their respective democratic revolutions and their sporadic alliance against Great Britain. Their alliance, however, was fraught with conflict at the most basic psychological and cultural levels, since most Americans were arguably more British than French, and for centuries France and England had operated as both political enemies and cultural foils. Mainstream American society embodied those differences in its simultaneous reverence for yet distancing

---

[17] Timothy J. Clark, *Image of the People: Gustave Courbet and the Second French Republic, 1848–1851* (New York: Graphic Society Ltd, 1973), 33.

[18] Siegal, *Bohemian Paris*, 11.

from French culture. The nouveau riche and newly middle-class Americans admired French fashions, books, plays, music, and language at the same time that they felt morally bound to critique them. American bohemians went a bit further by focusing on questions of sexuality raised in French literature.[19] Exploring such topics meant testing the parameters of social acceptance, something at which Menken excelled.

Menken probably found Pfaff's comfortably familiar. In many ways the atmosphere probably resembled her earlier life in New Orleans and East Texas, where respectable women could openly drink, smoke, and fraternize with men, as long as they recognized parameters established by Creole culture. The same was true at Pfaff's, although the parameters were loosely set by the surrounding culture. Menken particularly admired and emulated Walt Whitman and Ada Clare, and when she was in town, she went to Pfaff's to sit and chat with them, exchanging views on life and probably sharing confidences.

Adah Menken's friendship with kindred spirit Ada Clare was one of her most significant and enduring. They shared similar concerns about their public images and had similarly dramatic, elusive personalities. Although Clare was an essayist and Menken a poet and actress, they both self-consciously created public personae. In the early 1860s Clare, who was probably the older of the two, acted as Menken's sister/mentor, articulating views on politics, women's rights, morality, and literature that Menken would also voice in her essays. However, Clare enjoyed the benefits of a discretionary income brought by inheritance, while Menken supported herself, and those differences determined their respective routes to fame.[20]

Even though Clare cultivated a persona that many readers probably regarded as masculine, she considered herself significantly feminine. True, she adamantly expressed her opinions, traveled without a chaperone, openly claimed her illegitimate son, and spent time in the company of men to whom she was not married. But Clare also expressed a belief in women's "gentle influence." She voiced her ideal of bohemian womanhood when she wrote of her desire to emulate a particular French woman who lived a life "unconventional yet moral, free yet unselfish, artistic yet comfortable." Clare liked the freedom of bohemia but found filth and poverty distasteful. She explicitly defined her role as a "purifier and guardian of a better Bohemia."[21] In other words, she saw her mission as equivalent to that of the Victorian homemaker and reformer – not passive, pure, or pious, but definitely uplifting. Clare, although holding untraditional views on chastity, marriage, and gender equality, nevertheless worked within a conventional concept of woman's most valuable social role.

But Clare was also fearless in expressing her scorn for the absurd and constraining gender conventions emerging from domesticity. For example,

[19] Miller, *Bohemians and Critics*, 9.   [20] Parry, *Garrets and Pretenders*, 26–27.   [21] Ibid., 27.

in 1864, she published a parody of female prescriptive literature, entitled "The Man's Sphere and Influence," inverting the gender roles and saying, "The sacred precinct of home is the real sphere of man. Modesty, obedience, sobriety are the true male virtues. . . . We do not want man to be too highly educated; we want him sweet, gentle, and incontestably stupid . . . let not the sacred dumpling be neglected."[22] Clare lampooned Victorian ideals, and in her critique of women's subordinate position in American society, men and the "true women" who embodied domesticity served as her scapegoats. Clare wrote with strident, witty candor, free of the sentimentality that laced Menken's literary work, and offended (and therefore also thrilled) many.

Menken also felt a kindred bond with Whitman; he had succeeded in making himself into a multifaceted celebrity. Whitman created and performed his persona with as much deliberation as Menken. New Yorkers knew Whitman as a journalist for the *Brooklyn Eagle* before he exchanged that image for one of a free-thinking poet. Whitman's 1855 (debut) edition of *Leaves of Grass* had received several positive as well as scandalized reviews, and by the time his next edition went into print, in 1860, his notoriety had spread beyond New York. Whitman experimented with constructing images of himself, both through his poetry and photographic portraits. He was ever aware of the audience watching and evaluating him, whether they were readers, acquaintances, or people in the streets of New York.

Menken's acquaintance with Whitman influenced her work as a poet and may have helped her clarify convictions she held intuitively, for Whitman expressed beliefs that Menken echoed with her actions, if not her words. For example, the 1860 edition of *Leaves of Grass* abounds with images of women, sex, and the body, suggesting that the seeds of woman's social and personal liberation lay in sexual freedom. Whitman stated firmly, "[O]nly when sex is properly treated, talked, avowed, accepted will the woman be equal with the man, and pass where the man passes, and meet his words with hers, and his rights with hers." Menken never self-consciously formulated a connection between women's rights and sexual freedom, but her actions put her in sympathy with Whitman. Whitman's convictions described the essence of what she also advocated: candor, democracy, and an intellectualism comfortably housed within the body.[23]

"The shape-shifting, androgynous persona of Whitman's poetry" also paralleled Menken's public persona. Like him, Menken played parts within her poetry and prose, just as she played parts on- and offstage. In her early years as a poet she assumed the identities of either victimized woman or fearless leader against social injustice at the same time that she performed stage roles requiring convincing masculinity. Menken gauged public perceptions

[22] Ada Clare, "The Man's Sphere and Influence," in *No Rooms of Their Own: Women Writers of Early California*, ed. Ida Rae Egli (Berkeley: Heyday Books), 306–307.

[23] Reynolds, *Whitman's America*, 161, 213, 231, 344–345. *Leaves of Grass* went through four editions.

of masculinity and femininity and incorporated both into her public image, on- and offstage, in print and in action. She openly tested the fluidity of gender just as Whitman explored it in his poetry. She also explored sexually charged androgyny first onstage and later off, much as Whitman did in poetry and life. For Whitman his androgyny was not a *denial* of sexuality but of sexually codified identity; his androgyny was primarily sexual even as it worked against the notion of separate sexes.[24] Menken's androgyny would come to work much the same way, except that in public perception her androgyny heightened her attraction as the object of heterosexual desire; her sexually charged androgyny made differences between sexual bodies more explicit. The "I" in Whitman's verse was as subject to change as the narrator of Menken's; both performed personae within their written work, as well as through photographs and public behavior.[25]

Menken wanted the public to see her as Whitman's kindred spirit. She defended him in the essay "Swimming against the Current," published June 10, 1860, in the *Sunday Mercury*. Publicly supporting him established her bohemian identity, even though she was only one of several women who spoke out in favor of Whitman's work. The popular writer Fanny Fern, herself a formidable cultural critic and iconoclast, stated that "Whitman's sexual frankness was infinitely preferable to much popular religious and reform literature, in which sex was insidiously cloaked in piety" and that "sexual openness was a healthy contrast to the festive prurience of popular culture."[26] Whitman's verse proposed sexual freedoms for both sexes, and women lauding his work took a daring step when signing their names to those positive reviews.

Menken sent a message about herself when she defended Whitman, a man whom many Americans perceived as scandalous and culturally dangerous, and many others celebrated as a genius and culturally refreshing. The *Sunday Mercury* prefaced Menken's essay by saying that "though none can fail to admire the almost masculine energy of its terse sentences. . . . We are far from endorsing all its sentiments, and are astonished to observe that Mrs. Heenan indulges in a eulogium of that coarse and uncouth creature, Walt Whitman." Whitman combined his appreciation for American democracy and history with a celebration of human sexuality and emotion that both offended and thrilled an enormous number of people.

Menken was more than just thrilled; she identified with Whitman. She wrote that to swim against the current, one must have "individuality of intellect, and an affinity with God – not society." She expressed this same view of herself, of course, every time she was called to defend her actions.

---

[24] Ibid., 162. Reynolds argues that Whitman's professed affection for other men has been misconstrued as homosexuality – that is, he argues that a homosexual identity would be anachronistic, and Whitman's belief in love between same-sex individuals is culturally bound. Those around Whitman would probably not have perceived his words or actions as indicative of a same-sex preference.
[25] Ibid., 161–166.   [26] Ibid., 347.

Menken considered Whitman "too far ahead of his contemporaries; they cannot comprehend him yet." She predicted that though he and others like him, the "Messiahs of humanity," would die in pain from insults, disappointment, and ridicule, "marble statues will be erected over the remains of him whom they suffered to starve because he swam against the current."[27] Menken implied, of course, that she swam alongside him, and dismissing negative comments about Whitman meant removing the sting from insults directed at herself. Regardless of readers' opinions, Whitman was delighted with the piece and pointed it out to Clapp.[28]

How did this image work with her other poetic presentation, the sentimental victim, which was still the principal player in her verse? The private life that Menken portrayed in her poetry focused almost exclusively on her disillusionment or betrayal at the hands of her lover. She presented the kind of personal experiences that transcend social categories of race, class, gender, and religion. Most readers could identify with her sense of betrayal, even if they had experienced such emotions only in the realm of imagination. The bohemian image worked for Menken because it was implicitly at the center of the social class that most frequently read her poetic pain.

But Menken demonstrated her bohemian intellectual leanings more often in prose than poetry. Essays such as "Midnight in New Orleans," "The Real and the Ideal," and "Behind the Scenes" explore concepts of visibility, reality, sincerity, and performance. All of her essays suggest that there was more to Menken than met the eye. In "Midnight in New Orleans" the narrator guides the viewer to the windows of private homes to witness scenes of grief and poverty. "Who would dream to gaze upon thy lofty spires, and marble mansions," she archly questions, "that mystery and misery were dwelling in thy very midst?"[29] "The Real and the Ideal" focuses on "how vain and futile it is to expect" that the "dreamings and longings of the immortal soul" can be made real. Menken seems particularly struck by the fact that "time is too short, the world is too poor, to enable [man] to develop and expand the mighty energies of his god-like soul." Clearly, she herself feels trapped in reality, demanding: "[T]here must be something higher, grander, and wider, in which the struggling soul shall loose her fettered wings!"[30] "Behind the Scenes" also intimates that Menken has a side unknown to the public, and it was not coincidental that she chose to publish the essay in October 1860, a week after she was called a prostitute by Heenan's lawyers in court. Although Menken explicitly writes about a fictitious actress whose mother is dying, she is clearly meant to be seen as the subject of the essay: "O horror!

---

[27] AIM, "Swimming against the Current," *Sunday Mercury,* June 10, 1860.
[28] Walt Whitman to Henry Clapp, Jr., June 12, 1860, in *Walt Whitman: The Correspondence,* vol. 1: *1842–1867,* ed. Edwin Haviland Mille (New York: New York University Press, 1961). Whitman refers to her as "Mrs. Heenan," suggesting that the bohemians thought of her as the pugilists's wife.
[29] Mrs. A. I. Menken, "Midnight in New Orleans," *New Orleans Daily Delta,* May 21, 1858.
[30] AIM, "The Real and the Ideal," *Sunday Mercury,* Nov. 18, 1860.

The painted stage, the gaslight, called her to laugh and sing, whilst under the gold-'broidered vestment that poor, lonely heart was breaking!" Lest the reader miss the connection, Menken brings herself into the essay at the end: "Well, the mimic scenes are over, and, like the poor, heartbroken actress, whose glad, eager personations brought down the house, I, too, will go home to life's realities. Perhaps, alas! Many of us had better been there before."[31]

In "Women of the World" (October 1860), one of her most striking essays, Menken condemned "fashionable women," even though many considered her one herself. In fact, Menken probably wrote the essay for just that reason; by declaring that women's education and autonomy was more important than fashion, she meant to argue that she was not a "woman of the world" but, rather, educated and independent. Her essay advocates greater appreciation for women's roles outside the family. She stridently disagrees with the way most girls are raised: "To win for herself a wealthy husband is the lesson." She concludes, "There are other missions for women than that of wife and mother," urging female readers to "cultivate their mental faculties." While the many middle-class women writers favored women's education and frequently disparaged materialism, they must have found the dismissal of "woman's greatest role" (wife and mother) offensive. They may have found it yet more troubling when the notorious Menken stated without irony that women's gifts are "Virtue, Purity, and Love – jealously entrusted to her, by the Creator, to glorify rude souls of clay. . . ."[32]

Her most controversial essay was probably "Lodgings to-Let – References Exchanged," where Menken dared to express her opinion on the presidential election. Her decision to exercise a normally male prerogative by commenting on politics again suggests that the bohemian identity was becoming central to her image. The *Sunday Mercury* published the essay only reluctantly, stating: "Our comprehension of that elastic intuition known as 'Woman's Sphere' does not include politics among the debatable prerogative that females may indulge with impunity. As a general thing, Woman knows no more about politics than she does about metaphysics; and when she meddles with either, a very pretty muddle is apt to be the result."[33] But Menken took a light tone in the essay, despite her daring in taking on the subject, as she primarily pokes fun at the number of people desperate to find lodging in the White House. Lincoln had recently won the election, much to the dismay of most of New York, which had overwhelmingly supported George McClellan.[34] Menken spoke to a sympathetic audience when she prophesied: "I may say (looking through South Carolina spectacles), the gentleman

---

[31] AIM, "Behind the Scenes," *Sunday Mercury*, Oct. 14, 1860.

[32] AIM, "Women of the World," *Sunday Mercury*, Oct. 7, 1860.

[33] Newell's introduction to AIM, "Lodgings To-Let – References Exchanged," *Sunday Mercury*, Dec. 19, 1860.

[34] Ernest McKay, *The Civil War and New York City* (Syracuse: Syracuse University Press, 1990), 266.

who has succeeded in securing this house for the next term of years will not escape with his life."[35] For a woman stepping outside of her "sphere," Menken was uncannily accurate. South Carolina seceded from the Union one month later.

In 1861, while maintaining a grueling touring schedule, Menken began experimenting with bohemian ideas about sexuality and gender in her personal life. Indeed, she took a rather stereotypical bohemian approach by both embracing convention in action and defying it in words as she set out to seduce a man and a woman, and ultimately chose a traditional marriage. She began wooing Robert Newell, the editor at the *Sunday Mercury* who published her work with such enthusiasm, at the end of July in 1861, a little over a month after Menken's triumphant debut of *Mazeppa*. She sent him several letters from Milwaukee, where she performed at the Academy of Music, seducing him with the idea that he alone knew her true self, her unperformed self. One day, as if suddenly struck by the growing intimacy of their correspondence, she mused: "[H]ow little can we learn of the inner, hidden life of real natures! And how much we learn sometimes, even with the casual acquaintances, if they for a moment lift the veil which covers and conceals the workings of some master-motive, some spring of feeling, or source of permanent aspiration."[36]

She did not mention her feelings for Hattie Tyng, a sentimental poet whose latest collection of poetry, *Apple Blossoms*, had been Menken's most recent traveling companion. Menken's opening lines suggest that if she had even met the Wisconsin poet on a visit to Milwaukee three months earlier, they were at best no more than passing acquaintances. Menken now claimed, however, that Tyng's poetry compelled her to reach out, saying, "[F]or weeks and months I have read, not what you have written for the world, but what an uncontrollable magnetism of affinity told me that you had written for me, and that your heart bided some response." Tyng's verse became Menken's solace: "I waited and reasoned with this great magnetic influence, talked of the world, or society and its iron laws, tried to put you away among *others*, but you did not heed me, only came back more lovingly and seemed to put your arms around me in my most bitter hours of loneliness, and whisper of patience and peace." Using language almost identical to what she had written to Newell, Menken pondered the magic of people revealing their "innerselves" through unguarded behavior: "We can learn but little of any one from the external life they lead; but we learn much, if even for a moment the veil is lifted which covers and conceals the workings of motives, the springs of feeling, the sources of inspiration and the result to be labored for." Considering her own inability to give a straight answer, Menken's next words to Tyng are telling: "I think, dear lady, just in

35 "Lodgings-To-Let," *Sunday Mercury*, Dec. 2, 1860.
36 AIM to Newell, Milwaukee, 1861, quoted by Newell, "Adah Isaacs Menken."

proportion as others impart and we attain a true knowledge of the interior nature which lies behind all their visible life, just so much are they really *ours*."

That summer, Menken pursued both Newell and Tyng, two writers who, unlike the bohemians, advocated Victorian gender norms. Menken encouraged them to open their hearts to her, and appeared to initiate intimacy by sharing her deepest thoughts, while in truth she revealed little. Examined within the context of Menken's own life, what appear to be deeply personal letters instead reveal Menken's determination to experiment with her performance of a private or "true" Menken. They also suggest that Menken's participation in the bohemian circle affected her private life as well as her public image.

Menken's busy traveling schedule undoubtedly dictated that much of her personal life would have to take place in letters; she was rarely in one town for more than two weeks. After her debut as Mazeppa in Albany, Menken embarked on two years of constant travel. In July she went from Pittsburgh to Milwaukee – a journey of roughly 650 miles that took three or four days by train. In August and September, she starred again at the Pittsburgh Theatre before heading to St. Louis by rail and paddleboat to perform at De Barr's, the city's preeminent theater. By mid-November she was performing in Louisville. From there, Cincinnati was a quick jaunt up the Ohio, where she played at Wood's Theatre for two weeks. In January 1862, she again packed the Green Street Theatre in Albany before resting until March, when she repeated the same circuit as the previous fall. She spent the summer months of June through September at the Bowery Theatre in New York and Howard's Athenaeum in Boston, before heading south by train to Washington, D.C. Her longest stay in one city took place from late fall until early spring, 1863, when she starred at the Front Street Theatre in Baltimore.[37]

While audiences in cities such as Cincinnati and St. Louis had probably read quite a bit about her rendition of *Mazeppa*, they saw her perform a different array of male and female characters. She played Jack Shepard, Eagle Eye, and Dick Turpin, and strong women, such as Joan of Arc or the cross-dressing Mathilde of *The French Spy*, both of whom fit nicely with Menken's edgy self-presentation. All of these roles were considered the standard fare for sensation and involved cross-dressing and horse tricks, but they lacked the death-defying mountainous trek in *Mazeppa*. Nor did they require a horse trained to the level of the "wild, untamed steed," which must appear fierce while behaving predictably. Performing *Mazeppa* on tour would have

---

[37] Information on Menken gathered from a wide variety of sources, including newspapers and playbills. Travel information comes principally from Appleton's Companion (1862), 20; James E. Vance, Jr., *The North American Railroad: Its Origin, Evolution and Geography* (Baltimore: Johns Hopkins University Press, 1995), 102–114.

entailed transporting a horse – not just on one train, but from train to train, and by boat. Such mundane details may explain why Menken did not perform *Mazeppa* until she earned a longer contract. *Mazeppa* remained Menken's most famous role, but it was not her principal role until 1862, when she began earning longer contracts.

During these early years of national stardom, Menken chose roles already familiar to most audiences, so her stage work initially appeared to conform rather than to promote change, posing little threat to dominate taste makers. It would take another couple of years for cultural critics to see that Menken's success suggested a broadening of public taste enabled by economic shifts. Critics justifiably portrayed Menken as a woman determined to make money through sensation, and implied that she lacked legitimate talent. They presented her as a nine-day wonder, an opportunist, and the spurned wife of a pugilist who was quickly losing public appeal. But while Menken propelled herself into stardom by sheer determination, she also strove to portray herself as a woman of substance behind her public facade, and the bohemian image proved particularly useful.

Menken's correspondence with Robert Newell suggests how much intellectual pursuits figured into the persona she wished to play in her private life. She wrote to him from Milwaukee in the summer of 1861, saying, "Over a year ago I became deeply interested in the various topics of religion, and lost no opportunity to study them in all lights and shades; but having become settled in my conviction that the Reason and Conscience are God, and that to do Right is religion, I did not feel that enthusiasm for the multifarious branches of modern and ancient theology which I had once so delighted in mastering." But lest he think her unfeminine in her quest of knowledge, she adds with self-deprecating charm, "After reading Kant, Fichte, Paine, Cousin, Emerson and Andrew Jackson Davis, I became so confused as to grow absolutely tired of religious subjects, and was constantly asking myself, 'Where is the Truth?' I despairingly thought of renting a bungalow somewhere in Heathendom, and turning either Brahmin or Parsee." Newell had saved her with his wisdom, she suggested, saying, "You have done much to help me out of my quandary. By your words of perspicuous truth and advice to a poor lost child, I grew calm and good enough to see the True light." It was an intellectual yet feminine Menken who approached Newell by letter.

She also brought bohemian ideas into her private life when she sent a letter to Hattie Tyng. After speaking briefly of her need to reach out to a comparative stranger, she launched into what appeared to be an intensely personal expression of private desires: "I have had my passionate attachments among women, which swept like whirlwinds over me, sometimes, alas! Scorching me with a furnace-blast, but generally only changing and renewing my capabilities for love. I would 'have drunk their souls as it were a ray from Heaven' – have lost myself and lived in them. . . ."[38] Historians have suggested that passionate exchanges were common among close friends during this period, but Menken was not Tyng's friend. What purposes did Menken have for writing such an emotional letter to a woman she may not have even known? Was her letter meant to be read sexually or simply as one woman expressing passionate emotions to another based almost entirely upon their shared sex?

Despite a celebration of same-sex love in nineteenth-century culture, same-sex intimacy challenged the antebellum assumption that heterosexuality defined gender identity and the sexes worked in innate complement. Judith Butler points out the instability of such a structure when she argues that defining gender through behavior means relying on repetition of action to confirm itself. For heterosexual gender to persist as normative it must be performed over and over again; cessation or a change in the pattern suggests a need for new definitions.[39] Advocating absolute binary gender required that men act out masculinity and women perform femininity while repeating the process of heterosexual desire and activity. Thus, despite the fact that middle-class culture was creating separate and distinct male and female worlds, women desiring other women and entering emotionally and physically fulfilling relationships with them would seem to threaten a system dependent on male-female intimacy to define the "natural" genders. The situation created a paradox: Just as men and women found themselves bound by heterosexual norms, they experienced increasing isolation from the other sex.[40]

Menken and her bohemian friends avidly read the work of several French writers who explored the concept of same-sex passion as being significantly different from platonic friendship and heterosexuality. Unlike the American sporting press that focused on eroticism between men, the French bohemians of the 1830s focused on same-sex desire between women as having particular danger and allure. While the general American public tended to look to London for their reading material, Menken's bohemian friends favored the work of Honoré de Balzac, Charles Baudelaire, George Sand,

---

[38] AIM to Hattie Tyng, July 21, 1861, Walken House, Racine, Wisconsin; facsimile of the original letter in Kate Wilson Davis, "Adah Isaacs Menken – Her Life and Poetry in America," M.A. thesis, Southern Methodist University, 1944, appendix.

[39] Judith Butler, "Imitation and Gender Insubordination," in *Inside/Out: Lesbian Theories, Gay Theories*, ed. Diana Fuss (New York: Routledge, 1991), 21.

[40] Thomas Laqueur, *Making Sex: Body and Gender from the Greeks to Freud* (Cambridge: Harvard University Press, 1992), 8. Lacquer argues that the concept of two complementary sexes arose in the eighteenth century in response to parallel understandings of gender. See also Carroll Smith-Rosenberg, "The Female World of Love and Ritual," in *Disorderly Conduct: Visions of Gender in America* (New York: Knopf, 1985); Donald Yacovone, "Abolitionists and the Language of Fraternal Love," in *Meanings for Manhood: Constructions of Masculinity in Victorian America*, ed. Mark C. Carnes and Clyde Griffen (Chicago: University of Chicago Press, 1990), 85; David Reynolds, *Walt Whitman's America: A Cultural Biography* (New York: Vintage Books, 1995), 391–403.

and Théophile Gautier – writers whose heroines challenged the concept of male and female as two separate, distinct, and opposing genders.[41] Although fascinated with female homoerotic desire in particular, the term "lesbian" can be affixed to their heroines only cautiously, as these writers consciously created protagonists who looked female (physical self) but acted male (social self).

Gautier's *Mademoiselle de Maupin*, published in 1835, was particularly provocative and "became the bible of aesthetic-decadent literature," while the title character "became a prototype of the lesbian in literature for decades afterward." The heroine is "a beautiful young woman who looks equally stunning when dressed as a man" and "flaunts her sexual nature and refuses classification in either of the two sexes. . . . Yet she is a *femme fatale* as far as the men are concerned." At one point in the novel, Mademoiselle de Maupin declares that she belongs to "a third distinct sex, which yet has no name," with "the body and soul of a woman, the mind and power of a man."[42] A reflection of such ideas may also be seen in the work of Menken's closest friends from Pfaff's, Whitman and Clare, who frequently suggested that all selves combine both masculine and feminine characteristics.

The only evidence of Menken ever expressing what appears to be sexual desire for another woman is the 1861 letter to Hattie Tyng, although one can certainly argue that suggestions of homosexuality appear in several of Menken's poems and certainly in her story about Laulerack. It is possible that Menken had particular reasons for writing so provocatively to a woman who was at best an acquaintance. Tyng's poetry and short stories had appeared alongside Menken's own in the *Sunday Mercury*. Perhaps Menken had heard personal stories of Tyng through contacts at the newspaper before ever going to Wisconsin. In any case, Menken, no stranger to impertinent fan mail herself, suggests that Tyng unwittingly wrote the poetry for her – a revelation that "bided some response." Menken, usually the spectacle, becomes the spectator within this letter. The intimacy audiences regularly demanded of her she demands of another public female figure. She probes,

> Do you believe in the deepest and tenderest love between women? Do you believe that women often love each other with as much fervor and excitement as they do men? I have loved them so intensely that the daily and nightly

---

[41] Eric Hemberger, *The Historical Atlas of New York City: A Visual Celebration of Nearly Four Hundred Years of New York City's History* (New York: Henry Holt, 1994), 86; Miller, *Bohemians and Critics*, 9–10; Parry, *Garrets and Pretenders*.

[42] Lillian Faderman, *Surpassing the Love of Men: Romantic Friendship and Love between Women from the Renaissance to the Present* (New York: Quill, 1981), 264–66. Perhaps it is worth noting that Havelock Ellis and other so-called sexologists also used this term "third sex" in a very different way, to show an abnormality, rather than greater freedom from normative forms. John D'Emilio and Estelle Freedman. *Intimate Matters: A History of Sexuality in America* (New York: Harper & Row, 1988).

communion I have held with my beloved ones has not sufficed to slake my thirst for them, nor all the lavishness of their love for me been enough to satisfy the demands of my exacting, jealous nature.[43]

Menken puts herself in the role of the sexually hungry male aggressor, the lover whose desires cannot be slaked, and who demands absolute devotion. But she also identifies these affections as specific to female unions: "We find the rarest and most perfect beauty in the affections of one woman for another." She employs the sexually suggestive language found in sentimental romance novels:[44]

> [affection between women has] delicacy in its *manifestations*, generosity in its intuitions, an unveiling of inner life in its intercourse, marked by charming undulations of feeling and expression, not to be met with in the opposite sex. Freed from all the *grosser* elements of passion, it retains its energy, its abandonment, its flush, its eagerness, its palpitation, and its rapture – but all so refined, so glorified, and made delicious and continuous by an ever-recurring giving and receiving from each to each. The electricity of the one flashes and gleams through the other, to be returned not only in degree as between man and women, but in *kind* as between precisely similar organizations. And these passions are of the more frequent occurrence than the world is aware of – generally they are unknown to all but the hearts concerned, and are jealously guarded by them from intrusive comment. . . .

In the letter to Tyng, Menken, the ultimate performer of self, suggests that another self exists beneath the public mask. In fact, she implies that most women remain isolated behind masks: "[T]he world so curbs in a woman's inner being to its shadows, that few can be reached at all, and even then it is imperfectly that we must go back to the [unreadable] of our own individuality, disappointed and alone." Menken highlights her openness as if to compel Tyng to render herself equally vulnerable: "In the dumb pages of this poor, vague letter, you have the inner and most sacred folds of my heart. I wanted to give you some excuse in thus lifting to your stranger a veil so closely shrouded down to the rest of the world." Menken suggests that Tyng has already unveiled herself to Menken in poetry, and she, Menken, comes to offer her greater freedom yet. The image of the veil lifting to reveal the true self suggests rituals of marriage – with Tyng playing the part of the bride. Until Tyng lifts the veil she will remain "shrouded down," dead to the rest of the world. Like the bridegroom taking virginity or the prince kissing the princess to life, Menken is waiting on the other side of the veil, ready to impart vitality. Yet, as she gives herself a masculine role in the romance, Menken also emphasizes her identity as a woman of "precisely

---

[43] AIM to Tyng, July 21, 1861, Davis appendix.

[44] Patricia Anderson, *When Passion Reigned: Sex and the Victorians* (New York: Harper-Collins, 1995), 71–81.

similar organization." Further reinforcing the masculine role she is playing, she signs this personal letter tersely, "Yours faithfully, A. I. Menken" – as her former husband would have signed his name.[45]

But there is more to this story than meets the eye. On its surface, the letter appears simple enough: Tyng's poetry evoked a powerful chord in Menken, who audaciously expressed her desire. But once again, things were not as they seemed; the "essential" self Menken exposed was itself a performance. In the letter, Menken suggests that a woman can reveal her true self by simply lifting aside her social concealment. The images of passion, love, and pain Menken boldly paints imply that Menken has already unveiled herself to Tyng. Yet the phrases burning through the letter – supposedly emerging from "the inner and most sacred folds of [Menken's] heart" – came directly from an 1859 novel entitled *Ethel's Love Life*, written by the appropriately named Margaret J. M. Sweat.[46] Menken copied the paragraphs straight from the text, suggesting that she had the novel in hand when writing the letter. It is possible that another person forged the letter, but if so, the forger would have to have known Menken's handwriting; the letter abounds with the scripted flourishes Mark Twain once described as sized "of the doorplate order." Also, certain poetic (but less passionate) phrases from the novel turn up in a missive Menken wrote to her friend Ed James at roughly the same time. Menken had essentially turned Sweat's character into a part she could perform in her own private life.[47]

The novel Menken used complicates the notion that genteel Americans saw same-sex affection as a natural extension of women's identification with other women. Sweat, a Maine author who wrote several popular novels, creates a story of poisonous lesbian love framed within a redemptive hetero-sexual romance. In this epistolary novel, Ethel writes to her suitor, Ernest, whose wholesome love she credits with evoking memories of less worthy passions. The reader experiences her lovemaking along with her as Ethel relives moments with Leonora in detailed dreams: "[W]ith such glowing, almost painful intensity, she threw herself upon my neck and clasping me with fierce fondness of a lioness to her heart, till I felt its throbbings against my own, she bent over me with that longing, burning look... smothered me with hot kisses, and murmured in my ear." Despite her declared love for Ernest, Ethel describes her relationship with Leonora as immutable: "I knew

[45] AIM to Tyng, July 21, 1861, Davis appendix.

[46] Margaret J. M. Sweat, *Ethel's Love Life: A Novel* (New York: Rudd and Carleton, 1859), 82–86.

[47] Samuel Clemens to Pamela Moffett, March 18, 1864, Virginia City, Nevada Territory, in the Mark Twain Collection, Bancroft Library, University of California Berkeley; AIM to Ed James, n.d. (probably fall, 1862), from Power's Hotel, in Allen Lesser Collection (hereafter ALC), American Jewish Archives, Cincinnati, Ohio; Davis, *Actresses as Working Women*, 101–132. Kate Wilson Davis notes that Menken most often plagiarized from the work of Alice Carey and Ossian (a.k.a. James Macpherson); Gregory Eiselien adds that she also plagiarized from Penina Moise and "poached" a line from Whitman, see Gregory Eiselien, ed., *Infelicia and Other Writings* (Peterborough, Ontario: Broadview Literary Press, 2002), 30–31.

that a strange and irrevocable tie still bound us two together, and we could never really part." Yet in the next instant, her love for Ernest breaks this eternal connection: "I yearned, for a moment, with an overpowering desire for one more hour with her I had loved so well. But I look upon your picture, my beloved Ernest, and in that one instance, I regain my calmness." While Leonora represents carnal passion for Ethel, Ernest signifies peaceful, sublime love. Ethel perceives her love for Leonora as dangerously compelling: "[I]t is only through repeated proof of the poisonous nature of the plant I have cherished, that I find power to tear it out of my life."[48] The negative portrayal of Ethel's relationship with Leonora suggests that, despite a celebration of same-sex affection, at least some Victorians did not necessarily see same-sex relationships as innately pure, as so many historians have argued.

However, *Ethel's Love Life* can also be read as a double-entendre. Ethel's love for Ernest exists on a cool higher plane – one demanding self discipline and supplication. Considering the Victorian ethos of rationality and production, this love would appear to fit a proscriptive ideal. But Sweat concurrently undermines its redemptive promise. Ethel's passion for Leonora becomes a living, breathing thing: Her dreams of their union overtake her as she lies vulnerable in sleep. Ethel's love for Ernest lacks the carnality of her love for Leonora but also the excitement. Dreams of Leonora return again and again, and with them Ethel expresses desire for other women as well. Sweat portrays love between women as difficult to control, and capable of igniting liberating passion. In this sense, *Ethel's Love Life* is a lesbian fantasy contained in a novel of stultifying heterosexual love. It makes tangible the passion it condemns.

Looking at Tyng's sentimental poetry and Sweat's provocative novel, one must question what compelled Menken to bring the two together. Why did Tyng's verse, resonant with images of springtime, infant death, and love, inspire Menken to adopt Sweat's passionate depictions of what appears to be homoerotic desire? Again, this is the same Menken who publicly defended the iconoclastic sexuality of Walt Whitman's work, and brought sentimental images and romantic language together in her own poetry. With such choices, Menken suggests a connection between the sentimental and the sexual. It may help if we consider sentimental poetry another form of Victorian dress. In other words, just as fitted bodices over tightly laced corsets and crinolines swelling below impossibly tiny waists were a form of expression that emphasized the body they masked, so too did sentimental poetry convey passion and intimacy by cloaking it with particular language and images. Looking at Tyng's *Apple Blossoms*, one finds verse after verse of love, death, and fecund springtime until physical passion becomes almost palpable in its suggested absence. Menken suggests that sentimental poetry

[48] Sweat, *Ethel's Love Life*, 71–72, 76.

and overwrought passion were, in fact, the major and minor chords of Victorian sensibility.

Menken's letter also evinces conventions of the Victorian period when she begs Tyng's pardon before launching into a passionate ten-page effusion and ends with a prayer for God's blessing. A similar mixture of polite behavior and extravagant emotion can be found in throughout sentimental literature. In light of other letters exchanged by women during this period, Menken's effusive passion would have been less unusual had she expressed it to a close female friend.[49] Likewise, in popular novels such as Sophie May's *Cousin Grace* (1865), young women often symbolized the sanctity of their friendship by exchanging bejeweled rings and declarations of "everlasting fidelity."[50] Passion between women seems to have been accepted, as long as it did not threaten the more predominant image of marriage as women's ultimate goal. In literature and life, Victorians were not sexually repressed so much as struggling to define acceptable parameters for private and public behavior, and the need to contain simultaneously promoted the need to express. Along with evolving social restrictions emerged new means of expression, and thus "the boundaries between erotic expressiveness and reserve were shifting, problematic, almost impossible to map with any sense of finality."[51]

In print culture, American women did sometimes comment on the fact that marriage kept most women from fulfilling their nondomestic aspirations, and there may have been an unwritten understanding that lesbian relationships could provide an alternative. But most women's novels suggest that however deep female friendships and dear professional aspirations, marriage was still the paramount achievement for women. In *Cousin Grace,* for example, the young women take a vow never to marry so that they may be "certain of becoming distinguished" and become "doctors, judges or ministers, just as they liked."[52] Such a conclusion suggests that if one did not marry, then one was not "a woman" in the conventional sense, and could pursue other dreams. But the humorous tone of the author suggests that her heroines will soon grow out of their adolescent desire to become "distinguished," and realize the wonders of wifedom and motherhood. Many real women did, of course, choose to pursue nondomestic ambitions rather than marry. Catholic sisterhoods offered thousands of women the opportunity to pursue education, public service, and travel. Many Protestant women considered devotion to social reform an acceptable alternative to marriage. Several women with public careers, including actress Charlotte Cushman,

---

[49] Faderman, *Surpassing the Love of Men*; Smith-Rosenberg, "Female World."

[50] Sophie May, *Cousin Grace* (Boston: Lee and Shepard, 1865), 6–7.

[51] Michel Foucault, *History of Sexuality*, vol. 1: *An Introduction* (New York: Pantheon Books, 1978), 3–13; Peter Gay, *The Bourgeois Experience: Victoria to Freud*, vol. 2: *The Tender Passion* (New York: Oxford University Press, 1986), 3.

[52] May, *Cousin Grace*, 21–22.

earned respect for maintaining spotless personal lives – not because they lived alone, but because the public did not consider their female companions as sexual partners. Menken may have had the advantages of this lifestyle in mind when she wrote a second letter to Hattie Tyng in August of 1862, revealing that she still harbored passion for the poet, who had clearly chosen to ignore the first letter.

Given Menken's friendship with Walt Whitman and her reading material, she may also have been trying to realize an intellectual ideal. Although Menken's letter may suggest that she identified with Sweat's heroine's desires – that she, too, felt strong attraction to other women – it may merely indicate that she found the idea of such consuming passion captivating and set out to experience it. Her letter to Tyng proves little about Menken's proclivities, other than the fact that (once again) she imposed fiction on her real life.

Much like Sweat's heroine, Ethel, Menken sent fervent letters to Newell at roughly the same time she expounded the authenticity of female passion to Tyng. With her epistolary seduction of Newell, she pursued a man clearly wedded to Victorian ideals of morality, regardless of his cultural sophistication as a political satirist. Besides acting as the literary editor of the *Sunday Mercury*, Newell wrote tongue-in-cheek articles on wartime politics as "Orpheus C. Kerr" (office seeker), giving him just enough edge to suggest an appreciation for the unconventional. Yet it is clear from her self-presentation in letters that Menken recognized that gender norms marked the parameters of his tolerance. She consistently presented herself as intellectual but femininely vulnerable in her letters to Newell. For example, she described her poetic approach with unarming deprecation: "I have no literary adviser – have never known one worthy of the name. I work blindly, as it were. . . . I have only imagination to guide me . . . if you will continue your kindness, by advising me, and making such corrections in my manuscript as you deem necessary, I shall endeavor to bear myself so as not to shame your good counsel." She implied that she would be his Pygmalion whom he could reshape to conform to his ideals.[53]

Striving to live up to her portrayal of him as her savior, mentor, and hero, Newell subscribed to Menken's claims that some personal selves were more "real" than others. His later musings suggest that he truly believed her when she claimed, "I was not born for one hour of the life into which I have been forced – forced by cruel circumstances – until I have scarcely an agency in my own actions. I have always longed for the quiet of country life, far from the busy sins of the town. I detest the stage and all its associations." Her letters to Newell appeared deeply revealing, as she vividly described not only dreams and past tragedies, but also fears of madness and loathing for public life.[54] And perhaps, at some level, Menken could see the problems of public life

[53] AIM to Newell, quoted by Newell, "Adah Isaacs Menken."   [54] Ibid.

and longed to escape it. After all, she was only recently emerging from the scandal with Heenan, and she was well aware that public attention could be demeaning and painful. But she was beginning to attract admiring crowds again and remembering that the attention could also be intensely satisfying. Her intellectual reputation was growing; she was gaining attention for her work as an essayist and a poet. But it was her ability to draw theater crowds that supported her, gave her financial autonomy and a performance high. Newell was no bohemian, but he appreciated her intellectual side and marriage to him could provide a measure of social protection and respectability. It was a step away from sensationalism even if also a step away from social rebellion.

Newell and Menken were in the midst of their epistolary courtship when McHenry County, Illinois, finally certified Menken's divorce from John Heenan on April 3, 1862.[55] The story appeared alongside other tidbits of human interest and gossip, but news of Heenan no longer captured the headlines. War had pushed virtually everything else from the front pages of the papers by the spring of 1862. In April, a stunned nation read of the Battle of Shiloh, which left no victor despite its 25,000 casualties. Menken, meanwhile, began suffering from neuralgia, a painful spasm of the facial muscles that would torment her throughout the rest of her life. In letters to Newell, she bemoaned her life as an actress and addressed the stresses of the theater far more than the war: "I wish to be something more and something better than I am now. I have no opportunity . . . situated as I am now, wandering about the country, unsettled and dissatisfied. . . . I want to get out into a purer atmosphere. I must."[56]

Yet despite such claims, Menken promoted duality of gender more actively than ever. On July 24, 1862, while performing *Mazeppa* in Baltimore, she demanded that Gus Daly submit a publicity statement to the New York papers with terminology meant to accentuate her masculine traits. As if she were a theater critic, she reviewed *Mazeppa,* noting that "Adah with her usual spirit mounted" her horse and was ascending the mountain "when the 'red fire' was suddenly lighted just under the first run, blazed in the horse's eyes, which caused him to fall from the 2nd run (8 feet) to the stage with Adah under his feet." A chaotic scene ensued in which "Women fainted . . . every body [rushed] on the stage, thinking she was dashed to pieces, but before anyone could reach her, she was on her feet, and extricating her horse, which was frightened into almost spasms." But Adah, of course, "was cool, and calmed the horse, amid thunders of

55 "Adah I. M. Heenan v. John C. Heenan, Bill for Divorce," Judge Isaac G. Wilson, McHenry County Circuit Court, March Term A.D. 1862; "A Decree for Divorce Entered April 3, A. D., 1862," plaintiff Adah I. M. Heenan, defendant John C. Heenan, McHenry County Circuit Court, Woodstock, Illinois, copy made and sealed on May 20, 1938, by circuit court clerk Will T. Conn, copies in Kovach, vol. 6.
56 AIM to Newell, quoted by Newell, "Adah Isaacs Menken."

applause, and in an instant mounted up again" and dashed up the runs. With boundless admiration she added, "Nothing daunts this intrepid and fearless girl." Menken essentially emphasized her courage and masculinity in her performance of herself, the celebrity, as well as in the role of Mazeppa.

She also deliberately added the unladylike tidbit that she and R. E. J. Miles, "the most celebrated male Mazeppa, would be going to the race-track together that afternoon, 'for the purpose of losing their small change on the runners.'"[57] More than once, Menken had claimed that she played male roles because they filled the theaters, even though she preferred per-forming weightier female roles, such as "Bianca, Julia, Parthenia, Lady Gray, Rosalind, and Beatrice."[58] She swore to Daly that if financial reasons forced her to play male roles, then "in these parts I will create a new sensation."[59] Much of that "sensation" began to come from the creation of an offstage persona that correlated with her stage performances.

Menken's professed desires and convictions were elements of this offstage persona, and they were consistently inconsistent. In July 1862, Menken declared to Daly that "it [won't] do to be married," and a month later she wrote one last time to Hattie Tyng.[60] Again, she spoke with startling familiarity: "No sign from you to bid me spell out the letters of your name again, and yet something impels me to say over and over again that your heart is my heart and your life in some time has been my life, your Love my Love." This time she signed her feminine name: "faithfully yours, Adah I. Menken."[61] There is no other record of Menken ever again approaching Tyng – who apparently kept her silence as well as the letters.[62] Two months later, Newell proposed and he and Menken married in New York City on September 24, 1862.[63] Newell swam in the mainstream, and others (including Newell) may have mistakenly seen her marriage to him as a retreat to traditional values.[64]

Their marriage certainly allowed her greater manipulation of traditional values, as she turned to Newell for assistance on and off over the next few

[57] Menken to Augustin Daly, July 24, 1892, AIM Correspondence in ALS file (hereafter AIM ALS), Harvard Theatre Collection (hereafter HTC), Hougton Library, Harvard University, Cambridge, Massachusetts.

[58] Menken to Newell, quoted by Newell, "Adah Isaacs Menken"; Menken to Daly, July 18, 1862, AIM ALS HTC.

[59] Menken to Daly, July 18, 1862, AIM ALS HTC.

[60] AIM to Daly, July 18, 1862, AIM ALS HTC.

[61] AIM to Tyng , Aug. 29, 1862, New York. Facsimile of the letter can be found in Davis. Later, as Hattie Tyng Griswold, she later published two collections of essays on other authors – including ones Menken counted as friends – but did not mention Menken.

[62] It is not clear why Menken identified with Tyng's work. Tyng's poetry does not mention affection be-tween women, but dwells heavily on heterosexual romance, mothers, dead children, and descriptions of landscape, flowers, and wind. See Hattie Tyng Griswold, *Apple-Blossoms* (Milwaukee: Strickland, 1874).

[63] Letter from Board of Health Records, New York City, to Allen Lesser, ALC.

[64] AIM to Newell, quoted by Newell, "Adah Isaacs Menken."

months. There are two versions of the story explaining why the marriage
lasted nearly four years while their initial cohabitation lasted only a few days,
both appearing to have originated from Newell. One version has Newell
and Menken taking vows before a Christian minister, before returning to
his home in Jersey City. After a fierce argument over her theatrical career
Newell locked her in the bedroom, inspiring Menken to escape through
the window and return to New York.[65]

But Newell himself later claimed that they had married because of
Menken's "suddenly critical ill health" and the fact that she had no "living relative or intimate friend in the world upon whom she might call for
help."[66] Although Menken kept an active performance schedule that summer, unusually bad ticket sales in July and August suggest that illness may
indeed have affected her performance.[67] In letters to Edwin James, Menken
wrote of illness so severe that she could scarcely sit up in bed.[68] Newell
claimed that she suffered from "an incessant lung fever" that "defied the
best physicians of two cities" until the doctors themselves declared that only
the "fever and delirium of the stage" could save their patient.[69] A letter
from Menken confirms he had reason for believing that she only reluctantly
returned to the stage, when she wrote:

> I dreamed, night before last, of playing 'Mazeppa,' and of falling from the
> horse, feeling acutely the death-wound, and hearing my own voice moan
> out a low death-cry; then of darkness and undefinable chaos, and waking
> in a new world. There my first thought was to look upon my hand for my
> wedding ring, to make Heaven sure. I seemed to hold it in my hand, broken
> to pieces! Still, again, last night I dreamed the very same. What, oh, what
> must I think of it?

It is clear what Newell was to think: Menken's success with *Mazeppa* was
going to destroy their marriage. She chose not to reveal that she was in the
midst of experiencing financial success greater than any she had enjoyed
since the first months of the Heenan scandal. Instead, she commanded with
bittersweet understanding, "Never write a line favorable to any one or any
thing connected with its death-dealing and damning charnel house. Leave

[65] According to Board of Records, a reverend, Millikan, performed the ceremony, ALC. Allen Lesser
refers to a poem Newell wrote about Menken's flight out the window, see Allen Lesser, *Enchanting
Rebel: The Secret of Adah Isaacs Menken* (New York: Beechurst Press, 1947), 92.

[66] AIM to Newell, quoted by Newell, "Adah Isaacs Menken."

[67] Ticket sales for Menken's first week were respectable ($179), but dropped sharply over the next
four weeks to roughly less than half that amount. See receipt book of Wyzeman Marshall, manager
of the Howard Athenaeum and Boston Theatre, from Sept. 10, 1851 to July 25, 1864, HTC, TS
1544.279.99.

[68] AIM to James, May 20, 1862; AIM to James, n.d., AIM ALS HTC.

[69] AIM to Newell, quoted by Newell, "Adah Isaacs Menken."   [70] Ibid.

Photograph that circulated in San Francisco and Nevada during Menken's visit in 1863–64. The photograph alludes to Byron, with the loose collar, a similar arrangement of curls, and her large, slumberous eyes. This may be the image that Charles Warren Stoddard later described as having a "half-feminine masculinity that turned every head."

its criticism to other pens; defile not yours; for you will know the cause of my death – you will know why we were separated."[70] Menken wrote from new heights of success in Baltimore, where she finally revived *Mazeppa* and began her journey to fame and fortune.

Menken rarely returned to New York City after she left for Baltimore that fall, but her bohemian identity moved easily with her: She had re-crafted herself into a liberated intellectual. Once again, she found that social transgression increased her market value. There is no evidence that she ex-perimented with her sexuality other than writing to Hattie Tyng, if one accepts her advances to Tyng as sexual rather than intellectual. If indeed she did choose to pursue women privately, her plagiarized letters to Tyng suggest that she needed a model for that role as well. Menken was not an original, only unusual in her audacity to borrow and experiment. And in the midst of her pursuit of Tyng, she also wooed and married Robert Newell. Her marriage to Newell had the air of a business relationship for her, and did not effect her public image other than to perhaps boost her intellectual clout. There must be something more to her that meets the eye, Americans may have mused (just as they would a century later over Marilyn Monroe and Norman Mailer), if the witty "Orpheus C. Kerr" married her.

The image of the intellectual, private Menken would become incredibly important over the next few years as her offstage persona was soon over-shadowed by her identity as the Tartar prince. The bohemian elements of liberation would explain why she performed such a sensational role, while, for some, the intellectual aspects of her "true" personality would elevate the nature of the performance itself. Mazeppa became Menken's vehicle to fame, and she shaped perceptions of that role just as the daring nature of the role shaped public perceptions of Menken. Soon the two, Menken and Mazeppa, became inseparable.

Chapter 6

Becoming Mazeppa

In 1863, while playing on an extended contract in Baltimore, Menken was arrested as a Confederate spy; the resulting local fame filled seats at her performances for the next few months. In the process, Menken came to a truth she had been testing, but had never wholly embraced: Her status as a public celebrity would make her stage career a success. *Mazeppa* would not bring audiences to Menken, but rather "the Menken" would bring audiences to *Mazeppa*. From this moment on, Menken appeared to act on the understanding that she needed to be as daring and trangressive as the Mazeppa spectators saw on stage because they believed they were seeing Menken herself in the performance. In 1864, when she performed Mazeppa to California and Nevada audiences, Menken even began dressing as a man offstage as well as on, first as a disguise (with whiskers) and later as herself. She began performing Menken as Mazeppa, a romantically tragic figure created by an intellectual mind, a rogue and a hero, vulnerable at times and masterful at others.

The Tartar prince was the epitome of the romantic hero characterized by Byron: fearless, exotic, independent, brooding, and enigmatic, with deeply emotional undercurrents. In the cultivation of her celebrity persona, Menken was already as mysterious and defiant, but in 1863 she began taking her self-performance further still. Just as readers connected Byron to his narrative voice and saw his life as the model for his protagonists, audiences perceived Menken not only as an actress playing Mazeppa on stage but also as the embodiment of Mazeppa as she played him offstage. That is to say, Menken became, as one Californian put it, "an ideal duality of sex"; she combined the best of the two genders into a single captivating force.

In November 1862, Menken accepted her longest contract yet, performing for six months in Baltimore. Despite the fact that Menken came into national consciousness during the Civil War period, these six months marked the only point during which the war intruded into her spotlight. It is possible that Menken chose to go to Maryland with hopes that the warmer climate would improve her health, as the timing would suggest, but given Maryland's precarious political position, it was a dangerous place to choose. It is more likely that Menken went there because it was the only way she could hope to compete with the war, which was claiming newspaper space at a ferocious rate. Like the other border states of Kentucky and Missouri, Maryland suffered from its position as a buffer zone between the North and

South. Maryland was in a particularly bad position because it surrounded the nation's capital on two sides. It also possessed the northern characteristics of finance and commerce, but was socially and culturally southern. Such conflicting loyalties virtually paralyzed Maryland, and Menken was ideally suited to the task of capitalizing on that internal conflict.[1] After all, with her competing performances of virtue and vice as well as various fabricated life stories, she had been presenting herself as a contradictory persona since as least as early as 1857, and had considerable skill at playing to both sides.

Because of Maryland's geopolitical position, its citizens could advocate neither secession nor Union loyalty. This conflict was especially clear in the 1860 election, when Maryland voters had been evenly divided between supporting the Union and Southern Democrat parties, while Abraham Lincoln, the "Black Republican," had received a smattering of votes. Once southern secession was under way, Maryland was "bombarded with pleas and advice from the South," but the few hesitant steps taken toward secession were quickly blocked by opposing citizens. When the first volunteer Union soldiers began passing through Baltimore en route to the battlefields in April 1861, riots broke out, resulting in the death of forty-two soldiers and twelve citizens, with scores of others wounded. Out of desperation, Lincoln declared martial law throughout the state, even though such an action had no legal precedent. On May 14 the citizens of Baltimore awoke to find the Union army encamped overlooking the city; open resistance to the Union came to an end in Baltimore. Three days later Lincoln ordered the suspension of the *writ of habeas corpus* along the railroads that linked Philadelphia, Washington, and Annapolis. Although he faced opposition from the Supreme Court, the suspension allowed the Union army to "arrest any spies or Confederate sympathizers whose acts or statements were inimical to the United States government." Lincoln's actions were necessary to protect the Union capital, but they served to unite many southerners in the conviction that they were defending their right to liberty in the face of unconstitutional aggression.[2] With so many citizens longing to voice resistance but muzzled by various fears, Maryland was an ideal setting for a cultural rebel seeking publicity, but as Menken would see for herself, it was a dangerous place perform defiance.

Menken went to Baltimore shortly after the Battle of Antietam, not coincidentally when the city was swarming with journalists. In September, Robert E. Lee had brought his troops across the Maryland border to offer

[1] Kevin Conley Ruffner, *Maryland's Blue and Grey: A Border State's Union and Confederate Junior Officer Corps* (Baton Rouge: Louisiana State University Press, 1997), 29.

[2] Ibid., 30–31, 34; William A. Blair, "Maryland, Our Maryland": Or How Lincoln and His Army Helped to Define the Confederacy," In *The Antietam Campaign*, ed. Gary W. Gallagher (Chapel Hill: University of North Carolina Press, 1999), 75, 80; Scott Sumpter Sheads and Daniel Carroll Toomes, *Baltimore during the War* (Linthicum, Md.: Toomey Press), 31, 33.

assistance to its citizens who wished to regain their rights. By that point it was virtually impossible for Maryland to successfully secede, had its citizens been so inclined. Nine days later, McClellan's army attacked the Confederate invaders, resulting in Antietam, the bloodiest battle of the war. Baltimore became a medical center over night, and by October the city boasted the largest war prison in the Union. Although Maryland formally remained a state in the Union, it was the captive of the federal government and its military force.[3]

Menken began her six-month run in Baltimore by performing her usual favorites: cross-dressed pieces such as *The French Spy* and *Jack Sheppard* and burlesques such as *Tom and Jerry* and *Three Fast Women*. Advertisements in the *Baltimore Sun* promised that her performances were "Full of Fun, Flash, and Frolic," but she did no better than other local offerings, such as the "merry farce of Mischievous Annie...Mrs. W. J. Florence Assuming Five Characters, with Songs and Dances" offered at the Holiday Theatre in early November.[4] At the end of the first month she finally brought out *Mazeppa*, which proved such an overwhelming success that she performed only *Mazeppa* for the next month.

It was rare for an actor to perform the same role several times in one theater in such a brief period, and the fact that Menken continued playing only *Mazeppa* suggests that the piece kept filling the house. The Front Street Theatre even began adding matinee performances of *Mazeppa* in mid-December. By the end of that month, Menken was again performing other roles, but was including the climactic scene from *Mazeppa* as part of the evening's offerings.[5] Menken wrote to Ed James: "My business is still immense. It is really true that we must turn people away. Tonight is the 13th of 'Mazeppa,' and the house last night was crowded. Ladies crowd not only the dress circle, but the parquet. Such a run of a piece was never known in Baltimore."[6] It was a sunny early winter, and despite the ravages of nearby war and a chronic shortage of currency, the people of Baltimore found the means to appreciate a lively theater season.[7]

According to newspapers, the Baltimore public adored Menken in *Mazeppa*, and considered it a respectable drama. The *Baltimore Sun* reported that although the chief attraction was Menken's beauty and state of undress, her spirit kept the piece from appearing vulgar. "The undress is," the reviewer explained, "not to the extent common to the part in the hands of male representatives, and there is a dash and spirit, and *insouciance* about the

[3] Blair, "Maryland," 75; Sheads and Toomes, Baltimore, 51–62.

[4] Advertisements, *Baltimore Sun*, Nov. 12–15, 1862.

[5] Advertisements, *Baltimore Sun*, Nov. 21–Dec. 15. Matinees were added on Dec. 8.

[6] Adah Isaacs Menken (hereafter AIM) to Ed James, Dec. 1862, Baltimore, in Adah Isaacs Menken Correspondance in ALS file (hereafter AIM ALS) in the Harvard Theatre Collection (hereafter HTC), Houghton Library, Harvard University, Cambridge, Massachusetts.

[7] *Baltimore Sun*, Dec. 15, 1862.

personation which seems to disarm reproach while the Amazonian daring and nerve with which she performs the great exploit of the drama, surpasses conception." It is a statement that leads one to speculate: How far had male actors undressed for the part? There is no indication of anyone having previously expressed dismay over female spectators witnessing male undress. The *Baltimore Sun* stated that Menken played her part with "deep feeling and anguish of the spirit" and women filled the theater alongside the men "even down to the orchestra."[8] Indeed, the papers advertised the play as family entertainment: "Fathers! Mothers!! Daughters!!! Sons!!!! Grandfathers!!! Grandmothers!!! Uncles!!! Aunts!!! The Great Show Piece of Mazeppa! . . . The startling effects, the terrific horsemanship, of Adah Isaacs Menken lashed on the bare back of the Wild horse . . ."[9]

Menken's popularity and acceptance in Baltimore may have been based as much in her spirited support of the Confederacy as her performances. While living in the North, Menken had expressed Union patriotism, but she privately expressed Confederate convictions. In 1860, Menken wrote to Newell, "Oh, were I a man – a soldier – I'd march into the very midst of the battle, and, with voice of thunder and hands of iron, I'd shatter and cast down every chain that binds the glowing heart of the proud South to the pale, sneering sister who would crush her to the dust. . . . I love my country – the South."[10] But Menken had been living in the North, and made her living from the pocket money of its citizens. As usual, it is hard to know to which side Menken gave allegiance; she seems to have given allegiance only where and when it was profitable.

As an avid reader of daily papers she had undoubtedly seen stories of popular actors such as Maggie Mitchell, who were starring in southern cities when the war broke out, and thus made public shows of Confederate allegiance. After describing Mitchell singing Rebel songs in New Orleans, the *Sunday Mercury* warned darkly, "Of course, this outlaws [Mitchell] in all loyal communities for some time to come, and we advise her to remain among the rebels with whom she sympathizes."[11] In her sensational wartime biography, actress Pauline Cushman asserted that Confederates pressured entertainers to demonstrate southern loyalty onstage, suggesting that wartime expressions of allegiance should not be accepted on face value by the public.[12]

[8] "Miss Menken's Benefit," *Baltimore Sun*, Dec. 1862.

[9] Advertisement, *Baltimore Sun*, Dec. 5, 1862, p. 2.

[10] AIM to Robert H. Newell, quoted by Newell in "Adah Isaacs Menken," publication unknown, pasted into "Biography of Adah Isaacs Menken. Extra Illustrated," Harris Rare Books, 76-M545x, Brown University Library, Providence, Rhode Island.

[11] "Amusements," New York *Sunday Mercury*, Jan. 20, 1861, p. 3.

[12] Pauline Cushman, *The Romance of the Great Rebellion: The Mysteries of the Secret Service; A Genuine and Faithful Narrative of . . . Mrs. Pauline Cushman, the Famous Federal Scout and Spy* (New York: Wynkoop and Hallenbeau, 1864), 7–9. It is worth noting that P. T. Barnum owned the copyright to this book, not Cushman. It is equally interesting to note that Cushman looks exactly like Menken in her steel

Although there is no record of Menken's patriotism being questioned, she apparently believed that it soon would be, because on March 17, 1861, she published the densely worded "Pro-Patria" in the *Sunday Mercury* as a sign of her devotion to the Union, and supposedly had copies of the poem passed out at her performances.[13] And while in Baltimore, she even demonstrated her devotion to the cause by donating a gift from "local fans," a diamond bracelet, to raise Union hospital funds.[14]

Publicly professing Confederate allegiance gave Menken no advantage until she starred in Baltimore. In March 1863 she wrote Ed James that she had tucked his picture into "the edge of my large looking glass, in company with Jeff Davis, Gen. Van Dorn, and Gen. Bragg."[15] Various stories claim that Menken made her Rebel sympathies even more visible by hanging pictures of Confederate generals in her dressing room, sending gifts of champagne to celebrate southern victories, and declaring her feelings onstage.[16] Such actions would have been self-destructive in Union-occupied Baltimore, but she definitely did *something* to alert Union officials. As she wrote cheekily to James:

> On Monday I was arrested and brought before the Provost Marshall for being a secessionist. Of course, I did not deny that charge, but I denied having aided the [Confederate States Army]. They wanted to send me to "Dixie," but would not permit me to take but one hundred pounds of luggage. Of course I could not see that. So after a great deal of talk they concluded if I would take "the oath" to let me off. This I refused most decidedly. After all they let me off under "parole." I am to report myself to Provost Marshall Fish in 30 days. If I have continued my unlawful ways I can take my choice between the "oath" or going across the lines without any clothes.[17]

Records of the incident disagree with some of the details of Menken's version but confirm that she was arrested and questioned. The official record of her arrest in Baltimore states "that miss Adelaide Mankin" was reported to Provost-Marshall Fish on July 15, 1863, for burning a flag.[18] The date is

engraving, and gives a biography that sounds remarkably like one of Menken's: "Suffice it to say that, born in the city of New Orleans, on June 10th, 1833, of French and Spanish parentage, I inherited the adventurous spirit of my clime and race," 6.

[13] AIM, "Pro-Patria," *Sunday Mercury*, March 17, 1861.   [14] *Baltimore Sun*, Dec. 8, 1862, p. 1, c. 2.

[15] AIM to Ed James, March 1863, AIM ALS HTC.

[16] Allen Lesser, *Enchanting Rebel: The Secret of Adah Isaacs Menken* (New York: Beechhurst Press, 1947), 100; Wolf Mankowitz, *Mazeppa: The Lives, Loves, and Legends of Adah Isaacs Menken* (New York: Stein and Day, 1982), 90–91; Bernard Falk, *The Naked Lady: A Biography of Adah Isaacs Menken* (London: Hutchinson, 1967), 57.

[17] AIM to Ed James, March, 1862, AIM ALS HTC.

[18] Letter, C. H. Bridges to Allen Lesser, Dec. 8, 1932, Allen Lesser Collection (hereafter ALC), American Jewish Archives, Cincinnati, Ohio. Bridges wrote to Allen Lesser that the above description was the only one of Menken's arrest in military records.

clearly wrong (since by that point Menken was en route to California), but the description of her arrest and the Provost-Marshall's warning corresponds to Menken's account of the event.

In her letter, Menken proceeded gleefully, "I tell you, Ed, I gave them 'particular fits,' and all in good argument, too. Although for the sake of my business, the matter was kept out of the papers, it has done me a great deal of good, and helped me to knock Mr. and Mrs. Barney Williams 'higher than a kite.' I am now playing to crowded houses, and that in 'Mazeppa,' too, which you know had an awful big run here before. But there seems to be more excitement about the piece than ever." Menken credited the arrest, not *Mazeppa*, with increasing her audience, suggesting that a large proportion of Baltimore kept the story alive through hushed conversation and that many supported what they undoubtedly saw as courage. Like Mazeppa himself, to the public Menken rebelled fearlessly against the oppressor. And regardless of personal politics, Menken had proven herself to be as daring offstage as on. Menken was turning into Mazeppa to satisfy her public's desire.

Menken enjoyed success throughout her last three months in Baltimore before succumbing to another attack of neuralgia, and returning to recover at her husband's home in New York. In early July 1863, Menken and Newell began packing their trunks for the month-long journey to the California coast. Newell had arranged to write freelance for San Francisco's famous literary newspaper, *The Golden Era*, so that he could accompany her on the journey.

In retrospect, the timing of their departure makes it look like an evacuation. Just two days before Menken and Newell were scheduled to leave for California, on July 11, 1863, the draft riots broke out across New York City. Angry mobs rose up in opposition to the first conscription notice because it contained a clause allowing those with money to buy themselves out of service. The mobs destroyed property and targeted blacks as scapegoats for the war itself, assaulting or killing African Americans who had the misfortune to fall in their path. On the third day of the riots, Menken and Newell navigated their way through the chaotic city streets to board a steamer bound for Panama. Two days later the riots subsided, leaving 119 people dead and millions of dollars in property damage, while the conscription act remained unchanged. By that point, Menken and Newell were tucked in bunks aboard a ship moving stealthily down the southern coast, pushing through the dark nights without running lights for fear of attracting Confederate privateers.[19]

Menken and Newell first traveled to Aspinwall, now Colón, which marked the eastern end of the Panama Railroad. By 1863, the newly built railroad stretched from Aspinwall to Panama City, eliminating most of the

---

[19] Ernest McKay, *The Civil War and New York City* (Syracuse: Syracuse University Press, 1990), 197–209; Lesser, *Enchanting Rebel*, 106.

dangers of the trip that had once required passengers to travel by flatboat and pack mule.[20] Menken undoubtedly found Panama comfortably familiar; the steamy towns with liquor dealers selling quinine (to combat or cure malaria) must have reminded her of tropical East Texas and South Louisiana. Layers of corsets and crinolines rendered travels through Panama particularly miserable for women, but Menken recovered her health on this trip. Newell, on the other hand, having lived in New York all of his life and displaying little sense of adventure (other than marrying Menken) up to this point, undoubtedly saw the voyage as unmitigated torture. Accounts suggest that he suffered from sea sickness and heat while Menken thrived.[21]

On the western side of the Panamanian Isthmus they boarded yet another steamer and headed north toward California. A crowd of hack and omnibus drivers, hotel runners, and well-dressed Californians greeted the ship when it finally docked in San Francisco on August 7, 1863. Most of the crowd had come to see "the Menken" whom they had heard about from the brightly colored playbills promising her arrival that papered the fences, buildings, trees, lampposts and even rocks of the city for weeks.[22] Poet Charles Warren Stoddard recalled that her poster picture had a "half-feminine masculinity" that turned every head.[23] Meanwhile, local papers printed intriguing information about her fame as a "nude" actress and gifted poet, and noted her frequent marriages. Truthfully, most Californians already knew of Menken's public past; San Francisco papers had been reporting on her activities regularly since the Heenan marriage scandal of 1860.[24] In this way, Menken's public persona continued to guarantee her a robust audience for her stage performances.

The crowd cheered as Menken descended the plank in an eye-catching dress of yellow and black taffeta, an ornate hat tied jauntily under her chin. Perhaps she had heard from fellow bohemian Bayard Taylor how extravagance so defined female dress in California that "even servant-girls" wore silk dresses everyday.[25] She tripped down the plank in robust health for the first time in nearly a year, her husband teetering along behind her. As humorist Orpheus C. Kerr, Newell's impending arrival had also received

[20] Oscar Lewis, *San Francisco: Mission to Metropolis* (Berkeley: Howell-North Books, 1966), 89; Gene Smith, *American Gothic: The Story of America's Legendary Theatrical Family – Junius, Edwin, and John Wilkes Booth* (New York: Simon and Schuster, 1992), 32.

[21] Lesser, *Enchanting Rebel*, 107–109.

[22] Bayard Taylor, "San Francisco, after Ten Years," in *New Pictures from California* (Oakland, Calif.: Biobooks, 1951), 1–2. Taylor describes the crowd that greeted ships in 1859; J. Ross Browne, "Washoe Revisited," third installment, *Harper's New Monthly Magazine* (June 1865), 4.

[23] Charles Warren Stoddard, "La Belle Menken," *National Magazine* (Feb. 1905), 471.

[24] The earliest mention appears to be in the *San Francisco Call*, April 1, 1860, p. 1, c. 3, and regards the letter from Alexander Menken accusing Adah of bigamy. Information on her appears steadily throughout the next few years.

[25] Lesser, *Enchanting Rebel*, 107; Taylor, "San Francisco," 10.

notice, but excitement over his visit seems to have died as soon as he followed Menken down the plank.[26] Although Newell had intended to write for the *Golden Era*, he produced few articles by the time he left with Menken the following spring. Somewhere between New York and San Francisco, the marriage between Menken and Newell had foundered, and in the following months Newell seemed to shrink and virtually disappear in the light of his wife's ever-expanding celebrity.

Over those few months out west, as Menken's celebrity grew, she began performing a mix of male and female gender norms both on- and offstage. On stage, her Mazeppa became more feminized in his attire, while offstage her Menken exhibited masculinity. She first began by disguising herself as a man and gambling with friends on San Francisco's Barbary Coast. During the winter months on the Nevada Comstock, Menken's gender bending became even more pronounced, as she became "one of the boys" who fraternized in the saloons and gambling halls. There is no evidence that Menken ever affected male dress in New York City or Paris (as is sometimes suggested), but she clearly enjoyed wearing trousers out West. Dressing in male clothing provoked a reaction among the public in the west far different than it would have back east. Most residents of California and the Comstock celebrated rather than vilified Menken's gender play; in editorials and reviews they acknowledged "The Menken" as a woman in men's clothing, as a masculine spirit in a woman's body, and as an androgynous self who expressed a sexuality that both men and women found compelling. More than ever before, Menken came to inhabit a fluid space between genders, performing definitions of self that suggested a spectrum of gender, rather than a binary structure. And here a crisis of identification did not arise; the frontier culture embraced her as a singular creature of daring beauty in whatever shade of sex she chose to embody.

Menken had negotiated a favorable contract with California theater king Thomas Maguire, who met the couple at the wharf and escorted them into busy, dust-covered San Francisco. Maguire had several friends in common with both of them, and they probably exchanged news. Before leaving for California in 1850, Maguire had owned a legendary Manhattan pub called the Pewter Mug, where Walt Whitman had mingled with Bowery B'hoys, including George Wilkes.[27] But Maguire's willingness to give into Menken's unusually high contract most likely stemmed from his experience with Menken's cultural precursor, Lola Montez, ten years earlier. When Montez had arrived San Francisco in 1854, Maguire had tried to sign her, but she chose to star at a rival theater – which Maguire took as a personal

[26] Aug. 9, 1863, *Golden Era* (hereafter *GE*). This advertisement focuses on Newell, and mentions Menken only as his wife, "a young and beautiful actress, and gifted poetess."

[27] Peter George Buckley, "To the Opera House: Culture and Society in New York City, 1820–1860," Ph.D. dissertation, State University of New York at Stony Brook, 1984, p. 408.

affront. With Menken he took no chances, agreeing to turn over "one third of the nightly gross receipts and 50 percent of every matinée and Friday night."[28] With most starring actors surviving only on the proceeds from benefit night, the last night of the star's run, the contract with Maguire significantly raised Menken's commercial value.

By the time Menken and Newell arrived, San Francisco was well established as a site of extravagance and wild behavior. Less than a century before, the Spanish had founded the city as a mission, but the 1848 discovery of gold in nearby Sacramento motivated literally tens of thousands of fortune hunters from around the world to set up temporary residence in California. As the closest port, San Francisco blossomed into a thriving metropolis overnight.[29] When the gold slowly ran down to a trickle, the 1860 discovery of silver in the Comstock region – just west of Sacramento, in Nevada territory – kept the city growing.

But even as early as 1863, San Francisco had changed dramatically from its frontier mining days. Returning to San Francisco ten years after his first visit in 1849, Bayard Taylor wrote, "[T]here was not a Californian feature about the picture, if I except the morning-blanket of gray fog. . . . There were no wash-bowls to be seen; no picks; no tents; no wonderful patent machines; no gold-dust." Instead, he found a booming metropolis, with "flags in the breeze, church-spires, fantastic engine houses, gay fronts of dwellings, with the animation of the holiday crowds in the streets below." By contrast, Comstock resident Mark Twain depicted the city as "stately and handsome at a fair distance," but disappointing when a closer view revealed streets "made up of decaying, smoke-grimed wooden houses" and "the barren sand hills toward the outskirts" of town. But Taylor noted that immigrants had brought flora with them, and were in the process of transforming the sandy countryside with acacia, fuchsia, heliotrope, and geraniums. Only the expensive cost of living reminded Taylor that he was back in the land of gold.[30]

And although still depicted as a frontier city by East Coast Americans, San Francisco was as cosmopolitan as New York. An 1864 children's book exclaimed, "There certainly never was such a place got together before, as this San Francisco. The people are rushing in from all quarters of the world – from Europe, from the United States, from Canada, Mexico, South America, the Sandwich Islands, Oregon, and even from China."[31] Despite the fact that Spanish and Native American cultures had shaped the original mission town for over a century, Maguire escorted Menken and Newell through a vibrant

[28] Laurence Estavan, ed., "Lola Montez," in *San Francisco Theatre Research*, vol. 5 (San Francisco, 1938), 2, 104.

[29] Lewis, *San Francisco*, vii. San Francisco was named Yerba Buena until 1847.

[30] Taylor, "San Francisco," 2–4; Mark Twain, *Roughing It* (Berkeley: University of California Press, 1993), 387.

[31] Samuel Goodrich, *The Adventures of Billy Bump* (New York: Sheldon, 1863), 153.

city dominated by the get-rich-quick identity that had marked it for only a decade. With its relative youth, dense but culturally diverse population, and wealth of connections to trade, capital, and government, San Francisco was a cosmopolitan frontier city. Yet, despite its youth, sand-laden wind took the shine off new paint, making buildings look old and careworn before their time.[32] Summer winds covered the city with dust, and frequent rains turned the streets to mud.

Menken had heard much of San Francisco's thriving theatrical culture from her acting peers. There was more than one way to get one's gold, after all; just as gold attracted prospectors and speculators, it attracted others to feed, clothe, and entertain them. Theater had sprung up alongside the mining shacks, and by the mid-1850s the city had already earned a reputation as a "good theatre town" that rivaled established theater districts in New York and New Orleans.[33] In 1850, Thomas Maguire built the Jenny Lind, the most opulent theater in San Francisco. Decorated with deep rose velvet panels, a lavishly gilded ceiling, and a wide stage, the Jenny Lind was often filled to its capacity of 2,000. But like other structures in the dry, windy climate, it was vulnerable to fire and burnt to the ground twice in a single year, only to be rebuilt more lavishly a third time.[34] Meanwhile, Maguire used his eastern connections to lure stars to the Bay City. Several of Menken's peers had performed there before her, including Stephen Masset, Artemus Ward, James Murdoch, and Edwin Booth. Booth's brother, Junius Booth, Jr., came in 1852 and made a career as the city's best leading man before eventually starring with Menken in *Mazeppa*.[35]

By the time of Menken's arrival, in 1863, San Francisco could claim one of the most theatrically sophisticated audiences in the United States. And although virtually any kind of mainstream entertainment could be found there in any given week, San Franciscans as a whole preferred light entertainment, especially the lowly "variety show."[36] "Variety," a mix of comedy, song, dance, and often minstrelsy and pantomime, conflicted with middle-class ideals of self-improvement, making it markedly more popular with western audiences than eastern. Most of the city's inhabitants were more interested in improving their fortunes than themselves, and light-hearted entertainment gave them a welcome respite from days marked by extremes of boredom and danger. Maguire fully subscribed to P. T. Barnum's belief that "what gave pleasure to democratic audiences was good"; as long as the performance brought happiness (and money to his pocket), he considered it worthwhile.[37] His audience agreed, by purchasing tickets.

[32] Taylor, "San Francisco," 2.   [33] Lewis, *San Francisco*, 98.
[34] Constance Roarke, *Troupers of the Gold Coast; or, The Rise of Lotta Crabtree* (New York: Harcourt Brace and Co., 1928), 32–34.
[35] Smith, *American Gothic*, 51–53.   [36] Roarke, *Troupers*, 150.
[37] Neil Harris, *Humbug: The Art of P.T. Barnum* (Chicago: University of Chicago Press, 1973), 78.

The less vilified image of women in public San Francisco probably appealed to Menken as well, not only because it gave her greater freedom, but also because it felt familiar. Having spent her adolescence in French Louisiana, Menken would have been accustomed to women participating in "the sensuous atmosphere around them: drinking wine, enjoying music and literature, [and] wearing bright colors." Although there was a growing restraint among the California middle class, women in both New Orleans and San Francisco could partake in social freedoms considered inappropriate in other American cities because of the historic variables that had shaped their communities. New Orleans had a history of celebrating sensual pleasures and the arts. Likewise, the frenetic economy, scarcity of women, and multicultural population prevented a hegemonic response to women's public behavior in San Francisco until the late 1860s.[38] Unlike New Orleans, however, San Francisco's culture was overwhelmingly masculine, making Menken's onstage performances as a woman remarkable yet, somewhat paradoxically, making it easier for her to dress in male clothing offstage.

As Maguire escorted Menken and Newell about town he discussed his plans for *Mazeppa*. Most of San Francisco's residents made a living either mining or servicing the mining industry. Catering to a population of 60,000 that was mostly white, male, and twenty to forty years of age, San Francisco had "eight hundred liquor dealers, ninety-five hairdressers, eighty-four restaurants, seventeen banks, and twelve daily newspapers." Most migrants to California came without family; even the married men left their families behind, hoping to make a quick fortune and return home. These miners were hungry for entertainment, and written material was easy to transport to distant mining regions outside San Francisco. By 1860, some 132 periodicals had been started in San Francisco alone, "printed in six different languages, representing eight religious denominations and seven political parties."[39] A culture dependent on the media meant one enamored with celebrities. Maguire chose to use the familiar Menken paradox to foster her celebrity, portraying her as a mysterious woman whose life lay open for the public to read.

Menken hardly needed Maguire to explain the importance of newspapers, and wasted little time before hand-delivering samples of her poetry to

---

[38] Nancy Walker, "The Historical and Cultural Setting," in *Approaches to Teaching Kate Chopin's The Awakening*, ed. Bernard Koloski (New York: Modern Language Association of America, 1988), 70; for primary accounts of New Orleans, I recommend Grace King, *New Orleans: The Place and the People* (New York: Negro Universities Press, 1968), and Lyle Saxton, comp., *Gumbo Ya-Ya: A Collection of Louisiana Folk Tales* (Gretna: Pelican Press, 1987).

[39] Roger Austen, *Genteel Pagan: The Double Life of Charles Warren Stoddard* (Amherst: University of Massachusetts Press, 1991), 16; Linda Peavey and Ursula Smith, *Women in Waiting in the Westward Movement: Life on the Home Frontier* (Norman: University of Oklahoma Press, 1994), introduction and ch. 1; Walton Bean, *California: An Interpretive History* (New York: McGraw Hill Books, 1968), 185.

the *Golden Era*, an unpretentious literary paper that put comical social commentary alongside poetry, short stories, and theater reviews. Joe Lawrence, owner and editor of the paper, described her arrival: "'How do you do? I'm Adah Menken,' the Goddess said, as she paused in the entrance to our ink-stained office. At least a dozen of us were sitting around the room. We leaped to our feet, but none had the grace to reply to that vision of rare beauty in white."[40] Menken soon spent her spare hours getting to know the journalists who socialized as well as worked in the offices of the *Golden Era*. These self-proclaimed bohemians readily welcomed both Menken and Newell as kindred spirits.

Bret Harte, Charles Henry Webb, Ina Coolbrith, and Prentice Mulford formed the nucleus of the group. Although Mulford would eventually abandon the bohemians to write for the Purity League, a postwar organization dedicated to the moral uplift of San Francisco, the rest remained lifelong friends. Menken probably knew Webb from Pfaff's, before he joined the Union army. The Battle of Manassas had convinced Webb of the insanity of war, and he fled to San Francisco only months before Menken's arrival. Despite her work as a journalist, Coolbrith's greatest talent lay in poetry, and she would later became California's first poet laureate, before discovering and nurturing the talent of young Jack London. Harte attained the greatest fame of them all, achieving lasting recognition for his humorous depictions of mining life in stories such as "The Outcasts of Poker Flat." Although Harte left the West not long after Menken to pursue greater fortunes in the East, he maintained a lifelong correspondence with his fellow bohemians. He never warmed to Menken, though, and later sketched an unflattering parody of her in a short story called "Crusade of Excelsior."[41]

The group at the *Golden Era* were accustomed to temporary joiners, and readily accepted Menken as a fellow bohemian. Mark Twain frequently visited to seek respite from his job at the *Territorial Enterprise*, the newspaper of the Comstock region, and reviewed Menken twice before coming to know her personally. Joaquin Miller also dropped in and out of San Francisco, but his role in Menken's experiences is something of a mystery. Despite his claims of friendship, evidence suggests that he was in Europe in the fall of 1863. In any case, Miller shared Menken's theatrical sensibilities: He became famous as the "Singer from the Sierras" while touring Europe dressed as a caricature of a frontiersman in a "red shirt, high boots and a sombrero."[42] Humorist Artemus Ward considered himself a member of the bohemian

---

[40] Mankowitz, *Mazeppa*, 107.

[41] Albert Parry, *Garrets and Pretenders: A History of Bohemianism in America* (New York: Covici, Friede, 1933), 30; Richard O'Connor, *Bret Harte: A Biography* (Boston: Little, Brown, 1966), 70–71, 81; George Stewart, *Bret Harte: Argonaut and Exile* (Boston: Houghton Mifflin, 1931), 122.

[42] Joaquin Miller, *Adah Isaacs Menken* (1892; Ysleta, Texas: Edwin B. Hill, 1934); Bean, *California*, 192–193; M. M. Marberry, *Splendid Poseur* (New York: Thomas J. Crowell, 1953), 48–49.

circle whenever he returned to the West. Ambrose Bierce, embittered by war, visited for several months not long after Menken's departure. New York bohemian and journalist Ada Clare also visited as a contributor to the *Golden Era*. In fact, the group itself was only visiting in a sense; like most of the Anglo-American population, none of the bohemians were native Californians.

At Harte's urging, the San Francisco group called themselves "bohemians" and attempted to replicate the now famous gatherings at Pfaff's. Harte alluded to Henry Clapp, Jr.'s "*Feuilletons*"(Papers) by naming his *Golden Era* column "Bohemian *Feuilletons.*" He titled his collection of essays *The Bohemian Papers* and his later reminiscences of California *Bohemian Days.*[43] Ironically, Harte would have been the last person to draw up a chair in a smoky tavern like Pfaff's. A meticulous writer and (temporarily) devoted family man, Bret Harte rarely took part in social gatherings outside the offices of the *Golden Era*. Like Menken, Harte was creating and selling an image.

Harte's concept of "bohemian" highlights the fundamental differences between the social environments of San Francisco and New York. The bohemians were popular in California; they suited the culture, unlike the bohemians in New York, who functioned as a sort of protest group. As much as they tried, the Californians could not succeed in replicating the New York gatherings, because their audience responded too differently. They *resembled* those who filled Pfaff's tavern; nearly all of them wrote for their living and defined themselves as "those free and easy knights of the quill who are banded together in the bonds of good fellowship and minor journalism, and may be characterized as the 'unterrified Democracy of the Republic of Letters.'"[44] And like the New Yorkers, their eagerness to share social and political critique was often an excuse for a good time. However, unlike the bohemians in New York, the Californians could not rebel against their surrounding culture. The New York bohemians rebelled against middle-class social values and esthetics. But in California rebellion itself became conformity, since the mainstream population celebrated its rebels much more openly than on the East Coast. Even their literary forums reflected the difference: Unlike the snidely intellectual *Saturday Press,* the *Golden Era* had a breezy informality popular with miners, middle-class families, and intellectuals alike, making it the most successful literary journal in the West.[45] In essence, the minimal power of middle-class culture in San Francisco altered what it meant to be bohemian. Back east, New York bohemians depended on the existence of a larger restrictive culture to create the pleasure

[43] See humorous letter on Pfaff's as a celebrated hangout, *New York Saturday Press,* Sept. 23, 1865; O'Connor, *Bret Harte*, 70.

[44] "The Siege of Bohemia: Slaughter of the Innocents!," *GE*, Feb. 14, 1864, p. 4, c. 6.

[45] Bean, *California*, 185.

of rebellion, and middle-class Americans enjoyed the thrill of transgression the bohemians provided. But in San Francisco, if anyone was rebelling, it was the embryonic middle-class culture trying desperately to bring order to what they saw as chaos and moral depravation.

To be accepted as a fellow bohemian in the city's most vocal literary circle brought Menken distinct advantages. The *Golden Era* habitually overstated the triumphs of newcomers, and their write-up of Menken was over the top: "In every city on the other side of the Continent she has everywhere achieved brilliant successes. . . . the name of Adah Isaacs Menken is perhaps the surest and strongest attraction that now finds place upon the playbills of any theatre in the Atlantic states." The paper added that she "attracted wide attention and high critical commendation" for her poetry. In fact, before Menken had set foot on the western shore, editors at the *Golden Era* established her intellectual ability by publishing her wartime poem "Saved."[46] The California public supported the *Golden Era* and the *Golden Era* lauded Menken − an equation that enabled Menken to enter the higher realms of San Francisco's public arena with relatively little effort.

Besides a launching a formidable advertising campaign, Maguire had assembled a first-rate cast and scheduled two weeks of rehearsals before the box office began selling tickets at the end of the summer. By *Mazeppa's* opening night on August 24, 1863, the California public clamored to see her: "Washington street and all the adjacent thoroughfares were thronged with people, all intent on effecting the most desirable position − in fact any position, in Maguire's Opera House. . . . We doubt if a similar audience was ever gathered together on a like occasion." Interestingly, San Francisco papers had reported a nearly identical situation when Lola Montez had opened ten years before.[47] But unlike the case of Montez, Menken's debut received rave reviews. The critic for the *Alta* later asserted that Menken "showed herself more of an accomplished actress than we had been led to believe from the sensational notices which have beset her career." She is "calm, considerate, careful and judicious − one of the modern natural school."[48] Of course, regardless of her talent, the public knew that it was her notoriety that sold tickets. A week afterward, Webb quipped, "It had been privately whispered around that the play was an excessively improper one, and consequently every one went to see it."[49] The drama critic for the *Golden Era* remarked that tickets were sold out hours before the performance and hundreds were turned away nightly, and that Menken's audience included local officials, "ladies," journalists, and miners. Both the *Alta* and *Golden Era* focused on Menken's superlative athleticism and equestrian skill, with the latter commenting that "Miss Menken's acting is as free from the platitude

[46] "Adah Isaacs Menken," *GE*, Aug. 9, 1863.   [47] Estavan, ed., *San Francisco Theater Research*, 12.
[48] "The Debut of Menken," *Daily Alta,* Aug. 25, 1863.   [49] Inigo, "Things," *GE*, Aug. 30, 1863.

and commonplace of the stage as her poetry is from those of the language." It was telling that all referred to her as Miss Menken and not Mrs. Newell.[50]

A few unfavorable reviews also appeared in the city's newspapers, but they had no noticeable impact on Menken's popularity. For the most part, negative observers focused on Menken's impropriety on stage rather than the quality of her performance, and criticized the female public for attending the show. One editor sarcastically remarked, "Modesty has gone to Salt Lake City to see Brigham Young's harem, and the Menken is almost here. . . . Adah is young and festive, and rides bare-backed. Ladies will, of course, attend the performances."[51] The Sacramento *Union* described Menken as "a pretty, shapely Jewess, considerably more undressed than any actress yet tolerated on the American stage. . . . a crowded audience, illuminated with ladies applauded. Prudery is obsolete." Likewise, the San Francisco *Bulletin* commented: "A number of ladies were present, determined to know if the performance was a proper one for them to behold."[52] The reporters' comments on female attendance were designed to question the propriety of "ladies" at Menken's show, but also suggest that an unusual number of women (particularly given the small percentage of female residents) attended Menken's performances in California. The *London Illustrated News* paraphrased a San Francisco paper that stated that sensation pieces were corrupting the tastes of theatergoers. The reporter alluded to Menken as the chief culprit, saying, "[T]he boards had become debauched by adventurers in the profession, who, lacking the talents to secure pre-eminence, inaugurated a vulgar style of pieces, termed "spectacular" in which exposed limbs and indecent rant usurped the creations of mind; and illustrious authors were thrust aside for the accommodation of literary empirics."[53]

Mark Twain also attended *Mazeppa* that fall. Before seeing the performance, he had dismissed Menken as a "shape actress," who succeeded only because of her figure.[54] On September 13, 1863, he published one of the most descriptive reviews of *Mazeppa*, suggestively titled "The Menken – Written Especially for Gentlemen":

> When I arrived in San Francisco, I found there was no one in town – at least there was no body in town but "the Menken" – or rather, that no one was being talked about except that manly young female. I went to see her play "Mazeppa" of course. . . . She appeared to me to have but one garment on – a thin, tight white linen one, of unimportant dimensions; I forget the name of the article, but it is indispensable to infants of tender age. . . . Here

[50] "Maguire's Opera House, " *GE*, Sept. 20, 1863.   [51] Falk, *Naked Lady*, 66.

[52] Sacramento *Union* and San Francisco *Bulletin*, quoted in *Wilkes' Spirit of the Times*, Jan. 1, 1864.

[53] *London Illustrated News*, Nov. 26, 1864, noted in Nicholas Kovach Collection, Special Collections, University of Minnesota, Minneapolis.

[54] George Lyman, *The Saga of the Comstock Lode: Boom Days in Virginia City* (New York: Charles Scribner's Sons, 1934), 270.

every tongue sings the praises of her matchless grace, her supple gestures, her charming attitudes. Well, possibly these tongues are right. In the first act, she rushed on the stage, and goes cavorting around after "Olinska"; she bends herself back like a bow; she pitches headforemost at the atmosphere like a battering-ram; she works her arms, and her legs, and her whole body like a dancing jack; her every movement is as quick as thought; in a word, without any apparent reason for it, she carries on like a lunatic from the beginning of the act to the end of it. At other times she "whallops" herself down on the stage, and rolls over as does the sportive pack mule after his burden is removed. If this be grace then the Menken is eminently graceful.[55]

It is significant that although Twain renders Menken's performance ridiculous, he refrains from warning the public to avoid the show. Twain had already earned a reputation for meting out harsh criticism and condemning performances when he felt they deserved it. But in this review Twain deliberately emphasized sensual elements of the performance, as if to sell it to a sporting crowd. He also portrayed Menken's acting as absurd rather than simply bad, which suggested as much criticism of the enthralled audience as of the performer. What she did was deliberate, but their fascination with such a performance was ludicrous.

A lack of Victorian sensibility in early 1860s San Francisco may partially explain the city's celebration of Menken's controversial act. Middle-class social mores did not come to exert significant impact on San Francisco until later in the decade, when the newly completed railroad altered the city's demographics. Hence, Californians on the whole openly reveled in novelties; there was no need to criticize and sneer to mask one's enjoyment of the spectacle. Although Menken's *Mazeppa* unsettled accepted gender identities without explicitly challenging them, she did, in the words of Robert Allen, combine "spectacle, feminine sexuality, and speech – a combination that was for nineteenth-century bourgeois males particularly fascinating and potentially disconcerting."[56] Of course, the novelty of Menken's act was the famous horse ride.

By aggressively pursuing a woman out of his league before being stripped and forced to ride in passive pseudo-nudity, Menken's Mazeppa combined elements of gender performance in ways that California audiences particularly appreciated. Menken did not simply play a male role or even an androgynous one; she played a male *and* female role. She was both the male lover of the countess Olinska and the naked woman whom Olinska's father had lashed to the back of a horse. Menken's attraction was only heightened when she recovered her manhood, waged an aggressive battle, and won the heroine. Menken was no longer slim and boyish but volumptuously curved; she played up her physical changes on stage out west. In shifts and changes that blurred before the audience's eyes, she appeared to be the epitome of both masculinity and femininity. Reviews in the *Alta* and *Golden Era* consistently stress Menken's athleticism and equestrian skills as enhancing her beauty. One journalist effusively describes her as uniting "the more delicate muscular compactness of the masculine frame with the willowy elasticity of the feminine" and asserts that she is "thus admirably qualified to represent characters like Mazeppa . . . characters nominally masculine, but imbued by the dramatist with the poetic phrasing which amount to an idealized duality of sex."[57] In other words, Menken displayed male traits such as strength, agility, and self control without appearing "mannish."

This perceived "duality of sex," not once noted in New York but frequently observed by Californians, is particularly interesting since Menken emphasized the female contours of her body *more* in West Coast productions of *Mazeppa*. Back east, Menken simulated nudity in a body stocking and a flowing tunic that ended at mid-thigh. By Victorian standards the outfit was provocative, but still less suggestive of her shape than either the Greek *chiton* or the close-fitting chemise and shorts outfit that she adopted in California. In productions such as *Jack Shepard, Black-Ey'd Susan*, and *The French Spy*, Menken wore loose shirts, sailor outfits with wide-legged trousers, and enveloping suits. But photographs make it clear that the boyishly Menken of Cincinnati was now a shapely woman, who was at that time at least twenty-eight. Yet while Menken now emphasized her body more explicitly, Californians commented on her "masculinity." Their commentary indicates that they considered her "duality of sex" an essential characteristic of her image. They suggested, in fact, that Menken's female body encapsulated a masculine spirit, making her a combination of both regardless of which role she played.

Menken's success at presenting feminine and masculine traints on stage is especially apparent in reviews of her performances penned by women. Both Florence Fane and Tess Ardenne of *The Golden Era* focused particular attention on Menken's male impersonations. In an article dated September 27, 1863, Fane referred to Menken as Cassimer, suggesting that she had seen Menken in *Mazeppa* before attending a performance of *The French Spy*. Fane repeated comments made by a group of women whom she overheard exclaiming that "*she* was bewitching in the 'Spy,'" and exaggerated her disillusion upon hearing Cassimer described as female: "[L]anguage is inadequate to express my emotions. *She* indeed! My brave, my beautiful and suffering hero, *only* a woman?" She overheard the "Accidental Ladies" express appreciation for Menken's body: "They had the hardihood to declare that they

[57] "Dramatic and Musical," *GE*, Sept. 13, 1863, p. 8.

admired – nay, doted on Cassimer, knowing he was a woman! They said they didn't see why women might not see a woman in a military undress if they chose." But Fane would have none of it: "It is needless for them to excuse themselves by talking about the Greek Slave," she huffs, referring to Hiram Powers's controversial statue. "*She* didn't put on boy's clothes, and inveigle unsuspecting young ladies into feeling an interest for her sorrows." Fane playfully suggested that Menken shows her insensitivity by bewitching "all the world with her lovely nakedness" as a man, when she was in fact a woman.[58] Fane and the "Accidental Ladies" are clearly attracted to Menken as male, even knowing that she is female under her male persona.[59] Menken may have had the hips and breasts of a woman, but she clearly projected masculine beauty through expressions of aggression and physical prowess. Despite her flippancy, Fane acknowledged attraction to Menken, suggesting that the actress's "lovely nakedness" bewitched women as well as men.

After seeing Menken play the part of William the Sailor in *Black Ey'd Susan*, on April 24, 1864, Tess Ardenne felt compelled to defend Menken's frequently disparaged thespian talent. Ardenne, mixing gender pronouns with abandon, claimed that Menken as a man, is "handsome enough to turn the heads of all the girls in any port her ship may enter." She rhapsodizes over Menken's physical gestures: "[Y]ou never saw hands speak like hers; I knew before that they had a language of their own . . . I did not know that they could use so perfectly the language of affection." She described Menken's portrayal of William's love as "passion robbed of its earthly dross, loving the object for her own sake. . . . It is a conception of man's love in its highest form, such as makes a woman's heart beat with joy and pride to have inspired." [60] Ardenne stepped away from her ostensibly objective appreciation for Menken's talent and implied that Menken's portrayal of a man in love was appealing *because* she was a woman – that as a woman playing a man, she could love women the way they want to be loved. Her sentiments clearly echo those copied by Menken in her letter to Hattie Tyng. The deep identification between the self and the beloved deepened the quality of the relationship enjoyed by the participants, be they lovers or not.

Menken accessed cultural power by revealing social liminalities, but why did her bending of gender provoke the desire of men and women alike? The comments of Florence Fane, Tess Ardenne, and the "Accidental Ladies" in San Francisco contradicted the common assumption that breeches parts were merely used to show off a woman's figure. According to the various

[58] Florence Fane, "Florence Fane in San Francisco: About Poor Cassimer," *GE*, Sept. 27, 1863, p. 1, c. 2.

[59] I have not been able to find any explanation for what Fane meant to imply with the term "Accidental Ladies." Perhaps she meant to suggest women who aspire to a higher class, or prostitutes who dressed and behaved like ladies when at the theater.

[60] Tess Ardenne, "Black-Eyed Susan," *GE*, April 24, 1864, p. 5, c. 3.

descriptions supplied by Californian men and women, Menken looked and acted both male and female (to use normative terms). Surely, if she had appealed as overtly feminine, female reviewers would not have depicted Menken as a handsome boy; they would have recognized her as a woman dressed in revealing clothing, intended to entertain male viewers. This is not to suggest that the state of being appealing is a gendered one, but rather that audiences respond according to whether a presentation includes or excludes them. The female reviewers suggest that Menken targeted both sexes and that her success added to her celebrity appeal.

With her duality of gender, Menken tapped into a particular kind of sexual appeal that brought together society's preconceptions of masculine and feminine sexual expression. For over a century before her appearance, male thinkers had explored the "'peculiarities' of women," suggesting that woman were a source of mystery. Several decades later, Havelock Ellis defined "the male sexual impulse" as "open, aggressive, unproblematic" but the woman's as "elusive."[61] Menken, with her shifting identities and athletic performances, managed to strike a balance between these conceptual norms, enhancing her ability to appeal to a variety of viewers. Playing to the heterosexual male gaze, she could be excitingly open as well as mysterious. Yet she also enticed female viewers as a dashing, athletic young man able to express affection with the deep emotion shared only with female friends. If men and women were, as Henry James noted at the end of the century, becoming separated by an ever-widening chasm of gender norms, who could fill the needs of that society better than a Menken?[62] Her gender duality invited all to enjoy her spectacle.

Menken's appeal may also indicate sexual tensions in her predominantly white male audience. Many of her viewers came from mining camps outside San Francisco as well as from the city itself. By the 1860s, San Francisco had more women than the decade before, but sex ratios were far from even, and a significant proportion of those women worked in prostitution. Homosexual desire undoubtedly proliferated in isolated mining camps but also in the city, where white men inhabited a world separate from women of their social class. Such all-male environments may have created an atmosphere of unease, as men began to fear association with or – worse – attraction to other men. If this was the case, watching Menken's convincing performance of gender duality may have both evoked and released those tensions. In some ways, her performance reinforced the conventional images of masculinity and femininity, despite the fact that she switched genders. The male characters she played were masculine by virtue of their heroic aggression, and the

[61] Thomas Laqueur, *Making Sex: Body and Gender from the Greeks to Freud* (Cambridge: Harvard University Press, 1992), 226.

[62] Larzer Ziff, *The American 1890s: Life and Times of a Lost Generation* (New York: Viking Press, 1966), 275.

women signified themselves through dependence and vulnerability. In the imagined essentialism of the roles, men could find assurance that whatever they did for release, they would never forfeit their intrinsic masculinity. By identifying with Menken, they might also imagine themselves at once both the passive female and aggressive male, and thus play out same-sex desire in an unthreatening way. Finding pleasure in being both male and female at the same time would make *Mazeppa* particularly satisfying, as Menken rapidly transformed from male to female before the audience's eyes.

Menken further delighted her San Francisco audience by poking fun at her loose reputation by putting on a play with the particularly racy title *Three Fast Women*. Menken had performed this piece many times before but never to such an appreciative audience. Since performing the piece in 1861 in Louisville, she had made a habit of adapting *Three Fast Women* to include local references. It was a lightweight protean comedy in which she played several male and female roles. The show's chief attraction was Menken as the minstrel "Bones."[63] Outside San Francisco her impersonation of a male minstrel significantly departed from gender norms, as women rarely took part in minstrel shows. But the Bay City had seen other women play male minstrels, most notably, young Lotta Crabtree.[64] In other regions, men performed minstrel roles almost exclusively, and their exaggerated versions of black women were often the climax of the show. Indeed, female impersonators served to playfully highlight the homosexual element present yet normally subordinate in blackface minstrelsy and promoted an ambiguously licentious atmosphere that blurred conventional gender outlines for male spectators.[65] So what can we make of Menken, parodying the typical minstrel performer? In *Three Fast Women*, Menken not only traversed the gender line by playing five male and four female characters, but she complicated the image by introducing race as well – by poking fun at those white men in blackface. For all her audience knew, Menken may have been a free woman of color. So she may have been black, passing for white, parodying a white man in blackface. *Three Fast Women* became Menken's most popular San Francisco production after *Mazeppa*.

Menken played male characters so successfully onstage that her friend and co-star June Booth convinced her to dress in drag and accompany him to the Barbary Coast – at a time when going to the Barbary Coast was as daring for a woman as donning trousers. At that time, the Barbary Coast, a

---

[63] Playbills for "Three Fast Women," Dec. 3, 1861 (no place) and Louisville (n.d.), Playbill Portfolio, Billy Rose Theatre Collection, New York Public Library, Lincoln Center, New York (hereafter BRTC). Menken claimed to have written the play, but varying sources indicated that she merely rewrote an already existing British farce; Mankowitz, *Mazeppa*, 104–106. There was another play called *Three Fast Men* also being performed during this period.

[64] Roarke, *Troupers*, 136.

[65] Eric Lott, *Love and Theft: Blackface Minstrelsy and the American Working Class* (New York: Oxford University Press, 1993), 27.

nine-block area of saloons, brothels, and dance halls bordering the theater district, had not yet gained the notoriety it attained after the war, but it was clearly the city's epicenter of vice.[66] Menken hid her famous face behind a bushy mustache and cigar and joined a game of faro. She succeeded in fooling everyone enough to gamble undetected by the gossip mongers, and enjoyed that first evening so much that she continued to disguise herself as a man and frequent the gaming tables. When her friend Artemus Ward visited the city in the spring of 1864, they supposedly made the rounds together.[67]

As Menken moved toward masculine independence offstage she also moved away from expressing herself through poetry. In the first few months of her stay, Menken brazenly republished poetry from the *Sunday Mercury* as "written for the *Golden Era*." (One can only imagine Newell's reaction, as the former literary editor of the *Sunday Mercury*.) In reality, she contributed only three new poems to the *Golden Era*, the last ones she would ever write. In them the pious female voice of her New York poetry has vanished, and the poet's voice is confessional, naked in anger and grief. The poems are strikingly dramatic, intensely self-aware "and unsparing in [their] condemnation of a male-dominated world that restricts woman's freedom, mocks her expression of genius, and dooms her, body and soul to unhappiness." Ironically, they are also generally considered the most interesting ones she produced, outside "Judith." She included all three in *Infelicia*, opening her collection with her most controversial, "Resurgam," and closing with the last poem she ever published, "El Suspiro," renamed "Infelix." When William Rossetti put together his anthology, *American Poems*, in 1902, he included "Aspiration" and "Infelix" among her four best poems.[68]

Menken published "Aspiration," in September 1863, a month after her arrival. In it, she expresses the poet's desire and failure to transcend mortality through written expression. The narrator remains ungendered, suggesting that aspirations of the soul transcend the boundaries of sex. An unusually serene poem for Menken, "Aspiration" lacks the emotional self-exposure of her other two poems. Its noticeably shorter length, precision of language, and concise phrasing suggests that Menken was experimenting with poetic forms more than she had previously.

In late November 1863, "Resurgam" incited public commentary. Menken may have meant to allude to Walt Whitman's "Resurgemus," which he first published in the New York *Daily Tribune* on June 21, 1850, and later

[66] Josephine Baker Barnhart, *The Fair but Frail: Prostitution in San Francisco, 1849–1900* (Reno: University of Nevada Press, 1986), 32.

[67] Mankowitz, *Mazeppa*, 110.

[68] Joan Sherman, "Introduction" to *Collected Black Women's Poetry* (New York: Oxford University Press, 1988), xxv–xxxvi; William Michael Rosetti, ed., *American Poems* (London: E. Moxon, Son, 1925), 445–448.

renamed "Europe" in the 1860 edition of *Leaves of Grass*.[69] In his poem Whitman depicts brave young sons rising up against European despotism.[70] Menken's poem bears little resemblance to Whitman's except for her use of the word "Resurgam," which signifies his articulation of triumphant conviction. She cries "Resurgam!" again and again, throughout the seven stanzas depicting the poet's death through a lover's betrayal. But readers may also have understood "Resurgam" as an allusion to classical literature. While discussing the work of another artist, in 1868, the *New York Evening Post* defined "Resurgam" as "the old classic fable implicitly believed by the ancients, which teaches the rebirth or resurrection of the Phoenix from the ashes of its parent."[71] However, in Menken's poem the repetition of "Resurgam!" provides no hope but rather heightens the intense loneliness of a poem overloaded with melancholy. Made up of meaningful images, its overall meaning was paradoxically indecipherable. For example: "The stars were strangled, and the moon was blind/with the flying clouds of deep despair./Years and years the songless soul waited to drift out beyond the sea of pain where the shapeless life was wrecked." Once again, Menken portrays the first-person narrator as a white woman with flowing gold hair and wearing "crimson roses." She complicates her previously buoyant self-portrayal by describing herself as "Dead in this beauty!/Dead in this velvet and lace!/Dead in these jewels of light!/Dead in the music!/Dead in the dance!" "Resurgam" presents a Menken entirely different from the joyous, boy-like woman the California public had come to expect.[72]

A full month after Resurgam's publication, "Occasia Owen" remarked in her column, "Some folks pretend to like it. But I wouldn't be afraid to wager . . . that they are only putting on an 'extra thrill.' It is above their comprehension, but, presuming that it *must* mean something, they cry 'charming' to cover their ignorance." The name "Occasia Owen" (occasion owing) suggests that this review was meant to be taken in good humor, but it slowly grew less facetious. When Owen reached the end, she metaphorically threw her hands up in resignation: "I take back that word 'bosh,' as applied to 'Resurgam.' Yet I will not own it 'charming.' It is too pitiful to be pretty. The wail of a heart stung to madness, yet proudly wearing its grief. The despairing moan always resounding above the boastful 'Resurgam.'"[73] Owen's comments reflected the public debate over whether Menken was an unusual genius or a pseudo-intellectual. Once again, she defied others' attempts to categorize her.

---

[69] Walt Whitman, *Leaves of Grass: Comprehensive Readers Edition*, eds. Harold W. Blodgett and Sculley Bradley (New York: W. W. Norton, 1965), 266n.

[70] Whitman, "Europe," in *Leaves of Grass*, 268.

[71] "Resurgam," *New York Evening Post*, Aug. 20, 1868, p. 2, c. 1.

[72] AIM, "Resurgam," *GE*, Nov. 29, 1863, p. 4, c. 4.

[73] Occasia Owen, "Feathers. Pluck, No. 57," *GE*, Jan. 3, 1864.

It is impossible to say whether Menken *ever* stood unmasked before the public, but many readers probably assumed she did in "El Suspiro," a poem that suggests genuine pathos. Arguably one of her best poems, "El Suspiro" came at the end of Menken's dazzling season in San Francisco. By January 1864 she had earned a fortune, become the reigning celebrity of San Francisco, and ventured regularly into the city streets disguised as a man. She had achieved the independence she had so often depicted in her autobiographical stories but perhaps at great personal cost. If taken as an expression of her feelings, "El Suspiro" suggested to readers that she felt intense confusion over her goals: "I can but ever own my life is vain/A desert void of peace;/I missed the goal I sought to gain,/I missed the measure of the strain/That lull's Fame's fever in the brain,/And bids Earth tumult cease."

The last stanza focuses on the heartbreak the poet feels when confronting her public image. She suggests that her celebrity self has eclipsed her "real self," which is left behind, forgotten in the adulation the public pays to her projected self-creation. By expressing masculine characteristics, Menken acknowledges having successfully alienated herself from women and men alike: "Myself! alas for theme so poor/A theme but rich in Fear;/I stand a wreck on Error's shore,/A specter not within the door,/A houseless shadow evermore,/An exile lingering here." She suggests that pursuit of "fame" has given her exceptional freedom from social constraints, but also forced her into a restless, nomadic existence, cut off from a secure, fulfilling attachment to another person. She is in emotional exile. Her admiring public knew her as "The Menken," a restless spirit unfettered by conventional morality yet transcending common vice, a celebrity without a past or family, without those elements that had formed the basis of identity before the modern age of celebrities and cities. She had earned independence only to discover that it brought with it alienation. She watched from the margins without definition of race, region, religion, or gender.[74] She had traded intimacy for publicity.

Yet as tempting as it may be to accept that Menken exposed her internal convictions for the first time, her past actions should warn against such a conclusion. This is not to suggest that Menken did not feel the emotions she expressed, but rather that the act of writing is not the same as the act of publishing. Because she put it before the public, it was a performance. The decision to share "El Suspiro" in the popular local paper demonstrates Menken's desire for the public to recognize her as having sincere, deep feelings; it does not necessarily prove that those were her actual feelings. Her publicly expressed melancholy added dimension to her previous performances as a joyous femme fatale, a careless bohemian, and a "thing of beauty and a boy forever," as Webb once described her.[75]

---

[74] AIM, "El Suspiro" *GE*, Jan. 3, 1864, 3.   [75] O'Connor, *Bret Harte*, 75.

Menken may also have portrayed sorrow because her marriage was so obviously deteriorating; she might have found herself in need of public sympathy. It is impossible to get a sense of Menken's marriage to Newell; at times it appears to have been one of convenience, almost a business arrangement, and yet there is also evidence that both of them were caught up emotionally at different times. When wooing him, Menken professed warm feelings, and Newell appears to have expressed the same after they parted company a few months later, if not before. While out west, as Menken had become ever more transgressive, her relationship with Newell became combative. Even if middle-class gender norms did not determine social mores in San Francisco at large, Menken had brought along repressive society in the form of her husband. In Newell she had her own private Victorian. Menken described their marriage in a letter written to Ed James on January 29, 1864:

> With all my professional success there is not a day of my life that I do not pass the fiery ordeal of tears and prayers.... I cannot, in this letter, tell you all the cause, but suffice it to say that I married a "gentleman." Perhaps you do not know what the word means as I do. It means a far superior being to either you or me. It is a being who lives in a realm far above us, and who occasionally condescends to tell us what low, wicked and lost creatures we are.[76]

Newell consistently reminded Menken of what she could not have or be. He emphasized the futility of being anything but condemned for her independence.

Yet during this period of success and shifting gender identities, Menken also enjoyed public friendships with other female celebrities, suggesting that on the West Coast, female independence, while not exactly commonplace or wholly acceptable, was also not necessarily considered social deviant. Ada Clare, Menken's friend from Pfaff's, came out to California to capitalize on her friend's success, and wrote incendiary feminist editorials for the *Golden Era*. Ina Coolbrith, the poet and queen of California bohemian circles, was a quieter kind of local celebrity: beloved, respected, and remote. Friendship with Coolbrith gave Menken local validity as an intellectual and poet. Lotta Crabtree was an up-and-coming variety actress, an adolescent celebrity whom Menken publicly took under her wing, giving Menken an oddly maternal image. All four of these women emphasized contemporary gender ideologies even as they defied them in practice; they enjoyed careers and supported households, but gave careful attention to femininity in their public images. Clare and Coolbrith earned their money through writing, and Crabtree and Menken as variety actresses. These friendships are significant in that they were very public, and served to suggest that Menken was

[76] AIM to Ed James, San Francisco, Jan. 29, 1864, AIM ALS HTC.

not simply a sex symbol for male enjoyment but also capable of genuine female friendship. Menken had enjoyed close friendships with women before, but always privately. To many Americans on the East Coast, Menken had so profoundly "unsexed" herself that women endangered their own reputations by publicly recognizing her. In San Francisco, Menken enjoyed a female cohort unlike any she had experienced back east, and her decision to publicly claim such friendships indicates that she wanted them to shape her celebrity image. Just as she was claiming masculine freedoms, she was also publicly displaying female friendships.

In February 1864, Menken left this female circle in more ways than one, when she took *Mazeppa* to the silver-rich, woman-poor town of Virginia (later Virginia City) in Nevada Territory, and entered the most colorful phase of her life. But for once the town outstripped her for scandal, and that difference ended up forcing Menken to adjust her transgressive image. The significantly higher ratio of men to women, most of them prostitutes, meant that Menken was one of a small population of women who did not make her living from selling sexual intercourse. And yet, as an actress of undressed drama, she, too, sold sex, which put her in a low position on the social hierarchy. Wearing male clothing allowed Menken to enjoy the freedom of an overwhelmingly masculine society while avoiding the position of prostitute. By middle-class standards, it was wildly inappropriate, but her behavior once again suited her surroundings. Even though Menken behaved more unconventionally than ever before – openly dressing in men's clothing, gambling and carousing with male friends – her behavior did not shock the men on the Comstock, it only rendered her "'one of 'em.'"[77] And in the end, their whole-hearted acceptance of her as one of their own subverted her earlier play with gender boundaries. Their lack of resistance took the charge out of her rebellion; the more Menken pushed against convention, the closer she came to the hungry audience. On the Comstock she was a celebrity without distance from her audience, which proved to be exhausting.

Menken and Newell took a boat to Sacramento, and then traveled by stage over the dusty Sierra Nevada range to the region called "the Comstock" or "Washoe," and took up temporary residence at a hotel in the mining town of Virginia. She arrived when Washoe was riding high on the greatest silver boom in world history. At the time of Menken's visit, journalist J. Ross Browne wrote, "The silver mania had taken possession of the entire population, without distinction of age or sex. Washoe and the regions beyond had sprung up into a second California. Gold was nowhere now – it was all silver – above, below, everywhere."[78] Every month the Wells Fargo line carted off millions of dollars in silver bullion, while hopeful migrants

---

[77] Walter M. Leman, *Memories of an old Actor* (San Francisco: A Roman, 1886), 301.

[78] J. Ross Browne, "Washoe Revisited," *Harper's New Monthly Magazine* (May 1865), part 1, p. 682.

poured over the mountains from San Francisco. Like San Francisco a decade earlier, the town of Virginia came into being overnight. The explosive population growth led to buildings often being rented before they were built. In 1860 the census had recorded seventeen men to every woman on the Comstock, and the ratio became more disproportionate as the silver market boomed.[79] Most of the women who came without men earned their living as prostitutes, hurdy-gurdy girls (paid to dance with men), or card dealers, while a few ran boarding houses or made men's clothing.[80] Yet in the midst of this rough terrain, Thomas Maguire chose to build an Opera House in 1863, complete with billiard parlors and a mahogany bar inlaid with ivory.[81] Virginia's dense settlement, racially and ethnically segregated housing, and international population gave it an uncanny resemblance to Gold Rush San Francisco in the middle of an uncompromising desert.[82]

It took the average traveler thirty-six hours to get from San Francisco to Virginia, and yet despite uncomfortable conditions, the greater proportion of women in California traveled "prolific in crinoline and gorgeous in silks and satins."[83] When finally arriving, hot, tired, and filthy with dust, the traveler confronted a haphazardly erected city that scaled one side of craggy Mount Davidson. The surrounding mountains resembled great hills of yellow sand, with patchy green shadings of sage, scrub maple, and cacti, but the beauty of unfiltered sunshine turned evening sunsets into spectacular kaleidoscopes of color. Beneath turquoise skies of unusual depth and clarity the land stretched sandy and dry, desolate of water, with the town Virginia a lone oasis of human settlement.

Mark Twain later described Virginia as "roosted royally midway up the steep side of Mount Davidson" with a population of "of fifteen to eighteen thousand," half of which "swarmed the streets like bees and the other half swarmed among the drifts and tunnels of the 'Comstock,' hundreds of feet down in the earth," directly under the streets. The presence of the mines underlay day-to-day existence, and Twain recalled underground explosions jarring his chair in the newspaper office. The sides of Mount Davidson were so steep that parallel streets ran fifty feet above each other, with houses facing into the mountain, so that their fronts "were level with the street they faced, but their rear first floors were propped on lofty stilts."[84]

If Menken had chosen cultural frontiers before, she now entered a frontier culture. The many descriptions of the Comstock during this time suggest a community held together by the common malady of silver fever, with citizens attempting to amass fortunes through exhausting labor, and

---

[79] Paul Fatout, *Mark Twain in Virginia City* (Bloomington: University of Indiana Press, 1969), 52–57, 60. Virginia did not become Virginia City until after Menken's time.

[80] Marion S. Goldman, *Gold Diggers and Silver Miners: Prostitution and Social Life on the Comstock Lode* (Ann Arbor: University of Michigan Press, 1981), 27–29; Fatout, *Mark Twain*, 52.

[81] Fatout, *Mark Twain*, 75.   [82] Goldman, *Gold Diggers*, 5, 14.

[83] Browne, "Washoe Revisited," part I, pp. 684–685.   [84] Twain, *Roughing It*, 282–283.

snatching rest in flimsy, crowded houses. Browne said of Virginia, "All is life, excitement, avarice, lust, deviltry, and enterprise. A strange city truly, abounding in strange exhibitions and startling combinations of human passions." Through the rosy glow of hindsight, Twain describes the Comstock as "a glorious place, combining freedom and masculinity" with money so plentiful that "the trouble was, not how to get it, – but how to spend it, lavish it, get rid of it, squander it."[85] Menken was happy to be at the receiving end of such desperate spending, but performing in Virginia meant living in a topsy-turvy town without many socially recognized boundary lines.

Violence and alcohol were integral components of life in Washoe. Mining, on which the entire town subsisted in one way or another, required most of the population to work day and night in precariously built mining shafts that became virtual ovens when crowded with men and machinery. Miners used dangerous explosives to create new tunnels, despite the exhaustion, hunger, and heat that impaired their coordination and vision. For the women of the town, the mining industry meant intimate contact with men whose vocation fostered extreme emotions. The pressures of living in this kind of environment exacerbated violence and the desire to lose oneself in alcohol or distraction, and the revolver became "a popular settler of arguments, whether about a dog, a mine, a woman, or a drink." A *New York Times* correspondent complained that nights in Washoe were "hideous with the clamor of caterwauling drunks." The reputation of the Comstock became so well known that when San Francisco's charismatic preacher Thomas Starr King quipped that Washoe was a place of "big mines, little mines and whiskey shops: in other words, Ophir holes, gopher holes, and loafer holes," people far and wide knew exactly what he meant.[86]

Adding to its unique character, Washoe benefited from three of the most talented journalists on the West Coast working together at one paper: the *Territorial Enterprise*. Joe Goodman took leadership of the *Territorial Enterprise* in 1862 and began producing a daily paper so well written that eastern papers frequently gave it notice. Goodman also deserves enduring credit for "discovering" Samuel Clemens, who had come to Nevada in 1861 to escape the war and mine silver, and fought off boredom by sending outrageously silly letters to the paper. Goodman eventually tracked Clemens down and talked him into writing for money. Recognizing his failure as a silver miner, Clemens reluctantly agreed. The quiet and extraordinarily gifted William Wright (known to Washoe as Dan De Quille) taught Clemens the trade. Between Clemens and De Quille, the *Enterprise* quickly outstripped all other papers in clever pranks and bally-hoo. Most of Washoe considered De Quille the more talented of the two, and at best tolerated Clemens.

[85] Browne, "Washoe Revisited," part 2, p. 4; Twain, *Roughing It*, 293.
[86] Goldman, *Gold Diggers*, 20–21; Fatout, *Mark Twain*, 60, 73–74.

Enraged citizens forced Clemens (just beginning to write as Mark Twain) to flee the area more than once for besting them with an elaborate lie. De Quille, Goodman, and Twain conversed regularly at a local pub, but unlike the intellectuals at Pfaff's and the *Golden Era*, they approached life with little reverence and called themselves "companions of the jug."[87] Because of their many affiliations with the writers of the *Golden Era*, the bohemians in San Francisco spoke of the trio as honorary members of their circle.

As was true throughout the nation, tensions of war underlay the irreverent party atmosphere of the Comstock. Yet politics seldom resulted in violence between Anglo-Americans in Washoe. The Civil War in the West was instead a war against Native Americans, and the size and culture of Virginia made the violence against Native Americans hard to ignore – unlike in San Francisco, where urban living isolated its citizens from bloodshed. From 1861 to 1865, according to Alvin Josephy, "more Indian tribes were destroyed by whites and more land was seized from them than in almost any comparable period of time in American history." Exiled Native Americans wandered the streets of western towns such as Virginia begging for money, food, and liquor.[88] Expansion of the Union required the dispossession of Native Americans, and as the Union began to win the war in 1863, it took an active role in breaking remaining Native American control of the Far West. Thus, going west did not bring exemption from violence and war, only respite from choosing between the North or South.

Ever open to new distraction, Virginia immediately embraced Menken as both a celebrity and comrade. As usual, a few prominent citizens expressed disapproval, but most residents craved entertainment. Before she arrived, Maguire had pasted Washoe with over 1,200 advertisements for Menken. Colorful posters of a semi-nude Menken as Mazeppa on horseback greeted viewers from literally every turn: on rocks, trees, sides of buildings, and every other public space available. In a town of lonely men, photos of Menken baring arms and legs in classic Greek dress had a powerful impact. Despite the problems evident in their marriage, she and Newell arrived together by stage on February 27 to a town buzzing with anticipation. Menken emerged from the carriage like a queen, while Newell stepped down from "the top of the hind boot ... dressed in a black mustache, a plug hat, and a gray blanket" looking like a "Georgia major just returned from the war."[89]

Menken chose *The French Spy* for her opening performance on March 2, 1864, which was an old favorite of the sensational stage, since it involved several suggestive turns of identity, with the heroine going from European

---

[87] Fatout, *Mark Twain*, 7–8, 11, 33–37; Nells Drury, *An Editor on the Comstock Lode* (New York: Farrar and Rinehart, 1936), 217.

[88] Fatout, *Mark Twain*, 70; Alvin Josephy, *The Civil War in the American West* (New York: Alfred A. Knopf, 1991), xiii; Hinton Helper, *Dreadful California* (Indianapolis: Bobbs-Merrill, 1948), 40.

[89] Browne, "Washoe Revisited," part 2, pp. 6–7; Fatout, *Mark Twain*, 160.

male to Arab male to Arab girl to French wife. Twain, De Quille, and Goodman watched opening night from their customary front-row seats. Twain supposedly attended Menken's first Washoe performance prepared to "vivisect her, show her up" as a circus rider. He had seen her before, when he reviewed *Mazeppa* in San Francisco the previous fall. His skepticism fizzled as Menken managed, "without slighting her audience," to give special attention to the three journalists. Someone had warned her beforehand that the *Enterprise* had earned a formidable reputation for its theatrical reviews.[90] The three journalists supposedly attended performances together because they liked to compete to see who could write the most discerning review. In the competition to review Menken, Goodman won hands down for his bombastic flattery:

> When you have watched the dawn of a fresh emotion in her soul, which rises and glows till her whole being is suffused with its spirit, and trembles in her countenance with more than voiceful intelligibility, finding its ultimate expression in some action whose grace and significance scorn interpretation, you feel that words would be a miserable, meaningless mockery. It is no abstract conception of passion that Miss Menken delineates. It is the passion that springs from a profoundly emotional and womanly heart – a heart with all the finest sensibilities, quickest instincts, generous impulses, and noblest purposes, that ever animated or actuated mortal being.

Such an overblown account succeeded in winning Menken's affection, but also the ire of other journals. The *Virginia Union* described Menken's performance as "an exhibition without restraint and without shame of the most lascivious nature that lewd imaginations can invent, out to meet with the public reprehension."[91] The *Enterprise* leapt to her defense, attacking the *Union* as too shallow to perceive "divine conceptions." With their usual exuberant humor, De Quille and Goodman waged a war of compliments in the paper for the next week, motivating another editor to remark, "Both the editors of the *Enterprise* have gone crazy – but they didn't have far to go."[92]

Their competition to complement Menken led to a rather comical series of events that aptly conveys the level of boredom in Washoe. Once they ran out of effusive adjectives, they began elevating her work far above that of the surrounding talents of the supporting cast. Their reviews aroused such venom in her colleagues that one actor hurled verbal jabs at Goodman during a performance. When Menken demanded that the actor apologize to Goodman and he refused, she left the stage in the middle of the performance. Soon an antagonism developed among the reviewers at the *Enterprise*, other

[90] Lyman, *Saga of the Comstock Lode*, 271; Lesser, *Enchanting Rebel*, 125; Bean, *California*, 192.
[91] Fatout, *Mark Twain*, 162–63.
[92] *Stockton Daily Independent*, March 14, 1864, quoted in Ibid., 163.

papers, and the local theaters, and the skirmish persisted for months after Menken's departure in April.[93] The bickering in the press, however, seemed to make the public more determined to see her perform – again, and again, and again.

Not only did spectators pack the Opera House to the rafters every night, but they gave Menken a fortune in mining stocks and silver bullion. A fledgling company presented her with fifty shares of the suggestively titled "Menken Shaft and Tunnel Company" stock, and decorated the certificates with etchings of a nude woman on horseback. The local American Engine Company No. 2 elected her an honorary member and presented her with an ornamental belt stamped with their insignia. One group of provocative admirers renamed their mine "Mazeppa Mounting Ledge," and an entire district dubbed itself "The Menken." But perhaps the most dubious (and humorous) honor came from brothel owners who printed their names and addresses on flyers emblazoned with "Mazeppa" over a nude figure on horseback and the mock warning: "institutions to stay away from."[94]

Menken performed both extremes of gender in Virginia. According to Twain's memories, Virginia was an emphatically masculine town, unlike "the world has ever seen gathered together," with a population he described as "not simpering, dainty, kid-gloved weaklings, but stalwart, muscular, dauntless young braves, brim full of push and energy, and royally endowed with every attribute that goes to make a peerless and magnificent manhood – the very pick and choice of the world's glorious ones." He remembered "[n]o women, no children, no gray and stooping veterans." Of course, he exaggerated. There *were* women, but his comment suggests the importance placed on masculinity on the Comstock. Being male was not enough; one should display an absolute absence of femininity (no kid gloves). How did Menken the chameleon respond to this? She wore pants, "smoked and rode astride, and gambled with a freedom that was delightful to the men on the Comstock."[95] Newell isolated himself in the hotel, and Menken cavorted about town without escort. If masculinity was the thing to wear, then Menken would of course be in style.

At the same time, Virginia's heightened masculinity also intensified the impact of her femininity. On the Comstock, Menken liked to be one of the boys – admired, independent, making a fortune, and spending it on cards and whiskey. But she made that fortune by showing her female body to audiences hungry for the sight of a white woman. Western history of this period abounds with stories of men traveling hundreds of miles to see an

---

[93] Lesser, *Enchanting Rebel*, 125.

[94] Ibid., 123–24; David Dempsey, with Raymond Baldwin, *The Triumphs and Trials of Lotta Gabtree* (New York: William Morrow, 1968), 143.

[95] Twain, *Roughing It*, 392; Leman, *Memories*, 301.

Anglo woman – or even simply to see her clothing. The woman did not have to be young, beautiful, and half-dressed, as Menken was several nights a week. One can easily imagine the effect Menken's stage performances had on the Comstock audience.

Complicating the image was the fact that Menken could also descend from the stage and become not a man, exactly, but one of the boys. Menken may have originally donned male dress to protect herself from unwanted advances, but it quickly turned into her means of having autonomy. Without male clothing, what freedom could she have in a town mostly populated by prostitutes and miners? Wearing men's clothing may have suggested to the men around her that she had no interest in heterosexual attention, enabling her to socialize yet remain exempt from the mating game. Thus, in a sense, Menken's identity as a celebrity allowed her to express two genders as she never had before. Within the taverns and gambling parlors, Menken could join in the male social circles, yet still thrill audiences with her "symmetrical" figure in the Opera House. The fact that she often wore the same clothes as the actress Menken onstage and the boy Menken offstage suggests the importance of context in defining her gender.

Menken did not find acceptance from all residents of the Comstock; those harboring aspiration for respectability found her disconcerting. Menken and Twain, for example, maintained a wary friendship at best. A few weeks after her arrival, Twain described her to his sister on March 18, 1864:

> I took [the essay] over to show it to Miss Menken, the actress – Orpheus C. Kerr's wife – she is a literary cuss herself. Although I was acquainted with Orpheus, I didn't know her from the devil, & the other day . . . she sent a brief note couched in stately terms & full of frozen dignity, addressed to "Mr. Mark Twain," asking if we would publish a sketch from her pen. Now you ought to have seen my answer – because I took a good deal of pride in it. It was extravagantly sociable & familiar, but I swear it had humor in it, because I laughed at it myself. . . .
>
> I think I can safely say that the woman was furious for days. But that wasn't a matter of much consequence to me, & finally she got over it on her own accord, & wrote another note. She is friendly now.[96]

Twain respected Menken's opinion enough to show her his work, but he obviously found her manipulations laughable, and the *Enterprise* never printed any of her writings. But the most surprising thing about this letter is that Twain deliberately misleads his sister about his acquaintance with Menken. He implies knowing Menken only through her husband when in fact he had attended her performances several times. In fact, by the time of this letter he had probably shared drinks with her at Tom Peasley's saloon. His

[96] Samuel Clemens to Pamela A. Moffet, March 18, 1864, Mark Twain Collection, Bancroft Library, University of California, Berkeley.

prevarication suggests that he did not want his sister knowing he normally socialized with Menken, still seen as quite disreputable back east.

By the time Menken and Twain parted, De Quille believed "Mark disliked the Menken."[97] Several months after she left, Twain published what sounds like a parody of a favorable review: "A Full and Reliable Account of the Extraordinary Meteoric Shower of Last Saturday Night." He quipped, "[T]he whole constellation of the Great Menken came flaming out of the heavens like a vast spray of gas-jets, and a glory spread over the universe as it fell [N. B. I have used the term "Great Menken" because I regard it as a more modest expression than the Great Bear . . .]."[98] Twain was one of the few West Coast commentators who consistently described Menken as female.

But however Twain felt by the time she left, Menken had spent much of her spare time with De Quille, Goodman, and Twain, or gambling at Tom Peasley's saloon. She probably fell into comradeship with the "companions of the jug" because of her own literary aspirations. Reminiscences of Menken's visit consistently portray the actress as having a wonderful time "where red and white chips passed merrily from hand to hand."[99] Only Menken herself did not leave evidence that she remembered those same happy times. This may not be surprising, considering that a desire to avoid her husband probably motivated her seeking company elsewhere, as their marriage was clearly falling apart. In fact, after only two months in Washoe she abruptly cut off her engagement and returned alone to San Francisco without explanation. She either left Newell behind in Nevada or he had already returned to San Francisco.

She left without warning one evening after a party. As a tribute to his famous customer, Tom Peasley had her portrait painted and mounted between one of John Heenan and another of Lola Montez on the far wall of the saloon. Menken supposedly responded with good humor, challenging Dan De Quille to a boxing match on top of the bar, and declaring to her worshippers: "I began with a prize-fighter but I'll end with a prince!"[100] Shortly afterward she caught the next stage back to San Francisco. A doctor sharing the carriage, Allan McLane Hamilton, remembered her telling the stage master that an emergency demanded her immediate return to the city, and he noted that she traveled without baggage. The carriage ride from Washoe to San Francisco took thirty uncomfortable hours, and the early morning sunrise revealed Menken with heavy makeup blurred by layers of travel dust, looking "anything but attractive in all her frowziness."[101]

[97] Nigey Lennon, *Sagebrush Bohemian: Mark Twain in California* (New York: Paragon Books, 1993), 84–85.

[98] Peter Stoney, *Mark Twain and the Feminine Aesthetic* (Cambridge: Cambridge University Press, 1992), 164–165.

[99] Leman, *Memories*, 301.

[100] Sam Davis, "Dramatic Recollection," *Nevada Monthly* (July 1880), 229; Lesser, *Enchanting Rebel*, 127.

[101] Goldman, *Gold Diggers*, 12.

Once in San Francisco, Menken initiated plans to return to New York and then travel on to England. She informed acquaintances that she was busy translating *Mazeppa* into French. On April 17, 1864, she played *Mazeppa* one last time in Maguire's crowded Opera House. The *Golden Era* remarked: "The star that flashed across our Western Hemisphere from an eastern glow of triumph, lighting up the old time dullness of our theaters with a meteoric grace and brilliancy, is about to disappear from our gaze – we hope not forever. . . ." And the paper roundly chastised local critics of Menken, declaring: "Those whose morals would be effected, or whose delicacy of taste would be shocked by anything which is seen in 'Mazeppa' or 'French Spy,' had better retire from the rude gaze of the world."[102] When Menken and Newell left on the *Moses Taylor* on April 23, 1864, they were accompanied by June Booth and his daughter. A few days later, Lotta Crabtree and most of the remaining cast of *Mazeppa* followed on another ship.[103]

Oddly enough, Menken seems to have boarded the ship and never looked back. Even in her most emotional letters to Charles Warren Stoddard, she never mentioned the friends they shared. Perhaps the problem with the West, in terms of Menken's brand of celebrity, was that she was *too* intimate with her audience. Particularly in Nevada, she was perhaps too much, as one miner fondly remembered, "one of 'em."[104] Charles Warren Stoddard later exchanged letters with her about poetry, but he had been only a boy when she was in California, and they had not been friends. Bret Harte, Ina Coolbrith, Joaquin Miller, Charles Henry Webb, Mark Twain, and Dan De Quille maintained lively friendships with each other, but if they wrote to Menken, they did not keep her letters as they did the others.[105] However, their various writings suggest that they never forgot her; they remembered Menken as part of the San Francisco of their youthful years. As the *Golden Era* suggested, Menken seemed to pass through the western skies like a meteor, leaving them with memories of her brief but brilliant flare.

Out west, Menken had transformed her public self into Mazeppa, a daring figure that claimed both masculine and feminine freedoms. She became the independent hero of formula novels and literature – dashing, independent, self-made. Yet she remained a beautiful woman who earned a fortune by revealing herself to be physically what her actions suggested she was not. Overall, western audiences celebrated her as being the best of both genders, of having that "ideal duality of sex" that Theophile Gautier had so clearly described in *Mademoiselle de Maupin*. As a seductively androgynous celebrity

---

[102] "Adah Isaacs Menken – The Woman and the Artist – Her Triumphal Career in California," *GE*, April 7, 1864.

[103] *San Francisco Morning Call*, April 23, 1864, p. 2, c. 1.   [104] Leman, *Memories*, 301.

[105] The Bancroft Library at the University of California at Berkeley has extensive letter collections of Harte, Webb, DeQuille (Wright), and Twain (Clemens). The best collection for Miller can be found in the papers of his biographer, M. Marberry, at the American Heritage Center, University of Wyoming, Laramie. Coolbrith's letters were destroyed in a fire.

Menken shared traits with everyone in her audience, and could be desired and return the desire of all who surveyed her. Many westerners apparently considered her gender liminality a wonderful trait, and her performances in California and the Comstock earned her a sizable fortune.

Menken and Newell boarded the *Moses Taylor* together in San Francisco, but she arrived alone in New York at the end of May, when tender new leaves began to shade the walks and the spring air suggested fresh beginnings. Despite his constant presence in her life from New York to California and back, her marriage to Newell was apparently over in all but the legal sense. She returned an extremely wealthy woman, and perhaps anticipated admiration from the city that continued to scorn her. No crowd gathered at the pier to greet her arrival, however, and the New York press did not pay homage to her wealth. After all, it was 1864 and New York elites felt besieged by the nouveau riche of wartime industry. The presidential campaign started up in May as well, and many Americans were deeply concerned that Lincoln would not win reelection.[106] The war seemed to be without end. Menken left for London two months later, determined to gain admiration abroad.

---

[106] Earnest McKay, *The Civil War and New York City* (Syracuse: Syracuse University Press, 1990), 266.

Chapter 7

Becoming the Menken: 1864–1866

On July 23, 1864, Menken sat down in her room at the Brunswick Hotel in London to write a cheerful letter to Ed James, who now worked for the New York *Clipper*.

> My engagement is made with E. T. Smith, for the "The Theatre Royal Astley's," to open with theatre on the 26th of September. That being, you know the commencement of the proper fashionable season, my piece "Mazeppa" is to be produced in the most magnificent style. Everything is to be done for my success possible.[1]

"Theatre Royal Astley's" sounded grand, but by Menken's arrival Astley's had become a run-down amphitheater with a somewhat legendary past; only the grayest heads in London held memories of the theater's glory days as the site of magnificent equestrian drama. Nor was performing there Menken's first choice. She had originally planned to revise her stage image by working with playwright Dion Boucicault, of *Octoroon* fame. But by the time Menken arrived, financial difficulties had forced Boucicault to give up his dreams of revamping the ampitheater, and commercially savvy E. T. Smith had taken over management of Astley's.[2] Menken then tried to reshape her image by pursuing a contract at the Drury, known for highbrow drama rather than circus acts. Failing that, she returned to Astley's to negotiate a generous contract to perform *Mazeppa*. Menken had clearly hoped to create a more respectable reputation as an actress, but circumstance forced her to swallow those hopes, and she instead embarked on an incredible journey toward fame, wealth, and celebrity.

During Menken's European sojourn she became the Menken, an international phenomenon needing only one name. Now she played to two major audiences: the European one before her and the American press, which by extension meant the American public. During Menken's European period, her performances of self begin to say less about American society than before, since she no longer played principally to that audience. She continued to experiment with publicity and altered her image to suit a more

---

[1] Adah Isaacs Menken (hereafter AIM) to Ed James, July 23, 1864, Brunswick Hotel, London, Adah Isaacs Menken Correspondance in ALS file (hereafter AIM ALS), Harvard Theatre Collection (hereafter HTC), Houghton Library, Harvard University, Cambridge, Massachusetts.

[2] Henry Baker Barstow, *The London Stage, Its History and Traditions, from 1576–1888*, vol. 2 (London: 1889), 226.

Menken as a middle-class, respectable woman. Taken by Sarony, probably in 1866 or 1867. Note the conventional styling of Menken's dress, with its volu-minous skirts, and her lack of jewelry. Posing with books was popular among respectable women, both because reading was tied with middle-class prosperity and because it was an easy pose. (Harvard Theatre Collection)

cosmopolitan audience, noticeably leaving behind androgyny or duality of sex in favor of heightened femininity. But Americans' reactions to Menken become, if anything, more telling than before. Once Menken gained stature in Europe, she also gained it even more in the eyes of many hitherto scornful Americans. At the same time, once she reached that pinnacle of fame, her always controversial act became truly dangerous in the eyes of more conser-vative taste makers. Both her fame and infamy increased in American culture because of her reception in Europe. When she returned to the United States in 1865, to finally receive the adulation of the masses she felt was her due, she also found herself the target of vicious criticism.

Her changing status back home stemmed from changes in American society. The northern middle class was continually expanding, fueled in large part by economic changes wrought by war, and the hierarchy of signifiers was noticeably shifting. Fashion was beginning to surpass respectability as the most important sign of class. Not surprisingly, many reacted against such a shift while others furthered it by buying into the latest trends. In the eyes of the former, the Menken symbolized the disintegration of American culture. They objected to the muddying of social values with a lowly desire for pleasure and profit. How could she, a mediocre actress best known for scandal and sensation, have become so powerful unless society itself was in a downward moral slide? But the admiration of worthy Europeans added a level of legitimacy that confused the issue for many Americans. On the one hand, some Americans took Menken's elevated status in Europe to mean that there was more to this woman than they had thought. To others she was a proven menace, if not capable of destroying culture in both Europe and the United States, then at least signaling its demise. She became most famous during these years when she was perceived as most dangerous.

Menken was part of a larger trend in entertainment, of course, or she would not have been so threatening. By the time Menken reached England, sexualized burlesque was already filling theaters and inciting discussion. The famous leg show *The Black Crook* was breaking records on Broadway several months before her return in 1866. Sexualized burlesque provoked the audience at all levels, using wit and humor to intellectually challenge social politics (particularly, gender politics) at the same time that revealing costumes played to the male gaze. In the course of seemingly harmless and humorous skits, burlesque mixed up visual and verbal cues to make sharp social commentary on social relations of domination and subordination, spoofing on interactions between genders, classes, and races. Menken's *Mazeppa* employed costumes similar to those of the burlesque troops, but her challenge to gender politics was less verbal and therefore more subtle. Nevertheless, she was part of a larger trend of female performers using sex to sell tickets at theaters patronized by women as well as men. Indeed, many saw her as initiating such changes, since her success with *Mazeppa* had proven that well-heeled audiences would not merely tolerate but in fact flock to see such sensational fare.[3]

For the first two years in England, Menken made every effort to ensure that American newspapers carried stories of her socializing with royalty and hosting dinner parties attended by great men, such as Charles Dickens and Charles Reade.[4] Despite Americans' democratic outlook, Menken's patronage by famous men and aristocrats raised her market value back home. Of course, most Europeans felt they had nothing to lose by attending Menken's show; the aristocracy had a history of attending lower-class theaters of dubious moral character. Attending Menken's performance did not indicate one's position on the social scale. Not so in the United States; when she returned in 1866, the makeup of her audience became as much the subject of debate as Menken herself.

---

[3] See Faye Dudden's chapter, "The Rise of the Leg Show," in *Women in American Theatre: Actresses and Audiences, 1790–1870* (New Haven: Yale University Press, 1994), 149–181.

[4] Mabel Osgood Wright, *My New York* (New York: Macmillan, 1926), 131–132.

Because she became the Menken during these two years, this is also the image of Menken that has best endured. During this period, memories of Menken's scandal with Heenan persisted, but many other aspects of the former Menken – her poetry and prose, her Confederate leanings, her gender-bending in California and Nevada – moved to the background. While in Europe, Menken marketed herself as simply American, an identity exotic enough to preclude constant reinvention. To Europeans, "American" suggested a multiplicity of origins; she no longer had to pick and choose between marginal identities. She also gave more attention to marketing herself as a femme fatale, although many aspects of that image became confusing as she tangled stories of husbands and lovers to a point that Menken herself could not seem to follow. She excelled at cultivating the appropriate air of mystery, however. She first introduced herself to British society by riding her horse or carriage in "full livery" in the park at the same time of day as other socially prominent Europeans and then pointedly ignoring them, thereby piquing their interest.[5] This was also when Menken became notable for lavish spending and acts of astounding generosity; her new image required money to ride in grand carriages, dress exquisitely, throw sumptuous dinner parties, and support struggling artists and writers.[6]

For the most part, the British press portrayed her contradictory behaviors as more fascinating than scandalous. After all, she was not one of them; she was there to entertain. By the end of her two-year stay, the Menken had gained an identity that moved away from the ambiguities of her former fame. She still played with stories of her past and images of her "true" self because these evidently remained potent ways of controlling her image, but her ambiguity became less important than her identity as a celebrity sex symbol. She was known for being known. She was famous because she was.

Her success was in no way certain when she first went to Europe in 1864. E. T. Smith gambled heavily when he agreed to Menken's contractual demands. With the war raging at home, American entertainers had been fleeing to London in droves, but few could fill British theaters.[7] Smith must have sensed her unusual market appeal because not only did he agree to Menken's price, but he also hired a large supporting cast and built magnificent sets. He also immediately launched an advertising campaign, and apparently used the first *Mazeppa* poster he could find, one that featured an obviously male semi-nude prince. It turned out to be a useful if misleading choice; many onlookers believed that the barely dressed male Mazeppa was meant to be Menken – that she, too, would be wearing only a scrap of cloth

---

[5] Letter from J. H. Moore in *Athenaeum*, n.d., noted by Allen Lesser, see Allen Lesser collection (hereafter ALC), American Jewish Archives, Cincinnati, Ohio. Bernard Falk, *The Naked Lady: A Biography of Adah Isaacs Menken* (London: Hutchinson, 1952), 76. British biographer Bernard Falk provides the best material on Menken's stay in London, quoting newspapers, magazines, and letters verbatim.

[6] Falk, *Naked Lady*, 93–94. Falk recounts stories told by Robert Reece and Watts Philip.

[7] Ibid., 84–86.

around her hips.[8] The lithograph promised sex, danger, and a helpless rather than self-reliant hero, unlike her *Mazeppa* advertising back home.

The advertising initially provoked some concern. H. B. Farnie, editor of the London *Orchestra,* was the first in England to voice concerns over Menken's influence, in an editorial called "The Morals of American Art" that was guaranteed to make genteel Americans blanche. Farnie made an enduring connection when he quoted an American paper, *Watson's Weekly Art Journal,* as saying that *Mazeppa* belonged to a genre called "the naked drama," which was wholly of American origin. He went on to remark,

> It is to be hoped for the sake of decency . . . that the exhibition at Astley's is far from anything of this degraded order . . . there have been imported many corruptions from America already, corruptions in language, in religion, or at least that superstition which does duty for it − in art. It would be the more painful therefore to have to point out to a London manager that the public morals are not yet so sunk as to tolerate a performance which would be hooted everywhere save in a Yankee audience. . . .[9]

Farnie noted something that theater critics in the United States were just beginning to recognize: Menken's rendition of *Mazeppa* was not simply a nine-day wonder; its financial success suggested profound cultural changes.

Menken answered the *Orchestra* in true Menken fashion, and thus initiated a more intimate relationship with the British public. She began by reiterating Farnie's charges, ostensibly to deny their validity but in the process ensuring that readers would be compelled to think about Menken and determine their own point of view. She defended herself on the grounds that such observations were "calculated" to do her "serious injury" by a man who admitted he knew nothing of "the merits of the actress or her piece." As usual, her indignant response said as much as the letter itself: She was a highly literate, intelligent woman, not a frontier harlot without moral sense. Menken insisted that *her* Mazeppa was not "naked drama" − it was art, which viewers would recognize once they put aside their prejudice and judged her performance on its own merit. "I impersonate the hero," she added, "but my costume, or rather want of costume as might be inferred, is not in the least indelicate, and in no way more open to invidious comment than the dress worn by Cerito, Rosati, or even the grotesque garb employed by ladies in burlesque on the London stage."

She distanced herself from the growing phenomena of sexualized burlesque and music hall cross-dressing by speaking of them as lower art forms.

> I may add that my performance of Mazeppa had a most prosperous career in America, and as is usual in such cases my success created a host of imitators,

---

[8] J. H. Moore, ALC.

[9] H. B. Farnie, "The Morals of American Art," *The Orchestra: A Review of Music and Drama* (Aug. 20, 1864), 745.

and some of these ladies, I hear, have adopted a style of drapery inconsistent with delicacy or good taste.

"Mazeppa," like any other specialty, is easily vulgarized. Let "Les Sylphides" be scantily dressed, and ungracefully acted by an indifferent artist, and what will be more offensive? The critics find no fault with Mrs. Charles Kean's embodiment of Ixion, and the young ladies who exhibit their well-formed limbs in the Haymarket and Strand burlesques (notably in such parts as Cupid or Ixion) are not accused of indelicacy.

She made it clear that she was not the shallow one: "[D]o me the favor, as a stranger, to suspend your opinion of my representation, and after you witness it I am quite willing to abide by your criticism."[10] Her tempered acidity apparently pleased rather than stung Farnie, who was delighted to see their correspondence reprinted in papers throughout the United States and England.[11] Menken no doubt felt the same satisfaction.

But aside from this particular editorial, Americans usually read celebratory reports of Menken abroad. For example, in September, the *San Francisco Call* reported that Menken, who had left their coast on the *Moses Taylor* only four months earlier, was now thrilling London audiences and flirting with royalty: "Menken is in London. She rides on her fine black mare every afternoon in Hyde Park, with a groom in full livery in attendance, and sometimes she airs herself in an open carriage, with coachmen and footman in livery."[12] Menken's publishing friends, such as Daly, James, and Queen, kept her name before the American public. Amid reports of costly battles and prison camp atrocities, Americans read small notices that sparkled with news of Menken's dazzling success abroad and compelled them to remember her, and perhaps to reconsider her. Was she a genius as so many claimed? Or did the Europeans like her because she was an absurd American novelty – an embarrassing representation of New World culture who provided the Brits with a good laugh? Either way they saw it, she remained part of American culture from thousands of miles across the sea.

And theater was emerging as a site of competition between Americans and the British. Antebellum American theaters tended to produce British plays mainly because lack of an effective international copyright made it legal for American publishers to reprint British plays without compensating the playwright, making them cheaper to produce than American works.[13] The British undoubtedly took reliance on British playwrights as yet another sign of America's cultural poverty. Actress Olive Logan noted that the British seemed to imagine that "American audiences were composed in

---

[10] AIM to Editor, *The Orchestra*, Aug. 27, 1864   [11] Falk, *Naked Lady*, 78.
[12] *San Francisco Call*, Sept. 11, 1864
[13] Bruce McConachie, *Melodramatic Formations: American Theatre and Society, 1820–1870* (Iowa City: University of Iowa Press, 1992), 124.

great part of Pike's Peak miners sitting in the best boxes in their shirt-sleeves, and with their legs up," and went on to describe the elegance of the New York audience.[14] Rather than trying to defend American theaters and their patrons, journalist Junius Browne turned on the London version: "The theatres in London are, on the whole, inferior to the theatres of New York, both in the quality of the houses (externally and internally), and of the performance."[15] Even Americans who did not regularly attend the theater participated in the ongoing competition through their readership, and Menken's success in London therefore carried significant weight. There was something wonderful about seeing an American triumph in snooty British circles.

Despite the *Orchestra's* claims that corruption came from the New World rather than the old, British audiences had already proven themselves less prudish than Americans by flocking to performances of the "British Blondes," a burlesque troop that would descend on America four years later, in 1868. Menken pointed out the hypocrisy of the *Orchestra's* claims when she referred to performances of Cupid and Ixion. "Burlesque" had been around for decades, but the groups like the British Blondes infused it with sexuality and modern gender politics. In Lydia Thompson's version of *Ixion; or, The Man at the Wheel*, female performers cross-dressed in costumes as brief as the undressed Mazeppa and employed sexually suggestive language.[16] Thompson's production challenged as well as catered to the prurient gaze in ways that Menken's act did not. In 1869, *Appleton's*, a mainstream American magazine, characterized burlesque as setting out "with respecting nothing – neither taste, propriety, virtue, nor manners. Its design is to be uproariously funny and glaringly indecent. . . . The mission of burlesque is to throw ridicule on gods and men – to satirize every body and everything; to surround with laughter and contempt all that has been reverenced and respected."[17] Burlesque undermined cultural authority by celebrating "an upside-down version of the world" and denying "the legitimacy of rationality and its power to impose order and meaning."[18] Menken pointed out the hypocrisy of London critics calling *Mazeppa* a social threat, given the popularity of burlesque in London. *Mazeppa* differed significantly from burlesque in its relationship to the audience. While transgressing gender norms on stage, Menken did not force the audience to confront its own participation; she did not challenge the hypocrisy of prudish viewers who delighted in her disrobing.

[14] Olive Logan, *The Mimic World and Public Exhibitions. Their History, Their Morals, and Effects* (Philadelphia: New World Publishing, 1871), 357.

[15] Junius Henri Browne, *Sights and Sensations in Europe* (Hartford: American Publishing, 1871), 28.

[16] Dudden, "Rise of the Leg Show," 164.

[17] Robert C. Allen, *Horrible Prettiness: Burlesque in American Culture* (Chapel Hill: University of North Carolina Press, 1991), 136.

[18] Ibid., 147.

Menken's London debut on October 3, 1864, filled Astley's to capacity, and she continued to attract full houses through December.[19] Besides Menken's fame, Londoners appreciated seeing Astley's restored to its former glory. John Oxenford of the *London Times* noted nostalgically: "Horses are again at Astley's... when we see Mazeppa appear in more brilliant condition than ever, we are inclined to wonder that the capitol has been so long without an entertainment of the kind."[20] As for her lack of clothing, newspapers were quick to agree with Menken's sentiments that her undress was no more excessive than that of many other performers on the London stage. Oxenford asserted that her costume "is not a whit more objectionable than those of the female Highland boys and mythological beauties who are now accepted as matters of course."[21] The *Morning Advertiser* remarked that "the scanty drapery in which she carries in the main action of the drama is admittedly calculated to exhibit these physical capabilities for the part, while at the same time avoiding offensive display."[22] The London *Illustrated News* pointed out the fine line Menken walked, portraying Mazeppa as "a discreet compromise between the objectionable and the prudent; for, though the lady's figure is displayed on horseback, care has been taken that the rules of decency should not be too violently transgressed."[23] In the United States, Americans read notices such as one in the *San Francisco Call* that claimed, "The *Times*, *London Era*, *Reynold's Newspaper and Dispatch*, *News of the World*, *United Service Gazette*, *Morning Post* (The London "fashionable journal"), and *Belle's Life* all comment on Menken's appearance and all are unanimous in the opinion that she is lovely as an hour...."[24] Menken's press contacts made sure to let Americans know that she was an undeniable success abroad, even when the British public expressed ambivalence.

Not surprisingly, *Punch*, edited by Mark Lemon, expressed the most severe criticism in its own witty, sexually suggestive way. American magazines frequently quoted *Punch* because of its clever, naughty schoolboy humor, and Americans surely read the verse that ended:

> "Who live to please" – no need on us
> That stale excuse for thrusting –
> there is a way to please one-tenth,
> The nine-tenths by disgusting.
> Your shame why let these bills, wherewith

[19] "Astley's," *London Daily News*, Oct. 4, 1864; editorial, *London Times*, Oct. 7, 1864; these articles marked a significant departure in that most theater news in the *Times* was featured in the advertisement section.

[20] *London Times*. Oct. 4, 1864.   [21] Ibid.

[22] *London Morning Advertiser*, Oct. 10, 1864, as noted in Richard Northcott, *Adah Isaacs Menken; An Illustrated Biography* (London: Press Printers, 1921), 24.

[23] "Theatres," *Illustrated London News*, Oct. 8, 1864, noted by Nicholas Kovach in the Kovach Collection, University of Minnesota (hereafter Kovach).

[24] "La Menken," *San Francisco Call*, Nov. 27, 1864.

> You plaster London's wen, ken?
> "Bring forth the horses!" Yes, Mr. Smith,
> But don't bring forth the Menken![25]

By this point Menken had become accustomed to bad verse written on her behalf, since wits had been poetically expressing their opinions of her since the days of the Heenan scandal. Any mention of her, good or bad, was good advertising.

Menken and Smith understood that they were not selling tickets to see *Mazeppa* so much as to see the Menken, and they sold her by making her visible yet just out of reach. Menken attended publicized events with famous writers, rode in the London parks, and contributed to rumors about her personal life. Although she no longer wrote verse, she actively sought the friendship of intellectuals and literati. She became friends with Charles Reade, a popular novelist and playwright, and once remarked that John Oxenford was her "sole beau for theatres and operas."[26] Charles Dickens tried to attend her production in 1864 in an effort to distract himself from the oppressive heat of Indian summer, and discovered all the tickets were sold out. Because the ticket master recognized Dickens, he was offered Mr. Smith's private box, but he turned it down.[27] There is no evidence to back up the long-standing rumor that she used the opportunity to befriend him and provided him with a private box.[28] Menken was good friends with many of Dickens's friends, however, which suggest that they at least became social acquaintances, and the rumor of friendship with Dickens was more important to her image than an actual friendship. Menken's reputation as a brilliant woman grew exponentially as her new friends introduced her to their friends, and ever greater numbers of artists, writers, and actors enjoyed generosity at her table. The publicity, elaborate set, talented cast, and arduous rehearsals quickly paid off, and Menken reveled in fame and adulation that surpassed even her sojourn in California. As on the American West Coast, Menken's popularity manifested itself in popular songs such as the "Mazeppa Waltz" and "Mazeppa Gallop," and in light-hearted farces such as "Cream of Tartar."[29]

At roughly the same time that Americans began hearing of Menken's illustrious European friends, a host of Menken imitators scattered across the United States. None of them approached her success despite their increasing levels of undress. In August, Menken teased James, "No letter from your dear

---

[25] Falk, *Naked Lady*, 80.   [26] AIM to Gus Daly, London, Dec. 6, 1865, AIM ALS HTC.

[27] Letter from Charles Dickens to unknown correspondent, dated Oct. 8, 1864, quoted in John Forster, *The Life of Charles Dickens*, vol. 5 (Liepzig: Bernhard Tauchnitz, 1874), 303.

[28] B. W. Matz, "Adah Isaacs Menken," *The Dickensian*, vol. 13 (Sept. 1917), 241.

[29] Falk, *Naked Lady*, 84; *Clipper*, March 2, 1867. Indeed, when Dickens first attended her play he called her "Mrs. Heenan," suggesting that she was still more well known for the 1860 scandal than *Mazeppa*; see Forster, *Life of Dickens*, 303.

hands yet. . . . I presume some army of 'Mazeppas' have captured you."[30] She could afford to joke in 1864, but soon the army of Mazeppas threatened to take over England as well. When she left London to perform in England's smaller cities in 1865, she was forced to advertise that she was *not* appearing in London, making it clear that those "Menkens" were merely imitations.[31] Burlesques of Menken's *Mazeppa* had become popular all over the United States by this point, and upon Menken's arrival in England, they began to appear there as well. In November 1864, the Strand Theatre put on "Mr. Byron's" burlesque of *Mazeppa*. "Mr. Byron," the London *Illustrated News* explained, was a Mr. H. J. Byron – not Lord Byron, the inspiration behind Menken's version.[32] The imitators seem to enhance the value of the genuine article, but Menken had to appear frequently in order to keep a monopoly on the Menken image; others threatened not only to take over her business but also her identity.

Just as others were adopting Menken's name in various forms to capitalize on her notoriety, Menken was attemping to shake the name privately. She was transforming her private self into "Dolores," a name that translated into "sorrowful." In 1862 Menken had written to Newell that her father had called her Dolores, after her mother, and that she had chosen "Adah" as a stage name.[33] While still in California she began signing "Dolores" to letters addressed to Daly.[34] In the winter of 1865 she began using the same name in her letters to James before commenting in a long, rambling letter, "And so lives poor Menken with all her success, and the favor of Royalty, and the love of her one life – a Wreck." She suggested that only within her friends at the *Clipper* office "lives the remains of Dolores Adios Los Fiertes known as 'Adah Isaacs Menken.' So much for me."[35] From that moment on, Menken signed her personal letters "Dolores," "Dolo.," or "Infelix," meaning the unhappy one. She told European friends that her given name was Dolores, and that they should call her that. Thus, when she died, her friends abroad claimed that her real name was Dolores, just as vehemently as her American friends stated it was Adelaide. She revised her private self into a woman of lonely sorrow, a tragic figure of loss and alienation.

Menken also juggled husbands and lovers at a confusing rate. Behind the scenes, Menken herself seemed unable to decide upon which man she should bestow her public attention. During those two years in London she strove to put distance between herself and husband Robert Newell, reveled in the attentions of past husband John Carmel Heenan, lived with and eventually married stockbroker James Barkley, and may have exchanged

[30] AIM to Ed James, Aug. 21, 1864, AIM ALS HTC.   [31] *London Times*, April 17, 1865.

[32] *London Illustrated News*, Nov. 5, 1864, Kovach.

[33] AIM to Newell, quoted by Newell in "Adah Isaacs Menken," no publication noted, pasted in "Biography of Adah Isaacs Menken. Extra Illustrated," Harris Rare Books, 76-M545x, Brown University Library, Providence, Rhode Island.

[34] AIM to Gus Daly, Dec. 1863, AIM ALS HTC.   [35] AIM to James, London, n. d., AIM ALS HTC.

written vows with magician William Davenport. And a few years later, only months before her death in 1868, Americans were to hear of yet another past husband whom seemed to have slipped Menken's mind long before.

But if Menken was juggling suitors and husbands to capture the attention of the press, with a few notable exceptions, her efforts failed. Newell was in many ways the most interesting player in this farce, but his connection with Menken received no media attention until after her death, when his reading of her played a major part in reshaping her image. After returning from California, Newell had resumed his career as a journalist, novelist, and poet, and struggled for years to understand how things had gone awry between them.[36]

Menken had a very different reaction to their breakup. She enlisted Ed James's services in keeping tabs on her estranged husband and made it clear that she saw him as a threat to her safety. She wrote,

> Please find something of Mr. R. H. Newell's movements in N. Y. See if he is at the *Mercury* office, and see how he is getting on, and of his health. Don't fail to learn all you can for me. I am anxious to know if he contemplates visiting England. Do try to find out. You will do me a lasting favor. Set your wits to work, and be private in your inquiries.[37]

Perhaps she felt guilty, for no sooner had she left Newell than she found another lover on the steamer to England. Menken filled her letters to Ed James with effusions about James Barkley, referring to him as "the best man that ever breathed in God's World" and strangely said that she had "known him intimately for fourteen years. He was my child ideal."[38] According to various sources, Barkley's life followed a trajectory similar to that of Menken, if she had indeed been Ada McCord of Memphis; he had lived in Memphis during her girlhood, and later traveled to New York City and San Francisco.[39] In 1864 she wrote that she had known Barkley fourteen years, which was roughly the time that elapsed since McCord left Memphis. But it is more likely that Menken was being fanciful and suggesting that she had met her "soul mate."

Menken's manipulations of Ed James reveal how calculating she could be in personal relationships, even when not engaged in promoting her celebrity image. What Ed James thought of Menken's infatuations and affairs

[36] Newell, Menken Scrapbook, Brown University; "Orpheus C. Kerr, His Recent Death in Brooklyn and the True Facts of His Career," July 1901, publication not noted, article in Adah Isaacs Menken clippings file, HTC. Newell's demise poignantly highlights the loneliness of his final years: He died in his attic apartment during a July heat wave in 1901. Since he had no friends or relatives, no one discovered the decomposing body until ten days after his death.

[37] AIM to James, London, Aug. 8, 1864, AIM ALS HTC.

[38] AIM to James, London, Dec. 12, 1864, AIM ALS HTC.

[39] Allen Lesser, *Enchanting Rebel: The Secret of Adah Isaacs Menken* (New York: Beechhurst Press, 1947), 143.

is impossible to guess. Descriptions of him as "a fat, florid man, with a long hard face" who had difficulty keeping the discussion on one subject do not make him sound particularly appealing.[40] But Menken certainly valued his devotion and his handling of her American publicity. She flirted to keep his affection, once writing, "[W]hy all the flattery in the world could not make me proud of anything but your love."[41] And another time the teased, "[I]f you are tired of kissing the picture, why you shall kiss *me*. How will that do? But you need not give up the picture just for that; because you can kiss that as often as you like and you can kiss me only once."[42] Her letters to him vacillate between flattery and demand, even while she consistently emphasized having sisterly feelings for him. More often than not her letters to James are charmingly self-deprecating, as if she truly did consider him a confidante: "I mean to do everything that is right, pleasant, and proper. But you know what hell is said to be paved with. I believe that I am a very large shareholder in that pavement. I would like to sellout. But so many wretches have invested largely in the same stock that I fear it will be rather difficult to find a victim."[43] In spite her frequent teasing, she addressed him as "brother" and called herself his "devoted sister" – a practice that confused later biographers for quite some time.[44]

But now something shocking happened – something Menken could never have predicted, even with all of her calculating: Heenan came calling. If Ed James had romantic feelings for Menken, then their correspondence must have been painful. Besides her annoying insistence that he befriend Barkley while in New York, James was also doomed to read passionate descriptions of John Carmel Heenan's attempts to woo back Menken. Soon after Barkley returned to his business in New York in the fall of 1864, Heenan called on Menken. She and Heenan were now in reversed positions: She was the star, and a broken Heenan courted her favor.[45]

In 1865 she sent James a letter that reads as if written for public consumption. She neglects to mention Barkley (the central topic of her other letters of this period) and returns to language she employed during the bigamy scandal of four years before. Referring to Heenan as Lord Carmel, she writes:

> I know and perhaps you do, he never loved anybody but me. He never will. There is *only* one love to one life. Carmel would die for me tomorrow but

[40] Edmund Yates, *His Recollections and Experiences*, vol. 2 (London, 1884), 31.

[41] AIM to James, May 1863, "Sunday P.M.," Baltimore, transcript in ALC.

[42] AIM to James, May 11, 1863, AIM ALS HTC.   [43] AIM to James, Dec. 12, 1864, AIM ALS HTC.

[44] AIM to James, July 23, 1864, AIM ALS HTC.

[45] In "Probable End of Heenan," *San Francisco Call*, April 29, 1864, the reporter suggests that Heenan had suffered from an earlier "drugging" and "is now subject to convulsions, and suddenly falls down in the street in fits. . . . His day is over." In August the same paper noted that "Heenan was jumping out a train at Epham England in order to avoid a train collision, hurted his spine, now he is subject to fits," *San Francisco Call*, Sept. 11, 1864.

it is *too late*. He has been the ruin of what might have been a splendid life. It was he who taught me to disbelieve in man, it was he who made me callous and unfeeling. He seeks to revive that which is dead. Now Ed, it is *my turn* to inflict suffering. I do not mean to hurt the only man I ever really loved, but I can not help it. *It is too late*. I do not tell him all of myself, for when he is with me the old dead power comes up, and I am silent and let him talk of his love and the reward he thinks he can now bring me in his devotion and conscious faith. I know he is *now* true, but – too late. I can not believe again. He killed me. I died. There is no Resurgam. I can not tear the bandage from my eyes even to say: "*You crucified me*." He knows it, But he hopes. Alas!

Menken goes on in the same maudlin tone, wondering why she receives such devotion from James himself: "I can not imagine why anyone should be fond of me." She portrays herself as the woman of earlier poems: "I always tell [friends] not to love me. I am too cold and passionless since my crucifixion." Surely, this private letter was meant for an American audience; she had written of her "crucifixion" at the hands of Heenan too often in the past to return to the theme unconsciously. Indeed, the language of this letter echoed the death of the sentimental self she had long ago addressed in her suicide letter.

The story of Heenan wooing Menken did make the press, but only barely and never with the emotional depth Menken wanted to convey. Here was the man who had nearly destroyed her with rejection now begging for her forgiveness. But she did not want a private reconciliation; she apparently craved a public display, a public vindication. Unfortunately for her, Heenan's activities mattered little to American readers. He was a has-been, and her scandal with Heenan had already shaped her image irrevocably. His attempts to reconcile may have fed into Menken's ego, but they did little to repair damage done by the 1860 scandal.

Nevertheless, Menken played up the situation as much as she could. Perhaps to make the story more appealing, she tried to elevate his image a bit. She could not return him to his celebrity pedestal, so she gave him a title, calling him "Lord Carmel." Menken's association with royalty was not entirely a fiction – royalty attended her performances, sent her gifts, and counted themselves among her admirers – but the people whom she mentions in the letter were merely friends to whom Menken assigned royal titles.[46] For example, in the same letter she talks about Heenan, she also mentions "little Lord Stamford," sitting on the parlor carpet beside her.[47] Menken put little Lord Stamford at the center of an imaginary world, saying he is "only a boy of ten years. But do not scorn him. His baby voice is heard by the Queen herself! His fragile little fingers must sign document[s] of

[46] Falk, *Naked Lady*, 125; Lesser, *Enchanting Rebel*, 146. There are many articles on Menken and royalty. E.g., see *San Francisco Call*, Oct. 30, 1864.
[47] AIM to James, London, 1865, AIM ALS HTC.

importance to this well governed nation. His estates, and his mother's and sisters' incomes must bear the signature of this boy."[48] But researchers have found no evidence of a "Herbert Vane, Lord Stamford" and suggest that he might have been the son of actor Charles Fechter (he was too old to be Menken's).[49] The wording of the letter suggests that Menken intended James to share her news of "Carmel" with the public, but he kept it to himself.

Accompanied by the servant she titled "Lady Stuart," in August 1865, Menken returned briefly to the United States to divorce Newell.[50] She wrote to James, "You are aware, I believe that I have petitioned for a divorce from N.?...During my short stay in New York he did me many petty injuries, and insulted me and Lady Stuart with rude notes."[51] Menken soon left New York for Indianapolis, a city that was quickly becoming what Reno would be in the twentieth century: the national loophole for escaping an undesirable marriage.[52]

Menken had long made the most of a surprising acceptance of divorce that emerged between 1850 and 1870, probably because of gains in women's property laws and then, later, the upheaval of war.[53] Historian Norma Basch argues that "migratory divorce," the kind of divorce used by someone like Menken who married in one state and divorced in another, enabled women to be "independent, rights-bearing individuals who could negotiate the law to their own advantage."[54] Menken's constant returns to the altar and divorce court were undoubtedly threatening to a public that saw her as both undermining the sanctity of marriage and demonstrating a growing sense of autonomy in American women. Those who dismissed Menken as an immoral opportunist could not deny that she employed legal freedoms, but they were freedoms that frightened many Americans. Newspapers reported only the most sensational divorce cases, however, and the parting of Menken and Newell was apparently not interesting enough receive notice – particularly during the months following the end of the war.

At this point, Menken truly seemed to lose her emotional balance and to recast Newell into a sort of monster. Menken's earlier struggles with Newell in California suggest that, in her opinion, he was emotionally cruel, but there is nothing to suggest that he was physically violent. Nevertheless, Menken believed he would try to harm her, and wrote to James that upon hearing of her decision to divorce him, Newell "will be *furious*, notwithstanding his

[48] Ibid. [49] Lesser, *Enchanting Rebel*, 165.

[50] Lady Stuart was also a friend; she appears in pictures with Menken, with the two of them reading a book together. AIM photographs, HTC, and a labeled cartes de visite in Adah Isaacs Menken, Museum of the City of New York, New York.

[51] Ed James, Steamer "Persia," Queenstown, Aug. 16, 1865, AIM ALS HTC.

[52] Norma Basch, *Framing American Divorce: From the Revolutionary Generation to the Victorians* (Berkeley: University of California Press, 1999), 100.

[53] Ibid., 75. [54] Ibid., 60.

direct refusal to live with me, to support me, or even speak to me." She worried that he would "have his private opinion publicly expressed. . . . If anything is said that you know to be false of me, deny it in the *Herald* and *Clipper*. . . . Money in the matter of my reputation and honor is of no consequence." Was she suggesting it was possible to "buy" honor? She even requested that James spy on Newell, in case he should prepare to leave America – presumably to come after her. She underlined her words with thick slashes of ink: "*keep me posted about him (N.) He means mischief.* If he finds J. B. is in N. Y. he will take his life. Say nothing of this, but be my guardian angel in this matter as far as you can. I have no friend to confide in but you. The 'Prince' [Barkley] is my heart's blood."[55] And Newell was clearly now the villain in Menken's story. It was not a story that she tried to sell to the public however – or at least, it was not one that Ed James agreed to sell for her.

Menken returned to England and openly kept company with James Barkley when he was in London, but the public was far more interested in her rumored affair with magician William Davenport. Menken publicly denied marriage to Davenport more than once, in both England and the United States, but who was to know the truth? Menken may have started the rumors herself. After all, she and the two Davenport brothers were the sensational celebrities of the season; popularity coupled their names together long before rumors of marriage surfaced. A month after Menken's London debut in 1864, the New York *Times* ran news from London: "The chief excitements at this moment are Miss Menken bound to her fiery steed . . . and the brothers Davenport bound to their chairs."[56] In August 1865 she told the *Herald* that not only was she not married to one of the Davenport brothers, but, in fact, she had "never spoken to either of these gentlemen."[57] She may have denied an alliance because she did not want to be put in the same category as the Davenport brothers, who held seances and staged amazing feats of escape. To many, the unexplainable magic tricks and so-called spirit rappings aligned the Davenport brothers with both the occult and the spiritualist movement.[58]

But there was something to the story, and the public seemed to sense it. According to Davenport family legend, Boucicault brought Menken to one of the Davenport seances not long after she arrived in London, and soon the brothers "were accepted scenery at [Menken's] Brompton Road house as Menken's 'spiritual advisors.'" The great grandson of Ira Davenport, Ormus Davenport, later transcribed a handwritten statement he

[55] AIM to James, Dec. 1865, AIM ALS HTC.

[56] "Our London Correspondence," *New York Times*, Nov. 6, 1864, p. 3, c. 2.

[57] "*London Court Circular* of February 18, 1865," *San Francisco Call*, Aug. 6, 1865, p. 1, c. 4; New York *Sunday Mercury*, July 16, 1865; Menken to James Gordon Bennett, *New York Herald*, Aug. 27, 1865.

[58] Ann Braude, *Radical Spirits: Spiritualism and Women's Rights in Nineteenth-Century America* (Boston: Beacon Press, 1989).

found among the family papers, dated January 8, 1865, reading, "I, Dolores A. Fiertos acknowledge Wm. H. Davenport, as my only legal and beloved husband for all my future life, so help me God I believe to be my Father and of all earth. Signed by me, A. I. Menken. Richmond, England."[59] If authentic, Menken's decision to use what she was currently claiming as her birth name, Dolores A. Fiertos, may have been a way of assuring Davenport that their marriage, although not legal, was meaningful.

Like John Heenan, William Davenport was a handsome man with dark hair and a handlebar mustache. During this period Menken had photographs taken that show her wearing a brooch containing the portrait of a man of that description, but the image is too tiny to be identified.[60] One has to wonder whether the vague image on a picture sold for publicity was also one of Menken's ways of selling herself as mysterious, whether it was meant to tantalize the audience with evidence of an affair she had denied. And there was something alluring about the idea of a union between a man and woman who both specialized in deception and challenged the audience to engage in detection. Their marriage or affair contained the same elements of allusion, deception, detection, and mystery as they themselves embodied and performed.

Rumors of a marriage between William Davenport and Menken persisted for months in the United States. Like marriage to a pugilist, marriage to a magician tied Menken's name with the fashionable, rather than the respectable or cultivated. American papers had a field day with the bad, suggestive puns, such as the *San Francisco Call's* pointing out: "[I]t is remarked that 'they would find the matrimonial *knot* not easily untied.' Adah's antecedents would seem to prove that she had found that the wedlock is nothing but a *slip*-noose."[61] A friend of the Davenport brothers later claimed that Menken attended several "seances" in which others tied up the brothers to see them escape. Menken supposedly arrived with her horsewhip in hand, "declaring loudly she would punish anyone "who hurt the Davenports by tying the ropes too tight.[62] Either trying to fan the flames of publicity or sincerely wanting to untangle Davenport's name from her own, Menken

---

[59] Transcript of original in author's possession, 3. See also Ormus Davenport, "The Davenport Brothers and Adah Isaacs Menken," *The Linking Ring* (December 1993), 68; in this article Davenport dropped the "Dolores A. Fiertos" because he was not sure how to explain it. Davenport's claims are believable because he describes stationary that Menken did indeed use for a short time, examples of which may be found in the Harvard Theatre Collection. According to Ormus, the originals of the letters were destroyed several years ago. Magician Harry Houdini mentions the marriage of AIM and William Davenport in *A Magician among the Spirits* (New York: Harper and Brothers, 1827), based on stories told by Ira. Also, stories coupling Menken's name with Davenport appear in newspapers; see "The Beautiful Menken!" *San Francisco Bulletin,* Jan. 19, 1865; *San Francisco Call,* May 14, 1865, p. 1, c. 3; *San Francisco Daily Morning Call,* July 16, 1865, p. 1, c. 1.

[60] See AIM photographs, HTC.   [61] *San Francisco Call,* May 14, 1865, p. 1, c. 1.

[62] Wilbert Beale, *The Light of Other Days, Seen through the Wrong End of an Opera Glass,* vol. 2 (London: 1890), Kovach.

personally wrote to American newspapers denying marriage to William.[63] Menken went so far as to have lawyers publicly deny her participation in spiritualist gatherings in the *London Court Circular* of February 18, 1865.[64] But however Menken claimed to feel about spiritualists in 1865, only one year earlier she had dedicated a poem to British spiritualist Emma Hardinge, who was lecturing in San Francisco at the time. As in most things, Menken was as inconsistent as she was adamant.[65]

It may be inappropriate to impose reason onto Menken's self-performance in 1865, even if her decisions often appear to be sharp-witted marketing. Menken's rambling letters to James and a mysterious quarrel with Gus Daly suggest that she had a precarious hold on her emotions. It was during these last four years of her life that Menken earned her most enduring image: that of a faltering sex goddess, a person who later generations might look back on as a sad precursor to Marilyn Monroe, as ambitious and tough as Mae West or Madonna, but not nearly so strong. She monitored her image less carefully than before. Menken had smoked cigarettes since at least 1859, but now a journalist noted that Menken's clothing was "spotted with the ashes of cigarettes, which never quitted her lips."[66] She also began drinking more in public. The weight she had gained in California had long since rounded out her boyish figure, and she continued to gain at a visible pace. Always known for her quick temper, Menken was now labeled volatile and unpredictable, and stories of temper began to resemble tales of fiery Montez. In short, she began displaying the characteristics played up in twentieth-century stories of human Hollywood wreckage. She seemed to lose her footing in 1865, and her letters become overly dramatic ramblings, suggesting a fragile self searching desperately for stability while at the same time committed to the life that was bringing about her demise.

In the early spring of 1865, Menken took *Mazeppa* on a three-month tour through "the provinces," visiting small cities throughout England and Scotland, where people had read of her success but could not afford the journey into London.[67] She was performing in Glasgow when newspapers declared the end of the American Civil War, and a few days later, the assassination of President Lincoln – a tragedy which Menken had predicted in an essay five years earlier.[68] She left no records of her reaction to the war's end, but she would have known that it was now possible to return to her childhood home for the first time in years. In letters, she focused instead on

---

[63] Menken to James Gordon Bennett, *New York Herald*, Aug. 27, 1865.

[64] "*London Court Circular* of February 18, 1865," *San Francisco Call*, Aug. 6, 1865, p. 1, c. 4.

[65] AIM, "Dreams of Beauty" ("inscribed to Emma Hardinge"), San Francisco *Golden Era*, March 20, 1864.

[66] "La Menken," *Home Journal*, Sept. 1868, quotes an earlier observation by Adrien Marx.

[67] "The Beautiful Menken!" *San Francisco Bulletin*, Jan. 19, 1865; *San Francisco Call*, April 30, 1865, p. 1, c. 4.

[68] AIM, "Lodges to Let – References Exchanged," *Sunday Mercury*, Dec. 2, 1860.

her enchantment with James Barkley, who crossed the Atlantic several times to see her.[69] Meanwhile, Americans read glowing reports of her British tour, and reviews such as one from a Glasgow paper that suggestively dubbed her "Queen of the Gymnasts" and described her "as an artiste and actress of great power."[70]

While performing in small British cities in May 1865 she experienced a reaction to *Mazeppa* that foreshadowed what she would encounter in the United States the following year, and perhaps showed the impact she and the women of burlesque had already had on mainstream theater. Several citizens in Cheltenham disapproved of her lack of clothing, and a group of reform-minded women organized a boycott of the theater. At the same time, Menken suddenly faced the ire of viewers who considered her clothing too abundant. Believing that Menken would be naked, several spectators felt cheated when they saw her covered from head to toe in flesh-colored tights. A resident of Cheltenham wrote to the local paper that "beyond showing her well-proportioned arms and legs she was fully, classically, and even modestly dressed." In fact, "[a]n Irish friend, unable to restrain his rage, sprang out of his seat" and "angrily demanded his money back." The Irishmen stated that the show was a swindle: "I expected to see The Menken half-naked, according to the pictures of her, but, egad! she's as properly dressed as any of your respectable actresses – I'll not submit to such a contemptible fraud!"[71] Menken's reception in Cheltenham indicates changes in public perceptions of entertainment. Both supporters and detractors had come to expect undress from Menken. She could no longer please both sides. Viewers upset by the growing trend toward "leg shows" and burlesque protested against her. Meanwhile, those who had become accustomed to a display of women's bodies onstage demanded greater novelty and saw her act as promising something it did not deliver; few appreciated how she skirted agilely along the boundary between propriety and sensation.

Menken, meanwhile, was seeking for a new vehicle. She had taken the "provincial tour" only as a means of earning money while she waited for the play John Brougham was writing expressly for her, *The Child of the Sun*. Unfortunately, Brougham's script was not ready by the time she returned to London, which left her with once again performing *Mazeppa*. It now became clear that *Mazeppa* had ceased to be a novelty. Crowds no longer filled theaters to see it, even if they still found Menken intriguing. Yet when *The Child of the Sun* was finally staged at Astley's in October, it proved to be an utter disaster. Menken stated baldly to James: "[The] piece is a failure. Brougham has not written up my talent, it has no plot, nor any construction of interest in the three acts. But for my almost superhuman efforts the play

---

[69] AIM to James, Jan. 20, May 2, 1865, AIM ALS HTC.   [70] *Sunday Mercury*, March 26, 1865.
[71] Falk, *Naked Lady*, 103.

would have been taken off the bills long ago. I put my whole life in it."[72] She had certainly placed her hopes on it.

For once, neither Menken nor her clothing were the central topic of reviews; there were too many other elements to criticize. Brougham had attempted to capitalize on Menken's attractions by having her play several exotic male and female characters. Her gorgeous costumes made the most of her figure, and the extravagant sets signified that this was a first-class production, but the play simply did not hold together. Besides failing to supply the adrenaline rush of the treacherous horse ride, *The Child of the Sun* also lacked Menken's usual athletic display. It would have been reasonable for Menken to request a less arduous vehicle, as the three-hour performances of *Mazeppa* required exhausting gymnastics night after night. However, Menken's name had become synonymous with thrill and sensation, and this play lacked both. *The Child of the Sun* was simply another protean drama hiding behind magnificent sets of paint and paper-mache. After two months Smith pulled the show, and Menken was back to performing *Mazeppa*.

Perhaps needing to vent a little steam, Menken left for Paris "on a lark," hoping to meet Théophile Gautier and George Sand.[73] According to one biographer, the meeting with Gautier proved instrumental in connecting Menken with playwrights Anicet Bourgeois and Ferdinand Dugué, who later agreed to rewrite their play *Les Pirates de la Savanne* into a *Mazeppa*-like vehicle, by adding a version of the horse ride.[74] She also met George Sand, whom she had long admired, but it is doubtful that they had time to carouse through the streets of Paris wearing trousers and smoking cigars, as one biographer has suggested.[75] Sand and Gautier were both in their sixties, and living off the fame earned in earlier life. Sand now spent the days nursing her companion of twenty years, playwright Alexandre Manceau, who lay dying of tuberculosis in their home in Palaisant, a small village outside Paris.[76] Meanwhile, Gautier struggled to recover from financial losses incurred during the Revolution of 1848, bitterly describing himself as "an animal tied to the post of journalism."[77] He could not have been the light-hearted bohemian of thirty years before. Still, Menken had made contacts in Paris, and she left knowing that her agent was negotiating a contract there.

---

[72] AIM to James, 255 Brompton Rd., London, S. W. England (n.d.), Kovach.

[73] AIM to James, Dec. 19, 1864, AIM ALS HTC.   [74] Falk, *Naked Lady*, 130.

[75] The story of Menken and Sand as friends and possible lovers comes from a book by Sam Edwards, *George Sand: A Biography of the First Modern Liberated Woman* (New York: David McKay, 1972), 248. However, Edwards is also Paul Lewis (Noel Gerson), who confused Menken scholars for years by basing a biography called *Queen of the Plaza: A Biography of Adah Isaacs Menken* (1964) on a diary by Menken, which he later admitted never existed. See his confession in Wolf Mankowitz, *Mazeppa: The Lives, Loves and Legends of Adah Isaacs Menken* (New York: Stein and Day: 1982), 189. Mankowitz liked the idea of George Sand and Menken together, too, and falsely identifies Sand in a photograph. See ibid., 46.

[76] Ruth Jordan, *George Sand: A Biography* (London: Anchor Press, 1976), 315–316.

[77] Théophile Gautier, *Mademoiselle de Maupin* (London, n.d.), 8.

She finally returned to the United States in the spring of 1866, undoubtedly expecting a warm welcome from the public. She left for the States in March, when she received word that Barkley suffered from serious illness.[78] She sold all of her London possessions, including dogs and horses, indicating that she had no intention of returning.[79] By the time she arrived in New York, however, Barkley had recovered, and they began living together openly in a Seventh Avenue brownstone she named "Bleak House," after the novel by Dickens.[80] Menken supposedly turned Bleak House into a salon that summer, with businessmen, politicians, and intellectuals all attending her dinner parties.[81] Menken's success abroad and diligent publicity at home paid off handsomely; for a time it seemed as if New Yorkers finally recognized her success.

This time Menken had no problem securing a Broadway contract, despite her price of $500 a performance at a time when stock actresses considered themselves lucky to earn $60 a week and women in middle-class occupations, such as sales or teaching, cleared no more that $400 to $600 a year.[82] George Woods of the Broadway Theatre happily capitalized on Menken's international fame. Ironically, his sister-in-law was Olive Logan, the actress and moral reformer who soon became one of Menken's most tenacious critics, and his decision to book Menken divided the Logan family for years to come.[83] Olive Logan began publishing attacks on the "nude drama" throughout the 1860s and 1870s, asserting that "no woman who could have enchained an audience" without exhibitionism "would ever have descended to this baseness. But such women were never actresses in the true sense, and among the reputable members of the profession were . . . tabooed and avoided."[84] She shrewdly refused to mention Menken by name, thereby denying Menken extra publicity, but she alluded to her performances.

Logan and Menken actually held similar views on women's rights, even though they expressed their views differently. Logan fought from within the system, embracing respectability and domesticity. According to Logan, women would sacrifice equality if they lost their role as the moral arbiters of

[78] *London Weekly*, 1866, noted in papers of ALC. Article placed by Mr. Pender, who was acting as Menken's agent.

[79] *Sunday Mercury*, Aug. 13, 1865.

[80] Menken refers to her residence as "Bleak House" in a letter to Gus Daly, May 2, 1866, New York City, AIM ALS HTC.

[81] Mankowitz, *Mezeppa*, 157.

[82] Claudia Johnson, *American Actress: Perspective on the Nineteenth Century* (Chicago: Nelson Hall, 1984), 55–56.

[83] Mardia Bishop, "From 'Wax-Doll Prettiness' to a 'Lifeless Dough Doll': The Actress in Relation to the Images of Women in Mid-Nineteenth Century America," Ph.D. dissertation, Ohio State University, 1993, p. 223.

[84] Olive Logan, *Before the Footlights and Behind the Scenes* (Philadelphia: Parmalee and Company, 1870), 584.

society. She argued that feminine influence should only raise the morality of entertainment. Menken also spoke publicly in favor of women's rights, but she openly disparaged the domestic theory that wifely submission led to power. Despite or because of her many marriages, Menken seemed to put little faith in the virtues of the wifely role. In 1860 she had written in a essay, "What is God-created Woman's mission? The holy mission of building temples of the Beautiful, the Lofty, the Sublime...." And she argued for more rigorous female education, noting, "Intellectual women, occupied by serious studies and good of their fellow creatures" were less likely to pursue superficial goals, such as marrying a wealthy man.[85] Logan and Menken agreed that low expectations for women led to an unhealthy society, but they disagreed on the nature of those expectations.[86] Menken won unusual freedom by adopting nonconformist behaviors but paid a high price for her independence, in large part because of social critics such as Olive Logan.

In the spring of 1866 Menken expressed her doubts about domestic life to librettist Robert Reece, one of many friends she assisted financially.[87] With characteristic candor and self-mockery, Menken responded to news of his upcoming nuptials:

> I hear you are to be married. I am really glad of that. I believe all good men should be married. Yet I don't believe in women being married. Somehow they all sink into nonentities after this epoch in their existence. That is the fault of female education. They are taught from their cradles to look upon marriage as the one event of their lives. That accomplished, nothing remains.
>
> However, Byron might have been right after all: "Man's love is of his life apart; 'tis woman's whole existence." If this is true we do not wonder to find so many stupid wives. They are simply doing the "whole existence" sort of thing! Good wives are rarely clever and clever women are rarely good.

She saw marriage was detrimental to women because, once married, they stopped challenging themselves to excel. The problem was not that husbands wielded oppressive power, but rather that women focused so much attention on catching a man that once that was accomplished they were left without a purpose. Marriage limited women to a circumscribed ideological space that made them unable to be anything but wives. A clever woman, such as herself, could not be confined to such a narrow definition of womanhood. With actions as well as words she suggested that the role of helpmate limited women. Given such views Menken may have perceived her frequent marriages as a way of escaping the "'whole existence' sort of thing." Men enjoyed a different position, in her opinion; since men were held to an entirely different standard of "good" and not taught to see

[85] AIM, "Women of the World," *Sunday Mercury*, Oct. 7, 1860.   [86] Ibid.   [87] Falk, *Naked Lady*, 141.

marriage as "the event of their lives," marriage strengthened rather than weakened them. Despite her pride in being a "clever" woman unsuited to marriage, she signed the letter with an air of depression: "Yours, through all stages of local degradation. *Infelix*, Menken."[88]

Olive Logan had good reason to worry about Menken's financial success. "Nude drama" threatened the livelihood of "legitimate" actresses by moving the images of prostitute and actress closer together and by undermining the value of fully dressed performers. Logan feared that the status and high salaries enjoyed by talented actresses would disappear under an onslaught of legs. To those bent on reforming the theater, "nude drama" was a major setback that appeared to destroy recent advances in ridding theaters of vice, so that they might be suitable for respectable audiences. Years of reform had finally eradicated the notorious "third tier" of prostitution from mainstream theaters. But with "nude drama" the licentiousness of the "third tier" essentially moved to center stage. Men could no longer hire prostitutes in theaters, but – thanks to Menken and her imitators – they could enjoy the spectacle of women exposing their bodies on stage. Logan's reaction suggests that she understood spectatorship to be participatory; consciously or not, she realized that increasing emphasis on celebrities elevated the importance of fashion over respectability, which in turn preferenced an actress's marketability over her stage talent.[89]

Both Menken and Logan recognized that acting was a valuable yet vulnerable profession for women. Financially, it was unique: Men and women received equal pay for equal work in theater. Subsequently, by the 1870s, acting had become one of the most popular professions for women despite its dubious reputation. Perhaps as many as four times more women earned their living through acting than in literary and scientific fields (including nursing) combined. The only profession with more women was teaching.[90] Acting had the distinct advantage of not requiring an education beyond the ability to read, and paid the women while they trained.[91] Even a lowly chorus girl earned several times the wages of a factory worker, domestic, or seamstress, with less drudgery and greater autonomy. On the other hand, acting was rarely a steady profession, and when productions failed actresses often had to moonlight in other jobs.[92] Despite findings that suggest that many single women in urban areas used sexual favors as a means of earning "extras," such as clothing, entertainment, and luxury foods, even the lowest actress on the legitimate stage was unlikely to

---

[88] Ibid. The original of this letter may be found in the manuscript division of the Boston Public Library, Boston, Massachusetts.

[89] "Address of Miss Olive Logan," Seneca *The Revolution*, May 20, 1869.

[90] Joseph A. Hill, *Women in Gainful Occupations, 1870–1920*, quoted in Johnson, *American Actress*, 51.

[91] Johnson, *American Actress*, 54.

[92] Tracy C. Davis, *Actresses as Working Women: Their Social Identity in Victorian Culture* (London: Routledge, 1991), 84.

turn to prostitution because it would endangered her already precarious reputation.[93]

Some Americans viewed Menken's European triumphs with curiosity or nationalistic pride, while others began to see her as a threat to mass culture. They connected her with the changes wrought in American theater since the start of the war, as entertainment for its own sake became more important and widespread. The success of *The Black Crook,* which appeared on the New York stage in April 1866 and toured the country eight times between 1868 and 1892, heralded the change.[94] Most important, *The Black Crook* was staged at Niblo's Garden, New York's theater for respectable family entertainment, despite the fact that it featured a "leg show." The famous number appeared during a ballet piece, making use of one of the few (and only recently) acceptable excuses for displaying the female body. Magazines and newspapers expressed opposing opinions about *The Black Crook.* Undoubtedly because it appeared at Niblo's, and not the Bowery, several critics defended the piece. "The costumes are such as may be seen in any of the European theaters where such entertainments are given, and there is nothing to shock the modest or attract the unrefined in the deportment of the danseuses," the middle-class *Home Journal* assured readers. "It is the magnificence of the costumes; the perfect ensemble of the dancing . . . and above all, the gorgeous scenery, so appropriate and so tasteful, which prove so popular . . . in the 'Black Crook' all the senses are charmed. . . ."[95] But the fact that the *Black Crook* appeared at the epitome of respectable theaters indicated that it was now acceptable to the masses to expose female bodies on stage. To conservative eyes, moral and esthetic standards were dropping in favor of profit. *The Black Crook* generated enormous profits for an unprecedented fifteen months.[96]

Both European and American audiences legitimized Menken in a way she had not been before, and this put her into the middle of an emerging conflict over what signified middle-class identity. Due to the positive attention of Europeans, her performances came under greater scrutiny in the United States. Menken's highly publicized patronage by brilliant men made her harder to dismiss. When conservatives such as Logan dismissed Menken as merely vulgar, they also implicitly challenged the judgment of "great men," such as Charles Dickens (whether or not he actually supported her). Given Menken's acceptance abroad and the international popularity of this new kind of entertainment, attacks may have appeared prudishly provincial to many Americans. They were well received, however, by those

[93] Kathy Peiss, "'Charity Girls' and City Pleasures: Historical Notes on Working Class Sexuality, 1880–1920," in *Passion and Power: Sexuality in History,* eds. Kathy Peiss and Christina Simmons (Philadelphia: Temple University Press, 1989), 60.

[94] Susan Glenn, *Female Spectacle: The Theatrical Roots of Modern Feminism* (Cambridge: Harvard University Press, 2000), 149.

[95] *Home Journal,* Jan. 9, 1867.   [96] Dudden, "Rise of the Leg Show," 149.

who agreed that theater was being destroyed by crass upstart capitalists and the people who blindly bought tickets to whatever proved fashionable – that is, people who had money but no esthetic sense or training. Should money alone define class status? Were middle-class American values being destroyed? Clearly, the debate over Menken was about far more than Menken or theater, as was made clear by critics' preoccupation with the makeup of her audience.

The Broadway Theatre filled to capacity when Menken performed *Mazeppa* on April 30, 1866. That month, New York was approaching the end of a devastating cholera epidemic, and its people undoubtedly hungered for light entertainment. They had the money, thanks to a vigorous postwar economy. Seats sold out a week in advance, extra chairs were placed in the aisles, a number of people were permitted to stand in the orchestra pit, and some even stood on windowsills. The audience greeted Menken with a standing ovation as she entered the stage, and again when the curtain came down at the end of the final act.[97]

As usual, papers took opposing sides in evaluating Menken's talents, but this time reviews made a greater point of scrutinizing those who attended to the performance. Sporting papers that had long been friendly to Menken, such as Frank Queen's *Clipper*, celebrated her Broadway appearance. However, many mainstream papers published reviews that now emphasized Menken's lack of talent rather than clothing, before turning a critical eye on the audience itself. William Winter's blistering review in the *Daily Tribune* was widely quoted at the time and, rather unjustly, remains the most well known of all her reviews. He began boldy: "To announce that Miss Adah Isaacs Menken would appear at the Broadway Theater in the character of Mazeppa was to announce that a woman would exhibit herself, in public, in a condition closely bordering upon nudity, and such an announcement of course, was calculated to draw together an immense concourse of spectators." Winter immediately focused on the kind of spectators drawn to such fare: "The audience, composed chiefly of males, was the coarsest and most brutal assembly that we have ever chanced to see at a theater on Broadway. Every variety of dissolute life was represented in it." He waxed poetic: "The purple nose, the scorbutic countenance, the glassy eye, the bull head, the heavy lower jaw, the aspect of mingled lewdness and ferocity – all was there. Youths, whose attire exhibited an eruptive tendency toward cheap jewelry, lolled upon their seats, champing tobacco, and audibly uttering their filthy minds. . . . The air fairly reeked with vulgarity."

But Winter had plenty to say about Menken, as well. First, she had no talent: "To speak of Miss Menken as an actress would be to waste words. She has not the faintest idea of what acting is. She moves about the stage with no motive and, therefore, in a kind of accidental manner, assumes attitudes that are sometimes fine and sometimes ridiculous, speaks in a thin, weak voice, and with bad elocution; exclaims 'death!' and 'vengeance!' very much as a mild and hungry female might order tea and toast." The poor quality of her acting "invites critical attention, not to her emotional capabilities, her intellectual gifts, or her culture as an artist, but solely to her physical proportions." For once, Menken's beauty was of no importance, as Winter tersely agreed that her body, "a trifling topic," is "in many respects, beautiful." However, he added, "That any purpose connected with dramatic art is served by their public exhibition is offensive to good taste, we are distinctly certain." Winter clinched his vicious review with the most backhanded of compliments: "If Miss Menken serves no other purpose, she will at least warn her professional observers what to avoid." He summarized that Menken's act was "unmitigated trash": "The appearance of Miss Menken's Mazeppa at a theater on Broadway is nothing less than a grievous discredit to the acted drama in this Metropolis."[98] Unsurprisingly, Winter's was the worst review Menken ever received.

Scholars have taken Winter's review at face value, but, like Olive Logan, he had other reasons for attacking Menken and her fans. In the *Tribune* only the year before, Winter had expressed his conviction that American theater should play an active role in moral reform. He advocated that "the atmosphere of the theatre, on-stage and off, 'should be that of the drawing room where refinement prevails and where oaths and innuendoes and coarse jokes are never permitted.' "[99] Like Logan, Winter conceived of theater as an instrument of public reform, and his criticism of *Mazeppa* served that end. Winter's scathing review served to undermine Menken's triumphs abroad. His judgment of her audience consigned her admirers to the lowest common denominator of society.

Winter and Menken had never been friends, but the venom of his critique shocked and depressed her. Winter had known Menken since the early 1860s, when they attended bohemian gatherings at Pfaff's Tavern, and she courted the favor of Walt Whitman, whom Winter actively disliked. He undoubtedly remembered when Menken titillated New York with marriage to Heenan in 1860 and publicly defended Whitman's work.[100] On May 2, Menken wrote of Winter's comments to Daly, " '[M]isery loves company' after reading that *beastly* whack on me in the chaste and dignified *Tribune*. I am sad and depressed by the injustice and vulgarity of the article." She confided, "I am merely overwhelmed and grieved and discouraged. I know

[98] "Theaters, Mazeppa at the Broadway Theatre," *New York Daily Tribune*, May 1, 1866, p. 5.

[99] Bruce A. McConachie, *Melodramatic Formations: American Theatre and Society, 1820–1870* (Iowa City: University of Iowa Press, 1992), 236.

[100] Albert Parry, *Garrets and Pretenders: A History of Bohemianism in America* (New York: Covici, Friede, 1933), 39–41.

[the] article to be unjust and created through petty personal spite." She begged Daly to defend her talent.[101]

But however personal his feelings or strong Winter's bias, he was hardly alone in his opinion of Menken's *Mazeppa*. The *Home Journal* – a weekly periodical that declared as its motto: "We must all strive for beauty, because usefulness justifies itself" – published a review that sounded candid rather than malicious, and was therefore worse for Menken. Again, the critic was concerned with defining the spectators:

> There can be no doubt that she possesses a splendid form, as all may see; but she has as an actress, not even a claim to criticism. She simply attitudinizes, rides a well trained horse, and fences skillfully. Her elocution is faulty to a degree, and she has an unpleasant voice. . . . It would require a strong imagination to fancy any Polish page accoutered as Miss Menken when she first strides on as Cassimer. Her undress, when she is brought out as the ill-fated page doomed to the most barbarous death is still more absurd. The fringe of tassels around the scanty garment being the height of the ridiculous. In short, save beyond the fact that Miss Menken makes the most liberal display of her fine person, the whole performance is trash. It attracts certain classes, however. . . .[102]

The *Home Journal* made it clear that the whole production was disappointing, with overdone sets, impractical costumes, and a ill-prepared supporting cast. Descriptions of Menken's costume suggest that George Woods's desire to play up Menken's famous "fine form" contributed to the sense that *Mazeppa* at the Broadway was not a performance so much as a vehicle for capitalizing on public curiosity. Menken was a novelty and a celebrity, not an actress, and those who paid to see her could not claim the sensitivity of the more cultivated classes.

Three days later, she suffered a scathing review from yet another fellow bohemian, Bayard Taylor, now acting as the drama critic for *Wilkes' Spirit of the Times*. He wrote: "I will add that so far was the person called in the bills 'Mazeppa' is concerned, he (I use the gender of the character) is best *on* the mare and the worst *off* that I have seen or expect to see." From that point on, Taylor insulted Menken by basing his review on the horse's performance. By referring to Menken as "he," Taylor also implied that Menken had unsexed herself, lowering herself so basely that she could justly be compared with the (more talented) horse.[103]

Commentary on Menken's audience became standard as critics seemed to unite in their ire against Menken and the spectators who supported this kind of theater. Most common was the observation that only men attended her performances, as the *Herald* noted in May: "There was a very large crowd

[101] Menken to Gus Daly, May 2, 1866, AIM ALS HTC.
[102] "Theatricals," New York *Home Journal*, May 9, 1866.
[103] Bayard Taylor, *Wilkes' Spirit of the Times*, May 12, 1866.

present, mostly of the male portion of the community, the ladies being few and far between."[104] The *Evening Post* jabbed snidely: "Menken was last night greeted by an audience more numerous than select and accomplished very successfully what appears to be the main object in her public exhibitions"[105] Probably from Winter's pompous pen, the New York *Tribune* denounced the entire theater district, saying, "It is, we think, rather a remarkable fact that, at the present time, in the city of New York, there is not a single dramatic performance given which a person of taste and culture can witness with entire satisfaction.... And yet we have upward of eight prominent theatres in active operation."[106]

Many Americans, both male and female, paid no attention to the opinions of the critics and attended Menken's performances in droves. Although Taylor and the *Herald* had both stated that few women attended, the *Herald* later criticized its own statement, reporting on the presence of "a great proportion of ladies in the house, going far to contradict the censorious statements of some envious persons that the Menken could only cater to the roughest of the sterner sex, and that her stage attire merged closely on indecency."[107] Appreciating the market value of a good debate, James Gordon Bennett of the *Herald* decided to defend her, and he understood that female attendance was the key to Menken's legitimacy. In truth, newspaper accounts and theater records suggest that women had been attending Menken's performances all along, but their attendance seems to have increased significantly after her spectacular rise to prominence in Europe.[108]

An increase in female attendance may indicate that middle-class women considered Menken's fame as transcending her notoriety, but in fact women's theater attendance was increasing overall. Winter and Taylor both used language asserting that the women attending Menken's performances could not be "ladies." They implicitly supported the fact that "[a]ctresses had always been accepted by male society," and therefore "it was women's acceptance of an actress that carried significant social weight."[109] If women attended Menken's performances, then she was respectable enough for the mainstream. And if Menken was mainstream, then middle-class values were undergoing a profound and, in the eyes of many, disastrous change. Menken's acceptance highlighted that while some Americans were devoted to promoting "social purity," others financed an expanding popular culture that

---

[104] *New York Herald*, May 1, 1866.   [105] *New York Evening Post*, May 1, 1866, p. 2, c. 1.

[106] "The Decadence of Drama," *New York Tribune*, 1866, clipping in "Theatre Scrapbook, 1840–1877," Theatrical Scrapbooks Collection, box 68, item 532, HTC.

[107] "Adah Isaacs Menken at the Broadway Theater," *New York Herald,* May 16, 1866, p. 5.

[108] A variety of newspapers over the years commented on the number of women in the audience. Also see receipt book of Wyzeman Marshall, manager of the Howard Athenaeum and Boston Theatre, from Sept. 10, 1851 to July 25, 1864, HTC, TS 1544.279.99; Astley's Theatre, London, box office receipts during Miss Menken's engagement, Oct. 19–Nov. 26, 1867, HTC, TS 1529.291.

[109] Davis, *Actresses as Working Women*, 69–71.

directly challenged moral reforms.[110] Menken's successful performance on Broadway in 1866 implied significant loosening of social restrictions at the same time that it signaled a tightening of them.

Four months after Menken's departure from New York, a group of ministers introduced a bill to the New York legislature that would establish "a Board of Moral Health, 'to correct the indecencies of the American stage, and to secure that none but plays of an improving character shall be brought before'" the public. The *Herald* reporter took a sarcastic tone but was careful not to condemn the proceedings, suggesting that its readership was divided on the issue of morality in the theater. The *Herald* quoted "the Honorable Owen Murphy" as dramatically describing the dangers:

> [I]n the case of such plays as the "Black Crook" and Cendrillon, the arrow of lascivious suggestion pierces the vitals without warning; the best classes of our best youth, and of both sexes, suddenly find themselves engaged as passionate witness to spectacles in which every appliance of licentious and demoralizing imagery would seem to have been studied and prepared, regardless of expense, for the sole purpose of blunting the sensibilities of maiden modesty and giving to the evil passions of male spectators a stimulant and example which they only too little need. It is thus the simmering humors of the blood are made to boil over, delicious but dangerous fancies are first accepted and then caressed; and the hot pleasures which find admission through the eye, are made a conveyance of the soul's destruction.[111]

Clearly, Menken's performance in the summer of 1866, only a few months earlier, had come at a time when reform-minded Americans were turning their attention to popular culture. But at the same time that people such as Owen Murphy were organizing opposition to popular theater, Menken was selling out performances. Obviously, a large proportion of Americans were *not* concerned about the dangers that Murphy later described so vividly. In fact, critical reviews seemed only to make New Yorkers more curious about America's newest international celebrity. The theater had become a site of contention between established taste makers and the ticket-buying public. Newspapers such as the *Herald*, which relied on mass support, tried to play both sides until the winner of the argument became clear.

Menken catered to the public, but she also used her box-office advantage to gain more influence in the world beyond the theater. She paradoxically transcended the limits of her sex by playing up her body. By performing male roles, she was managing to live out fantasies of independence customarily available only to men. She made a fortune sword fighting, vaulting onto

---

[110] Timothy Gilfoyle, *City of Eros: New York City, Prostitution, and the Commercialization of Sex, 1790–1920* (New York: W. W. Norton, 1992), 185–187.

[111] *New York Herald*, Jan. 8, 1867, p. 11, c. 1.

horses, initiating romantic situations, and allowing herself to be helplessly stripped and bound to the back of a horse. She became rich by playing both aggressive and passive roles. But the cultural milieu in America was changing rapidly. By 1866 the Civil War had ended and a cultural war had begun over who would control public entertainment. Menken succeeded financially in the United States, but those who bought tickets to her performances did not control the press. Despite all the publicity about her success abroad, by the end of the summer she was a critical failure in the United States.

Once again she became deeply despondent. Besides her public humiliation, some of her melancholy might be attributed to the fact that she was now pregnant again. Either Barkley or Davenport had conceived a child with her earlier that spring, while still in England. Although her pregnancy was not yet visible, she felt its effects; nearly a month into the New York run, she fainted one night just before the curtain fell. Woods reluctantly released her from her contract when doctors determined that she had "strained her heart." It is possible that Menken played up her illness to escape the gaze of the New York press because she rested only a few days before organizing a Midwest tour for June. Despite the nausea and fatigue that often accompany early pregnancy, she performed to full houses in Cincinnati, Nashville, and Louisville.

Her return to Cincinnati surely set off memories for her, when she arrived to perform at Wood's Theatre. Her name, still Adah Isaacs Menken, had such different connotations than when she had lived there eight years before. She now arrived as a scandalous international entertainer rather than a young Jewish wife with poetic ambition and dreams of stardom. No friends came to greet her at the theater. Did she look for her ex-husband or former in-laws? If she did, she had no luck. Alexander had left the city in 1861, never to return, and Menken and Sons Dry Goods had filed for bankruptcy. Alexander's brothers had moved to Memphis, the only major southern city untouched by the war, and opened another dry goods company, Menken Bros.[112] Menken cut short her visit, citing exhaustion and ill health, and returned to New York to begin packing her trunks for Paris.

At the end of July, she confided to her new publicist and secretary, Susette Ellington, that she was expecting a child.[113] Now in her fifth month of pregnancy, she could no longer conceal her condition. She must have told James Barkley at roughly the same time, for despite all her avowals to never

---

[112] Menken Brothers stayed in business in Memphis until the 1890s. Alexander joined his brothers in 1871, accompanied by his new bride Mary Rowe. He clerked for another business, and died without fanfare by 1877. Ohio, vol. 80, Tennessee, vol. 43, R. G. Dun & Co. Collection, Harvard Business School, Cambridge, Mass.; marriage certificate, Alexander Menken to Mary Rowe, Aug. 16, 1871, Probate Court Records, William Howard Taft Center, Cincinnati, Ohio.

[113] Lesser, *Enchanting Rebel*, 181; I have been unable to locate the papers of Susette Ellington to substantiate this claim.

Here Menken looks like a proud mother with her son Louis Dudevant Victor Emmanuel Barkley (1867). This was a carte de visite meant for public sale. Note the naturalness of her smile – not a common sight in photographs of the 1860s. No one is sure what became of her son; he disappears from public record later that year. (Harvard Theatre Collection)

marry again, Menken married for the last time on August 19, 1866. They exchanged vows in the Bleak House parlor on Sunday, and three days later, Menken left for Paris.

According to Ed James, on the morning of her intended departure, Barkley and Menken fought "violently," and she had to be carried to the steamer "ill from an overdose of poison, whether to soothe her nerves or for self-destruction was never perfectly ascertained." It is just as likely that she took the poison in an attempt to abort the fetus, but that kind of specu- lation would never have made it into print. A delirious Menken was tucked into her stateroom bunk, and James notes mournfully that "the last we saw of this strange genius was when she could recognize nobody."[114] Menken never saw Barkley again; no evidence of their correspondence remains; and

---

[114] Ed James, *Biography of Adah Isaacs Menken* (New York: Ed James, 1869), 10.

she never again mentioned him in her letters or in verse, but she did give her child his last name. After her death, Barkley gave generously to erect a monument on Menken's grave in Paris. Whether he did so as an expression of affection or through a desire to confirm his claim on a famous woman cannot be determined; he left no personal papers.

Menken never returned to America.

Chapter 8

Finale

On ne disait plus: Nous allon à la Gaité mais bien: nous allons à Menken. Assister à ce spectacle etait plus qu'une affaire de curiosité, plus qu'un plaisir intellectuel et artistisque, c'etait un veritable satisfaction des sens.[1]

In September 1866, Menken went to Paris and became La Menken, a cosmopolitan celebrity, available for private viewing in photographs, but living on a distant, brilliant plane. She was now an international figure and marketed her image through photography with a savvy never seen before, creating a kaleidoscope of images to tantalize the public. Yet her letters suggest it was in this period, shortly before her death, that she privately began to pull away from the exterior image. She once commented to an admirer, poet Charles Warren Stoddard,: "I am still a vagabond, of no use to anyone in the world – and never shall be. . . . The body and soul don't fit each other; they are always in a 'scramble.'"[2] Her feelings of discordance reveal themselves in her publicity and public actions as she engineered scandal and flaunted personal liberation to increase visibility and yet also seemed to slip further away. From her beginnings in Cincinnati, the Menken image had been crafted like a mask; now its wearer seemed to grow weary of the sticky inner contours and long to set it aside. She set to work on substantiating her intellectual image as her celebrity identity grew tiresome and worn.

But however burdensome the celebrity image came for Menken to perform, she continued to promote it through photographs. Despite residing in Europe, Menken's image became more available in America than ever before. She was one of the first entertainers to use photography as a marketing device, and by 1866 she had become the most widely photographed woman of the period. By that summer Americans could purchase copies of her different images in theaters, card shops, newsstands, and photography studios across the country. But the technology that made her an internationally recognized face and figure also had the power to destroy her. Once photographs were in the hands of viewers, she lost control over her own image; she could

---

[1] *Profils Contemporaires: Miss Addah Menken* (n.p., n.d., but clearly written in early 1867 because it describes her performance in *Pirates de la Savane*). Hand copied ts. in Nicholas Kovach Collection, Special Collections, University of Minnesota, Minneapolis (hereafter Kovach).

[2] Adah Isaacs Menken (hereafter AIM) to Charles Warren Stoddard, Vienna, June 1867, noted in Allen Lesser Collection, American Jewish Archives, Cincinnati, OH (hereafter ALC).

manipulate the image, but she could not determine public reception. Nor could she control which pictures reached the marketplace, since photographers rather than subjects owned rights to the images. This final chapter of her life explores how she used photographic cartes de visite to promote intimacy with her fans while she performed on a distant stage, and the role of this new medium in both the rise and fall of her self-creation.

Menken performed within her photographs, just as she did in print and on stage, using contradictory images. The public could buy pictures of Menken smiling sweetly, like the girl next door, or sprawled suggestively in her nearly bare Mazeppa costume. She performed respectability by adopting the poses favored by middle-class women in their pictures. Lost in contemplation of a book or absorbed in her writing, her head propped comfortably on one hand, she looked educated and thoughtful. Smoking a cigarette or posed in men's clothing, with a fan of cards in her hand, she was daring and defiant. At turns she charmed, challenged, reassured, and titillated. Which was the real Menken? A viewer could choose among any of several images to give evidence of whatever he or she wanted to see. The spectrum of images protected her mystery and promoted her complexity.

Complications arose when pictures began circulating of Menken with her most famous, and controversial lovers, first Alexandre Dumas *père* and later Algernon Charles Swinburne. The public reacted against the pictures in part because they offended bourgeois sensibility by advertising Menken's sexual affairs. The public had heard of her affairs for years, but now they could actually see them in all their commonplace, fleshy detail. But there was more at stake in these pictures than an insult to propriety. They violated the relationship that Menken, as a celebrity and as a particular character, had established with her audience. In her other pictures, Menken fulfilled the desires of the viewer; she was dangerous, sweet, learned, vampish, or modest. The pictures were not about Menken so much as what the audience wanted her to be. These other pictures, however, were not about Menken's relationship with the viewer but rather Menken's relationship with her lover; the viewer was thrust into the position of voyeur. Voyeurism provided a different kind of pleasure that made it possible to enjoy a spectacle at a distance while disallowing the sense of personal connection fostered by celebrity. Voyeurism made it easier to criticize and mock because there was no longer that illusory personal relationship between the viewer and the viewed. The viewer was privy to intimacy, but no longer the subject of intimacy. Also, Menken's juxtaposition with men made her own subordinate gender position clear for the first time. Her image of independence was replaced with one of weakness, dependence, and sordid sexuality.

Menken entered the world of photography just as it was entering the mass media. Photographers and cultural critics alike wrestled with the implications of photography: Was it about authenticity or artistry? She may have discussed the topic with Walt Whitman, who had a lifelong obsession with photography as both medium and metaphor. He explored and experimented with photography in both his creation of self and his poetic philosophy. On the one hand, he saw himself as a voyeur of life whose poetry served the same purpose as a photograph. He described *Leaves of Grass* as his "definitive *carte visite* to the coming generations of the New World."[3] At the same time, he explored self-representation and creation through portraiture, choosing different versions of how he wished to be seen. He once commented, "I meet new Walt Whitmans every day. There are a dozen of me afloat. I don't know which Walt Whitman I am."[4] His quote suggests that photographs were more authentic, more Whitman than Whitman himself. He recognized the power of photography to subsume the original, to produce something greater than the original. But while Whitman explored the possibilities of photography as an instrument of democracy and self-presentation, Menken was more in tune with the commercial possibilities of photography. She attempted not to achieve accurate representation of herself, but rather to create a spectrum of images that maintained her overall image of complexity and contradiction.

Celebrity portraits capitalized on the notion that photographic portraiture conveyed the soul of the subject. Pictures of Menken in costume were obviously meant to depict her in the roles for which she had become most famous; they did not suggest intimacy, but rather captured an event. In these pictures she is much like the many pictures of Roman ruins that so delighted midcentury Americans: She is a spectacle, a cultural artifact available for viewing in the privacy of one's own home. But Menken had more pictures taken of her as Menken than as Menken playing a theatrical role. Photographs of Menken's face, full body shots of her in the private act of reading or thinking, images of her sitting politely or defiantly were meant to convey her as a person rather than a distant star. Fans could read her character in her face. Indeed, they could *own* her face and know her soul. She was available for intimate viewing whenever the owner of the picture desired. Even if nineteenth-century photography was "founded on an understanding of the medium as an illusion," as Miles Orvell demonstrates, the power of the human face belied the art behind the photography.[5] The poses and props might be artificial, but the face conveyed authenticity. Portraits allowed viewers to look into Menken's eyes and fantasize that they knew her better than those controlling the media.

[3] Quoted in Ed Folsom, *Walt Whitman's Native Representations* (New York: Cambridge University Press, 1994), 104.

[4] Ibid., 161. The chapter "Whitman and Photographs of the Self" is a wonderful exploration of the power of portraiture, 127–177.

[5] Miles Orvell, *The Real Thing: Imitation and Authenticity in American Culture, 1880–1940* (Chapel Hill: University of North Carolina Press, 1989), 77. "Photography and the Artifice of Realism" is one of the best discussions I have found on nineteenth-century cultural understanding of photography, 73–102.

Menken's photographic celebrity was made possible by the invention of photographic cartes de visite and the subsequent creation of their market demand. Cartes de visite, small pictures approximately six by eight centimeters pasted to card stock slightly larger, were the first easily reproduced, inexpensive photographs available. The daguerreotype, invented in 1839, was printed onto a glass plate coated with photo emulsion and impossible to replicate. The singularity of daguerreotypes, and the expense of its precursor, hand-painted miniatures, infused portraiture with value that went beyond the sentimental. Cartes de visite began much the same way; first introduced in Paris in 1854, they immediately became a popular novelty among the French and British upper classes. Photographic "visiting cards" were exchanged like typographic calling cards, and were virtually the same size.[6]

Efficient technology made cartes de visite easy to mass-produce, making them ideal for the larger population. Two advances made them possible: the invention of a multilens camera able to record several images at once, and albumen paper, onto which pictures could be printed from the original glass plate. The tremendous popularity of the stereoscope, a hand-held viewer through which one's eyes blended two prints into one three-dimensional image, had provided the financial incentive for inventing a camera able to take both pictures in one shot. It was a simple adjustment to create the standard cartes de visite camera, which took four images at once. By 1860, so-called cartomania had taken over France and England, and would soon sweep through the United States, as people began buying, trading, and collecting cartes.[7] Menken had her first publicity cartes de visite taken in a New York studio as early as 1859, dressed as a Civil War Zouave for *The French Spy*.[8] She was slightly ahead of the others; the trade in celebrity cartes de visite took off in 1861, when an American photographer, J. E. Mayall, began mass-producing celebrity photographs for sale.[9] By the spring of 1860, dozens of photographers were taking portraits of clients in New York, Philadelphia, and Boston. In England alone, 300 to 400 million cartes de visite were sold every year from 1861 to 1867.[10]

By 1863, at only twenty-five cents per carte, Americans could buy several different images of Menken, including Menken as the French Spy in tights and a brief toga-like costume (1862), a contemplative Menken looking remarkably like Byron (1862), and a flirtatious Menken peeking up from

[6] William C. Darrah, *Cartes de Visite in Nineteenth Century Photography* (Gettysburg: W. C. Darrah, 1981), 1–4.

[7] Ibid.

[8] Adah Isaacs Menken photographs (hereafter AIMP), Harvard Theatre Collection, Houghton Library, Cambridge, Massachusetts (hereafter HTC).

[9] Darrah, *Cartes de Visite*, 6.

[10] Ibid., 4. I could not find statistics for the United States, but I would speculate that sales of cartes were slightly lower because it took longer for the technology to spread to America's interior cities.

under the bird wing affixed to her dashing black hat (1863).[11] These early photographs were either portraits, taken from roughly ten feet away, or full body shots of Menken standing in empty space. Until late in 1864, Menken was quite slender, and when dressed in male or military clothing, she appeared beautifully androgynous. Several of the cartes de visite taken in California show her dressed in male clothing while striking feminine poses, playing up the "ideal duality of sex" so admired out west. To emphasize her literary persona, other pictures show her reading a book while propped against the kind of stuffed-velvet furniture found in middle-class parlors. Several head shots have her smiling sweetly, revealing dimples and even, pretty teeth. The charm and ease of her captured images is remarkable; although cartes de visite took only fifteen seconds to one minute of exposure time – a fraction of the time needed to take a daguerreotype – maintaining an air of relaxation was challenging. The wooden-faced cartes of other actors and celebrities of the period suggest that Menken had particular talent for posing. Her theatrical pictures convey emotion and action, whether as a courageous male character or as her tender, womanly self. Indeed, she may have been the only person to dare a smile until the late 1860s.

In 1868, American photographer Napoleon Sarony opened a studio in New York, having already established himself as a popular celebrity photographer on the opposite side of the Atlantic. Sarony mastered the art of creating lifelike portraits long before anyone else, and Menken was his first celebrity client. According to his own well-worn story, in 1865 Menken entered his studio in Birmingham, England, saying, "[A]ll attempts to photograph me as Mazeppa have been failures. Now I want you to take me in eight poses," but only on the condition that she pose herself.[12] The exchange worked to their mutual benefit: When working with celebrities, the photographer who took the picture would give the subject a large selection of prints without charging a fee; in exchange, the photographer would keep all rights to the photographs, which he or she could then mass-produce for profit.[13] Sarony agreed to allow Menken to pose herself as long as she would sit for another eight poses of his directing. Naturally, she came to recognize that he was the master of setting poses (this is Sarony's story, after all), and happily posed for many more cartes de visite. "Setting the pose" was the sole art of the photographer – he hired someone else to actually take the picture, which meant only opening and closing the shutter.

Sarony had the right to brag; he was the first photographer to achieve natural-looking portraits. He used careful staging to create images so relaxed or, conversely, so active, that the viewer studying the photograph could

---

[11] AIMP HTC.

[12] Ibid.; also in Ben L. Bassham, *The Theatrical Photographs of Napoleon Sarony* (Kent: Kent State University Press, 1978), 11.

[13] Bassham, *Theatrical Photographs*, 4.

forget about the process involved in taking it. His subjects look like people who would laugh and talk when not posing; they lack the stiff, unhappy camera face found in early photographic portraiture. Sarony relied heavily on props to achieve realism. His brother, Oliver, constructed a metal "posing frame" to hold the subject in position. Photographs of the frame – which Sarony fondly referred to as his "iron instrument of torture" – show a short, curved bar used to hold the person's head in position and another to prop up an arm or shoulder, allowing subjects to relax into seemingly natural poses. Sarony also introduced the use of painted backdrops and interesting accessories. Since the box camera had a shallow depth of focus, Sarony closed in the space by using painted backdrops and emphasized the foreground by casting interesting shadows onto the subject's clothing. Many of the seemingly personal items in Menken's pictures, such as her hat, writing desk set, and small statuary horses, were props that can be seen in other celebrity photographs by Sarony.[14]

Sarony's captivating cartes de visites of Menken transformed her into someone Americans easily recognized even if they had never been within a hundred miles of Menken herself. Sarony, meanwhile, became known as *the* celebrity photographer. He became so famous for his pictures of Menken that when he finally established a studio in Manhattan in 1868, he used the recently deceased Menken as his chief advertising device: "[On] a visit to the elegant, jewel-toned rooms of Messrs. Sarony & Co., at No. 680 Broadway . . . [t]here may be found the rarest posthumous works of the late Adah Isaacs Menken – something like hundred different studies of her, in every possible variety of posture and costume. . . ."[15] Sarony's pictures of Menken had been selling all over the United States for the past seven years. Both he and Menken had used her photographs to build reputations on both sides of the Atlantic.

Like other photographers, Sarony sold his photographs wholesale to other stores and traveling salesmen, who then took the photographs everywhere in the country. Cartes became less expensive as the technology became more widely used, augmenting their popularity. A person could buy his or her own cartes de visite for $1.50 to $3.00 a dozen. People began collecting them, pasting images of famous figures alongside those of friends and family in photograph albums – a recent innovation created by the desire to display cartes de visite. By the early 1860s, Americans could buy pictures not only of stars, but also of politicians, reformers, and writers – virtually any public figure, including some whom had died long ago. In the case of the latter, photographers aimed their cameras at the painted portraits of sacred historical figures, such as Martha and George Washington. And, unsurprisingly, the Civil War made cartes de visite photography more popular than

---

[14] Sarony's studio album, uncatalogued, HTC.
[15] "An Artist Photographer," New York *Home Journal*, Oct. 7, 1868.

ever before, because it allowed Americans to send their pictures to loved ones.[16] Cartes de visite were vulnerable to water, but they were lighter and less fragile than daguerreotypes and could be easily carried in a pocket or tucked between the pages of a diary or Bible.

Beginning with Sarony's photographs in 1865, the pictures of Menken that fans pasted into albums showed a voluptuously curved woman. Because of changes in theater fare as well as the more generous contours of her own body, Menken's cross-dressing now became more about showing off her curves than playing up androgyny. A tight belt defined rounded hips and a soft bosom that made the sex of even the fully dressed Cassimer perfectly obvious. Sarony also took several portraits of Menken dressed in her barest Mazeppa costume, which at this point resembled a waist-length toga over a pair of brief shorts. Sarony's most suggestive portrait shows the nearly-bare Mazeppa splayed horizontally against a bank of pillows, with her arms thrown over her head in a pose of passionate abandon, her eyes closed and her feet crossed primly at the ankle.[17] Sarony played up Menken's rebel image when he took a picture of her holding a cigarette with plumes of smoke wafting from the tip. Interestingly, this last carte is particularly rare, suggesting that either Menken did not want it sold or salesman did not believe it would sell and purchased few copies.[18] When Menken dressed in character, Sarony portrayed her as either a femme fatale or as a light-hearted "beautiful boy," whose laughing eyes invited the viewer to enjoy the fun with her. When dressed as Menken, he alternately portrayed her as sweet-faced, scholarly, or contemplative.

Menken was often posed with books: holding books, reading books, sharing a book with a female friend, or possibly writing one of her own. Cartes de visites of other socially prominent women suggest that middle-class women found posing with books particularly appealing.[19] Reading signified that the woman enjoyed a rich internal life as well as status above the laboring classes. Besides, it was an easy pose to hold and gave the reader something to do; for the many people who felt uncomfortable before the camera, it also meant not having to smile into the inhuman camera box with its four watchful eyes. Menken's image as a reader and writer implied a conventional middle-class identity that belied the sordid image presented in the American theater reviews of 1866.

Cartes de visite suggested an intimacy that earlier forms of portraiture did not. Before cartes, a few particularly famous individuals, such as George Washington, had several portraits painted, but viewers had to travel to visit such paintings – a formal process that emphasized the viewer's distance from

[16] Darrah, *Cartes de Visite*, 19.
[17] AIMP HTC. This photograph can be found in most collections of Menken photographs.
[18] Sarony studio album, HTC. I have never seen this photograph anywhere else.
[19] Cartes de Visite collection, "women," American Antiquarian Society, Worcester, Massachusetts (hereafter AAS).

the subject even as it allowed for the intimacy of seeing Washington's face at close range. Popular lithographs of Washington were widely available, but the variety of images remained small and, even when presenting him within a family setting, did not suggest a personal relationship with the viewer.[20] The relaxed images available on cartes de visite were a new phenomenon. It was the first time that subjects were pictured involved in tasks, rather than looking back at the viewer, suggesting that the viewer was in a privileged private space. Pictures such as the ones of Menken absorbed in writing at her desk implied that the scene took place within her own home, and therefore the picture image was of the private, "real" Menken. Although such images were staged, the setting and pose implied that here the camera caught Menken unmasked, allowing willing believers to fantasize unfettered by reality. Cartes enhanced the illusion of intimacy necessary for celebrity, allowing the purchaser to enjoy a one-sided, seemingly personal relationship with the subject. The small size of the pictures also meant that they were viewed individually; even if one viewed cartes in an album, or in the company of others, the act of viewing was generally a one-to-one, private experience. And they were sized for a secret, to be passed among friends, tucked under a pillow, or slipped into a pocket or book to be kept close at all times, for viewing or kissing.

Menken's ability to convey her personality only enhanced the intimacy of the viewer's experience. In pictures of her reading and writing, she looks genuinely involved in the work before her; if one thought she only played at intellectual pursuits, her cartes say otherwise. Furthermore, when posing as herself, she dressed head to toe in the requisite corsets, crinolines, and yards of fabric that hid the famous "symmetrical" build and distanced her from stage images. Her portrayal of Menken as a woman of sensibility is conveyed by sober shots of her fixing sad eyes on a distant point, as if her mind is truly focused inward. In a few rare pictures, she smiles sweetly, with joy in her eyes and fleeting dimples flashing, conveying an image quickly caught, as if the picture itself will change when one looks away. And finally there are shots of Menken fully dressed in respectable clothing but challenging the viewer with a daring glance that belies domestic ideals. As the French Spy she alternately poses as a beautiful young woman with a dreamy face or a fierce young soldier dressed for battle. As Jack Shepard she is a dandy in a stovepipe hat, holding a fan of cards, smirking at the camera with cocky male arrogance. But, of course, her most famous poses were as Mazeppa, in costumes that became increasingly bare yet more ornate as the years passed. In later pictures of Menken as the Tartar prince, she stands in command, holding her spear like a staff, the upward-pointing crescent moon of her headdress stressing Orientalism. Or she is Mazeppa

---

[20] Scott Casper earns credit for my knowledge of images of Washington; he was working on that subject for his upcoming book when we were both at AAS in 1998.

at his moment of weakness, when he is stripped of his clothing and remains suspended between boyhood and manhood, looking vulnerable and tender whether reclining or standing. The beauty of cartes de visite photography was that these many different images of Menken could be found at local theaters and newsstands even when the Menken herself was far away, riding horses across the Parisian stage or holding court in a London hotel. They suggested that she was never absent, regardless of geographic location.

Some of the first photographs Menken had taken in Paris in 1866 were with her new son. For the first time since striving for stardom, in September 1866, Menken arrived without fanfare, and waited out the last three months of her pregnancy. In November 1866, she gave birth to the son she named Louis Dudevant Victor Emmanuel Barkley and, according to her publicist, went against all her former claims to Judaism by baptizing him Catholic.[21] Menken had married Barkley presumably to legitimize their child, but there is no record of Barkley ever meeting his son, and the possible liaison between Menken and William Davenport suggests that the child may just as easily have been his.[22] Indeed, no official records exist of Louis Barkley's birth, death, or christening.[23]

Although Menken was still calculating and still performed her image with an eye to particular outcomes, she also gives evidence of deep depression during these years. Her letters are both melancholic and melodramatic, and by 1864, she had moved beyond renaming herself and those in her past and was now renaming those around her, referring to them with aristocratic titles or as her own sisters or brothers. She called even her dressing woman "mother." Those around her also participated in the seemingly harmless practice. One of the most ironic examples of this, given contemporary questions of Menken's racial identity, was her African American maid who renamed herself Minnie Menken.[24]

One of Menken's son's many middle names, "Dudevant," was the name of George Sand's first husband.[25] By naming her son Dudevant, Menken was probably trying to make a claim of intimacy with Sand; she probably thought, as did many, that Dudevant was Sand's maiden name. But it is extremely improbable that, as so many biographers have suggested, Sand became the child's godmother. For one thing, there is no concrete evidence

[21] Susette Ellington to the New York *Clipper*, March 19, 1867 (letter dated one month earlier).

[22] AIM to Wm. Davenport, Feb. 27, 1866, Swan Hotel, Bolten, England, ts. of letter in author's possession; AIM to Elizabeth Faye (wife of Davenport's manager), Feb. 21, 1866, ts. in author's possession. Originals no longer in existence.

[23] Letter from L. K. Keena to Allen Lesser, American Consul General, Paris, Feb. 24, 1933, ALC. She says that they checked records from Jan. 1, 1860, to Dec. 31, 1872.

[24] Wolf Mankowitz, *Mazeppa: The Lives, Loves and Legends of Adah Isaacs Menken* (New York: Stein and Day, 1982), 127.

[25] Ruth Jordan, *George Sand: A Biography* (London: Anchor Press, 1976), 19–33.

that Menken and Sand were close friends; Menken later referred to Sand as a dear friend but Sand herself never mentioned Menken in either her letters or diaries.[26] Also, the notion that Sand convinced Menken to baptize her child Catholic is questionable, given the fact that a year after the baptism of Menken's son, Sand's own devoted son and daughter-in-law chose to baptize their children in the Protestant faith, and Sand made no attempt to dissuade them.[27] The story of his baptism came from a letter by Menken's publicist, Susette Ellington, who wrote about the event to the *Clipper*, describing the child's baptism "at the grand cathedral, with a prince for a godfather, and his godmother one of the first authoresses of Paris."[28] It is possible that the entire story of his baptism was a fabrication meant to suggest a relationship between Sand and Menken, and nothing more.

However, if true, baptizing her son in a Catholic cathedral was a strange move for Menken to make, considering how vehemently and frequently she had claimed Jewish identity. But little Louis's christening would not have been Menken's only departure from her chosen faith: Several pictures of Menken taken over the next year show her wearing a cross.[29] It is true that anti-Semitism in France was particularly virulent at this point, and it is possible that Menken baptized her son out of a desire to escape public ire. Despite social freedoms that Menken exploited as much as possible in Paris, France was actually going through a relatively conservative, though joyous period. The so-called second Revolution, in which George Sand and other artists and writers had played a large role, was long since dead. Under Napoleon the third and his prefect, Georges Haussman, in only thirteen years Paris had been refashioned into a modern city, with a railroad system, straight, wide thoroughfares, and newly organized public spaces. Menken arrived just as the city was preparing to host the 1867 Paris Exposition, the "'open day' when [Napoleon III] invited the world to view the transformation."[30] Perhaps she worried that, with the eyes of the world on Paris, latent anti-Semitism would work against her. Yet her switch to a Christian persona remains unclear. If baptized, Louis would have been Catholic, but his mother wore crosses, never crucifixes. Meanwhile, the biography sold at Théâtre de Gaîté during her performances states her usual claim that she

---

[26] AIM to Charles Warren Stoddard, Adah Isaacs Menken Collection, Library of Congress.

[27] Jordan, *George Sand*, 314. The story of Sand as godmother was first raised by Allen Lesser in *Enchanting Rebel: The Secret of Adah Isaacs Menken* (1947), who later admitted, "George Sand's alleged role as godmother of Adah's son is a pure guess on my part." Furthermore, he wrote, "So far as concrete evidence is concerned, such as letters, contemporary newspapers, etc. there is nothing to show that Adah even knew George Sand." See Lesser to *American Weekly*, accusing Gene Couglin of plagiarism, ALC, 11.

[28] Ellington to Queen, transcript of original letter, Paris, Feb. 19, 1867, ALC.   [29] AIMP HTC.

[30] F. W. J. Hemmings, *Culture and Society in France, 1848–1898: Dissidents and Philistines* (New York: Charles Scribner's Sons, 1971), 124–132.

was born Jewish.[31] Why Menken chose to perform different religious faiths is open to speculation; she left no explanation.

In late December, only a month after her son's birth, Menken opened at the Théâtre de la Gaîté with the hastily revised *Les Pirates de la Savane*. The play was preferable to a French translation of *Mazeppa* because it was a pantomime, suggesting that Menken's often claimed French fluency was questionable. If possible, Menken's reception in Paris surpassed any she had experienced before; although a huge star in San Francisco and London, she became an idol overnight in Paris. She took nine curtain calls after the opening performance on December 29, 1866, and woke the next morning to find reviewers in raptures over her performance. Menken undoubtedly thrilled at the review in *L'Univers Illustré*: "Menken's career is ten times more romantic and fuller of episode than the life of the famous Lola Montez."[32] King Charles of Württemberg soon came to court her, much to the delight of the American public as well as the French.[33] Menken became a star celebrity in the most modern sense of the word: The media became obsessed with providing her images for public consumption, and, as always, she gave the people what they wanted.

During this period, Menken also suffered a series of accidents on stage that heightened her popularity and strengthened the image of her as daring and courageous. Reviewing *Les Pirates* for *Le Moniteur Universel* in early January, Théophile Gautier commented on allure of watching the dangerous spectacle: "If [the horse's] foot slipped, if a plank broke, the audience would have the pleasure of seeing a superb beast and a charming woman of intelligence, level-headedness and bravery, break together to bits. What greater attraction could one imagine?"[34]

During the second week of performances the horse did lose its footing while ascending the scaffold mountain and plunged to the floor. Luckily, Menken let go of the strap holding her to the horse and fell clear, and neither she nor the horse was injured. Two weeks later the incident replayed itself, only this time Menken was knocked unconscious and narrowly missed landing under the horse. The manager dismissed the audience

[31] Theatre de la Gaite, *Notice Biographique sur Miss Adah Isaacs Menken*, Artiste Américaine (Paris: Morris et compagnie, 1867), 1, HTC.

[32] Bernard Falk, *Naked Lady: A Biography of Adah Isaacs Menken* (London: Hutchinson, 1952), 149. Falk quotes a slew of notices following her Dec. 31, 1866, debut, and is careful to note the authors of the various reviews. Falk is the most reliable biography on reactions to Menken in Europe because he relies so heavily on newspaper and magazine articles, quotes them verbatim, and usually investigates the writers.

[33] Ellington to *Clipper*, Feb. 1867; Mankowitz, *Mazeppa*, 170–171. They may have been lovers, but they did not secretly marry, despite some biographers' wishes to the contrary (e.g., Elizabeth Brooks, *Prominent Women of Texas* (Akron, 1896)).

[34] Theophile Gautier, *Le Moniteur Universel*, Jan. 7, 1867, quoted in Kari Weil, "Purebreds and Amazons: Saying Things with Horses in Late Nineteenth-Century France," *Differences*, reproduced online at www.indiana.edu/~iupress/journals/differences/dif11-1.html.

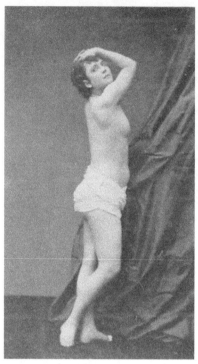

One of the famous two nude photographs of Menken. It was probably taken in Paris in 1867. Note that it is a carte de visite, meant to be replicated. (Harvard Theatre Collection)

as doctors filed backstage to determine the extent of the damage, fearing internal bleeding. Despite having suffered two broken fingers, a torn ear, sprained wrist, and a mild concussion, Menken insisted on returning to the stage two days later. She was forced to take thirteen curtain calls that night before an appreciative audience. It took nearly two months for her wounds to heal, but the incident increased the fervor of her fans' devotion.[35]

At some point while in Paris, Menken also posed for a series of semi-nude photographs, wearing only a swaddling of fabric around her hips. The rarity of these cartes de visite suggest that they were not for public sale. Some historians suggest that the photographer superimposed Menken's face on a nude body, but such a scenario is unlikely, given that all three were taken on the same set in Paris and were never published.[36] If authentic, their existence certainly demonstrates Menken's reckless daring. In France the

[35] *Clipper*, Feb. 16 and 23, 1867.
[36] Faye E. Dudden, *Women in American Theatre: Actresses and Audiences, 1790–1870* (New Haven: Yale University Press, 1994), 163; Mankowitz, *Mazeppa*, 175.

pictures would have seriously damaged her career; in America they would have destroyed her completely. Surprisingly, it took nearly a decade for pornography to flourish in America; most mid-nineteenth century porno-graphic cartes came from Paris and Italy, and were presumably smuggled in by those returning from travels abroad.[37] Cartes de visite were, of course, the perfect medium for pornography, as they were cheap to produce and easy to hide. The nude pictures of Menken confirm her comfort with nudity, and support journalist Adrian Marx's description of Menken as having "not the body of classical Venus, but the body of some peculiar Venus . . . with round, obtrusive, almost thick outlines."[38] From a modern standpoint, semi-nude Menken looks like a rather ordinary woman of middling stature, with heavy hips and thighs, a small bosom, and a rounded tummy. More captivating than her form is the daredevil expression on her face, inviting the viewer to share in the wickedness of her undress.

Ironically, a far more benign photograph precipitated Menken's fall from Parisian public grace, marking the point at which Menken truly lost control over her image. Menken had long been a fan of the celebrated French author Alexandre Dumas, whose *Three Musketeers* and *Count of Monte Cristo* have become classics. By the 1860s, Dumas was less well known for his plays than was his son, Alexandre Dumas *fils*, but he remained active in the theatrical world. When he decided to pay Menken a surprise first visit backstage in 1867, she reportedly gazed at him for a moment in silence before embracing him passionately.[39] He was sixty-three, corpulent, grizzled with years of decadence, and spoke little English. The son of a French father and Jamaican mother, Dumas was also biracial, and socialized with other black Frenchmen and expatriated Americans who lived in Paris. According to every available source, Confederate-loving Menken and visibly biracial Dumas immediately became fast friends, and probably lovers. They attended parties and plays, hosted dinner gatherings, and stayed together at his villa in Bougival.[40]

Despite her southern roots, Menken apparently ignored Dumas's black identity. It is possible that Dumas's accomplishments transcended race in Menken's mind, or that she, too, had African ancestry, as would later be sug-gested. Regardless of her own personal history, Menken's relationship with Dumas surely brought her into contact with the New Orleans quadroon poets who had expatriated to Paris. Over twenty years earlier, in 1845, sev-enteen quadroon poets in New Orleans had published a celebrated collection of their poetry, *Les Cenelles*. In the 1850s, when sectional tension increased and Codes Noir became more oppressive, many of these poets relocated to France. At least two of them, Pierre Dalcour and Camille Thierry, became

[37] Serge Nazarieff, *Early Erotic Photography* (Koln, Germany: Benedikt Taschen, 1993), 6–11.

[38] Adrian Marx, quoted in "La Menken," *Home Journal*, Sept. 16, 1868.

[39] Falk, *Naked Lady*, 162.   [40] Ibid., 175.

close friends with Dumas.[41] One can easily imagine Menken enjoying the camaraderie of peers from her distant home city.

In April 1867, *Le Figaro* remarked that "there are to be seen just now in the shop windows a series of astonishing *cartes-de-visite* of Mme. Menken and Alexandre Dumas, jointed together in *poses plastiques*. Can M. Dumas be her father? In one of the series he is in his shirt sleeves. Oh, for shame!"[42] Sure enough, portraits of Menken and the elderly Dumas appeared in shop windows throughout the city. Some of the images were tender, seeming to suggest that Dumas did indeed have paternal feelings toward Menken. However, the most compromising image depicted Dumas seated with his shirt open at the throat, his eyes smiling at the viewer, with Menken perched on a stool at his knees, her cheek against his open collar, gazing contentedly into the camera.[43] The pose and the sleepy peace of its subjects suggested privacy, intimacy. It was not a sexualized image so much as a romantic one, but still devastatingly personal.

Worse still, the initial photographs soon gave way to crass imitations, with the heads of Dumas and Menken superimposed on bodies in more compromising positions.[44] When defending herself against words, Menken could refute in kind what others had written about her and posit an alternative image, but she had no way to fight the appropriation of her photographic image. Even when the pictures had been of her alone, she could create a relationship with the viewer by presenting herself in particular ways. But in a photograph with another, the image became about her relationship with the other person, and no longer an exclusive bond between herself and the viewer. Superimposing her head on another image suggested she was entirely at the mercy of others' ideas about her. Commentary and photographic parody worked together, depicting Menken and Dumas as a joke, a pleasurable commodity for public consumption.

The photographs also sparked comment in America. Although they demanded attention, and in that sense increased her popularity, many Americans considered them inexcusably vulgar because of Dumas's racial identity. Mark Twain described the photographs to readers of the San Francisco *Daily Alta*: "In one of them Dumas is sitting down, with head thrown back, and great, gross face, rippled with smiles, and Adah is leaning on his shoulder and just beaming on him like a moon – beaming on him with the expression of a moon that is no better than it ought to be." Twain saw the photographs as most revealing of Menken's ambitions and manipulations.

[41] Charles Barthelemy Rousstève, *The Negro in Louisiana: Aspects of His History and His Literature* (New Orleans: Xavier University Press, 1937), 68; Arna Bontemps and Jack Conroy, *They Seek a City* (Garden City, N.Y.: Doubleday, Doran, 1945), 106.

[42] Horace Wyndham quoting from *Le Figaro*, *Victorian Sensations* (London: Jarrold's, 1933), 184–185.

[43] Article quotes Dumas *fils's* reaction to photograph, *Le Figaro*, Jan. 3, 1931, ALC; also quoted in Falk, *Naked Lady*, 175.

[44] Falk, *Naked Lady*, 176.

One of the two famous photographs of Menken with Alexandre Dumas *père*.
This photograph scandalized the public with its suggestion of intimacy and
destroyed Menken's reputation in France, perhaps because Dumas was biracial.
(Harvard Theatre Collection)

He points out patterns of her behavior: "I begin to regard Menken's conduct
as questionable, occasionally. She has a passion for connecting herself with
distinguished people, and then discarding them as soon as the world has
grown reconciled to the novelty of it and stopped talking about it." He lists
her past lovers and husbands and then his language takes on racist overtones:
"And now comes the great Mulatto in the Iron Mask, and he is high chief
for the present. But can he hold his position against all comers? Would he
stand any chance against a real live gorilla from the wilds of Africa?" To
Twain, at least, Dumas's racial identity was the greater novelty; the fact that
Dumas was one of the most celebrated writers in Europe seems to have
meant little when Menken snuggled up to his dark-skinned, kinky-haired
self. But Twain ends on a more generous note, expressing what would come
to bother so many upon Menken's death: "Menken is a good hearted, free-
handed, charitable soul – a woman who does white deeds enough, kindly
Christian deeds enough, every day of her life to blot out a swarming mul-
titude of sins; but, Heaven help us, what desperate chances she takes on her
reputation!"[45] The fact was, he saw the good side of Menken and implied
that most of his readers liked her, but it was pathetically obvious to him what

[45] Mark Twain, San Francisco *Daily Alta*, June 16, 1867, noted as "Letter Seventeen," on the website
www.twainquotes.com.

Menken was doing when she posed for those pictures. Twain's disgust was tempered compared with that of many Americans, and the outrage appeared to have as much to do with Dumas's race as the intimacy of the pose.

Slander against Menken and Dumas was racially inflected from the beginning of the scandal. Although Dumas's fame as a writer had the potential to strengthen Menken's image as an intellectual woman, his race, age, and reputation as a womanizer undermined any benefit she received from the publicity. Ditties in the French, British, and American press dubbed Dumas "L'Oncle Tom," although Menken could hardly be constructed as one of the domestic ladies of Harriet Beecher Stowe's novel.[46] Dumas's son, the celebrated playwright, had his name pulled into the affair as well, when journalists alluded to his play *La Dame aux Camélias*, which had for a time been censored because it depicted a "courtesan with a heart of gold."[47] Not surprisingly, newspapers also began referring to Menken as Dumas' Lady of Camellias.[48]

Stung by the negative references to his own work, Alexandre Dumas *fils* demanded that his father show more respect for his family.[49] Alexandre père then concocted an elaborate story that Menken had been visiting his daughter when, on a whim, the three of them stopped into a studio and innocently posed for pictures. The cartes were intended only for private viewing, Dumas argued. The photographer who sold compromising pictures to the public did so without their permission, and seeing no money to be made by including pictures of Dumas's daughter, printed up only those of Menken and Dumas. This was Dumas's story, but there are no pictures of his daughter to substantiate that part of his claim.[50] By April 17, 1867, Dumas *père* took the photographer to court for unlawful use of the pictures, and eventually stopped their sale, but the damage was done.[51] Americans read about his actions in their daily newspapers: "The elder Dumas is not ambitious of figuring in public with Miss Adah Isaacs, however much he may in private court her society, and accordingly he asks for damages and an injunction, which are certain to be granted; for in this *country truth* is no excuse . . . for a libel of any kind."[52] The scandal not only broke apart the relationship between Dumas and Menken, but also marked the end of her popularity in Paris and further damaged her image in the United States.

Evidence suggests that at this point the woman behind La Menken became extremely depressed. That is to say, she did not perform dramatic melancholy

[46] Mankowitz, *Mazeppa*, 172–174.   [47] Hemmings, *Culture and Society*, 44–47.

[48] Falk, *Naked Lady*, 174–76.

[49] Andre Marois, *The Titans: A Three Generation Biography of the Dumas* (New York: Harper Bros., 1957), 358; Claude Schopp, *Alexandre Dumas, Genius of Life* (New York: Franklin Watts, 1988), 481.

[50] Dumas *fils* retold the story in a letter to Mme. Wright, and the letter was quoted in *Le Figaro*, Jan. 3, 1931, ALC.

[51] Falk, *Naked Lady*, 177; *Journal Des Débates*, May 4, 1867, ALC.

[52] *San Francisco Daily Evening Bulletin*, June 12, 1867, noted in Kovach, vol. 2.

as part of her image, but rather exhibited signs of depression in her letters. Probably wanting to escape Paris until the scandal cooled, she accepted a month-long contract in Vienna. Unhappily, the Viennese found *Piraten der Savanna* absolutely devoid of humor; they disliked and shunned both Menken and her play. Menken's letter to poet Charles Warren Stoddard resonates with despair: "I have today fallen into the bitterness of a sad, reflective and desolate mood. You know I am alone, and that I work, and without sympathy; and that the unshrined ghosts of wasted hours and of lost loves are always tugging at my heart." Alone in her sumptuous Viennese hotel room, she contemplated her situation, "I have long since ceased to contend with the world; it bores me horribly; nothing but hard work saves me from myself."[53]

Also, something mysterious happened to Menken's son around this time. He may have died, as is commonly believed, or her busy schedule compelled her to send him away to the French countryside for safekeeping.[54] Most biographers believe that the child died, but there is no information on his death; he simply disappears from all public record in the summer of 1867.[55] She herself never commented on her child, but the pictures she took with him suggest pride and love. Why was Menken so silent on her role as a mother, especially when the mother was such a powerful image? Perhaps she felt that a crucial part of the Menken identity was that she appeared unfettered. Perhaps her motherhood was an identity she did not want to share. It is impossible to know, because of her inexplicable silence on the subject, but losing him (in whatever fashion) may have contributed to her depression.

By midsummer, Menken began signing her letters "Infelix," announcing her deep unhappiness. Reviews of her performances confirm that she now lacked the vital energy that had previously inspired such admiration. She may have sensed the onset of serious illness, because she began actively compiling her best poems into a collection.[56] This was no small task; she did not own any copies of the New York poems and badgered James to collect back issues of the *Sunday Mercury*.[57]

In October, she returned to London to secure a publisher for her poetry collection. Once again, she performed *Mazeppa* at Astley's, and initial reviews sparkled: "Enthusiastic reception of Adah Isaacs Menken who was greeted on Saturday night with an ovation never equaled within the walls of old Astley's. The success attending the revival of the splendid spectacle of

---

53 AIM to Charles Warren Stoddard, Vienna, June 1867, noted in ALC.
54 Davenport family legend, author's conversations with Ormus Davenport, Aug. 1999.
55 L. J. Keena, American Consul General to Allen Lesser, Paris, Feb. 24, 1933, ALC.
56 AIM to Stoddard, Sept. 21, 1867, Adah Isaacs Menken Correspondence in ALS file (hereafter AIM ALS), HTC.
57 AIM to James, no date, AIM ALS HTC.

Mazeppa is unparalleled."[58] In the United States, papers such as *Wilkes' Spirit of the Times* told a similar tale: "The inimitable Menken has made her reappearance in London at Astley's to such houses as are rarely seen. . . . The fair American was repeatedly encored and cheered by her enthusiastic auditors. Menken's photographs are the most widely sold in Europe."[59] According to excerpts from British papers reprinted in America, Menken was better than ever: "In her attitudes, this actress of the New World is excellent."[60] But despite all the puffery in the press, the offstage Menken still exhibited signs of depression.

In December 1867, one of her newest friends, painter and poet Dante Gabriel Rossetti, suggested that Menken pay a visit to his friend Algernon Charles Swinburne. Rossetti later joked that he offered Menken ten pounds to seduce Swinburne. Although nearly thirty years old, Swinburne had never slept with a woman but regularly paid for flagellation at the hands of prostitutes in St. John's Wood.[61] Menken undoubtedly knew Swinburne's work well; his *Poems and Ballads* had shocked and thrilled the public with its graphic sensuality.[62] No doubt Menken accepted Rossetti's dare because she recognized an opportunity. According to a letter from Swinburne to a friend, Menken showed up at the house in Chelsea armed with her poetry. She spent the night, and in the morning proposed to read him her verses, to which he replied, "'My darling, a woman with such beautiful legs should not bother about poetry.'" Swinburne's habitual flippancy makes it hard to tell how he felt toward Menken, but such derogatory comments certainly convey little respect.[63]

Swinburne knew Menken's reputation before she showed up on his doorstep; he had recently attended a performance of *Mazeppa* and had heard of her poetic ambitions. Menken's impropriety undoubtedly endeared her to him, since Swinburne operated on the assumption that "imaginative separation from and rebellion against conventional pieties is itself a source of power."[64] His verse also suggests that he also greatly admired female beauty. However, according to Rossetti, Menken eventually returned the ten pound note, admitting that she had failed to seduce Swinburne, adding, "'I can't make him understand that biting's no good.'"[65] Swinburne and Menken continued their "affair" for the next three months. No one knows whether

---

[58] *London Times*, Oct. 22, 1867.   [59] *Wilke's Spirit of the Times*, Nov. 9, 1867.

[60] "From an English Exchange," *Wilkes Spirit of the Times*, Nov. 23, 1867.

[61] Jean Overton Fuller, *Swinburne: A Biography* (New York: Schocken Books, 1971), 163.

[62] Laurence Binyon, "Introduction," in *Selected Poems by Algernon Charles Swinburne* (Westport: Greenwood, 1980), vii.

[63] Julian Field to Edmund Gosse, quoting Swinburne, in Algernon Charles Swinburne, *Adah Isaacs Menken: A Fragment of Autobiography* (London: printed for private circulation only, 1917).

[64] David Riede, "Swinburne and Romantic Authority," in *The Whole Music of Passion: New Essays on Swinburne*, eds. Rikky Rooksby and Nicholas Shrimpton (Cambridge, England: Scolar, 1995), 23.

[65] Fuller, *Swinburne*, 163.

their relationship became sexual or not. Swinburne may have used the connection with Menken to kill rumors of homosexuality and bestiality, and Menken used Swinburne to validate her image as an intellectual.

Rossetti and Swinburne were "pre-Raphaelites," subscribing to an esthetic somewhat related to Emerson's transcendentalism and Whitman's celebration of the sexual and sensual, with "nature" and idealized romance as its defining elements.[66] Rossetti's gothic paintings of strong women with haunted eyes, lush lips and tumultuous tumbles of hair became the hallmark of the pre-Raphaelite movement. Resonant with passion, they illustrated scenes from Bible and the days of King Arthur. Swinburne's poetry became a literary parallel, infusing classic themes of love and death with sexual passion and pain. Swinburne and Rossetti shared a home in Chelsea, and enjoyed friendship with other pre-Raphaelite artists and poets as gifted as themselves, including Ford Madox Brown and William Holman Hunt. Dante's older brother William, a renowned literary critic, helped to publicize their work. Friendships with the Rossettis and Swinburne gave Menken entree into a peculiarly intellectual and iconoclastic branch of elite society.

Despite their obvious differences, the friendship between Menken and Swinburne was rooted in a shared love of rebellion. They differed drastically in their backgrounds; while Menken was growing up in poverty, Swinburne enjoyed all of the benefits of aristocracy. He never had to fight for recognition; he was born and educated into an elite intellectual circle. However, his provocative subject matter made his work controversial for many years. Poet R. H. Stoddard defended Swinburne eloquently in 1866, saying that "Mr. Swinburne is not coarse, indecent and shocking . . . but, on the contrary, a young man of brilliant and beautiful genius, who dares much in his poetry because it is dramatic, and who, while occasionally handling subjects which the world is just now pleased to consider immoral, is always scholarly, imaginative, and poetical." Stoddard then quoted Swinburne's own response to criticism, in a statement that reveals much about the poet:

> The question at issue is wider than any between a single writer and his critics, or it might well be allowed to drop. It is this: whether or not the first and last requisite of art is to give no offense; whether or not all that cannot be lisped in the nursery or fingered in the schoolroom is therefore to be cast out of the library; whether or not the domestic circle is to be for all men and writers the outer limit and extreme horizon of their world. For to this we have come; and all students of art must face the matter as it stands.[67]

Swinburne saw the contemporary artist as fettered by Victorian morality, and that to bend to propriety was to limit oneself. To this day, Swinburne remains

---

[66] Susan P. Casteras, *English Pre-Raphaelitism and Its Reception in America in the Nineteenth Century* (Rutherford: Fairleigh Dickinson University Press, 1990), 34–36.

[67] R. H. Stoddard quoted in New York *Evening Post*, Dec. 6, 1866.

a controversial poet because of his interest in sexual perversion and the shock value of much of his work, yet he is also recognized as a master of poetic forms. Menken's work never approached the artistic quality of Swinburne's, yet the two held interests that they probably shared with few others – most notably, an fascination with sexuality outside normative behavior.

The link between them can be found in their literary tastes; both Menken and Swinburne revered the work of Dickens, Byron, Sand, Baudelaire, Gautier, and Balzac. Like Menken, Swinburne had read Gautier's *Mademoiselle de Maupin* and expressed intense curiosity about portrayals of sexual ambiguity.[68] Menken's association with Dickens probably impressed Swinburne as well. He so admired Dickens that he later made reading his work a daily ritual.[69] Menken and Swinburne spent countless hours in conversation, and considering their shared interests, they probably focused a substantial amount of attention on literature, gender, and sex.

No doubt Menken and Swinburne approached their reading differently. Menken exhibited romantic sensibility, while Swinburne, although the more critical reader, invariably responded to both life and literature with humor. In 1862, he managed to procure copies of Marquis de Sade's twin novels, banned in England: *Justine ou les Malheurs de la Vertu* and *Juliette ou les Prospérités de la Vice*. Swinburne described his reaction to *Justine*: "I really thought I must have died or split open or choked with laughing. I never laughed so much in my life. I couldn't have stopped to save the said life." Swinburne's determination to obtain a copy of the book and his comical response to it suggest his irreverent approach to just about everything. He immediately recognized de Sade's novels as pure sensation, explaining to his friend, "I looked for some sharp and subtle analysis of lust – some keen dissection of pain and pleasure," but de Sade "takes bulk and number for greatness . . . as if a number of pleasures piled one on another made up the value of a single great and perfect sensation of pleasure."[70]

Sometime later, Swinburne began writing his own novel of exquisite pleasure and pain, but the posthumously titled "Lesbia Brandon" remained unfinished and unpublished. He was writing the novel when he met Menken in 1867, and several elements suggest her influence. The "novel" – four loosely connected sections that Swinburne never took time to rewrite into one piece – centers on Herbert and Margaret, a brother and sister who look startlingly alike. Lesbia Brandon, a woman who becomes the recipient of Herbert's unwanted attention, is only a secondary character in the novel. The central conflict of the novel is not lesbianism, but rather an incestuous romance of "sharp and subtle" pain and pleasure between Herbert and his

[68] Philip Henderson, *Swinburne: Portrait of a Poet* (New York: Macmillan, 1974), 95.
[69] Clyde Kenneth Hyder, *Swinburne's Literary Career and Fame* (Durham: Duke University Press, 1933), 102.
[70] Fuller, *Swinburne*, 62.

sister. Swinburne wrote the character Margaret to resemble his first cousin Mary Gordon, the love of his young life. The relationship of Margaret and Herbert apparently allowed Swinburne to play out feelings he harbored for his cousin. With mothers who were sisters, and fathers who were first cousins, Mary Gordon and Swinburne were as close to siblings as cousins could be; Swinburne could not hope for anything more than fantasy.[71] He portrays Herbert as young, slim, and beautiful and Margaret as a feminine version of Herbert, but older by at least a decade and married with children.

Two characters in the novel appear linked to Menken: Lesbia Brandon and Leonora Harley. In a fine turn of gender transgression, Swinburne introduces Lesbia during a game of charades, for which Herbert is dressed as a girl who Margaret playfully calls "Helen." Lesbia develops a crush on the Helen, only to have her hopes dashed when Helen proves to be male. Herbert experiences similar pain several years later when he professes love to Lesbia and she replies that she cannot feel that way about a man.[72] Lesbia, "a horsewoman who writes poetry," clearly resembles Menken.[73] Swinburne presents Lesbia as Herbert's only love interest other than Margaret, a scenario that paralleled Swinburne's own complicated feelings about Menken and Gordon. Lesbia is "dark and delicately shaped; not tall, but erect and supple; she had thick and heavy hair growing low on the forehead, so brown that it seemed black in the shadow; her eyes were somber and mobile, full of fervor and of dreams . . . she was as warm and wan as a hot day without sun."[74] Swinburne wrote these sections of the novel when he was with Menken, and his depiction of Herbert's frustrated love seems to have been inspired by his own complex feelings.

Several literary scholars suggest that Menken inspired a minor secondary character named Leonora Harley. One has to wonder whether Menken told Swinburne about her letters to Hattie Tyng during one of their many late night conversations – or was his use of the name "Leonora" only coincidental? Swinburne describes Leonora: "There was afloat in London about this time a lady of aspiring build, handsome beyond average and stupid below the intellect of her profession. She had a superb and seductive beauty, some kindness of nature, and no mind whatever. Tall, white-faced, long limbed, with melancholy eyes that meant nothing and suggested anything."[75] Menken was not stupid, tall, white-faced, or long-limbed, but she was afloat in London and uncommonly attractive. Swinburne portrays Leonora as having a mesmerizing quality that both attracts and repels Herbert, much as Ethel described Leonora to her betrothed. Perhaps, in describing her letter from *Ethel's Love Life* to Swinburne, Menken unwittingly suggested another character for his book, possibly modeled loosely on herself.

---

[71] Henderson, *Swinburne*, 87.   [72] Fuller, *Swinburne*, 139.   [73] Henderson, *Swinburne*, 97.
[74] Fuller, *Swinburne*, 138.   [75] Ibid., 167.

Menken and Algernon Charles Swinburne, 1867. Swinburne insisted on having
their picture taken and was surprised by the scandal that followed, echoing the
earlier reception of Menken's photographs with Dumas. Menken looks ill in
this picture, perhaps with the affliction that would kill her a few months later.
(Harvard Theatre Collection)

At Menken's urging, Swinburne called her "Dolores," causing many to
later speculate that he wrote one of his most famous poems, "Dolores" with
her in mind. But in fact, "Dolores" appeared in *Poems and Ballads* before
Swinburne had even met Menken.[76] But, whatever role Menken played
in Swinburne's life, he harbored significant feelings for her – or for what
she represented to him: the possibility of a heterosexual relationship with
all the romantic trappings. Meanwhile, Swinburne proved to be the literary
connection Menken sought; he urged his own publisher, James Hotten,
to consider Menken's collection of poetry. Within a few months, Hotten
offered Menken a book contract and she began collecting her poems in
earnest.[77]

In April, Swinburne insisted that they pose for pictures together – as
if in reference to her earlier spectacle with Dumas only one year before.
Once again, Menken's photograph with another person undermined her

[76] Algernon Charles Swinburne, *Poems and Ballads: Including Atalanta in Calydon* (New York: Hurst,
n.d.).

[77] Menken did little more than collect old poems together for her volume; the poems in *Infelicia* differ
very little from the original versions found in the *Israelite* and *Sunday Mercury*.

careful portrayals of self. The photographs of Menken and Swinburne are clearly meant to suggest a romantic connection; despite their fascination with the unconventional, they posed like stereotypical lovers. Yet even in these faded, poorly executed, black and white pictures Menken's exhaustion and ill health is distressingly clear. Their supposedly romantic pairing conveys deep unhappiness on the part of Menken and smug arrogance in Swinburne, as he stands beside her seated form, her right hand resting tenderly on his left shoulder, her left hand enveloped in his. Despite the fact that she was seated, Menken looks like a giantess next to diminutive Swinburne, the top of her head level with his shoulder, so that he looks more like a son than a lover. The setting of the pose is shallow and dull, with no attempt on the part of the photographer to make use of drapery of her gown or provide a suitable backdrop. At the time, many saw it as a laughable commentary on Menken, but in hindsight the photograph is poignant, even tragic. Menken looks like the fallen star she was about to become.

Once again, the photographs immediately appeared in shop windows, and the publicity soon had Swinburne wishing he had not insisted on having the picture taken. By April 17, Swinburne wrote to a friend: "[P]aper after paper has flung pellets of dirt at me, assuming or asserting the falsehood that its publication and sale all over London were things authorized or permitted or even foreseen by the sitters."[78] Once again, a photograph destroyed another relationship and more deeply buried Menken's already ruined reputation.

Adding to Menken's distress was E. T. Smith's decision to break her contract at Astley's. By December, it had become clear that *Mazeppa* and Menken could no longer fill the theater. Menken took Smith to court for breach of contract in March 1867, but the trial was postponed several times.[79] On May 11, she leased Sadler's Wells Theatre Royal with the intention of performing *Mazeppa* under her own management and direction. However, after a month of poor ticket sales, she closed the show. Regardless of her ambition, Menken was beginning to show signs of illness, and probably could not cope with the athletic demands of the play. According to Ellington, Menken now wrote a will requesting a Jewish burial with a simple service and a plain coffin. She said that she wanted only her name and the words "Thou Knowest" inscribed on a modest marker.[80]

Between taking Smith to court and initiating her own production, Menken received other shocking news from America: She was still legally married to Alexander Isaac Menken, and he was finally suing her for divorce. Apparently, Alexander had not initiated the divorce as he had declared he would in the letter to Wilkes, back in 1860. Having met another woman he wished to marry, he now took his case to the Cincinnati Court

[78] Fuller, *Swinburne*, 165.
[79] "Action by Miss Menken," New York *The Last Sensation*, vol. 1 (March 28, 1868), 211, Kovach.
[80] Mankowitz, *Mazeppa*, 234–235.

of Common Pleas and brought forth witnesses to prove that Menken had lived as the wife of John Carmel Heenan in New York, from 1859 to 1860. He won the case on grounds of adultery.[81] Alexander's divorce suit finally supported what Menken herself had tried to prove by divorcing Heenan in 1862, that Heenan *had* claimed her as his wife before the scandal had erupted. However, it also meant that Adah's marriages to Newell and Barkley had been as illegal as her marriage to Heenan. She had been a bigamist for the past eight years. Perhaps more distressing to Menken, news of the divorce incited little comment.

An ill and melancholic Menken rallied her spirits when word came from Paris that theater manager Louis Dumaine had rented the Théâtre du Chatelet with the hopes of having her perform the lead in *Theodorus, Roi d'Abyssinie*. The promise of appearing in Henri Rochefort's newest play gave Menken hope. *Mazeppa* now seemed to disgust audiences in London and Paris – couldn't the Menken do anything else? The play that had initially won Menken such freedom now imprisoned her in unending humiliation, toil, and boredom. And of course her money was fast running out; Menken had a history of lavish spending. Indeed, generosity and overspending had been part of her image. Despite all of the money she had made, she had little savings. She returned to Paris with high hopes, only to discover Rochefort's play delayed. It was the fiasco of *The Child of the Sun* all over again, and she agreed without protest to play her old role in *Les Pirates de la Savane*.

But despite her rather heroic efforts to push on, at the end of the first week's rehearsal she collapsed onstage. The management postponed rehearsal for a few days, hoping she would display her legendary powers of recuperation. But this time Menken suffered from an illness more serious than just bruises and sprains. Journalist Adrian Marx visited while she lay in her small hotel room, obviously depressed and in pain. He later said that Menken understood her situation and told him baldly, "'I have received my death wound. I am lost to art and to life.'"[82]

She attended rehearsals again a week later, and struggled through one day before collapsing onstage the next morning. Attendants brought her back to the hotel, and several doctors attempted to revive her. Various journalists theorized a vague collection of maladies: consumption, appendicitis, dysentery, internal injuries, cancer.[83] Physicians reportedly found an abscess on her side "of at least three or four years' growth," which may have been caused by one of her many falls from the horse.[84] Whatever the cause of her illness, nothing could save her. According to Ellington, Menken spent her few cognitive moments obsessed with the production of *Infelicia*.

---

[81] "The Gushing Menken in a New Role," Boston *The Town: A Sensation Paper*, vol. 1 (April 25, 1868), 15, Kovach.

[82] Mankowitz, *Mazeppa*, 237.

[83] Collection of obituaries from various papers (*London Telegraph*, n.d.; *London Star*, Aug. 12, 1868; *New York World*, Aug. 20, 1868; *Sunday Mercury*, Aug. 30, 1868), ALC

[84] James, *Biography*, 43.

Henry Wadsworth Longfellow paid a deathbed visit to Menken, at the request of her friend Charles Reade, but she had few visitors considering the size of her entourage only months before. The height of summer in Paris, it was traditionally the time when those who could afford it, left the city for cooler climes.

Menken died on August 10, 1868, in her Paris hotel room. She was at most thirty-three years of age and left no money or valuables. At her request, she had a rabbi in attendance and was interred without an autopsy within seventy-two hours, as Jewish custom dictated. She was buried in the Jewish section of Père Lachaise cemetary on August 13, with forty people and her last horse in attendance.[85]

Given Menken's complicated self-performances, it seems fitting that with her death, officials began the long struggle to label her. According to cemetery records, she was "Dolores Feurtos Barclay," while the Parisian death certificate called her "Menken Adèle Isaac Barclay."[86] A year later, Ed James struggled to collect money to rebury her under a more fitting monument. Dumas and Swinburne, among others, refused to support the cause, but James Barkley made the venture possible with a substantial donation. On April 21, 1869, Ed James had Menken reburied in the Jewish section of Montparnasse Cemetery. Because he broke Jewish law by reburying the body, James decided not to publicize the second burial, although pictures of her tombstone soon made it to the United States. The front of the Montparnesse monument read: "Adah Isaacs Menken/Born in Louisiana, United States of America/ Died in Paris, August 10, 1868." On the south side were the words Menken had requested: "Thou Knowest."[87]

With that epitaph, Menken left the world one last tantalizing clue to the woman behind the Menken mask. "Thou Knowest" suggested to the viewer that he or she knew *something*, yet, of course, most viewers would read the words and feel at a loss. Biographers attribute the lines to Swinburne's poem about death and burial, "Ilicet," found in *Poems and Ballads*. Menken admired Swinburne's work, and may have identified with the stanza:

> No soul shall tell nor lip shall number
> The names and tribes of you that slumber;
> No memory, no memorial.
> "Thou knowest" – who shall say thou knowest?
> There is none highest and none lowest,
> An end, an end, an end of all.[88]

---

[85] Notice in a French paper, publication not noted, in the extra-illustrated collection, HTC.

[86] June 22, 1909, reissue of the Bulletin de décès for Dolores Feurtos Barclay, Republique Francaise, Ville de Paris, copy of certificate in the Adah Isaacs Menken Collection, Manuscript Division, Library of Congress; Mankowitz, *Mazeppa*, 242–243.

[87] Willoughby Maycock, "Adah Menken's Burial-Place," *The Referee*, June 27, 1909; James, *Biography*, 44–45; Mankowitz, *Mazeppa*, 244. According to all reports, the monument no longer exists.

[88] Swinburne, *Poems and Ballads*, 173.

The provocative lines suggest Menken's wish to die with the mask on, yet also emphasizes her membership in the larger group of dead who remain unnumbered, unnamed, with "No memory, no memorial." She may have meant to emphasize the frailty of fame, as she "the world's delight" now joined the unnamed dead; she knew that she would be buried under the name she had created. To scholars focusing on her African American legacy or Jewish identity, the epitaph and Swinburne's verse imply other exciting possibilities. They suggest that Menken may have included the references as a final symbolic act, to reconnect herself with her forgotten African ancestors or the many Jews destroyed by centuries of persecution. Yet, of course, the epitaph leads to no answers, despite its power of suggestion.

But Swinburne's phrase also appears in a poem already beloved by Menken: Lord Byron's "Cain."[89] Swinburne asks, "'Thou knowest' – who shall say thou knowest?" Byron's work, written forty years earlier, provides the answer: Adah (after whom Menken named herself) is the one who says thou knowest:

> Cain:
> ...He contents him
> With making us the nothing which we are:
> And, after flattering dust with glimpses of
> Eden and immortality, resolves
> It back to dust again – for what?
>
> Adah:
> Thou know'st –
> Even for our parents' error.[90]

Adah in the poem is referring to their parents, Adam and Eve, and their fall from grace. Menken left a clue, after all: She told the world that even her name "Adah" came from a poem, just as she had created her public persona from popular novels and bohemian literature. When Cain asks Adah about the point of life, he suggests Menken's own ascendance into fame: Though God had flattered "dust with glimpses of Eden and immortality," Menken remained mortal. By requesting the inscription "Thou Knowest," Menken told the world that she knew – had known, in fact, since she added that "h" to her name – that success in life is fleeting by virtue of mortality. Menken lived out that philosophy; when she died in August 1868, she left little behind: no known kin, money, assets, or clues.

However, she left one last bid for immorality: *Infelicia*. Two weeks after Menken's death, Swinburne's London publisher, James Hotten, released the

[89] Kate Wilson Davis, "Adah Isaacs Menken: Her Life and Her Poetry in America," M.A. thesis, Southern Methodist University, 1944, p. 14.

[90] Truman Guy Steffan, *Lord Byron's "Cain": Twelve Essays and a Text with Variants and Annotations* (Austin: University of Texas Press, 1968), 232.

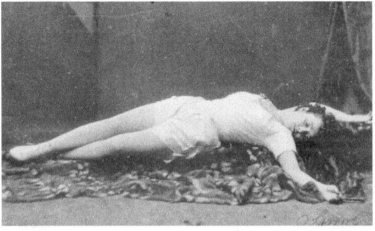

Photograph by Napoleon Sarony of Menken posed in her "nude" Mazeppa costume, probably 1866. Her body is vulnerable to the viewer in this unusually inactive depiction of her as Mazeppa. Her pose may be seen as suggesting passion, with her legs crossed and her upper body open, or alluding to Christ, with her cross-like arrangement. (Harvard Theatre Collection)

collection of thirty-one poems. It included a facsimile of Charles Dickens's letter accepting her dedication of the book to him, and the frontispiece contained an engraved portrait of Menken and lines that Swinburne had once written for her:

> Leaves pallid and somber and ruddy
>   Dead fruits of the fugitive years;
> Some stained as with wine and made bloody,
>   And some as with tears.[91]

Given the notoriety of Swinburne and his recent relationship with Menken, critics soon suggested that he or his secretary, John Thomson, had written *Infelicia*. Due to Menken's notoriety and unexpected death, the book received formidable attention. At first the reviewers focused on the debate surrounding its authorship, but, citing the poems' many flaws, both the public and critics soon accepted Menken as the poet. Now reviews began to focus more on Menken herself – and she could no longer misbehave and undermine the sensitivity conveyed in personal photographs. They believed they saw the true Menken, unmasked. Her untimely death, poems of tragic loss, and the cartes de visite of her writing at a desk, reading a book, or staring sadly into space, all contributed to reshaping her image. In obituaries, eulogies, and memories, Americans and Europeans began the process of rewriting Menken.

---

[91] Adah Isaacs Menken, *Infelicia* (London: Hotten, 1868), frontispiece.

Chapter 9

Remembering and Rewriting Menken

The Menken is dead. The bare-faced, bare-limbed, reckless, erratic, ostracized, but gifted, kind-hearted, successful, yet ill-starred Menken is no more. . . . She has no more lacqueys, no more toadies, no more flatterers now. No critics shall eat her dinners and then abuse her in their papers; no authors shall borrow money of her and then lampoon her.[1]

Americans learned of Menken's death on August 12, 1868, when newspapers across the nation printed information they had received by telegraph. News of her death initially took up little space in the papers, since it competed with both the passing of Senator Thaddeus Stevens and a cattle plague that threatened to destroy the United States beef industry.[2] The debate over Menken's character began two weeks after her death, when *Infelicia* first arrived in London bookstores, and it gathered momentum when the volume appeared in the United States two months later. First there was the death of Menken, then the reviewing of her poetry, and finally the process of remembering and rewriting her, which continues today. Images of Menken changed over time, as she receded into the past. Eventually, many would claim to see the "true Menken" behind the performance of celebrity, but they saw different things. The contradictory images that she herself had fostered, and her many marriages and famous liaisons, made her an ideal subject for those interested in mining the social and cultural margins of the past as well as for those simply looking to sell print. Within a century, journalists, scholars, and biographers established Menken as a Jewish poet, black poet self-centered femme fatale, early feminist, tragic heroine, lesbian cross-dresser, Texas legend, and the actress who introduced "nude drama." In the nineteenth century, Menken was famous for what she had done, but in the twentieth century, scholars became more preoccupied with who she "was"; they began giving more attention to her identity than her exploits.

Following her death, Menken was written into two basic forms: the siren and the victim. The siren image dominated her obituaries; the victim did not become popular until after publication of her book. In obituaries that August 1868, journalists, friends, and acquaintances began where the

[1] Unidentified newspaper clipping, Harvard Theatre Collection (hereafter HTC), Houghton Library, Harvard University, Cambridge, Massachusetts.
[2] *New York Tribune*, Aug. 12, 1868; *New York Herald*, Aug. 13, 1868.

most recent theater reviews had ended: She was a lousy actress who had made a fortune through exhibitionism. Even in her obituary the New York *Times* referred to her as "Miss Adah Isaacs Menken, as she was popularly called," and summarized her last seven years of unprecedented fame by recounting her different marriages and describing her as an actress with "little if any merit." The journalist added that she "made some pretensions to a literary reputation," but her contributions had been confined "to one or two minor weekly papers of no[t] very good repute." Only in the end did the writer begrudgingly add: "She was generous to a fault, and in consequence [her death] will be regretted by many."[3] The New York *Tribune* carried a less subjective notice of her death, describing her as "the actress to whose example may the successful origin of the nude drama be attributed" and focusing on her professional rather than personal choices.[4] The *Herald* covered the event a day later, and not surprisingly, James Gordon Bennett printed the most hyperbolic obituary of any of the major papers, describing her as "an actress of only meager ability" who, "[f]ailing as an actress in this country," tried her fortune in Europe, where she "created quite a furor, though her acting was severely criticized and condemned."[5]

However, if the largest New York papers presented her as a talentless, corruptive influence, others depicted her as a victim, albeit of her own making. Contrary to claims in the *Herald*, reviewers in Europe had portrayed her much more favorably than the mainstream New York press, and their obituaries expressed more regret than criticism, calling her "*pauvre* Menken" and describing her life as a captivating adventure.[6] In London, where she had most recently performed, the *Daily Telegraph* reported that Menken had died of that most genteel and literary disease, "consumption." The journalist marveled that her life had been as "adventurous as that of the equally celebrated Lola Montes."[7] Several smaller American newspapers were equally adulatory. The *Clipper*, still owned by Frank Queen, printed a long obituary, stating that "the record of Miss Menken's generosity and kindness to others is unwritten, but how many living witnesses there are who participated in her constant deeds and kindness."[8] H. B. Farnie, the London journalist who initially condemned Menken in England, sent details of her death overseas. Now calling Menken a comrade, Farnie reported her "exquisite suffering," saying, "Food she scarcely tasted, and she drank nothing but iced water." He also protested against "the ghastly pleasantries which are bandied over that poor, dear woman by certain portions of the Press. . . . She was a woman of an excellent heart – somewhat careless and

[3] "Adah Isaacs Menken," *New York Times*, Aug. 12, 1868.   [4] *New York Tribune*, Aug. 12, 1868.

[5] "Obituary: Adah Isaacs Menken," *New York Herald*, Aug. 13, 1868.

[6] Clipping from an unnamed French newspaper, HTC.

[7] "Death of Adah Isaacs Menken," *London Daily Telegraph*, Aug. 12, 1868

[8] "The Late Adah Isaacs Menken – By Arrival of the Steamship City of Antwerp," New York *Clipper*, Aug. 29, 1868, p. 166, c. 3.

prodigal, it is true, but ever unselfishly."[9] A few months later, the *Clipper* later carried Ed James's celebratory biography of Menken, which he eventually had published and sold as a cheap paperback.[10]

R egrets saturated obituaries printed after the first notices, as if to make up for the less than charitable judgments made initially. The *Galveston Bulletin* asserted that "her eccentricities and her vices have obscured her virtues and her genius. She has filled a place in the world's history that will not allow the journalist to pass her death in silence."[11] A memorial poem in the *Clipper* warned: "in this presence do not dare/To curse the helpless girl who lies/With death's deep shadow in her eyes,/ Pass on! She had her faults, and we have ours as well...."[12] One journalist remarked that "a mournfully ignoble celebrity was, by her own act and consent, attached to Menken's name" but she "had talents for something better, and a nature not ungenerous. Poor woman, she knew to what her life was leading her."[13]

In the New York *Tribune* on August 15, Robert Newell initiated a significant reshaping of Menken's public image when he advocated that she be shown pity rather than scorn, but he used language that essentially linked Menken with popular stories of prostitutes. Here Menken was a victim but also a siren. He recast her as the sad figure she had suggested through her poetry, yet added a volatile edge. He told of Menken's struggles to support her family when she was just a girl, and argued that her adult improprieties stemmed directly from her experiences as a child actress. Portraying the young Menken as "deprived of every sacred influence by which the female character is guided and guarded to the pure and gentle royalty of home life," he argued that it was not surprising that "she grew into the wild, volatile, improvident creature of a life as unstable and inconsistent" as depicted in the popular press. Newell expressed the desire that the public have "pity for her as the victim" of "wanton deception and heartless abuse." Yet in the process of acknowledging Menken's flaws, Newell condemned her behavior as harshly as her shrillest critics and described his ex-wife as ruled by "a rank, untrained nature."[14] Now that Menken could no longer misbehave, Newell could finally reconceptualize her as the woman who had so captivated him:

---

[9] Farnie's comments reprinted in George Lippard Barclay, *The Life and Remarkable Career of Adah Isaacs Menken, the Celebrated Actress* (Philadelphia: Barclay, 1868), 43–44.

[10] Ed James, "Adah Isaacs Menken," *Clipper* (1868); published in paperback form in 1869 for private distribution, and in 1881 for public sale.

[11] "Death of Ada Menken," *Flake's Semi-Weekly Galveston Bulletin*, Aug. 19, 1868, p. 6, transcription in the Adah Isaacs Menken Collection, Sam Houston Regional Library and Research Center, Liberty, Texas.

[12] H. J. D., "In Memoriam: Adah Isaacs Menken," reprinted in Barclay, *Life and Remarkable Career*, 45–46.

[13] *News of the World*, Aug. 16, 1868, p. 5, in Allen Lesser Collection (hereafter ALC), American Jewish Archives, Cincinnati, Ohio. Nearly every reminiscence of Menken after 1868 begins on this note of pity and judgment.

[14] Robert H. Newell, *New York Tribune*, Aug. 15, 1868.

a victim, good-hearted but misguided, and innocent because she was raised in ignorance. In the ensuing weeks and months the scornful depictions of Menken began transforming to again resemble the Menken of her poetry and letters.

Critics in London greeted the first edition of *Infelicia*, published within two weeks of her unexpected death, with a mixture of criticism, surprise, and poignant sympathy.[15] American newspapers printed reviews from across the Atlantic, and eagerly awaited the American release. With the publication of *Infelicia*, Menken's image as a victim began to overtake the disparaging commentary that had met her death, and it grew stronger as reviewers on both sides of the Atlantic began to wonder about the "real Menken," the person behind the fame. She was no longer the victim of her own making; she became instead a victim of modern society. Rarely did reviewers suggest that the poetry, the expression of the "real Menken," was itself performance; rather, Menken became a symbol of social ills. The London *Pall Mall Gazette* stated that Menken's poetry provided "singular proof of the way in which the world is prone to misunderstand its greatest women. Any one reading those verses must feel surprised that the writer should only have been known when living in connection with scanty clothing and equestrian drama." However, the journalist added quickly, from "a merely literary point of view the book is worthless." The reviewer for the London *Queen*, a women's magazine, wrote, "We took up this volume with an inclination to laugh at the bizarre notion of reading poems from the pen of the famous Mazeppa at Astley's. But we have laid it down with very different feelings. . . . Adah Menken, the pugilist's wife, the heroine of the circus . . . had within that finely molded form a heart of more than common tenderness, a brain of rare activity, fine tastes and lofty aspirations." Like the *Gazette*, the *Queen* quickly admitted the poor quality of Menken's work, saying: "In itself, and apart from the history of this author, the poetry is not much above the average of magazine verses. . . . It is the tone of these lamentations that impart them such interest as that they possess."[16] Newspapers reported that supplies of copies in London were "exhausted in a few days."[17]

Initially, several critics thought that Swinburne had either written the poems or strongly influenced them.[18] Actually, Newell was negotiating a contract for his own book with Hotten while he and Menken were making each other miserable in California, so Hotten and Menken had probably heard of each other long before her tryst with Swinburne.[19] But attributing Menken's work to Swinburne was perhaps understandable; although

[15] "Miss Menken's Poems," *Every Saturday*, Sept. 12, 1868, ALC.

[16] "Books and Authors," New York *Home Journal*, Sept. 16, 1868.

[17] "Doings and Saying of People and Papers Abroad," *Home Journal*, Oct. 7, 1868

[18] *Every Saturday*; Wolf Mankowitz, *Mazeppa: The Lives, Loves and Legends of Adah Isaacs Menken* (New York: Stein and Day, 1982), 199–200.

[19] *National Union Catalog Pre-1956 Imprints*, vol. 417 (London: Mansell Information, 1975), 107.

Menken's poetry lacks the intellectual depth and meticulous attention to poetic detail that marks Swinburne's work, they both use extensive biblical allusion and shocking images of pain commingled with beauty.[20] After acquitting Swinburne, critics pointed the finger at John Thomson, an alcoholic journalist who had copied out the poems for Menken to submit to Hotten. Although his authorship was easily disproven, rumors of Thomson's influence would persist for decades.[21] Obviously, few remembered Menken's work from the New York *Sunday Mercury* or the Cincinnati *Israelite*. If they had taken a look at her earlier work, they would have noticed that, other than a few title changes, she made few revisions for *Infelicia*.

Once critics accepted that Menken had indeed written the poems, they began critiquing them in light of her scandalous public images, and many responded with surprise and reluctant sympathy. Those who found artistic merit in her work agreed that its strength lay in its unusually stark images and confessional tone, the implied baring of her soul. When William Rossetti later anthologized her poetry in 1902, he said that her verses "express a life of much passion, and not a little aspiration; a life deeply sensible of loss, self-baffled, and mixing the wail of humiliation with that of indignation – like the remnants of a defeated army, hotly pursued. It is this life that cries out in the disordered verses, and these have a responsive cry of their own."[22]

Once *Infelicia* appeared in Menken's home country in September, American reviews ran the spectrum, sounding much like their British counterparts. Some asserted that her unexpected death brought the poetry greater recognition than it deserved. The critic for the San Francisco *Evening Daily Bulletin* asserted, "Had this volume appeared during the life time of the author it would have been thrown aside with indifference and forgotten in a month. It is true Miss Menken wrote some melodious verses, but so do hundreds of other women who cannot get a hearing before the public." This critic saw her written work as similar to her other performances: "We look in vain for those exhibitions of genius claimed by her admirers. The collection bears unmistakable evidence of having emanated from a diseased nature. The tone is low and sensuous." In fact, this reviewer considered her confessional style almost immoral, writing that "her exhibitions of moral nudity are hardly less indecent than her exhibitions of physical nudity on stage. There is too much casting off of drapery, too much emotional *dishabille*." This was a rare reviewer, who critiqued her work as performance rather than expression, writing, "[T]he display she makes of her interior life is

---

[20] Laurence Binyon, "Introduction," in *Selected Poems by Algernon Charles Swinburne* (Westport: Greenwood, 1980), vii.

[21] George R. Sims to "XYZ," introduction to Swinburne, *Adah Isaacs Menken: A Fragment of a Biography* (London: For Private Distribution, 1917), vii, fn; a series of letters regarding *Infelicia* from *The Referee*, Nov. 29, 1903–Jan. 3, 1904, pasted into one of the scrapbooks in the Theatrical Scrapbooks Collection, HTC.

[22] William Michael Rossetti, *American Poems* (1902; London: E. Moxon, 1925), 444–445.

by no means inviting. We fail to discover the tokens of that deeper and better self she prates so much about. Her 'naked soul' as revealed in these poems is anything but virgin." This journalist argued that the inner self she exposed served to confirm her moral bankruptcy: "We see the sources of those unhealthful fires that made her career scandalous.... If her outward conduct was bestial, it was because she was saturated through and through with vice."[23]

The middle-class *Home Journal* printed a long discussion of her character and poetry on October 7, 1868, that summarized public discussion on the subject:

> Who believes that this woman, the sport of fame and fortune, the paramour of black-legs and prize-fighters, reckless in the worst dissipation, the victim of her own wild appetites and passions, the heroine of ribald midnight orgies, the unblushing pet of the habitués of the amphitheatre, the boldest amazon of a vitiated horse-drama, had heart, soul, emotions, aspirations, like others of her sex who chanced to be born with different natures, and surrounded by circumstances more propitious to womanly delicacy and purity? We all believe it theoretically; but practically – not one of us; else should we make her memory something besides a butt for ridicule, sneers, scorn, contempt, reproach, and every conceivable indignity.

The writer asserts that Menken's sad ending and life are but a sign of the times – that she was created and supported by the world around her: "Adah Menken's sad career was the direct result of a diseased social system – a social system which, as a whole, tends to encourage rather than condemn, virtually if not literally, a life like hers.... When we wish to put out a fire we do not feed it with fresh fuel, or pour upon it streams of oil." The events of Menken's life and death exposed unpopular truths in contemporary life that needed to be acknowledged, in the opinion of this journalist: "There is a hot fever of indulgence, excess, excitement, licentiousness, burning in the very heart of what we call society. It is weak and cowardly to attempt to disguise the fact by saying that, all in all, the world is probably better than ever before, and the people in it more advanced, enlightened and progressive. This is true in a certain sense, but it does not alter the truth of the other assertion." Finally, the review turned to *Infelicia*, the supposed proof of her better nature, and asserted that the poetry showed "that she was a woman like other women," albeit "with stronger passions and greater aspirations than many." Like others, Menken was simply "thrown out alone upon the broad, turbulent sea of life by uncontrollable circumstances, and dashed hither and thither by impulses as that mysterious influence we call fate." Her poetry showed that "her heart was warm and tender; that she was generous to a fault," but she was also "passionate as a spoiled child, and quick to resent

[23] The San Francisco *Evening Daily Bulletin*, Oct. 31, 1868.

real or fancied injury . . . her appetites were stronger than her ambition, and her sensuality much more fully developed than her spirituality." And finally, the reviewer saw that "beneath the gaudy glitter of a shameful career there existed always, unresting, ever striving, that yearning for good and truth and right which underlies all human existence."[24]

Those who disparaged *Infelicia* wrote of her poetry as reminiscent of her public image, but those who appreciated her verse described her poetic persona as divergent. One of the best examples of the effect of *Infelicia* on Menken's posthumous public image appears in *Putnam's Monthly Magazine of Literature, Science, Art and National Interests*. The review of *Infelicia* opened with severe criticism of Menken: "[H]er name has been associated, in the public mind, only with theatrical performances in which the limit of shamelessness was reached and overleaped, and with rumors of a private life that was popularly believed to have matched in lawlessness and dissoluteness all that was known of her in public." However, the writer's image of her began to shift in the process of analyzing her poetry. He tried to remain critical, writing, "[A]s for her book of poems, it is but fair to say that while the greater number of them are allied in their structure to the rhapsodical, fragmentary, and often incoherent verses of Ossian, and Walt Whitman," he had to admit that "they do often show the possession of the poetical sense, and are interesting not only from their origin but in themselves." The review ends on a note of bemusement: "In truth, these poems have left a far deeper impression on our mind, as we have read them, than any thing in their literary execution, or even the ideas that the writer labors, in vain for the most part, to express with clearness, would make appear reasonable."[25]

The outward appearance of the book itself undoubtedly surprised and influenced readers. Both British and American versions were slim and small; Hotten's edition was bound in green cloth with gilt edges, while the American version boasted a burgundy leather cover embossed with *Infelicia* in Menken's own looping script, and her signature, "Menken," underlined in curlicues of gold.[26] By appearance alone, her book was as tasteful as many felt Menken had been crass. Given her notoriety, the public probably expected a paper-covered, penny-press version of her life, with a few poems appended (ironically, the form used most by her nineteenth-century biographers). But *Infelicia looked* like literature. Inside the leather-bound cover American readers turned creamy pages containing first a letter from Charles Dickens accepting Menken's dedication of the book, then a rather unglamorous portrait of Menken (which she disliked and tried to have changed), a title page that read only "*Infelicia* by Adah Isaacs Menken," a fragment of

[24] "La Menken," *Home Journal*, Oct. 7, 1868.

[25] "Table-Talk," *Putnam's Monthly: Magazine of Literature, Science, Art and National Interests* (Nov. 1868), 639.

[26] *National Union Catalog*, 287; Adah Isaacs Menken, *Infelicia* (Philadelphia: Lippincott, 1868).

verse (later attributed to Swinburne), and finally thirty-one poems.[27] No nudity, horses, or false biographies; no mention of fame, lovers, or travels; only Menken's poetry, to be read on its own merit. Of course, the fact that Menken's verse was packaged as literature and sold at prices affordable only to those who could buy leather-bound books *implied* merit. The appearance of *Infelicia* was so far removed from Menken's most famous public personae that it suggested a whole new side to this already controversial figure. Menken had spent the past few years constructing herself as a mystery, and the refined appearance of *Infelicia* implied what the poems reaffirmed: Here in the reader's hands was Menken's internal world – here was the real Menken, and she was not what they had imagined at all.

Ironically, middle-class white women, who had (verbally at least) steered clear of Menken and all that she represented, now came to her defense. Their commentary suggested that Menken's poetry revealed to them a woman's heart, regardless of how unfeminine her behavior. They questioned whether her behavior had been in reaction to a world that failed to reward her intelligence or allow her suitable means to meet her ambitions. On October 1, Elizabeth Cady Stanton and Susan B. Anthony's suffrage newspaper, *The Revolution*, published notice of her death within a review of *Infelicia*. Stanton herself reviewed the book, and introduced a renovated Menken to her female readers:

> Poor Adah! When she died she left the world a book of poems that reveals an inner life of love for the true, the pure, the beautiful, that none could have imagined in the actress whose public and private life were alike sensual and scandalous. Who can read the following verses from her pen, without feeling that this unfortunate girl, a victim of society, was full of genius and tenderness, and that under more fortunate circumstances, she might have been an honor to her sex. How sad and touching is this confession of the failure of her life.

Stanton presents Menken's story as a tragic reminder that "nobler virtues than we shall ere possess are found to-day among the poor children of want and temptation." Menken would have been gratified (and perhaps amused) to see Stanton suggest her as an "evangel," a savior of girls tempted by fame: "In death, poor Adah speaks sweet words of love and purity that will help to ennoble the life of many a girl that might have followed the paths she led."[28] Of course, at the time of this review, many considered Stanton and Anthony radicals themselves – and in fact, they would soon come to embrace the controversial and charismatic Victoria Woodhull, who shared some of

---

[27] Menken, *Infelicia* Menken wrote to James Hotten: "I am satisfied with all you have done except the portrait; I do not find it to be in character with the volume. It looks affected. Perhaps I am a little vain – all women are – but the picture is certainly not beautiful. . . . Do tell me, mon ami, can we not possibly have another made?" AIM to Hotten, reprinted in Algernon Charles Swinburne, *Adah Isaacs Menken: A Fragment of Autobiograph* (London: private printing, 1917), viii.

[28] Elizabeth Cady Stanton, "Adah Isaacs Menken," Seneca *Revolution*, Oct. 1, 1868, pp. 201–202.

Menken's flair for publicity.[29] But Stanton and Anthony exhibited middle-class sensibility, and they spoke to women of that social and economic class.

Stanton expressed an evaluation of Menken's poetry that many other women seemed to share. They could identify with the tragic Menken who expressed frustrations with a world that stifled her potential – a world that, in fact, vilified her every attempt to move beyond the prescribed confines of her life. They understood her self-hatred and self-mockery. She became a sister in her futile struggle to capture beauty within herself. Shortly after Stanton's review appeared, a woman named Millie Carpenter submitted a poem to the *Sunday Mercury* reinforcing Stanton's evaluation. The final stanza of Carpenter's "Infelicia" reads:

> Thou knowest! Ay! He knows and sees
>   How deep within that wayward soul
> Faith tended on her cloistered knees
>   Hopeful despite truth's meagre dole,
> The sacred fire upon the hearth
>   By which we now with clearer eyes,
> See her in her poet-worth
>   And grow through charity, more wise.

Carpenter and Stanton's eulogies to Menken express chastened apology. With her poetry, Menken motivated middle-class white women to reenvision her as a sort of martyr to women. Stanton, Carpenter, and the many women who purchased *Infelicia* enjoyed Menken's lesson. Women, in particular, responded to Menken's "Thou Knowest" at a level not expressed by male readers. Margaret J. M. Sweat, author of the novel Menken had plagiarized in mash notes to Hattie Tyng years before, published a poem decades later called "Saddest Is Safest," which began: "Thou knowest, dear, that when our life was gay/when sunshine smiled and flowers were everywhere/That shadows hovered in the cloudless day."[30] Women seemed to relish Menken's sorrow as voluptuous, finding something fascinating and authentic in the suggestion of tragedy lurking behind carnival. Despite the harsh criticism meted out by male reviewers (ironically, the social group who most enjoyed her performances), *Infelicia* went through over a dozen editions and remained continuously in print in the United States until 1902.

With her death and the publication of *Infelicia*, the public rewrote Menken into two basic forms: the sexual siren and the sensitive victim. But despite the

[29] Goldsmith, Barbara, *Other Powers: The Suffrage, Spiritualism, and the Scandalous Victoria Woodhull* (New York: Alfred A. Knopf, 1998).

[30] Margaret J. M. Sweat, "Saddest Is Safest," from her 1890 book of poetry, *Verses*, quoted in Connie Burns, "Private Sphere/Public Sphere: Rethinking Paradigms of Victorian Womanhood Through the Life and Writings of Margaret Jane Mussey Sweat," M.A. thesis, University of Southern Maine, 1993, p. 49.

bipolar simplicity of such categories, these portraits were not uncomplicated. As a siren Menken sometimes resembled the "whore with a heart of gold" found in westerns, a concurrently emerging genre of fiction. Yet as often as not, she was depicted as another Lola Montez: a tough-minded, self-centered, unprincipled woman who collected and discarded men as she did clothing and money. The tragic victim, on the other hand, fit roughly within the parameters sketched out by Newell, Stanton, Carpenter, and Menken herself: Menken as a genius wasted by the pervasive immorality of her environment. The debate that Menken had initiated over her character in 1860, during Heenan scandal, grew more heated upon her death – in large part because she herself was no longer the central issue.

The public soon discovered that now that Menken was dead, they could use her many images as tools for taking apart or putting together their own arguments on a surprising variety of issues. At the time of her death, Americans advocating social purity could point to Menken as a tragic consequence of society's immorality. Ironically, those arguing against vice could use Menken's painful and impoverished demise as an example of poetic justice.[31] Both contemporaries and, later, historians could turn to Menken's popularity as proof of America's moral hypocrisy. Articles and books were published on Menken every decade following her death, from the 1860s to the present. In the 1870s, writers tended to assume that readers knew of Menken, usually referring to her as a means of illustrating changes in society since her death. In the 1870s the debate over her true character ceased, and the public seemed to accept her as an unsolvable mystery.[32] By the 1880s she had become a subject dear to collectors of popular culture, and began turning up in memoirs of actors and privately circulating albums.[33] Her image was still popular enough that Lippincott in Phildelphia put out five editions of *Infelicia* that decade, and Chattos and Windus of London bought out Hotten's rights to the book, to release a new edition in 1888.[34] Meanwhile, Ed James decided to reprint his Menken biography, which had last been published in 1869.[35]

---

[31] Virtually every notice of her death goes one of these directions or the other. For an example, read "La Menken," *Home Journal*, Oct. 7, 1868; Adrian Marx, quoted in "Books and Authors," *Home Journal*, Sept. 16, 1868.

[32] I have run across several sideline references to her as contraditory or mysterious. An example of one may be found in S. W. Duffield, "Todd and His Double," *Overland Monthly and Out West Magazine*, vol. 15, no. 2 (1875), p. 155. Duffield writes, "His verses were the reflection of his better moods, and they reminded one of that strange contradiction, Adah Isaacs Menken."

[33] The most famous of the albums is one published for private distribution: Richard E. Sheppard, comp., *In the Album of Adah Menken* (Richard E. Sheppard, 1883). But individuals also put together scrapbooks collecting articles, pictures, and signatures, such as those found in "Biography of Adah Isaacs Menken. Extra Illustrated," Harris Rare Books, 76-M545x, Brown University Library, Providence, Rhode Island, which contains several original letters and signatures.

[34] *National Union Catalog*, 287–288.

[35] Ed James, *Biography of Adah Isaacs Menken* (New York: Ed James, 1881).

As public memories of her receded, depictions of Menken began to share a common trait: They focused on one of her identities at the expense of the others. In the Gay '90s, a decade when both burlesque and the corporate capitalism flourished, Menken resurfaced in several newspaper and magazine articles as a fun-loving sex symbol, and an aberration in Victorian times.[36] Menken's career as a Texas legend gained viability when Elizabeth Brooks pulled together scattered stories into a biographical sketch proclaiming Menken as one of the *Prominent Women of Texas*. The stories stemmed from fabrications by a former "Texas ranger, Confederate Hero and Congressman," Thomas Ochiltree, who claimed that they grew up together in Nacogdoches. As a legend, of course, Menken was not a manipulative and opportunistic siren, but rather a brilliant beauty who naturally won the hearts of kings and princes in Europe.[37] Although no evidence supports the story, literally dozens of articles on Menken's Texas origins would be published over the next century. Likewise, she became a popular topic in memoirs of California and Nevada's silver days. Most of these fond memories were recorded by men who almost uniformly remembered her as both a lady and one of the boys.[38] In California history, many saw her as a comet that swept across the western skies to briefly light up their world.[39]

By the early twentieth century, friends began sharing stories of emotionally intimate relationships with her. Poet Charles Warren Stoddard admitted that he first fell in love with her "Byronic" poster portraits when she arrived in San Francisco when he was still a teenager. He later exchanged several letters with her, which he reprinted in a flattering article. In Stoddard's article, Menken is a wholly generous, world-famous celebrity who took time to encourage an insecure, fledgling poet.[40] Joaquin Miller, who was in Europe when Menken was in San Francisco and probably never met her, made up tales of their days together on the California coast.[41] He began by saying, "Little is known about her except lies," and then preceded to tell some more. He described her vividly, saying that "Like Lord Byron . . . she was always

[36] A good example is "She Had Dumas at Her Feet, and Swinburne Was an Ardent Worshipper: The Sensational Career of Beautiful Adah Isaacs Menken," [Boston] *Sunday Globe*, Nov. 30, 1890, clipping in Adah Isaacs Menken Clippings, Billy Rose Theatre Collection, New York Public Library, New York.

[37] Elizabeth Brooks, *Prominent Women of Texas* (Akron: Warner, 1896), 156–157; Francis Edward Abernethy, ed., *Legendary Ladies of Texas* (Dallas: E-Heart Press), 86.

[38] Among several others: Walter M. Leman, *Memories of an Old Actor* (San Francisco: A Roman, 1886); Nells Drury, *An Editor on the Comstock Lode* (New York: Farrar and Rinehart, 1936); George D. Lyman, *The Saga of the Comstock Lode, Boom Days in Virginia City* (New York: Charles Scribner's Sons, 1949).

[39] Mark Twain, "The Great Bear Menken," first printed in the *Territorial Enterprise* and quoted in Peter Stoney, *Mark Twain and the Feminine Aesthetic* (Cambridge: Cambridge University Press, 1992), 164–165.

[40] Charles Warren Stoddard, "La Belle Menken," *National Magazine* (Feb. 1905), 477–488.

[41] M. M. Marberry, *Joaquin Miller: Splendid Poseur* (New York: Thomas J. Crowell, 1953).

Menken dressed as the undressed Tartar Prince. Note the conflict of masculinity and femininity in this pose: The crossed arms suggest masculine strength, but the bent leg, downcast eyes and defined waistline suggest femininity. Menken was clearly no longer aiming to suggest she played a man with this role. Photograph probably taken by Sarony in 1866. (Harvard Theatre Collection)

trying to make believe she was dreadful bad," but her "outer life . . . was one continuous ripple of laughter." Perhaps unwittingly he added to rumors of her having an African heritage by telling of the day that they raced each other down to the sea, where the sand piled high and the "horses plunged in and wallowed belly deep." Delighted, his fictional Menken cried, "I was born in that yellow sand once, sometime, and somewhere; in the deserts of Africa, maybe."[42] Reading his memories of her, one almost has to give him credit: they were clearly kindred spirits; she could not have remembered it better herself.

In the history of popular culture, Menken is presented as an actress rather than a poet. Because of her fame as Mazeppa, the undressed Tartar, Menken continues to hold her own in theater history. Robert C. Allen and Faye

[42] Joaquin Miller, *Adah Isaacs Menken* (Ysleta: Edwin B. Hill, 1934).

Dudden, among many others, acknowledge Menken as the precursor to burlesque.[43] Her sexual provocation is particularly important when she is studied as a cultural icon. In *American Beauty*, Lois Banner credits Menken with renewing the public's appreciation of voluptuous female forms.[44] Because of her marriage and scandal with John Carmel Heenan just as he was making pugilistic history Menken still figures in histories and stories of boxing.[45]

Oddly enough, Menken has also become a standard figure in the world of magic because of her supposed marriage to magician William Davenport.[46] Although Davenport himself never made any public claims to Menken, his brother and business partner, Ira, told the story to Harry Houdini, who began his career of famous escapes by imitating those of Davenports. Since Houdini remains the most celebrated magician in American history, it is perhaps not surprising that the story of Menken and William Davenport continues to find its way into print.[47] The strength of Menken's celebration in the world of supernatural studies is most humorously demonstrated by the strangest piece of Menken memorabilia in existence: a 1913 volume of poetry entitled *Believest Thou This*, which its unnamed scribe claimed Menken had dictated through a psychic medium, as a sequel to *Infelicia*.[48] Menken has also been the subject of works of fiction, numerous plays, a movie, and even an opera, none of which have proven successful.[49]

However, in terms of rewriting Menken as a character, nothing competes with the work of Noel Gerson, a.k.a. Samuel Edwards, a.k.a. Paul Lewis.

---

[43] Robert C. Allen, *Horrible Prettiness: Burlesque and American Culture* (Chapel Hill: University of North Carolina Press, 1991); Faye E. Dudden, *Women in American Theatre: Actresses and Audiences, 1790–1870* (New Haven: Yale University Press, 1994).

[44] Lois Banner, *American Beauty* (New York: Alfred A. Knopf, 1983).

[45] Elliot Gorn, *The Manly Art: Bare-Knuckle Prize-Fighting in America* (Ithaca: Cornell University Press, 1986); Nat Fleischer, *Reckless Lady: The Life Story of Adah Isaacs Menken* (New York: C. J. O'Brien, 1941); Harry Carpenter, *Boxing, an Illustrated History* (New York: Crescent Books, 1982); Richard O'Brien, *The Boxing Companion, An Illustrated Guide to the Sweet Science* (New York: Mallard Press, 1991).

[46] "Some Notes on the Davenport Brothers," *The Magician Monthly* (Aug. 1911), 174–177; "Davenport Brothers," New York *Mahatma* (Aug. 1895).

[47] Harry Houdini, *A Magician among the Spirits* (New York: Harper & Brothers, 1827), 19, fn.

[48] Agnes Procter Deltwyn (supposedly dictated to her by AIM), *Believest Thou This* (Chicago: M. A. Donohue, 1913).

[49] See the film *Heller in Pink Tights* (1960), directed by George Cukor and starring Sophia Loren. Norman Dello Joio wrote an opera named "Blood Moon" based on the life of AIM. "Here she is rechristened Ninette La Fond.... She is an octoroon who passes for white, loved by a wealthy young Southerner who pursues as her career takes her to New York and eventually Paris," according to Alan Rich of the *New York Times*, dated only Sept. 19, clipping in Adah Isaacs Menken folder, Billy Rose Theatre Collection, New York Public Library, New York. Ian Morison published *The Sensation: A Novel Based on the Life of Adah Isaacs Menken* (New York: New York Library, 1963) and Victor Milan *Adah: The World's Delight* (New York: Ace Books, 1982). But there are other examples; I have stumbled across many mentions of works in progress – movies, plays, operas, and novels – but I did not keep track of them, assuming that most of them never came to fruition.

Gerson saw in Menken true potential for sensational biography and came up with several imaginative ways to capitalize on his instinct. As Paul Lewis, he published *Queen of the Plaza: A Biography of Adah Isaacs Menken* (New York, 1964). A year later, he published the same text under the same title in London, but as Samuel Edwards. Gerson based his biography on Menken's diary, which he claimed to have found in the Harvard Theatre Collection. According to the diary, Menken had starred in Havana as she had often claimed, and occasionally turned to prostitution for supplemental income. In the late 1970s, a biographer named Wolf Mankowitz began researching Menken and was understandably keen on seeing that diary. After long talks with irate Harvard archivists who had been denying the existence of the diary for twenty years, Mankowitz confronted Gerson. Surprisingly, Gerson readily confessed he had made up the story of the diary, saying, "[I]t takes a pro to smell out a pro. . . . I must confess to you that the A. I. M. diary, which proved irresistible to write, is the product of my own imagination. So be it. . . . It is high time the hoax was exposed."[50] It was a hoax that Menken herself would probably have appreciated, since it stemmed from her own hyperbolic stories. Unfortunately, by that point, scholars had used Gerson's work in several articles, dissertations, and theses, and the damage to Menken's biographical paper trail had been done. Also, although Mankowitz exposed the lies of Paul Lewis, he overlooked publications under Gerson's other pseudonym, Samuel Edwards.

It was as Edwards that Gerson published the 1972 biography *George Sand: A Biography of the First Modern, Liberated Woman*, which stated that Menken had enjoyed several lesbian relationships, including one with Sand.[51] Gerson had no knowledge of Menken's letters to Hattie Tyng, rather, he claimed that Sand had written of the relationship herself. Given Gerson's other sins, it may not be surprising that in fact Sand and Menken had probably met only briefly and socially. Sand makes no references of Menken in her journals, and comments in her letters suggest that she did not particularly respect Menken. She certainly sympathized with Alexander Dumas *fils* about the embarrassment of his father's affair.[52] Ironically, Gerson's depiction of Menken as lesbian has created more interest amongst scholars than his stories of her steamy nights in Cuba.[53] The truth is, given Menken's

---

[50] Gerson to Mankowitz, in Mankowitz, *Mazeppa*, 189.

[51] Samuel Edwards, *George Sand: A Biography of the First Modern, Liberated Woman* (New York: David McKay, 1972).

[52] Claude Schopp, *Alexandre Dumas: Genius of Life*, trans. A. J. Koch (New York: Franklin Watts, 1988), 481.

[53] The most notable up to this point is a smart essay by Noreen Barnes-McLain, "Bohemian on Horseback: Adah Isaacs Menken," in *Passing Performances: Queer Readings of Leading Players in American Theatre History*, eds. Kim Marra and Robert A. Schanke (Ann Arbor: University of Michigan Press, 1998), 63–79. She balances her discussion of Menken as lesbian and/or a cross-dresser with skepticism toward the sources on which she is forced to rely.

letters to Hattie Tyng in 1861 and 1862 (which have never been mentioned
before in a published source), her portrayal of male characters, and her offstage cross-dressing in California and Nevada, she *should* be examined by
scholars interested in probing sexuality and gender identity. However, such
evidence must be handled extremely carefully. It is problematic enough
to explore sexuality and presentation of gender in terms of a past century's culture without it being further undermined by false tales aimed at
sensation.

Gerson defended his actions to Mankowitz by agreeing that Menken
had muddled identities and misrepresented her past until she left little solid
ground for biographers to stand upon.[54] How could one actually write her
life story – that is, establish "truth" – when everything about her early
life remained a mystery? In an odd way, although Gerson's biography of
Menken was fictional, it was only marginally more so than most others on
the market.

As the fields of lesbian and transgender history begin to bloom, Menken's
identity as a lesbian or transgender performer is becoming important to
many scholars, but two other identities truly dominate Menken's biographies in the twenty-first century: Menken as Jewish and Menken as black.
Both identities have little evidence to back them, and seem to somehow
share a connection – although perhaps not through Menken but rather
through those looking to her for evidence. The Jewish identity stems from
the work of Allen Lesser and the black identity from an article written by
John Kendall, both of whom published their first sketches of Menken in
1938.

Physician Allen Lesser wrote a book substantiating Menken's Jewish identity within a larger tribute to nineteenth-century Jewish Americans, *Weave a
Wreath of Laurel*. He followed it nine years later with a full-length biography
of her life, entitled *Enchanting Rebel: The Mystery of Adah Isaacs Menken*. Since
her death, American writers had routinely dismissed her claims of Jewish
heritage as being merely another facet of her complicated self-creation.[55]
Lesser believed otherwise, and wrote several articles and two books between
1930 and 1940 that set out to prove her importance as a Jewish poet. He also
wrote the sketch for the *Dictionary of American Biography*, which unequivocally stated that Menken was born Jewish. Lesser's sketches of Menken
were the most well researched up to that point. Certainly, no one else had
ever considered her years in Cincinnati, particularly not the poetry she had
published in the Cincinnati *Israelite*. And unlike other biographers, Lesser
steered clear of sensation, and used interviews and textual sources to back

[54] Mankowitz, *Mazeppa*, 189.

[55] Gus Daly, introduction to Adah Isaacs Menken, "Adah Isaacs Menken: Some Notes of Her Life in
Her Own Hand," *New York Times*, Sept. 6, 1868, p. 3; Edward James, *Biography of Adah Isaacs Menken
with Selections from Infelicia* (New York: Ed James for Private Distribution, 1869); Thomas Allston
Browne, "Adah Isaacs Menken," *History of the American Stage* (New York: Benjamin Blom, 1870).

up his claims. Although by modern standards his footnotes are inconsistent and only marginally helpful, Lesser was the first to use them in a Menken biography. All of these details marked his work as scholarly and dependable, and Lesser's argument continues to be accepted by many Jewish historians even today. Few people have checked his sources.

Despite his diligence as a researcher, Lesser wrote with a serious bias that undercuts his drive for truth. He truly wanted Menken to be Jewish, and he made her Jewish based on her claims and against the evidence. After all, Isaac Mayer Wise had stated unequivocally in 1864 that she was not Jewish. He asserted that she could not have been born Jewish because she asked to be converted, which he refused. It is true that Wise could have made such a declaration out of embarrassment; by 1864 many considered Menken shamelessly immoral. However, in 1924, when morals had shifted substantially and Menken could not possibly be seen as threatening to the image of Reform Judaism, his son Leo Wise told a similar version of his father's story but based on his own memories from childhood.[56] Lesser's observations only add up to speculation by comparison.

Lesser also deliberately downplayed Menken's life as an actress to focus more attention on her poetry. Had he wanted a Jewish actress, he would have done better to focus on Rose Eytinge, who had performed for President Lincoln, won critical praise, and lived a more respectable life.[57] But Lesser wanted the literary Menken, and in the process of trying to reclaim her as a poet, polished up her tarnished image with several other unsupported claims, including enduring love for Alexander Isaac Menken and a distaste for alcohol. Lesser argued that the "real Menken" could be found in her poetry, and that the other images had been a marketing device she had used to survive in the fickle world of entertainment. Thus, Lesser's work not only established Menken's Jewish identity, but also made her a far more sympathetic figure.

Other Jewish historians have had little incentive to disprove Lesser's claims; she serves a worthwhile purpose as scholars continue to struggle to establish Jewish American history. After massive migrations of Eastern European Jews at the turn of the century, America could claim several notable Jewish women, but earlier history yielded few despite the long presence of Jews in America. Had Menken remained only a tawdry circus-rider she would not have attracted the attention of historians such as Jacob Radar Marcus and Leo Shpall, but thanks to Lesser, they could virtually ignore her life as a celebrity and study her as an activist Jewish poet.[58]

---

[56] Brazo, "The Christmas Present Santa Clause Brought to Tom Ochiltree: A Romance of the Youth of the Brilliant Texas Lawyer and Adah Isaacs Menken," *St. Louis Globe Democrat*, ts. in the Sam Houston Regional Library and Research Center, Liberty, Texas.

[57] Browne, "Rose Eytinge," in Brown, *History of the American Stage*; Rose Eytinge, *The Memories of Rose Eytinge* (New York, 1905).

[58] Leo Shpall, "Adah Isaacs Menken," *Louisiana Historical Quarterly* (Jan. 1943), 2–3.

But Bernard Falk, a British biographer with no particular interest in Jewish history, also supported Lesser's claims in *The Naked Lady: A Biography of Adah Isaacs Menken*, published in 1952. He declared that he was won over by Lesser's logic, but his introduction implies that he also owed a debt to Lesser, who shared his research without reservation. Although the *Naked Lady* gives skimpy support of Menken's American experiences and relies on formulaic depictions of Menken as a sympathetic siren, it provides wonderful coverage of Menken's life across the Atlantic. Falk documents her European life with extensive use of newspaper and magazine sources that make the *Naked Lady* a valuable resource, despite its many flaws. Unfortunately, Falk's easy acceptance of Lesser's argument perpetuated the Jewish image without providing any more proof.

In terms of public knowledge, Menken also became a free woman of color shortly after she died, but that identity, like the Jewish one, did not truly take root until 1938. There is no evidence that anyone thought of Menken as black during her lifetime, although given her mysterious past the thought undoubtedly crossed a lot of minds. But there is no evidence. What do we make of an identity based almost entirely on rumor, hearsay, and wishes? For now, in the twenty-first century, Menken's most publicized identity is black. And it is undeniably enticing to think of Menken, the reigning celebrity of the Civil War period, as a free woman of color. The very thought changes the way we read her poetry and her life story; it reveals nuances in her written words, adds another layer of meaning to her Jewish identity, and shifts the way we interpret her constant prevaricating. But there is no evidence or, at least, not of the textual sort that historians normally accept as evidence. How do we unravel the convolutions of fact and fiction she knotted of her past and determine what may be accepted as evidence? The process should also prod us to question when it may be worthwhile to investigate rumor. Not all truths are visible, after all. We should question why Menken's racial identity has assumed such importance in the present day.

Despite the story not taking root until 1938, the tale of Menken's African ancestry first came into print in 1868; we cannot know whether rumors had circulated during her lifetime, but that would not have been unusual. Capitalizing on the drama of Menken's unexpected death and surprising book of poetry, sensation writer George Lippard Barclay (not to be confused with George Lippard) hustled her biography out within the year. He stated that Menken had claimed to be the daughter of a free man of color named Auguste Theodore.[59] Surprisingly, questions about Menken's racial origins did not resurface in print for another seventy years when another sensation writer, John S. Kendall, deduced a remarkably similar theory. Kendall also stated that Menken was the daughter of Auguste Théodore, but he based his

---

[59] Barclay, *Life and Remarkable Career*, 25.

argument on New Orleans public records and made no mention of Barclay's biography.[60] Kendall's work has become the basis of Menken's black identity today.

But investigation of New Orleans public records yields a still more fascinating story than the ones told by Barclay and Kendall, one that raises questions about how we determine race when looking back to another time and place. Once again, following Menken's trail leads not to clarity but to a more complicated set of truths. Her black identity has the advantage of allowing her to keep the other identities she claimed outright; Menken could have been a free woman of color and still be Spanish, Irish, British, or Jewish. The irony is that in American culture the same would not be true in reverse; by nineteenth-century American conventions (to which many Americans still adhere), if Menken claimed to be Irish, Jewish or Spanish, she could not also claim to be black. Trying to determine whether Menken was black requires examining how we define that identity, as well as exploring available records. If proving that Menken's parents were black is the only means of establishing her as an African American woman, then we simply do not have the evidence. But at the same time, aspects of Menken's behavior suggest she came from a racially mixed culture. South Louisiana culture was a racial hybrid, making African cultural elements available to people of European descent. Was Menken a white woman signifying black or a black woman passing for white? And how do we read the information if we can never know her heritage?

In 1868, Barclay said that Robert Newell was the one who gave him the information on Menken's true parentage. He begins, "On April 11, 1835, Marie Theodore, the wife of August Theodore gave birth to a daughter in the living quarters of the family tiny general store in Milneburg, Louisiana. . . . the baby was christened Adah Bertha."[61] He asserts that in 1863, Adah "in one of her more expansive moods, told a group of abolitionists" that her father had been a "free man of color." He goes on, "There may be some substance to the claim, for she told Newell, while married to him that 'I cannot, as the daughter of an octoroon, sympathize with the cause of the Confederacy.'"[62] The biggest obstacle with Barclay's "proof" is a letter that Newell included in his own memorial to Menken. Newell quoted Menken's letter, saying:

> I am an ultra Southerner; I cannot fraternize with the negro – I cannot feel with Abolitionism. . . . Oh, were I a man – a soldier – I'd march into the very midst of the battle, and, with voice of thunder and hands of iron, I'd shatter and cast down every chain that binds the glowing heart of the proud South

---

[60] John S. Kendall, "'The World's Delight': The Story of Adah Isaacs Menken," *Louisiana Historical Quarterly* 21 (July 1938).

[61] Barclay, *Life and Remarkable Career*, 25–26.   [62] Ibid., 25.

to the pale, sneering sister who would crush her to the dust. . . . I love my country – the South. Oh, that, like Judith, I could go to the tent of this black Holofernes and save my people![63]

Also, in February 1863, when Menken was briefly arrested as a Confederate sympathizer in Baltimore, she accepted that accusation proudly.[64] Her many statements supporting the Confederacy undermine contemporary concepts of black identity, which rest precariously on racial solidarity, but they actually put her on par with many free people of color. Louisiana Creoles were the people of French or Spanish ancestry born in the New World, and their community predated that of the Americans, making the free Creoles, or free people of color, among the oldest settlers in the region. The free Creoles were a community proud to be African and French or Spanish; their heritage emphasized the intimate relationships between subordination and domination in pre-American Louisiana, and it came with a limited amount of lingering social power. A number of free people of color were invested in the plantation system, and owned slaves themselves.[65] The free Creoles recognized they would face losses on many levels should slavery be abolished.

The free black community that surrounded Menken as she was growing up, whether she was legally black or white, was significantly different from those in the rest of the American South. Because of economic and cultural advantages, the free people of color of New Orleans appear to have occupied a higher rung on the social ladder than the Cajuns, who were technically white (of French Canadian ancestry) and lived in poverty in the swamps and bayous of the back country. Legally, however, the Cajuns held a higher place on the scale because of their racial status. It is important to recognize that in South Louisiana it was common knowledge that free people of color could be more fair in coloring than white Creoles or Cajuns. Anywhere in the country, of course, one could be legally black and yet be blond and blue-eyed, or legally white with an olive complexion, black hair, and black eyes, but the differences between legal identity and color were much more well recognized and therefore socially structured in French Louisiana. Cultural constructions of color in French Louisiana were so complicated that outsiders could rarely follow them. In many ways, then, the Creoles, black and white, had a fluid identity that slipped across cultures easily even in ordinary day-to-day living, as they worked and lived in towns divided between American or Creole dominance, traced out in nuances of color.

---

[63] AIM to Newell quoted in Robert Henry Newell, "Adah Isaacs Menken," no publication noted, pasted into Adah Isaacs Menken, "Biography . . . and other information," Harris Rare Books, M545x-76, John Hay Library, Brown University, Providence, Rhode Island.

[64] AIM to Ed James, n.d., Adah Isaacs Menken Uncatalogued Correspondence file, HTC.

[65] There's a good description of slavery under gens de couleur in John Blassingame, *The Slave Community: Plantation Life in the Antebellum South* (New York: Oxford University Press, 1979).

Kendall entered this confusing world of color and race in an effort to establish Menken's parentage. He began his search for Menken's past with the assumption that she was born in New Orleans, as she claimed. After compiling the names of possible fathers, he then dismissed each as never having appeared in birth, death, court, or parish records of Louisiana. Her most widely accepted claim of being Adelaide McCord collapsed quickly because he could not find records of a James McCord. Yet looking through census records I discovered that while there is no record of a James McCord in New Orleans during Menken's childhood years (1830 and 1840), a James McCorde shows up in the 1850 census, and a James McCord in the 1860 census.[66] Stranger still, James McCord makes an appearance in the New Orleans *Times-Picayune* as the late father of an Addie McCord who died in 1894, and her younger sister Annie, who died in 1897.[67] Menken was obviously not this Addie McCord (since she died in 1894, and Menken died in 1868), yet Menken had often claimed her father was named James McCord and her younger sister was named Annie.

Kendall found records of a distinguished physician named George W. Campbell, "a relative of the Duke of Argyle," who resembled Menken's description of Josiah Campbell, so he dismissed the Campbell story as yet another fanciful fabrication.[68] But in 1994 another scholar, John Cofran, discovered that the names McCord and Campbell appear together in the 1850 New Orleans census records: C. Campbell as the widowed head of household with a fifteen-year-old daughter named Ada C. McCord, born in Tennessee, a fourteen-year-old boy named John W. McCord, and an eleven-year-old girl named Josephine McCord, both born in Mississippi. Tracing these McCords back to Memphis, Cofran found that the 1840 Memphis census records list Richard McCord, married to an unnamed woman, with three unnamed children whose ages match those of Ada, John, and Josephine listed in the 1850 New Orleans census. Cofran also found a listing in Memphis marriage records that Catherine E. McCord married Josiah E. Campbell on June 22, 1848. From these findings, Cofran concluded that "Adah Isaacs Menken was born Ada McCord on 15 June 1835 . . . she was born in Memphis. She was the first child of Richard and Catherine McCord. After Richard's death (which probably occurred in 1842), Catherine married Josiah Campbell in 1848 and moved to New Orleans" where Josiah died shortly afterward.[69] If true, then Menken had been born a white Presbyterian, and her mother, Catherine A. McCord, ran

---

[66] *Louisiana 1850 Census Records: Orleans Parish*, 257; *Louisiana 1860 Census Records: Orleans Parish*, 407.

[67] "Addie McCord," New Orleans *Times Picayune*, April 4, 1894, p. 4, c. 7; "Annie McCord," *Times Picayune*, Oct. 7, 1897, p. 4, c. 7, and Oct. 10, 1897, p. 4, c. 6.

[68] Kendall, " *The World's Delight*," 848.

[69] John Cofran, "The Identity of Adah Isaacs Menken: A Theatrical Mystery Solved," *Theatre Survey* 31 (May 1990): 53–54. *Louisiana 1850 Census Records for the City of New Orleans*, 12; *Tennessee 1840 Census Record for Shelby County*, 202.

a successful dry goods and millinery shop in New Orleans until she remarried around 1851.[70] Cofran's version of the Menken biography echoes the version told by Ed James in 1868. By backing his theory with documented information, Cofran makes the most persuasive claim to Menken's origins. Cofran did not pursue his research further, hence there is no evidence that he knew of the other Addie McCord (daughter of James) living in New Orleans. His explanation of Menken's origins remains the most believable because of documentation but still leaves questions unanswered.

According to Memphis census records, in 1840 Richard McCord headed a household of eleven: himself, a wife, two daughters, a son, a free black man between twenty-four and thirty-six, a male slave the same age, two slave boys under ten, a slave girl under ten, a young slave woman between ten and twenty-four, and a slave woman aged twenty-four to thirty-six.[71] This information tells us that the McCord family had been prosperous until suffering financial loss between 1840 and 1850, and that Ada McCord spent at least part of her life sharing a home with a slave family that almost mirrored her own. The two slave girls were near the ages of Ada McCord and her sister, and they, too, had brothers and a mother and father close to the age of Richard and Catherine McCord. If Menken was this Ada McCord, the close presence of the slave family might explain her contradictory ability to identify with cultural minorities while maintaining Confederate allegiance. Menken's fascination with dark and light sisters might have stemmed from the fact that she grew up with a slave girl near her own age, perhaps sharing a sisterly relationship during childhood.

Cofran himself suggests the remaining problem with his construction of her puzzle: How do we explain the strange coincidences surrounding Menken's decision to go by the name Théodore and, in particular, the consistency in her brother's name. Menken was more consistent about her brother's name than that of anyone else in her past – stating that his name was Auguste or John August three separate times: to Newell in 1862, in "Notes of My Life" (1861–65), and in the 1860 *Illustrated News* article. More convincing yet is her poem "To My Brother Gus," which appeared in the *Liberty Gazette* in 1855. The persistent pairing of "Theodore" and "Auguste" suggests that Barclay and Kendall's findings continue to be relevant to Menken's story.

Having dismissed the McCord and Campbell stories as insupportable, Kendall turned to the only remaining name: Ada Bertha Theodore – the name she claimed to have appeared under as a child in the New Orleans theater. Ada Theodore married twice under that name, once to W. H. Kneass and later to Alexander Isaacs Menken, both times in Texas – which

[70] R. G. Dunn and Co. Collection, Louisiana, vol. 10, p. 345, Baker Library, Harvard Business School, Cambridge, Mass.
[71] *Tennessee 1840 Census Records for Shelby County*, 202.

certainly proves that Adah Isaacs Menken went by the name Ada Theodore at that point in her life.[72] Menken later stated that Theodore was a stage name she adopted while in New Orleans, but this explanation is disproven by the fact that Ada Theodore appears as a writer in East Texas newspapers long before there is evidence of her performing on stage.[73] In fact, there is no evidence of her *ever* performing as Ada Theodore in New Orleans.

Kendall believed that Menken was probably born a Théodore, so he focused his attention on the two Théodores he found in the New Orleans city directories in 1838: Mme. Théodore at 41 Condé Street and Auguste Théodore at 35 Bagatelle. One was white, and the other a free man of color. Kendall discovered that the New Orleans Board of Health had records of only two children born to any Théodore: Philomène Croi and Bénigne, born in 1839 and 1848, respectively, to Auguste and his wife Magdaleine Jean Louis Janneaux, a native of Pensacola. Kendall believed that Menken might have been one of these girls, arguing that African ancestry would explain her bizarre stories and actions. He theorized that Menken wanted to conceal her past because she was legally black and that she probably left Louisiana to marry a white man in Texas, where she would not be recognized.[74]

The most obvious problem with Kendall's proposition is something that he himself readily admits: Public records were a mess in nineteenth-century New Orleans, full of inaccuracies and lacking organization. He also seems to have not understand French Louisiana culture. Church documents were kept in French, and government ones in English, and if free blacks and free people of color made the unusual decision to record a birth, they usually turned to their church rather than the government.[75] Furthermore, Kendall went on the assumption that people wanted to record their personal information. An examination of a religious community during the racially turbulent 1830s to 1860s – when legal restrictions against free people of color increased dramatically – shows that free people of color might sometimes deliberately misrepresent themselves or a given situation to sustain a sense of autonomy and anonymity.[76] What Kendall perceived to be laxity may have been a

---

[72] Kendall, "*The World's Delight*," 849; Mankowitz, *Mazeppa*, 33.

[73] Catherine H. Leach, "Adah Isaacs Menken: The Biography of an American Actress," (M.A. thesis, Louisiana State University, 1937, p. 20. Leach accepts the now disproven argument that Adah's stepfather was a Scottish army surgeon. She states, "Adah adopted the name of Bertha Theodore for the stage." Mankowitz found four poems, an advertisement for Shakespearean readings, and a personal letter all from "Ada Bertha T–e" in a variety of east Texas newspapers all in 1855, several months after her first marriage to W. H. Kneass; Mankowitz, *Mazeppa*, 36–37. I found several poems written by Adah Theodore in the 1855 Texas *Liberty Gazette*, see Chapter 1 of this book.

[74] Kendall, "*The Worlds Delight*," 850–52.   [75] Ibid., 852.

[76] Renée M. Sentilles, "Forgotten Pioneers: A Comparative Study of the Sisters of the Holy Cross of Utah and the Sisters of the Holy Family of Louisiana," M.A. thesis, Utah State University, 1991, pp. 106–129.

wise sense of self-preservation. This makes Théodore's certification of his daughters' births unusual, but it does not in any way rule out the possibility that other Théodores had children during those years.

In fact, surviving city directories from 1805 to 1861 indicate a sizable population of Théodores residing in New Orleans. While Kendall is correct in citing only two addresses listed in 1838, other years can yield as many as many as six separate Théodore households. A Madame Théodore, comedienne, is listed in 1823 as living on St. Ann Street and shows up again in 1832 as residing at the Orleans Theatre. It is possible that Mde. Théodore was Menken's relative, or perhaps as a girl she admired the entertainer and longed to emulate her; either case could explain Menken's attraction to theater. Unfortunately, no other records of the woman exist in the city's public documents. It is also significant to note that most of the Théodores are listed with changing racial identities over the years. For example, Auguste shows up as "fmc," free man of color, in 1835 and 1849 but has no such indicator after his name in 1823 or 1846, unlike others listed on the same page.[77] Listing August Théodore without a designation after his name suggests that he may have looked white.

The Theodore connection, although not as well documented as the path to Ada McCord of Memphis, still holds a few startling coincidences with Menken. Was it simply chance that she claimed a brother with the same name as a free man of color who had a daughter her age? Was it also coincidence that she named her son Louis – one of Magdaleine Théodore's family names?[78] Barclay, claiming that his information came from Robert Newell, also refers to August's wife as "Marie Theodore."[79] The mother's name as "Marie" also crops up in various stories, including one told by Menken herself. She never claimed to have a mother named Catherine, but she did name herself and her mother as Marie in the "Notes" she sent to Gus Daly.[80] On April 25, 1855, a marriage license was issued for Benjamin Lerouge and Marie Théodore in Orleans parish – the same year that Ada Theodore first surfaces in Texas.[81] Perhaps she left home because of her mother's marriage. This route from Magdaleine Théodore to Adah Menken is long and unstable, but it suggests a wealth of possibilities, including the probability that Menken knew the Théodores.

Kendall did not check the census records of Auguste Théodore, or he would have noted that in 1840, Théodore was the sole provider for a household of twelve: three boys, three girls, two men, three women, and one elderly woman.[82] This suggests that he probably fathered more than the two girls listed in the Board of Health Records. Auguste Théodore also

[77] City directories, 1805–61, New Orleans Public Library, New Orleans, Louisiana (hereafter NOPL).

[78] Mankowitz, *Mazeppa*, 164.   [79] Barclay, *Life and Remarkable Career*, 26.

[80] Adah Isaacs Menken, "Adah Isaacs Menken: Some Notes of Her Life in Her Own Hand" (hereafter "Notes"), *New York Times*, Sept. 6, 1868, p. 3, c. 2.

[81] New Orleans marriage license, NOPL.   [82] *Louisiana 1840 Census: Orleans Parish*, 161.

moved every year, usually within Marigny, the district just beyond the Vieux Carré, where the white Théodores lived. His family size corresponded well with his neighbors, who were also free people of color. They also usually claimed anywhere from five to twenty household members, and most families reported having only one wage earner.[83] Marigny and the Vieux Carré were the Creole suburbs during the antebellum period, and by the 1850s, free Creoles dominated Marigny because the lots were small and inexpensive. By the Civil War, "three quarters of the sites in the fauborg had been owned at least at one time by gens de couleur libres."[84] Marigny is significant to Menken's story because the Pontchartrain Railroad passed through the fauborg. A few biographers have stated that Menken claimed to have been born on the "Chartrain," which they took to mean the tiny town of Milneburg, which had once existed at the end of the railroad line. However, it is just as likely that she meant she was born along the rail line or on the Pontchartrain lake front.

Death records indicate that when Auguste Théodore died in 1849 he was survived by "Magdelaine Jeannot."[85] In the 1850 census, "Magdelaine de la Auguste" appears as the head of a household of six, supported by fifteen-year-old Anthony, who worked as a "Segar Maker." We know that this is Auguste's wife because Philomene, age eleven, is listed under Anthony. Under Philomene is Annette, also eleven, and Belleria, age four. It is possible that Menken was part of this Théodore family, which was large and turns up only sporadically in public records. Menken might have been Philomene, with Annette as the sister she later called "Annie." Complicating such a scenario is the census taker, who designated the two girls as "B," for black, rather than "M," for mulatto, suggesting that Philomene and Annette did not appear white. However, the census could have based that decision on information he received from others. And, of course, Menken may *not* have been an actual Théodore, but shared a remarkable similarity of names and dates with that family. She could also have been one of the white Théodores, who most likely *were* related to Auguste and his family. Or maybe Menken was not the daughter of Auguste Théodore but his niece or a friend or neighbor well acquainted with the Theodore family.

It is tempting to imagine the three girls, Philomene Théodore, Addie McCord, and Ada McCord, playing together in the streets of New Orleans, sharing stories and perhaps wishing their friend's family was their own. When Ada McCord's father, Richard, died, his wife Catherine and her new husband Josiah Campbell might have moved her whole household, slaves and

---

[83] "Mayor's Office Register of Free Colored Persons Entitled to Remain in State, 1840–1857," unpublished, NOPL; Death Records, NOPL ; *Louisiana 1840 Census: Orleans Parish*, NOPL.

[84] Friends of the Cabildo [Sally Kittredge Evans], *New Orleans Architecture*, vol. 4: *The Creole Fauborgs* (Gretna: Pelican Press, 1974), 27.

[85] "Auguste Théodore," Death Records, NOPL, 615.

her own children, to New Orleans.[86] Her oldest daughter, Adelaide, could have maintained contact with her childhood companions and through them came into contact with the free Creole Théodores. Or perhaps Adelaide became friends with Addie McCord because of the similarities in their names, and through Addie met the Théodores. It seems likely that the girl who would grow up to be Menken must have known these other girls, because so many specific details of their all lives are woven into her life story.

Yet this path is impossible to follow – it might have happened, but we can never know. Attempting to establish patterns in the city directories, census records, and other registrations makes it clear that New Orleans records are riddled with inaccuracy. Names are spelled several different ways, dates conflict, and place names change. Sometimes a researcher has to pull things together, which encourages one to follow Kendall's example and shape the data to fit the imagination. But such conclusions are not "evidence." For example, in 1841, an A (indecipherable) Theodore aged forty-four registered himself on the "Mayor's Office Register of free Colored Persons Entitled to Remain in the State 1840–1857" as a merchant who came to New Orleans from New York in 1829.[87] This date corresponds fairly well to the Auguste Theodore who died in 1849 at forty-seven years of age, but the latter's death records indicate that he was a native of New Orleans.[88] There are simply too many roads to know which one led to Ada Bertha Theodore in Livingston, Texas, in the mid-1850s. And the truth is that Menken herself may not have known her own ancestry, so how can we?

Even if Menken was not born in New Orleans, everyone agrees that she spent her adolescence there. Whether or not she had African ancestry, she emerged from the Creole culture of New Orleans, a society shaped as much by West African and West Indian legacies as by French and Spanish colonization. Attempting to define Menken's racial identity in such an environment calls into question how these definitions functioned outside Louisiana. "Race" itself is, of course, a problematic term. In Menken's case, both she and her biographers defined race by ancestry. They said her father was Irish, Jewish, or African American, indicating that Menken must therefore share those identities. But "race" as a biological definition is maddeningly inconsistent, like Menken herself. Race is indeed the very opposite of what biology purports to be: a system that relies on consistent physical markings. As historian Barbara Fields points out, "race" as an

---

[86] According to credit records, Mrs. C. A. Campbell owned a "Fancy Goods and Millinery" shop, which she closed in 1851 or '57 (writing is unclear), when she "advanced from widowhood to matrimonial affiliation." See Louisiana, v. 10, p. 345, R. G. Dun & Co. Collection, Harvard Business School, Cambridge, Mass.

[87] "Register of Free Colored Persons," NOPL.   [88] Auguste Theodore, Death Records, NOPL.

absolute physical difference works only if blacks and whites do not have children together. Once they do, "Any attempt to carry the concept further than that collapses into absurdity: for example, a child belonging to a different race from one of his parents, or the well-known anomaly of American racial convention that considers a white woman capable of giving birth to a black child but denies that a black woman can give birth to a white child."[89] America has a contextual ideology of race "that tells people which details to notice, which to ignore, and which to take for granted in translating the world around them into ideas about that world."[90] In a culture as racially mixed as Louisiana, the cultural signifiers of race become even more contentious.

The clearest example of Menken signifying on the culture of *gens de couleur libres* was when she married Alexander Isaac Menken and added an "s" to her married name, making her Adah Isaacs Menken. Adopting a man's name with an added "s" or "e" was a strategy practiced by the quadroon mistresses of white Creoles in New Orleans. Whites and blacks could not legally marry in Louisiana, but since the earliest French settlement it had become common practice for white men to enter social contracts with quadroon women called *plaçage*. Within these arrangements, the couple essentially acted as man and wife, complete with a household and children. It was not a legal union, and it was not uncommon for white men of means to support two households, one with a white wife and the other with a quadroon mistress. Taking on the man's name with a slightly modifying letter allowed the quadroon woman to claim an official connection to her white provider without running foul of legal barriers. Menken could have recognized this when she chose to add the "s" to her name – a practice that she adopted from the beginning and from which she never wavered. It suggested a marriage that was not real; it claimed a union and yet denied it at the same time.[91] Why Menken chose to adopt a quadroon method of naming is impossible to know; it may have been her way of being both married and not married simultaneously. She certainly seemed to distrust marriage as much as she wanted to be in one.

Menken's identity as a black poet gained validity in 1988, after the story had been told and retold by several scholars. In 1945, Arna Bontemps and Jack Conroy elaborated on Kendall's thesis in *They Seek a City*, asserting that Menken was one of over 10,000 Louisiana quadroons who crossed over to white identity between 1850 and 1860.[92] Their support led to the inclusion of *Infelicia* in the Black Heritage Collection in 1971. But

---

[89] Barbara J. Fields, "Ideology and Race in American History," in *Region, Race and Reconstruction: Essays in Honor of C. Vann Woodward*, eds. J. Morgan Kousser and James M. McPherson (New York: Oxford University Press, 1982), 150.

[90] Ibid., 146.   [91] Friends of the Cabildo, 27.

[92] Arna Bontemps and Jack Conroy, *They Seek a City* (Garden City, N.Y.: Doubleday, Doran, 1945), 98.

the theory of Menken's black origins did not gain a larger following until African American studies became established in universities nationwide, and the story appeared in Wolf Mankowitz's *Mazeppa: The Lives Loves and Legends of Adah Isaacs Menken*, arguably the most otherwise well-researched Menken biography of the twentieth century.

A Hollywood screenwriter by profession, Mankowitz wrote *Mazeppa* to make money, but he did more original research than her previous biographers. Allen Lesser shared his manuscript papers with Mankowitz, which the latter employed heavily in *Mazeppa*. Yet Mankowitz was the first demonstrate that Lesser's reasoning could not be accepted as evidence – that, in fact, there was more to disprove Menken's Jewish heritage than to prove it. And Mankowitz ferreted out other, less obvious deceptions. For example, he produced enough evidence to forever dismiss the idea that Menken had performed in Cuba before she turned up in Texas, in the mid-1850s. He also added a new piece to Menken's life by looking for clues to explain her years in Texas, shortly before she married Alexander Isaac Menken in Galveston. All of this research suggested that Mankowitz's version of Menken's life could be trusted as factual, despite the fact that he included no footnotes and had appended an incomplete bibliography. *Mazeppa* is a commercial biography that portrays Menken as a capricious and opportunistic predator of men, but Mankowitz included just enough hard evidence and skepticism to make it the most trustworthy biography of Menken available by the 1980s.

Menken's black identity moved into scholarly acceptance when Mankowitz's text convinced prominent African American scholars that black ancestry was enough of a possibility to include her in the literary cannon. In 1988 the Schomberg Library Series on black women writers of the nineteenth century, under the editorship of Henry Louis Gates, jr., and Joan Sherman, republished *Infelicia*. In the eyes of many, the endorsement of Gates and the Schomberg Library established Menken's black identity. Reliable scholars, such as Joan Sherman and Daphne Brooks, are careful to remind their audiences that Menken's racial identity is not certain. But such scholarly writings have at the same time convinced less judicious writers that Menken is black. She now appears as a black woman on hundreds of Internet websites. In many ways, Menken became black at the end of the twentieth century and that identity becomes more accepted as scholars move away from the original research, that of Kendall, without looking at his sources.

Menken created a patchwork quilt of ethnic and racial identities to cover her past. It is doubtful that anyone will ever substantiate her racial heritage, and the act of trying to do so should make us question why it is important to so many contemporary scholars. Menken has been rewritten through time so that one seldom finds all of her images in one source. Instead, biographers have tended to break her into more coherent parts: scandalous, virtuous, Jewish, black, lesbian. Silenced by death, Menken's stories have become useful in others' lives. Depending on how we read them, her identities may reveal little about the woman and more about our own social and cultural concerns: fear of historical erasure, the desire to see ourselves reflected in the past, and perhaps the fantasy that representations appearing in surprising places will ameliorate our anger or guilt about the past that has led to our place in the present. Whether or not Menken "really was" black or Jewish is important to us because, even as we suggest that society is constructed and identities performed, we continue to speak with the language those constructions have created. Emerson said this much earlier: "As I am, so I see; use what language we will, we can never say anything but what we are."[93] Given our own inability to see beyond the confines of our own context, Menken is infinitely useful: Her ambiguity privileges the perspective of the viewer over the subject. As we move farther away from her own time period, the viewer can ignore the opinions of Menken's contemporaries, and see reflected in her a foreshadowing of the future. Who Menken "was," as a singular identity, is impossible to discern. Does it matter?

Her constant play on gender, race, religion, social class, and propriety that made her challenging to categorize in the nineteenth century make her particularly useful a century later. If she cannot be placed into categories, she cannot be excluded, either, and thus when historians of the present turn to Menken, they see suggestions of formerly invisible groups included in nineteenth-century public life. Menken's various images suggest representation in a period when for many groups there is little, and yet, upon close examination, even those shadows of possibility retreat.

And so here, in the end, we have a picture of Menken, the celebrity persona: a series of images created in response to an audience that kept expanding to the point of having few parameters. She began by projecting images locally, through performances on stage and in print. As she became more famous, her audience widened and became more complex – and, therefore, so did the Menken. After she died the images became yet more valuable, as they were subject no longer to Menken's whims, but now to those of anyone else. As the subject of this historical biography, as a vehicle for examining nineteenth-century American culture, Menken reveals a complex world of performances on- and offstage, in print or in action, by signifiers and statements. The irony, of course, is on us, for her images are still provocative, still fascinating. In her persistence, Menken demonstrates what Tony Horowitz has suggested of the Civil War itself: The past remains in our present for a variety of social, cultural, and political reasons that are

---

[93] Ralph Waldo Emerson, "Experience," *Essays by Ralph Waldo Emerson*, 2nd series (1876; rpt.: Boston: Houghton Mifflin, 1998), 79.

still in play.[94] The Menken performs for us yet because we are still captivated by the images she used to provoke the public in the century before
our grandmothers. And sometimes the questions are worth more than the
answers, as thou knowest.

[94] Tony Horowitz, *Confederates in the Attic: Dispatches from the Unfinished Civil War* (New York: Vintage, 1998).

Bibliography

NEWSPAPERS

Albany, N.Y.	*Standard*
Baltimore, Md.	*American Commercial Advertise, Daily Gazette, Sun*
Brooklyn, N.Y.	*Daily Eagle*
Cincinnati, Ohio	*Israelite, Commercial Advertiser, Die Deborah, Independent*
Galveston, Tex.	*Daily News*
London, Eng.	*Times, Tribune*
Milwaukee, Wis.	*Sentinel*
Nacodoches, Tex.	*Sentinel*
New Orleans, La.	*Daily Delta, Times-Picayune*
New York, N.Y.	*Sunday Mercury, Herald, Clipper, Times, Tribune, Wilke's Spirit of the Times, Illustrated News, Home Journal*
San Francisco, Calif.	*Golden Era, Californian, Daily Alta, Call, Bulletin, Evening Bulletin*
Sacramento, Calif.	*Bee*
Seneca, N.Y.	*Revolution*
St. Louis, Mo.	*Missouri Republican*
Liberty, Tex.	*Liberty Gazette*

ARCHIVES AND COLLECTIONS

American Antiquarian Society, Worcester, Massachusetts
American Jewish Archives, Hebrew Union College, Cincinnati, Ohio
Amistad Research Center, Tulane University, New Orleans, Louisiana
Baker Library, Harvard Business School, Cambridge, Massachusetts
Bancroft Library, University of California, Berkeley
Boston Public Library, Boston, Massachusetts
British Library, London, England
California State Library, Sacramento, California
Charlotte Cushman Center, Philadelphia, Pennsylvania
Cincinnati Public Library, Cincinnati, Ohio
Harvard Theatre Collection, Harvard University, Cambridge, Massachusetts
Historic New Orleans Collection, New Orleans, Louisiana
John Hay Library, Brown University, Providence, Rhode Island
Library of Congress, Washington, D.C.
Mariner's Museum, Newport News, Virginia
Massachusetts Historical Society, Boston, Massachusetts

Museum of the City of New York, New York
Nacogdoches Depository, Nacogdoches, Texas
New Orleans Public Library, New Orleans, Louisiana
New York Historical Society, New York
New York Public Library, New York
Special Collections, University of Minnesota, Minneapolis
Special Collections, University of Wisconsin, Madison
Sam Houston Regional Library, Liberty, Texas
Theatre Museum, London, England

PUBLISHED SOURCES

Aaron, Daniel. *Cincinnati: Queen City of the West.* Columbus: Ohio State University Press, 1992.

Abbott, Jacob. *Virginia; Or, A Little Light on a Very Dark Saying.* New York: Harper & Brothers, n.d. (probably 1855).

Abernathy, Frances Edward. *Legendary Ladies of Texas.* Dallas: E-Heart Press, 1981.

Agger, Lee. *Women of Maine.* Portland, Me.: Guy Gannett, 1982.

Allen, Robert C. *Horrible Prettiness: Burlesque and American Culture.* Chapel Hill: University of North Carolina Press, 1991.

Anderson, Patricia. *When Passion Reigned: Sex and the Victorians.* New York: Harper-Collins, 1995.

Andres, Cherry. *The Soldier's Daughter: A Comedy in Five Acts.* New York: Charles Wiley, 1825.

Arthur, Timothy Shay. *The String of Pearls for Boys and Girls.* New York: Burdick Brothers, 1857.

Asbury, Herbert. *The French Quarter: An Informal History of the New Orleans Underworld.* New York: Alfred A. Knopf, 1936.

Ashkenazi, Elliot. *The Business of Jews in Louisiana, 1840–1875.* Tuscaloosa: University of Alabama Press, 1988.

Austen, Roger. *Genteel Pagan: The Double Life of Charles Warren Stoddard.* Amherst: University of Massachusetts Press, 1991.

Babinski, Herbert F. *The Mazeppa Legend in European Romanticism.* New York: Columbia University Press, 1974.

Baker, Thomas N. *Sentiment & Celebrity: Nathaniel Parker Willis and the Trials of Literary Fame.* New York: Oxford University Press, 1999.

Banner, Lois. *American Beauty.* New York: Alfred A. Knopf, 1983.

Barclay, George. *The Life and Remarkable Career of Adah Isaacs Menken, The Celebrated Actress.* Philadelphia: Barclay, 1868.

Barnhart, Josephine Baker. *The Fair but Frail: Prostitution in San Francisco, 1849–1900.* Reno: University of Nevada Press, 1986.

Basch, Norma. *Framing American Divorce: From the Revolutionary Generation to the Victorians.* Berkeley: University of California Press, 1999.

Baum, Charlotte, Paula Hyman, and Sonya Michel. *The Jewish Woman in America.* New York: Dial Press, 1976.

Baym, Nina. *Feminism and American Literary History: Essays.* Rutgers: University of Rutgers Press, 1992.

Bean, Walton. *California: An Interpretive History.* New York: McGraw Hill, 1968.

Beecher, Henry Ward. *Lectures to Young Men on Various Important Subjects.* Salem, Mass.: John P. Jewett, 1846.

Bennett, Paula Bernat. "'The Descent of the Angel': Interrogating Domestic Ideology in American Women's Poetry, 1858–1890." *American Literary History* 7 (1995): 591–610.

———. *Nineteenth-Century American Women Poets: An Anthology.* Malden, Mass.: Blackwell, 1998.

Bennett, Susan. *Theatre Audiences: A Theory of Production and Reception.* London: Routledge, 1997.

Berlin, Ira. *Slaves without Masters: The Free Negro in the Antebellum South.* New York: Oxford University Press, 1974.

———. *Many Thousands Gone: The First Two Centuries of Slavery in North America.* Cambridge: Harvard University Press, 1998.

Bontemps, Arna, and Jack Conroy. *They Seek a City.* Garden City, N.J.: Doubleday, Doran, 1945.

Boorstin, Daniel J. *The Image; or, What Happened to the American Dream.* New York: Atheneum Press, 1962.

Bo-Peep Story Books: Hans in Luck, The Nose Tree . . . The Jew in the Bush. New York: Leavitt and Allen, n.d. (not before 1852).

Bradbury, Oscar. *The Belle of the Bowery.* Boston: H. L. Williams, 1846.

———. *The Modern Othello; or, The Guilty Wife: A Thrilling Romance of New York Fashionable Life.* New York: Robert M. Dewitt, 1855.

———. *Julia Bicknell; or, Love and Murder! Founded on a Recent Domestic Tragedy.* Boston: Henry L. Williams, 1845.

———. *Therese, the Iroquois Maiden: A Tale of City and of Forest Life.* New York: Samuel French, 1852.

Braudy, Leo. *The Frenzy of Renown: Fame and Its History.* New York: Oxford University Press, 1986.

Britten, Emma Hardinge. *Autobiography of Emma Hardinge Britten.* London: John Heywood, 1900.

Brodhead, Richard. *Cultures of Letters: Scenes of Reading and Writing in Nineteenth-Century America.* Chicago: University of Chicago Press, 1993.

Brooks, Daphne A. "Lady Menken's Secret: Adah Isaacs Menken, Actress Biographies, and the Race for Sensation." *Legacy: A Journal of American Women Writers* 15 (1998): 68–77.

Brooks, Elizabeth. *Prominent Women of Texas.* Akron, 1896.

Brooks, Stewart. *Civil War Medicine.* Springfield, Ill.: Charles C. Thomas, 1966.

Browder, Laura. *Slippery Characters: Ethnic Impersonators and American Identities.* Chapel Hill: University of North Carolina Press, 2000.

Brown, Bill, ed. *Reading the West: An Anthology of Dime Westerns.* Boston: Bedford Books, 1997.

Brown, Thomas Allston. *History of the American Stage.* New York: Benjamin Blom, 1870.

Browne, J. Ross. "Washoe Visited." *Harper's New Monthly Magazine* (May and June 1865).

Browne, Junius Henry. *The Great Metropolis: A Mirror of New York.* Hartford, Conn., 1869.

Buckstone, J. B. *Green Bushes.* New York: 1844.

Bullough, Vern L., and Bonnie Bullough. *Cross Dressing, Sex and Gender.* Philadelphia: University of Pennsylvania Press, 1993.

Buntline, Ned. *Mysteries and Miseries of New York.* New York: Berford, 1848.

Burge, James C. *Lines of Business: Casting Practice and Policy in the American Theatre, 1752–1899.* New York: Peter Lang, 1986.

Burrows, Edwin, and Mike Wallace. *Gotham: A History of New York City.* New York: Oxford University Press, 1999.

Bushman, Richard L. *The Refinement of America: Person, Houses, Cities.* New York: Alfred A. Knopf, 1992.

Buszek, Maria-Elena, "Representing 'Awarishness,' Burlesque, Feminist Transgression, and the Nineteenth-Century Pin-Up." *Drama Review* 43 (Winter 1999): 141–161.

Butler, Judith. *Gender Trouble: Feminism and the Subversion of Identity.* New York: Routledge, 1990.

Butsch, Richard. "Bowry B'hoys and Matinée Ladies: The Re-Gendering of Nineteenth-Century American Theatre Audiences." *American Quarterly* 46 (1994): 375, 391.

————. *The Making of American Audiences: From Stage to Television, 1750–1990.* New York: Cambridge University Press, 2000.

Buttrick, George Arthur, ed. *The Interpreter's Dictionary of the Bible,* vol. 2. New York: Abingdon Press, 1962.

Carnes, Mark C., and Clyde Griffen, eds. *Meanings for Manhood: Constructions of Masculinity in Victorian America.* Chicago: University of Chicago Press, 1990.

Casteras, Susan P. *English Pre-Raphaelitism and Its Reception in America in the Nineteenth Century.* Rutherford: Fairleigh Dickinson University Press, 1990.

City Sights for Country Eyes. Philadelphia: American Sunday School Union, n.d. (probably between 1854 and 1857).

Clare, Ada. *Only A Woman's Heart.* New York: M. Doolady, 1866.

Clark, Suzanne. *Sentimental Modernism: Women Writers and the Revolution of the Word.* Bloomington: University of Indiana Press, 1991.

Clark, Timothy J. *Image of the People: Gustave Courbet and the Second French Republic, 1848–1851.* New York: Graphic Society, 1973.

Clemmer, Mary. *Men, Women and Things.* Boston: Ticknor, 1886.

Clinton, Catherine, and Nina Silber, eds. *Divided Houses: Gender and the Civil War.* New York: Oxford University Press, 1992.

Cofran, John. "The Identity of Adah Isaacs Menken: A Theatrical Mystery Solved." *Theatre Survey* (May 1990): 47–54.

Cohen, Daniel A. "'The Female Marine,' in an Era of Good Feelings: Cross-Dressing and the Genius of Nathaniel Coverly, Jr." *Proceedings of the American Antiquarian Society* 103 (1994): 359–394.

Cohen, Rev. A., ed. and trans. *Joshua Judges: Hebrew Text & English Translation with Introductions and Commentary.* London: Soncino, 1976.

Condit, Carl W. *The Railroad and the City: A Technological and Urbanistic History of Cincinnati.* Columbus: Ohio State University Press, 1977.

The Converted Jewess: A Memoir of Maria. New York: G. Lane and P. P. Sanford, 1843.

Cooke, James W. *The Arts of Deception: Playing with Fraud in the Age of Barnum.* Cambridge: Harvard University Press, 2001.

Cooke, Miriam, and Angela Woollacott, eds. *Gendering War Talk.* Princeton: Princeton University Press, 1993.

Cossé-Bell, Caryn. *Revolution, Romanticism, and the Afro-Creole Protest Tradition in Louisiana, 1718–1868.* Baton Rouge: Louisiana State University Press, 1997.

Cott, Nancy. *The Bonds of Womanhood: "Woman's Sphere" in New England, 1780–1835.* New Haven: Yale University Press, 1977.

Cott, Nancy, ed., et al. *Root of Bitterness: Documents of the Social History of Women.* Boston: Northeast University Press, 1996.

Cowells, Emilie Marguerite. *The Cowells in America: Being the Diary of Mrs. Sam Cowell during Her Husband's Concert Tour in the Years 1860–61.* London: Oxford University Press, 1934.

Coyne, J. Stirling. *Unprotected Female.* N.p., n.d.

Crouthamel, James L. *Bennett's New York Herald and the Rise of the Popular Press.* New York: Syracuse University Press, 1989.

Curtis, Newton M. *The Matricide's Daughter: A Tale of of Life in the Great Metropolis.* New York: W. F. Burgess, 1850.

———. *The Star of the Fallen: A Tale.* New York: Williams Brothers, 1848.

———. *The Victim's Revenge: A Sequel to "The Matricide's Daughter" and "The Star of the Fallen."* New York: Williams Brothers, 1848.

Cushman, Pauline, *The Romance of the Great Rebellion: The Mysteries of the Secret Service: A Genuine and Faithful Narrative of . . . Miss Major Pauline Cushman, the Famous Federal Scout and Spy.* New York: Wynkoop and Hallenbeau, 1864.

Davis, Angela. *Women, Race and Class.* New York: Vintage Books, 1983.

Davis, Sam. "Dramatic Recollection." *Nevada Monthly* (July 1880): 229.

Davis, Tracy C. *Actresses as Working Women: Their Social Identity in Victorian Culture.* London: Routledge, 1991.

De Grave, Kathleen. *Swindler, Spy, Rebel: The Confidence Woman in Nineteenth-Century America.* Columbia: University of Missouri Press, 1995.

Dekker, Rudolf M., and Lotte C. Van de Pol. *The Tradition of Female Transvestism in Early Modern Europe.* New York: St. Martins, 1998.

D'Emilio, John, and Estelle Freedman. *Intimate Matters: A History of Sexuality in America.* New York: Harper and Row, 1988.

Dempsey, David, with Raymond Baldwin. *The Triumphs and Trials of Lotta Crabtree.* New York: William Morrow, 1968.

Denison, Mary Andrews. *Edna Etheril; or, The Boston Seamstress.* New York: Burgess, Stringer, 1847.

Denning, Michael. *Mechanic Accents: Dime Novels and Working Class Culture in America.* New York: Verso, 1987.

Diner, Hasia R. *A Time for Gathering: The Second Migration, 1820–1880.* Baltimore: Johns Hopkins University Press, 1992.

Dinnerstein, Leonard. *Uneasy at Home: Antisemitism and the American Jewish Experience.* New York: Columbia University Press, 1987.

Discher, M. Willson. "Fierce and Luxurious Dolores." *Theatre Arts Monthly* (September 1930): 780–788.

Domínguez, Virginia R. *White by Definition: Social Classification in Creole Louisiana.* New Jersey: Rutgers University Press, 1986.

Douglas, Ann. *The Feminization of American Culture.* New York: Knopf, 1977.

Drury, Nells. *An Editor on the Comstock Lode.* New York: Farrar & Rinehart, 1936.

Dudden, Faye E. *Women in American Theatre: Actresses and Audiences, 1790–1870.* New Haven: Yale University Press, 1994.

Dyer, Richard. *The Matter of Images: Essays on Representations.* London: Routledge, 1993.

The Dying Jewess. New York: Daniel Coolidge, n.d. (probably between 1833 and 1837).

Dytch, Meredith M. "'Remember Ellsworth!': Chicago's First Hero of the American Civil War." *Chicago History* 11 (1982): 15–25.

Edgeville, Edward. *Castine.* Raleigh: William B. Smith, 1865.

Edmonds, Emma S. *Nurse and Spy in the Union Army: Comprising the Adventures, and Experiences in Hospitals, Camps, and Battle-fields.* Hartford: W.S. Williams, 1865.

Edwards, Samuel. *George Sand: A Biography of the First Modern, Liberated Woman.* New York: David McKay, 1972.

———. *Queen of the Plaza: A Biography of Adah Isaacs Menken.* London: A. Redman, 1965.

Egli, Ida Rae. *No Rooms of Their Own: Women Writers of Early California.* Berkeley: Heyday Books, n.d.

Eiselien, Gregory, ed. *Infelicia and Other Writings.* Peterborough, Ontario: Broadview Literary Press, 2002.

Elfenbein, Andrew. *Byron and the Victorians.* New York: Cambridge University Press, 1995.

Elfenbein, Anna Shannon. *Women on the Color Line: Evolving Stereotypes and the Writings of George Washington Cable, Grace King, and Kate Chopin.* Charlottesville: University of Virginia Press, 1989.

Elliott, Mary. "When Girls Will Be Boys: 'Bad' Endings and Subversive Middles in Nineteenth Century Tomboy Narratives and Twentieth Century Lesbian Pulp Novels." *Legacy* 15 (1998): 92–97.

Epstein, Julia, and Kristina Straub, eds. *Body Guards: The Cultural Politics of Gender Ambiguity.* London: Routledge, 1991.

Estavan, Laurence, ed. *San Francisco Theatre Research.* San Francisco, 1938.

Ewing, Elizabeth. *Dress and Undress: A History of Women's Underwear.* New York: Drama Book Specialists, 1978.

Eytinge, Rose. *The Memories of Rose Eytinge.* New York, 1905.

Fabian, Ann. *The Unvarnished Truth: Personal Narratives in Nineteenth-Century America.* Berkeley: University of California Press, 2000.

Faderman, Lillian. *Surpassing the Love of Men: Romantic Friendship and Love between Women from the Renaissance to the Present.* New York: Quill, 1981.

Falk, Bernard. *The Naked Lady: A Biography of Adah Isaacs Menken.* London: Hutchinson, 1952.

———. *Naked Lady; or, Storm over Adah.* London: Hutchinson, 1934.

———. *Rachel the Immortal, Stage Queen: Grand Amoureuse, Street Urchin: Fine Lady.* New York: Appleton, 1936.

Fatout, Paul. *Mark Twain in Virginia City.* Bloomington: University of Indiana Press, 1969.

Faust, Drew Gilpin. "Altars of Sacrifice: Confederate Women and the Narratives of War." *Journal of American History* 76 (1990): 1200–1228.

The Female Wanderer: A Very Interesting Tale. Wells River, Vt.: White and Reed, 1826.

Ferris, Lesley, ed. *Crossing the Stage.* London: Routledge, 1993.

Fleischer, Ned. *Reckless Lady: The Life Story of Adah Isaacs Menken.* New York: O'Brien Press, 1941.

Folsom, Ed. *Walt Whitman's Native Representations.* New York: Cambridge University Press, 1994.

Foucault, Michel. *History of Sexuality*, vol. 1: *An Introduction.* New York: Pantheon Books, 1978.

French, Benjamin Brown. *Witness to the Young Republic: A Yankee's Journal.* Hanover, N.H.: University Press of New England, 1989.

Friedenberg, Robert. *"Hear O Israel": The History of American Jewish Preaching, 1654–1970.* Tuscaloosa: University of Alabama Press, 1989.

Friends of the Cabildo [Sally Kittredge Evans]. *New Orleans Architecture*, vol. 4: *The Creole Fauborgs.* Gretna: Pelican Press, 1974.

Fuller, Jean Overton. *Swinburne: A Biography.* New York: Schocken Books, 1971.

Fuss, Diane, ed. *Inside/Out: Lesbian Theories, Gay Theories.* New York: Routledge, 1991.

Gallagher, Gary W. *The Antietam Campaign.* Chapel Hill: University of North Carolina Press, 1999.

Gamson, Joshua. *Claims to Fame: Celebrity in Contemporary America.* Berkeley: University of California Press, 1994.

Garber, Marjorie. *Vested Interests: Cross-Dressing and Cultural Anxiety.* New York: Routledge, 1992.

Gautier, Théophile. *Mademoiselle de Maupin.* London: published for the trade, n.d.

Gay, Peter. *The Bourgeois Experience: Victoria to Freud,* vol. 2: *The Tender Passion.* New York: Oxford University Press, 1986.

_____. *Pleasure Wars: The Bourgeois Experience: Victoria to Freud.* New York: W. W. Norton, 1998.

Gerber, David, ed. *Anti-Semitism in American History.* Chicago: University of Illinois Press, 1986.

Giddons, Anthony. *The Class Structure of Advanced Societies.* New York: Harper and Row, 1973.

Gildersleeve, Mrs. C. H. [Rachel Longstreet]. *Remy St. Remy; or, The Boy in Blue.* New York: James Okane, 1865.

Gilfoyle, Timothy. *City of Eros: New York City, Prostitution, and the Commercialization of Sex, 1790–1920.* New York: W. W. Norton, 1992.

Gilman, Sander L. "Black Bodies, White Bodies: Toward an Iconography of Female Sexuality in Late Nineteenth-Century Art, Medicine, and Literature." *Critical Inquiry* 12 (1985): 204–242.

_____. *Inscribing the Other.* Lincoln: University of Nebraska Press, 1991.

Ginsberg, Elaine K., ed. *Passing and the Fictions of Identity.* Durham: Duke University Press, 1996.

Goffman, Erving. *The Presentation of the Self in Everyday Life.* Garden City, N.Y.: Doubleday, 1959.

Golden, Hymann E. *The Jewish Woman and Her Home.* New York: Hebrew Books, 1978.

Goldman, Marion S. *Gold Diggers and Silver Miners: Prostitution and Social Life on the Comstock Lode.* Ann Arbor: University of Michigan Press, 1981.

Goldsmith, Barbara. *Other Powers: The Suffrage, Spiritualism, and the Scandalous Victoria Woodhull.* New York: Alfred A. Knopf, 1998.

Gorn, Elliot J. *The Manly Art: Bare-Knuckle Prize-Fighting in America.* Ithaca: Cornell University Press, 1986.

Gossett, Thomas F. *Race: The History of an Idea in America.* Dallas: Southern Methodist University Press, 1963.

Green, Rayna. "Pocahontas Perplex: The Image of Indian Women in American Culture," *Massachusetts Review* 16 (Autumn 1975): 698–714.

Griswold, Hattie Tyng. *Apple-Blossoms.* Milwaukee: Strickland, 1874.

Habegger, Alfred. *Gender, Fantasy, and Realism in American Literature.* New York: Columbia University Press, 1982.

Haines, J. T. *The French Spy; or, The Siege of Constantina.* New York: Samuel French, n.d.

Hall, Gwendolyn Midlo. *Africans in Colonial Louisiana: The Development of Afro-Creole Culture in the Eighteenth Century.* Baton Rouge: Louisiana State University Press, 1992.

Hall, Stuart. "Notes on Desconstructing the Popular." In *People's History and Socialist Theory,* ed. Raphael Samuel. London: Routledge, 1981.

Haltunnen, Karen. *Confidence Men and Painted Women: A Study of Middle-Class Culture in America, 1830–1870.* New Haven: Yale University Press, 1982.

————. *Murder Most Foul: The Killer and the American Gothic Imagination.* Cambridge: Harvard University Press, 1998.

Hardinge, Emma. *American and Her Destiny: Inspirational Discourse through Emma Hardinge by the Spirits.* New York: Robert M. De Witt, 1861.

Harris, Neil. *Humbug: The Art of P. T. Barnum.* Boston: Little, Brown, 1973.

Harwell, Richard Barksdale. "Brief Candle: The Confederate Theatre." *Proceedings of the American Antiquarian Society* (April 1971): 44–48.

Hawthorne, Nathaniel. *The Complete Novels and Selected Tales of Nathaniel Hawthorne.* New York: Modern Library, 1937.

Hazel, Harry [Justin Jones]. *Virginia Graham: The Spy of the Grand Army.* New York: American News, 1867.

Headley, Phineas Camp. *A New Series of Question Books on the Heroines of the Bible; or, The Women of Sacred History.* Boston: Henry Hoyt, n.d. (probably 1867).

Hearn, Jeff, and David Morgan, eds. *Men, Masculinities, and Social Theory.* London: Unwin Hyman, 1990.

Hebrew Customs; or, The Missionary's Return. Philadelphia: American Sunday School Union, 1838.

Heller, Max. *Jubilee Souvenir of Temple Sinai, 1872–1922.* New Orleans: American Printing, 1922.

Helper, Hinton. *Dreadful California.* Indianapolis: Bobbs-Merrill, 1948.

Hemberger, Eric. *The Historical Atlas of New York City: A Visual Celebration of Nearly Four Hundred Years of New York City's History.* New York: Henry Holt, 1994.

Hemmings, F. W. J. *Culture and Society in France, 1848–1898: Dissidents and Philistine.* New York: Charles Scribner's Sons, 1971.

Hemphill, C. Dallett, *Bowing to Necessities: A History of Manners in America, 1620–1860.* New York: Oxford University Press, 1999.

Henderson, Mary C. *The City and the Theatre: The History of New York Playhouses – A 235 Year Journey from Bowling Green to Times Square.* Clifton: James T. White, 1973,

Henderson, Philip. *Swinburne: Portrait of a Poet.* New York: Macmillan, 1974.

Heschel, Susannah, ed. *On Being a Jewish Feminist: A Reader.* New York: Schocken Books, 1983.

Hyder, Clyde Kenneth. *Swinburne's Literary Career and Fame.* Durham: Duke University Press, 1933.

Horowitz, Helen Lefkowitz. "'Nous Autres': Reading, Passion, and the Creation of M. Carey Thomas." *Journal of American History* 79 (1992): 68–95.

Horowitz, Tony. *Confederates in the Attic: Dispatches from the Unfinished Civil War.* New York: Vintage Books, 1998.

Houdini, Harry. *A Magician among the Spirits.* New York: Harper & Brothers, 1827.

Howe, Daniel Walker, ed. *Victorian America.* Philadelphia: University of Pennsylvania Press, 1976.

Huet, M. M. *Silver and Pewter: A Tale of High Life and Low Life in New York.* New York: H. Long & Brother, 1852.

Illustrated Dictionary and Concordance of the Bible. New York: Macmillan, 1986.

James, Ed. *Biography of Adah Isaac Menken.* New York: Ed James, 1869.

Jerrold, Douglas William. *Black Ey'd Susan; or, All in the Downs. A Nautical Melodrama in Five Acts.* New York: R. H. Elton, 1830.

Johannsen, Albert. *House of Beadle and Adams and It's Dime and Nickel Novels: The Story of a Vanished Literature,* vol. 1. Norman: University of Oklahoma Press, 1980.

Johnson, Claudia. *American Actress: Perspective on the Nineteenth Century.* Chicago: Nelson Hall, 1984.

Jordon, Ruth. *George Sand: A Biography.* London: Anchor Press, 1976.

Josephy, Alvin. *The Civil War in the American West.* New York: Alfred A. Knopf, 1991.

Kaplan, Marion A. *The Making of the Jewish Middle Class: Women, Family, and Identity in Imperial Germany.* New York: Oxford University Press, 1991.

Kasson, John. *Rudeness and Gentility: Manners in Nineteenth-Century Urban America.* New York: Hill and Wang, 1991.

Kasson, Joy. *Marble Queens and Captives: Women in Nineteenth-Century American Sculpture.* New Haven: Yale, 1990.

Kelley, Mary. *Private Woman, Public Stage: Literary Domesticity in Nineteenth-Century America.* New York: Oxford University Press, 1984.

Kendall, John S. "The World's Delight': The Story of Adah Isaacs Menken." *Louisiana Historical Quarterly* 21 (July 1938): 846–68.

———. *"The World's Delight": The Story of Adah Isaacs Menken.* New Orleans: Thomas J. Moran's Sons, 1938.

Kibler, M. Alison. *Rank Ladies: Gender and Cultural Hierarchy in American Vaudeville.* Chapel Hill: University of North Carolina Press, 1999.

King, Grace. *New Orleans: The Place and the People.* New York: Negro Universities Press, 1968.

Kirkham, E. Bruce, and John W. Fink, comps. *Indices to American Literary Annuals and Gift Books, 1825–1865.* New Haven: Research Publications, 1975.

Knight, Helen. *Reuben Kent's First Winter in the City.* Philadelphia: American Sunday School Union, 1845.

Knoper, Randall. *Acting Naturally: Mark Twain in the Culture of Performance.* Berkeley: University of California Press, 1995.

Knowles, James Sheridan. *The Hunchback.* N.p., n.d.

Koloski, Bernard ed. *Approaches to Teaching Kate Chopin's* The Awakening. New York: Modern Language Association of America, 1988.

Kousser, J. Morgan, and James M. McPherson, eds. *Region, Race and Reconstruction: Essays in Honor of C. Vann Woodward.* New York: Oxford University Press, 1982.

Laqueur, Thomas. *Making Sex: Body and Gender from the Greeks to Freud.* Cambridge: Harvard University Press, 1992.

Lears, T. Jackson. *No Place of Grace: Antimodernism and the Transformation of American Culture, 1880–1920.* New York: Pantheon Books, 1981.

Leman, Walter M. *Memories of an Old Actor.* San Francisco: A Roman, 1886.

Lennon, Nigey. *The Sagebrush Bohemian: Mark Twain in California.* New York: Paragon Books, 1993.

Lesser, Allen. "Adah Isaacs Menken: A Daughter of Israel." *American Jewish Historical Society* 34 (1937): 143.

———. *Enchanting Rebel: The Secret of Adah Isaacs Menken.* New York: Beechhurst Press, 1947.

———. *Weave a Wreath of Laurel: The Lives of Four Jewish Contributors to American Civilization.* New York: Coven Press, 1938.

Lewis, Oscar. *San Francisco: Mission to Metropolis.* Berkeley: Howell-North Books, 1966.

Lewis, Paul (Noel Gerson; a.k.a. Samuel Edwards). *Queen of the Plaza: A Biography of Adah Isaacs Menken.* New York: Funk and Wagnalls, 1964.

Lindberg, Gary. *The Confidence Man in American Literature*. New York: Oxford University Press, 1982.

Lippard, George. *The Empire City; or, New York by Night and Day*. New York: Stringer and Townsend, 1850.

Lipton, Eunice. *Alias Olympia: A Woman's Search for Manet's Notorious Model and Her Own Desire*. New York: Charles Scribner's Sons, 1992.

Little Miss Consequence. New York: McLoughlin Bros. n.d. (between 1859 and 1862).

Loftis, Anne. *California: Where the Twain Did Meet*. New York: Macmillan, 1973.

Logan, Olive. *Before the Footlights and Behind the Scenes*. Philadelphia: Parmalee, 1870.

Looby, Christopher. "George Thompson's 'Romance of the Real': Transgressions and Taboo in American Sensational Fiction." *American Literature* 65 (1993): 651–672.

Lott, Eric. *Love and Theft: Blackface Minstrelsy and the American Working Class*. New York: Oxford University Press, 1993.

Lowe, Alfred D. *Jews in the Eyes of Germans: From the Enlightenment to Imperial Germany*. Philadelphia: Institute for the Study of Human Issues, 1979.

Magdol, Edward. *Owen Lovejoy: Abolitionists in Congress*. New Brunswick: Rutgers University Press, 1967.

Malone, Bobbie. "New Orleans Uptown Jewish Immigrants: The Community of the Gates of Prayer, 1850–1860." *Louisiana History* 32 (1991): 239–273.

Mankowitz, Wolf. *Mazeppa: The Lives, Loves and Legends of Adah Isaacs Menken*. New York: Stein and Day, 1982.

Marberry, M. M. "The Naked Lady, or, Don't Take Your Sisters to Astley's," clipping in Billy Rose Theatre Collection.

———. *Splendid Poseur*. New York: Thomas J. Crowell, 1953.

Marcus, Alan I. *Plague of Strangers: Social Groups and Origins of City Services in Cincinnati, 1819–1870*. Columbus: Ohio State University Press, 1991.

Marcus, Jacob R. *The American Jewish Woman, 1654–1980*. New York: KTAV Publishing House, 1981.

Marois, Andre. *The Titans: A Three-Generation Biography of the Dumas*. New York: Harper Bros., 1957.

Marsh, Jan. *The Pre-Raphaelite Sisterhood*. New York: St. Martin's Press, 1985.

Marty, Martin E. *Pilgrims in Their Own Land: 500 Years of Religion in America*. New York: Penguin, 1984.

May, Caroline. *The American Female Poets: with Biographical and Critical Notices*. Philadelphia: Lindsay and Blakiston, 1849.

May, Max B. *Isaac Mayer Wise: The Founder of American Judaism: A Biography*. New York: G. P. Putnam's Sons, 1916.

May, Sophie. *Cousin Grace*. Boston: Lee and Shepard, 1865.

Mayne, Ethel Colburn. *Enchanters of Men*. London: Metheuen, 1909.

McConachie, Bruce A. *Melodramatic Formations: American Theatre and Society, 1820–1870*. Iowa City: University of Iowa Press, 1992.

McDonnell, Colleen. *The Christian Home in Victorian America, 1840–1900*. Bloomington: University of Indiana Press, 1986.

McKay, Earnest. *The Civil War and New York City*. Syracuse: Syracuse University Press, 1990.

Menken, Adah Isaacs. *Infelicia*. London: Hotten, 1868.

———. *Infelicia*. Philadelphia: J. B. Lippincott & Co., 1873, 1876, 1885.

———. *Infelicia*. Philadelphia: J. B. Lippincott, 1888.

_____. *Infelicia.* Philadelphia: Lippincott, 1888, 1890, 1902.

_____. *Infelicia.* Freeport, N.Y.: Books for Libraries Press, 1971. Black Heritage Collection Series.

_____. *Infelicia.* In *Collected Black Women's Poetry,* vol. 3 of the Schomberg Library of Nineteenth Century Black Women Writers, ed. Henry Louis Gates. New York: Oxford University Press, 1988.

Merrill, Lisa. *When Romeo Was a Woman: Charlotte Cushman and Her Circle of Female Spectators.* Ann Arbor: University of Michigan Press, 1999.

Metzger, Bruce, and Michael D. Coogan, ed. *The Oxford Companion to the Bible.* New York: Oxford University Press, 1993.

Milan, Victor. *Adah: The World's Delight.* New York: Ace Books, 1982.

Mille, Edwin Haviland, ed. *Walt Whitman: The Correspondence,* vol. 1: 1842–1867. New York: New York University Press, 1961.

Miller, Joaquin. *Adah Isaacs Menken.* 1892; Ysleta, Texas: Edwin B. Hill, 1934.

Miller, Tice L. *Bohemians and Critics: American Theatre Criticism in the Nineteenth Century.* Metucken, N.J.: Scarecrow Press, 1981.

Milman, Henry Hart. *Fazio: A Tragedy in Five Acts.* New York: Samuel French, n.d.

Milner, Henry M. *Mazeppa; or, The Wild Horse of Tartary: A Romantic Drama in Three Acts.* New York: Samuel French, nd.

Moncrief, W. T. *The Jewess; or, The Council of Trent.* N.p., n.d.

Montez, Lola, *Lectures of Lola Montez (Countess of Landsfeld), Including Her Autobiography.* New York: Rudd and Carleton, 1858.

Moore, Madeline. *The Lady Lieutenant; or, The Strange and Thrilling Adventures of Miss Madeline Moore.* Philadelphia: Barclay, 1862.

Morgan, Henry. *Ned Nevins, the News Boy; or, Street Life in Boston.* Boston: Lee and Shepard, 1866.

Morison, Ian. *The Sensation: A Novel Based on the Life of Adah Isaacs Menken.* New York: North American Library, 1963.

Morris, Clara. *Life on the Stage: My Personal Experiences and Recollections.* New York: McClure, Phillips, 1901.

Mortimer, Favell Lee. *The Young Jew: A History of Alfred Moritz Myers, Adapted for Children.* Philadelphia: American Sunday School Union, 1848.

Mullenix, Elizabeth Reitz. *Wearing the Breeches: Gender on the Antebellum Stage.* New York: St. Martin's Press, 2000.

Murdoch, James. *The Stage; or, Recollections of Actors and Acting from an Experience of Fifty Years: A Series of Dramatic Sketches.* Philadelphia: J. M. Stoddart, 1880.

Nead, Lynda. *Myths of Sexuality: Representations of Women in Victorian Britain.* Oxford, Eng.: Basil Blackwell, 1988.

Niehaus, Earl F. *The Irish in New Orleans: 1800–1860.* Baton Rouge: Louisiana State University Press, 1965.

Nevins, John Williamson. *A Summary of Biblical Antiquities; Compiled for the Use of Sunday-School Teachers, and for the Benefit of Families.* Philadelphia: American Sunday School Union, 1829.

Newcomb, Pearson. *The Alamo City.* San Antonio: Standard Printing, 1926.

Newton, Esther. *Mother Camp: Female Impersonators in America.* Chicago: University of Chicago Press, 1972.

Northcott, Richard. *Adah Isaacs Menken: An Illustrated Biography.* London: Press Printers, 1921.

Norton, Mary Beth, ed. *Major Problems in American Women's History.* Lexington, Mass.: D. C. Heath, 1989.

O'Connor, Richard. *Bret Harte: A Biography.* Boston: Little, Brown, 1966.

Odell, George C. D. *Annals of the New York Stage.* New York: Columbia University Press, 1931.

Orvell, Miles. *The Real Thing: Imitation and Authenticity in American Culture, 1880–1940.* Chapel Hill: University of North Carolina Press, 1989.

Ostriker, Alicia Suskin. *Stealing the Language: The Emergence of Women's Poetry in America.* Boston: Beacon Press, 1986.

Oursler, Fulton. *The World's Delight.* New York: Harper & Bros., 1924.

Paige, John C. *A Special History Study: Pennsylvania Railroad Shops and Works.* Altoona: U.S. Department of the Interior, 1989.

Parry, Albert. *Garrets and Pretenders: A History of Bohemianism in America.* New York: Covici, Friede, 1933.

Peavey, Linda, and Ursula Smith. *Women in Waiting in the Westward Movement: Life on the Home Frontier.* Normon: University of Oklahoma Press, 1994.

Peiss, Kathy, and Christina Simmons. *Passion and Power: Sexuality in History.* Philadelphia: Temple University Press, 1989.

Peskowitz, Miriam, and Laura Levitt. *Judaism since Gender.* London: Routledge, 1997.

Phelan, Peggy. *Unmarked: The Politics of Performing.* London: Routledge, 1993.

Poovey, Mary. *Uneven Development: The Ideological Work of Gender in Mid-Victorian England.* Chicago: University of Chicago Press, 1988.

Porter, Betty. "The History of Negro Education in Louisiana." *Louisiana Historical Quarterly* 25 (1942): 729–736.

Raphael, Marc Lee. *Profiles in American Judaism: The Reform, Conservative, Orthodox, and Reconstructionist Traditions in Historical Perspective.* San Francisco: Harper & Row, 1984.

Reilly, Bernard F. Jr. *American Political Prints, 1766–1876: A Catalog of the Collections in the Library of Congress.* Boston: G. K. Hall, 1991.

Reinharz, Jehuda, and Walter Schatzberg. *The Jewish Response to German Culture.* Hanover: University Press of New England, 1985.

Richarz, Monika. *Jewish Life in Germany: Memories from Three Centuries.* Trans. Stella and Sydney Rosenfeld. Bloomington: University of Indiana Press, 1991.

Roarke, Constance. *Troupers of the Gold Coast, or the Rise of Lotta Crabtree.* New York: Harcourt Brace, 1928.

———. *Trumpets of Jubilee.* New York: Harcourt Brace, 1927.

Roberts, Brian. *American Alchemy: California Gold Rush and the Emergence of Middle-Class Culture.* Chapel Hill: University of North Carolina Press, 2000.

Roberts, W. Adolphe. "Swinburne's Delightful Dancer: The Career of Adah Isaacs Menken, Adored by Great Men and Herself a Poet." *Dance Magazine* (Dec. 1929): 15–57.

Reynolds, David. *Walt Whitman's America: A Cultural Biography.* New York: Vintage Books, 1995.

Rooksby, Rikky, and Nicholas Shrimpton, eds. *The Whole Music of Passion: New Essays on Swinburne.* Cambridge, Eng.: Scholar Press, 1995.

Rossetti, William Michael. *American Poems.* London: E. Moxon, 1925.

Rotundo, E. Anthony. *American Manhood: Transformations in Masculinity from the Revolution to the Modern Era.* New York: Harper Collins, 1993.

Roussève, Charles Barthelemy. *The Negro in Louisiana: Aspects of His History and His Literature.* New Orleans: Xavier University Press, 1937.

Ruffner, Kevin Conley. *Maryland's Blue and Grey: A Border State's Union and Confederate Junior Officer Corps*. Baton Rouge: Louisiana State University Press, 1997.

Rutherford, Jonathan. *Identity: Community, Culture, Difference*. London: Lawrence and Wishart, 1990.

Sachar, Howard M. *A History of Jews in America*. New York: Vintage Books, 1992.

Said, Edward W. *Orientalism*. New York: Vintage Books, 1978.

Sarna, Jonathan, ed. *The American Jewish Experience*. New York: Holmes and Meier, 1986.

————, ed. *Ethnic Diversity and Civic Identity: Patterns of Conflict and Cohesion in Cincinnati since 1820*. Urbana: University of Illinois Press, 1992.

Sarna, Jonathan, and Nancy H. Klein. *The Jews of Cincinnati*. Cincinnati: Center for the Study of the American Jewish Experience, 1989.

Saxton, Lyle, comp. *Gumbo Ya-Ya: A Collection of Louisiana Folktales*. Gretna: Pelican Press, 1987.

————. *Old Louisiana*. New Orleans: Crager, 1950.

Schappes, Morris U., ed. *A Documentary History of Jews in the United States, 1654–1875*. New York: Schoken Books, 1971.

Schiller, Dan. *Objectivity and the News: The Public Rise and Fall of Commercial Journalism*. Philadelphia: University of Pennsylvania Press, 1981.

Schopp, Claude. *Alexandre Dumas: Genius of Life*. New York: Franklin Watts, 1988.

Schudson, Michael. *Discovering the News: A Social History of American Newspapers*. New York: Basic Books, 1978.

Schweninger, Loren. "Antebellum Free Persons of Color in Postbellum Louisiana." *Louisiana Historical Quarterly* 30 (1989): 345–357.

Scott, Sir Walter. *Ivanhoe*. New York: Oxford University Press, 1996.

Seigel, Jerrold. *Bohemian Paris: Culture, Politics, and the Boundaries of Bourgeois Life, 1830–1930*. New York: Viking Press, 1986.

Senelick, Laurence. "Boys and Girls Together: Subcultural Origins of Glamour Drage and Male Impersonation on the Nineteenth-Century Stage." In *Crossing the Stage*, ed. Lesley Ferris. London: Routledge, 1993.

————. *The Changing Room: Sex, Drag and Theatre*. London: Routledge, 2000.

Seymour, Bruce. *Lola Montez: A Life*. New Haven: Yale University Press, 1995.

Sheads, Scott Sumpter, and Daniel Carroll Toomes. *Baltimore during the War*. Linthicum, Md.: Toomey Press, 1997.

Showalter, Elaine, ed. *Feminist Criticism: Essays on Women, Literature and Theory*. New York: Pantheon Books, 1985.

Shpall, Leo. "The First Synagogue in Louisiana." *Louisiana Historical Quarterly* 21 (1938): 518–531.

Sklar, Kathryn Kish. *Catherine Beecher: A Study in American Domesticity*. New York: W. W. Norton, 1976.

Smith, Daniel, comp. *Anecdotes for the Young; or, Principles Illustrated by Facts*. New York: Carlton and Phillips, 1854.

Smith, Gene. *American Gothic: The Story of America's Legendary Theatrical Family – Junius, Edwin, and John Wilkes Booth*. New York: Simon and Schuster, 1992.

Smith, Henry Nash. *Virgin Land: The American West as Symbol and Myth*. Cambridge: Harvard University Press, 1973.

————, ed. *Mark Twain of the Enterprise: Newspaper Articles and Other Documents 1862–1864*. Berkeley: University of California Press, 1957.

Smith-Rosenberg, Carroll. *Disorderly Conduct: Visions of Gender in Victorian America.* New York: Alfred A. Knopf, 1985.

Soderholm, James. *Fantasy, Forgery, and the Byron Legend.* Lexington: University of Kentucky Press, 1996.

Sorkin, David. *The Transformation of German Jewry, 1780–1840.* New York: Oxford University Press, 1987.

Soulé, Frank, John Gihon, and James Nisbet. *The Annals of San Francisco.* New York: D. Appleton, 1854.

Spann, Edward K. *The New Metropolis: New York City, 1840–1857.* New York: Columbia University Press, 1981.

Spell, Lotta M. "The Theatre in Texas before the Civil War." *Texas Monthly* (April 1930), 291–301.

Stansell, Christine. *American Moderns: Bohemian New York and the Creation of a New Century.* New York: Henry Holt, 2000.

————. *City of Women: Sex and Class in New York, 1789–1860.* New York: Alfred A. Knopf, 1986.

Steffan, Truman Guy. *Lord Byron's "Cain": Twelve Essays and a Text with Variants and Annotations.* Austin: University of Texas Press, 1968.

Stein, Leon. *Lives to Remember.* New York: Arno Press, 1974.

Sterkx, H. E. *The Free Negro in Antebellum Louisiana.* Rutherford: Fairleigh Dickinson Press, 1972.

Stevenson, Louise. *The Victorian Homefront: American Thought and Culture, 1860–1880.* New York: Twayne, 1991.

Stewart, George. *Bret Harte: Argonaut and Exile.* Boston: Houghton Mifflin, 1931.

Stoddard, Charles Warren. "La Belle Menken." *National Magazine* (Feb. 1905): 471, 478.

Stoney, Peter. *Mark Twain and the Feminine Aesthetic.* Cambridge: University Press, 1992.

Sweat, Margaret J. M.. *Ethel's Love Life: A Novel.* New York: Rudd & Carleton, 1859.

Swinburne, Algernon Charles. *Adah Isaacs Menken: A Fragment of Autobiography.* London: private printing, 1917.

————. Poems and Ballads: Including Atalanta in Calydon. New York: Hurst, n.d.

————. *Selected Poems by Algernon Charles Swinburne.* Westport: Greenwood, 1980.

Swisshelm, Jane Grey Cannon. *Letters to Country Girls.* New York: J. C. Riker, 1853.

Taylor, Bayard. *New Pictures from California.* 1894. Rpt. Oakland, Calif.: Biobooks, 1951.

Taylor, Bernard, ed. *Mark Twain's San Francisco.* New York: McGraw-Hill, 1963.

Tebbel, John, and Mary Ellen Zuckerman. *The Magazine in America: 1741–1990.* New York: Oxford University Press, 1991.

Thayer, William Makepeace. *The Bobbin Boy; or, How Nat Got His Learning: An Example for Youth.* Boston: J. E. Tilton, 1860.

Thompson, George. *The Mysteries of Bond Street; or, The Seraglios of Upper Tendom.* New York, 1857.

————. *The Outlaw; or, The Felon's Fortunes.* New York: Frederick A. Brady, n.d.

Truettner, William H., ed. *The West as America: Reinterpreting Images of the Frontier, 1820–1920.* Washington: Smithsonian Institute, 1991.

Tucher, Andie. *Froth and Scum: Truth, Beauty, Goodness, and the Ax Murderer in America's First Mass Medium.* Chapel Hill: University of North Carolina Press, 1994.

Turner, Mary M. *Forgotten Leading Ladies of the American Theatre.* Jefferson, N.C.: McFarland, 1990.

Twain, Mark. *Roughing It*. Berkeley: University of California Press, 1993.

Underhill, Lois Beachy. *The Woman Who Ran for President: The Many Lives of Victoria Woodhull.* New York: Penguin Books, 1995.

Vance, James E. Jr. *The North American Railroad: Its Origin, Evolution, and Geography.* Baltimore: Johns Hopkins University Press, 1995.

Velazquez, Madame Loreta Janeta. *The Woman in Battle: A Narrative of the Exploits, Adventures, and Travels of Madame Loreta Janeta Velazquez, Otherwise Known as Lieutenant Harry T. Buford, Confederate States Army.* Hartford: T. Belknap, 1876.

Volo, Dorothy Dennean, and James M. Volo. *Daily Life in Civil War America.* Westport: Greenwood, 1998.

Walker, Cheryl. *The Nightingale's Burden: Women Poets and American Culture before 1900.* Bloomington: University of Indiana Press, 1982.

Wallys, Philip. *About New York: An Account of What a Boy Saw in His Visit to the City.* New York: Dix, Edward, 1857.

Warren, Joyce W. *The American Narcissus: Invidualism and Women in Nineteenth-Century American Fiction.* New Brunswick: Rutgers University Press, 1984.

Wasowicz, Laura. "The Children's Pocahontas: From Gentle Child of the Wild to the All-American Heroine." *Proceedings of the American Antiquarian Society* 105 (1996): 377–315.

Watson, Margaret G. *Silver Theatre: Amusements of the Mining Frontier in Early Nevada, 1850 to 1864.* Glendale, Calif.: Arthur H. Clark, 1964.

Wermuth, Paul C. *Selected Letters of Bayard Taylor.* Lewisburg: Bucknell University Press, 1997.

Wheelwright, Julie. *Amazons and Military Maids: Women Who Dressed as Men in Pursuit of Life, Liberty, and Happiness.* London: Pandora, 1989.

White, Richard. *It's Your Misfortune and None of My Own: A New History of the American West.* Norman: University of Oklahoma Press, 1991.

Whitman, Walt. *Leaves of Grass: Comprehensive Readers Edition.* Eds. Harold W. Blodgett and Sculley Bradley. New York: W. W. Norton, 1965.

Winsor, Justin. *The Mississippi Basin: The Struggle in America between England and France, 1697–1763.* Boston: Houghton, Mifflin, Riverside Press, 1895.

Wise, Isaac M. *Reminisences.* Trans. David Philipson. Cincinnati: Leo Wise, 1901.

Woodson, Carter G. *The Education of the Negro Prior to 1861.* Washington, D.C.: Associated Publishers, 1919.

Wright, Mabel Osgood. *My New York.* New York: Macmillan, 1926.

Wyatt-Brown, Bertram. *Southern Honor: Ethics and Behavior in the Old South.* New York: Oxford University Press, 1992.

Wyndham, Horace. *Victorian Sensations.* London: Jarrold's, 1933.

Yates, Edmund. *His Recollections and Experiences*, vol. 2. London, 1884.

Ziff, Larzer. *The American 1890s: Life and Times of a Lost Generation.* New York: Viking Press, 1966.

UNPUBLISHED SOURCES

Bishop, Mardia. "From 'Wax-Doll' Prettiness to a 'Lifeless Dough Doll': The Actress in Relation to the Images of Woman in Mid-Nineteenth Century America." Ph.D. diss, Ohio State University, 1993.

Buckley, Peter George. "To the Opera House: Culture and Society in New York City, 1820–1860." Ph.D. diss, State University of New York at Stony Brook, 1984.

Burns, Connie. "Private Sphere/Public Sphere: Rethinking the Paradigms of Victorian Womanhood through the Life and Writings of Margaret Jane Mussey Sweat, 1823–1908." M.A. thesis, University of Southern Maine, 1993.

Cutter, Barbara. "Devils in Disguise, Angels on the Battlefields: American Womanhood, 1800–1865." Ph.D. diss., Rutgers University, 1998.

Davis, Kate Wilson. "Adah Isaacs Menken – Her Life and Poetry in America." M.A. thesis, Southern Methodist University, 1944.

Goldman, Karla. "Beyond the Gallery: The Place of Women in the Development of American Judaism." Ph.D. diss., Harvard University, 1993.

Hart, Sister M. Francis Borgia. "Violets in the King's Garden: A History of the Sisters of the Holy Family." 1976. Archives of the Sisters of the Holy Family, New Orleans, Louisiana.

Klinko, Donald W. "Antebellum American Sporting Magazines and the Development of a Sportsman's Ethic." Ph.D. diss., Washington State University, 1986.

Leach, Catherine. "Adah Isaacs Menken: The Biography of an American Actress." M.A. thesis, Louisiana State University, 1935.

Mostov, Stephen G. "A 'Jerusalem' on the Ohio: The Social and Economic History of Cincinnati's Jewish Community, 1840–1875." Ph.D. diss., Brandeis University, 1981.

Otto, Kirsten. "The Image of Women in Isaac Mayer Wise's Die Deborah between 1855 and 1874." M.A. thesis, University of Cincinnati, 1993.

Sentilles, Renée M. "Forgotten Pioneers: A Comparative Study of the Sisters of the Holy Cross of Utah and the Sisters of the Holy Family of Louisiana." M.A. thesis, Utah State University, 1991.

Index

CPSIA information can be obtained
at www.ICGtesting.com
Printed in the USA
LVHW05s0711180718
584094LV00002BA/178/P